BVR's Guide to Valuing Dental Practices

First Edition

Stanley L. Pollock,
BS, DMD, MS, PHD, JD,
MCBA, MCMEA, ABAR

Editor

BVR
What It's Worth

Business Valuation Resources, LLC
1000 SW Broadway, Suite 1200
Portland, OR 97205
(503) 291-7963 Fax (503) 291-7955 www.BVResources.com

BVR

What It's Worth

Acquisitions Editor: Colin Murcray

Chair and CEO: David Foster
President: Lucretia Lyons
Vice President of Sales: Lexie Gross
Managing Editor: Janice Prescott
Customer Service Manager: Stephanie Crader

ISBN: 978-1-935081-75-3

Table of Contents

Introduction

Welcome to *BVR's Guide to Valuing Dental Practices*. This reference includes overviews of the dental practice valuation process by two leading practitioners, an essay on the qualitative factors that go into valuation—complete with checklist—a chapter focusing on the special requirements of orthodontic valuations, a chapter on goodwill from a leading healthcare valuation practitioner, and a summary of recent legal cases involving dental practice valuations, as well as two full dental practice valuation reports.

Our first overview was written by Dr. Stanley Pollock, a dentist and oral surgeon based in Pittsburgh, Pennsylvania, who also holds degrees in hospital administration, law, and business, as well as credentials in business valuation. His perspective is followed by another author, L. Norton Hindley, ASA, who has been a business appraiser for 40 years with a specialty in healthcare. His approach is somewhat different from Dr. Pollock's, but that's what makes this field interesting.

The essay on the qualitative aspects of dental practice appraisal and accompanying checklist was written by Sarah K. Lynch, a managing partner at Jim Kasper Associates LLC in New England, who specializes in appraisals and sales of dental practices. The chapter on orthodontic practice valuations was written by Dr. Thomas Ziegler, who was a practicing orthodontist before attending law school and founding Ziegler Practice Transitions, one of the leading practice transition companies in the nation.

The chapter on goodwill was written by Robert J. Cimasi, president of Health Capital Consultants in St. Louis, a leader in the field of healthcare appraisals. From our own files, BVR shares a series of 10 recent valuation cases involving dental practices—most of them in a divorce context. The abstracts presented here are based on our coverage of the valuation world in *BV Update*.

We present two real dental practice valuations. In Chapter 7, Timothy Brown, a dental appraiser and broker based in Vancouver, B.C., introduces his valuation report, shown in Appendix A. This report has been set up to be used as a valuation template. The second valuation, in Appendix B, was produced by Bill Sipes, who has more than 40 years of experience in business valuation, management consulting, and accounting and tax work. We have changed the names in both reports to protect the confidentiality of the clients.

Finally, Appendix C is a BVU teleconference and accompanying slides on the valuation of dental practices.

Stuart Weiss, CPA/ABV, CVA, ABAR, PFS

Chapter 1

The Art of Dental Practice Appraisal

By Stanley L. Pollock, BS, DMD, MS, PHD, JD, MCBA, MCMEA, ABAR

The appraisal or valuation of dental practices has become increasingly widespread during the past few decades and the number of appraisers involved in professional practice appraisal has increased accordingly. During this time, professional practice appraisal has developed from a rather crude, formula-driven art form into a mature, multi-method process. In the 1970s and '80s, dental practices were valued and sold at 100% of the latest 12 months' gross revenues. In the 1990s, when large corporations believed they could manage dental practices efficiently—at the very least, better than doctors—practices were valued and sold at inflated numbers.

But then the dental practice bubble began to leak. Dental practices, as a rule, sold at only 65%[1] of collected revenues in the 2000s. As reported in the 2006 and 2007 supplements of *Valuing Professional Practices & Licenses,*[2] general dental practices sold in arm's length deals at 57% of the latest annual gross revenues. Gross revenues, of course, were higher than in previous decades and certain pockets across the United States saw prices remain strong while other areas were negatively affected. The same situation holds true today.

What became apparent during those decades was that many appraisers and individuals were still seeking simple guideline formulas while other, more studious ones gathered a great deal of relevant and applicable appraisal information. Organizations began to compile important and much-needed data, most notably the Institute of Business Appraisers (IBA) Market Database, Pratt's Stats,® BIZCOMPS,® Done Deals, the Goodwill Registry, the American Dental Association, the Risk Management Association, and trade organizations. Brokers of all types began to market their services and realized the necessity for reliable data and the magnitude of the task of accumulating it. Authors published significant articles and treatises. Seasoned appraisers provided training programs and new and established organizations launched them for enthusiastic, neophyte appraisers.

On April 27, 1987, the Ad Hoc Committee on Uniform Standards of the Appraisal Standards Board (ASB) of The Appraisal Foundation developed and copyrighted the *Uniform Standards of Professional Appraisal Practice (USPAP).*[3] USPAP, adopted by the major appraisal organizations in North America, represents the generally accepted and recognized standards of appraisal practice in the United States. Today, there are four recognized, legally constituted professional appraisal associations in the United States and one in Canada: the Institute of

1. Cox, H. A., *Are You Prepared to Retire?* Dent. Econ. 1995:85(7) 36-45.
2. Pollock, Stanley L., DMD, JD, MCBA, *Valuing Professional Practices & A Guide for the Matrimonial Practitioner*, Wolters Kluwer, Austin, TX, Third Edition, 2008 Supplement.
3. Appraisal Standards Board. *Uniform Standards of Professional Appraisal Practice*, 155 15th Street, NW, Washington, DC 20005.

Business Appraisers (IBA), the National Association of Certified Valuation Analysts (NACVA), the American Institute of Certified Public Accountants (AICPA), the American Society of Appraisers (ASA), and the Canadian Institute of Chartered Business Valuators (CICBV). The CFA Institute also offers a respected and applicable Chartered Financial Analysts designation (CFA), although the CFA focuses on the analysis of publicly traded companies. At this time, the IBA, NACVA and AICPA have reached accord in the long standards unification process.

Although most dental practices would be considered small businesses under any definition of revenues or earnings, they typically generate profitability rivaling that of almost any industry. In the following 2010 statistics presented by the Virginia-based National Society of Certified Healthcare Business Consultants,[4] profitability ranged from 34% to 52% depending on specialty.

Figure 1. Profitability of Dental Practices by Specialty

Practice Type	Gross Receipts	Overhead	Cash Flow	Cash Flow
General dentistry with hygienist	$772,677	-$511,841	$260,836	34%
Endodontia	752,901	-362,743	390,158	52%
Oral & maxillofacial surgery	1,230,035	-621,253	608,782	49%
Orthodontics	1,085,327	-679,248	406,079	37%
Pediatric dentistry	974,100	-595,284	378,816	39%
Periodontia	823,438	-512,906	310,532	38%
AVERAGE	**$939,746**	**-$547,213**	**$392,534**	**42%**

Because of the degree of profitability, dental practices are highly desirable to own. The American Dental Association's 2008 Survey of New Dentists[5] reports that of new dentists buying practices, 24.5% purchased an existing practice as a partner, 37.7% purchased an existing practice as the sole owner, and 37.7% started a new practice. There was little variation in the amount spent to establish or purchase a practice. Among new dentists who purchased an existing practice as a partner, as a sole owner, and who started a new practice, the average amount spent was $472,390, $471,930 and $457,600, respectively.

Robert J. Cimasi, CBA, AVA, FCBI,[6] president of Health Capital Consultants, LLC in St. Louis, Mo., clearly outlines pertinent differences between medical, dental, and other professional business valuations. In his publications and presentations, Cimasi lists certain differences which specifically impact dental practice valuations. A few are:

4. *Statistics*, National Society of Certified Healthcare Consultants & Academy of Dental CPAs, Suite 130, 12100 Sunset Hills Road, Reston, VA 20190.
5. 2008 Survey of New Dentists, American Dental Association, 210 East Chicago Avenue, Chicago, IL 60611.
6. Cimasi, Robert J., MHA, ASA, CBA, AVA, CM&AA, CMP, Health Capital Consultants, 1143 Olivette Executive Parkway, St. Louis, MO 63212.

- Dentistry is heavily regulated by governments and third-party payers
- Although the practice may be owned by a non-dentist, the actual care of patients is limited to licensed dental professionals
- There is a sharply decreasing supply of dentists
- Goodwill and non-compete covenants play a large part in the valuation process
- Acquiring a dental education and advanced training is long-term and extremely expensive
- The cost of starting and acquiring a dental practice is extremely expensive
- The cost of operating a practice is very high
- Technology plays a major part in a dental practice
- Efficient management, more than ever, is required to operate a dental practice
- The average practice staff consists of four to five highly skilled individuals per dentist

In January 2010, the Florida-based Institute of Business Appraisers[7] promulgated its Certified Business Appraiser Body of Knowledge. This highly detailed, all-inclusive document is an excellent guide for appraisers who are genuinely interested in providing quality dental valuation services to clients. Like each appraiser and each appraisal, each dentist and each dental appraisal is unique. A great deal depends upon the purpose and function of the appraisal and the training, knowledge, skills, education, experience and ethics of the appraiser. However, the following is a brief summary of the procedures that go into a dental practice appraisal.

- Compile and present a Letter of Engagement
- Present a signed Confidentiality Covenant
- Include Assumptions and Limiting Conditions
- Determine type of practice, e.g., general, specialty, solo, group, etc.
- Determine purpose for appraisal
- Determine if there is a conflict of interest

---

7. Institute of Business Appraisers, P O Box 17410, Plantation, FL 33318.

- Request three to five years of tax returns and financial statements, depreciation schedules, production and other operational reports, fee schedule, history of practice and practitioners, and personnel including title, salary, benefits, length of service, etc.
- Date of valuation and date of report
- Potential users of appraisal and report
- Complete a site visit to inspect tangible assets
- Hold confidential discussion with doctor(s) and/or administrators regarding future plans, including forecasts, transitions, demographic and economic factors, leases, previous sales
- Determine scope of work
- Determine exactly what is being appraised, included, and not included
- Determine if real estate or equipment appraisals are necessary
- Determine applicable standard of value—fair market, fair, investment, intrinsic, etc.
- Determine premise of value—going concern, liquidation, etc.
- Perform normalization of income & expenses and balance sheets
- Forecast receipts, expenses, cash flows
- Determine and apply multiple appropriate approaches and methods
- Explain why inappropriate methods were not used
- Determine appropriate discounts and premiums
- Weight the determinations of value
- Consider tax affecting
- Check for reasonableness
- Conclusion(s)
- Executive summary
- Justification
- Compile and present reports

Appraisers value practices in different ways depending upon the purpose and function of the valuation; the training, experience, style, and, of course, integrity of the appraiser; the location, size and type of the practice; the business form of the practice and many other factors. Dental practice valuations pose many differences from other businesses, and even from other professions. This chapter and book address certain differences and similarities in dental practice appraisal that have developed over the past few decades and include many appraisal approaches, techniques, and comments.

Normalization

Financial statements, tax returns, and depreciation, section 179, and amortization schedules are paramount in the valuation of a dental practice. Because of the accelerating changes in the dental health environment and the overwhelming influences of third-party payers, three years of tax returns and financial statements are normally appropriate and sufficient. Normalization is the adjustment of financial statements for items that are not representative or truly necessary for the operation of the present going-concern status of the practice. The appraiser must adjust or "normalize" balance sheets and income statements in four general categories: comparability, non-operating, non-recurring, and discretionary adjustments. Normalization addresses and characterizes unusual, over- or understated, operating and non-operating, and recurring and nonrecurring items. It also addresses excess and contingent assets and liabilities. Normalization brings reasonableness and consistency into the valuation process.

Normalizing the Balance Sheet

The balance sheet, also known as the statement of financial position, reports at a given point in time the assets of the dental practice, its liabilities and the owner's equity or ownership. The balance sheet is an historical report which presents the cumulative results of past transactions. It illustrates the basic accounting equation, assets minus liabilities equal owner's equity, or, in most dental practice appraisals, the net tangible asset value (NTAV).

The adjusted balance sheet reflects current market values and is superior to an historical balance sheet which considers original costs and accumulated depreciation. The sources of data for the adjustments to balance sheets are the latest three to five years' tax reports, financial statements, depreciation, amortization, and Section 179 schedules, as well as the appraiser's valuation of tangible and special assets. Not infrequently, the practice's balance sheet will show and the appraiser must address other current assets such as prepaid assets and doctor's and employee's loan receivables which the appraiser will have to find out if they will or will not be paid. Since the balance sheet and its values can change quickly and sometimes dramatically, the appraiser should try to obtain and recast the balance sheet as close as possible to the valuation date.

Normally, cash, accounts receivable and payable, vehicles, and liabilities are not included in dental practice sales and purchases. In associate buy-ins and buy-outs, and mergers and acquisitions, they may or may not be included. They are included in most divorce valuations. Whether handled separately or included in an appraisal, accounts receivable should be adjusted or aged.

A reasonable approach is to value accounts receivable according to age in that the older the receivable, the less likely that it will be collected. As you can see in Figure 2, receivables that are were booked in the past 30 days are likely to be collected, but receivables that are more than four months old are not.

Figure 2. Likelihood of Collection of Accounts Receivable by Age

Accounts Receivable Aging	Collection
Up to 30 days	92%
31-60 days	85%
61-90 days	75%
91-120 days	65%
121 days +	25% or less

Orthodontic practices have an added current asset to address—Contracts Receivable, which is the amount remaining and due for services which the orthodontist and patient have contracted to complete, but which have not been completed. Thomas F. Ziegler,[8] DDS, MS, ABO, JD addresses and provides an excellent method to calculate contracts receivable in his chapter in this book. Another method, developed by Bill Sutton,[9] a respected healthcare consultant, is to subtract overhead and the cost to complete the service to arrive at Contracts Receivable value, as shown in Figure 3:

Figure 3. Arriving at a Contracts Receivable Value

Contracts Receivable	$650,000
Less: Normal Overhead (62%)	-403,000
Less: Cost to Complete (30%)	-195,000
Value of Contracts Receivable	$52,000

Normalizing Operating Expenses

In most dental practices today, the amount paid for operating supplies (the inventory) is quite large and can run from 6% to 12% of gross revenues. It is arduous, but possible, for dental

8. Ziegler, Thomas F., DDS, MS, ABO, JD, 6520 Kenwood Road, Cincinnati, OH 45243.
9. Sutton, William, 3 McAllister Place, Greensboro, NC 27455.

practice personnel to calculate the cost of clinical and clerical supplies on hand. Instead, a reasonable method for estimating the value of such inventory is to calculate the amount actually paid during the past 12 months and divide by six, which is the equivalent of two months' inventory. This method saves the time and effort of actually counting X-ray film, local anesthesia carpules, cotton rolls, and so on. The appraiser should consider separately counting any large supplies of gold, amalgam, implants or other expensive supplies and materials on hand.

Fixed Asset Appraisal

Tangible or physical assets and their values play an important part in the valuation of a dental practice. For years, appraisers utilized simple methods such as: a) calculating book values shown on the balance sheet (original costs less accumulated depreciation) and adding one-third to one-half of the accumulated depreciation to the book value; b) calculating major equipment on a 10 to 12 year depreciation schedule and furniture on a five-year depreciation schedule rather than the more rapid accountant's depreciation or economic schedule; c) engaging the services of a dental supply company or equipment dealer to determine the value of the tangible assets.

All too often, equipment dealers value only those items that they originally sold or that are obvious in the office but overlook the expensive computer, telephone, communication, technology, anesthesia, vacuum, and other systems, as well as the expensive office furniture. Most of the time, the dealer omits the so-called "minor" equipment such as high-speed drills and hand instruments. Not infrequently, in today's modern dental practice, tangible asset appraisals by a qualified machinery and equipment appraiser are required for the equipment, furniture, computer, office and technology, and other assets. To be accurate, the appraisal must include all major and minor tangible assets at their current fair market values in good working condition, including shipping, taxes and installation. The balance sheets and depreciation, amortization and Section 179 schedules will reveal if the equipment is new or obsolete and may require replacement or updating.

Tangible assets classified as "major" include dental chairs, dental lights, X-ray and implant units; assets classified as "minor" include hand pieces, hand instruments, forceps, calculators and syringes. It is critical to understand that dental equipment and office furniture, whether major or minor, are unique, expensive to purchase and to maintain, but depreciate and lose their values rapidly. The premises of equipment value in dental practice appraisals are:

- *In place/in use value,* which assumes that the asset will be fully and continually utilized as part of the operating enterprise. This is also known as the "highest and best use."
- *Depreciated replacement-cost value,* which assumes the current cost to replace the same, similar, or like-kind asset including depreciation and an allowance for the length of time that it has been in service.

Be aware that with the rapid and large Section 179 IRS write-offs allowed for the past few years, many major items do not appear on the balance sheets but should still be included in the fixed-asset appraisals. In addition, genuine antiques, certain artwork, vehicles and personal items generally are not included, and may be valued at original cost or have to be valued by a competent personal property or vehicle appraiser.

In dental practices, leasehold improvements are generally extensive, expensive and amortized over 39 years. For normalization, however, a 15-year amortization write-off (6.67% per year) is appropriate. Additionally, reviewing the depreciation and amortization schedules provides the appraiser an opportunity to determine the age, condition and obsolescence of the various tangible assets and whether replacement may be indicated. In today's modern dental technology era, new equipment for patient care and efficient practice management is constantly appearing on the market, which requires a constant source of commitment, purchasing and borrowing, regardless of favorable tax write-offs.

Like dental practice appraisal, the appraisal of dental tangible assets has become specialized and has risen to a higher level. Comprehensive dental practice valuation is appropriate and encompasses a detailed tangible asset valuation, especially with the large costs of purchasing and maintaining the equipment. John Harris, president and founder of the National Equipment and Business Brokers Institute[10] (NEBBI) in Wichita, Kansas, has been a leader and advocate and has been instrumental in training professional appraisers in the specialized field of machinery and equipment appraisal. The NEBB Institute addresses the appraisal of dental equipment. It trains, certifies and supports Certified and Master Certified Machinery and Equipment Appraisers (CMEAs, MCMEAs). CMEAs and MCMEAs prepare and deliver comprehensive and detailed Certified Appraisal Reports consistent with the ethics and guidelines mandated by the Uniform Standards of Professional Appraisal Practice (USPAP). A USPAP-compliant Certified Appraisal Report includes, but is not limited to:

- Purpose, function and type of appraisal
- Scope of services including
    - Economic factors which affect property
    - Data research
    - Type & extent of analysis applied in arriving at opinions and conclusions
    - On-site inspection and its depth
    - Highest and best use

10. NEBB Institute, 2014 West 13th Street, Wichita, KS 67203.

- Statement of limiting conditions
- Methods of valuation
- Additional and special considerations
- Final value summary and reconciliation
- Appraiser certification and qualifications

Figure 4 is a sample Adjusted Balance Sheet at Fair Market Value. Note that the tangible asset value is the sum of the equipment, furniture and fixtures, or $58,193 + $12,275 + $15,728 + $2,831 = $89,027 (no accounts receivable).

Figure 4. Adjusted Balance Sheet at Fair Market Value

Assets			
Current			
Cash	$500		
Accounts receivable	55,209		
Allowance for doubtful accounts	(11,738)		
Supplies - clinical, clerical	10,916		
TOTAL CURRENT ASSETS		54,887	
Fixed			
Equipment - major, section 179	58,193		
Equipment - minor	12,275		
Furniture, fixtures - major	15,728		
Furniture, fixtures - minor	2,831		
Leasehold improvements	5,650		
TOTAL FIXED ASSETS		94,677	
TOTAL ASSETS			$149,564
Liabilities			
Current			
Accounts payable	20,928		
Other	6,111		
TOTAL CURRENT LIABILITIES		27,039	
Long Term			
Note payable	20,190		
TOTAL LONG-TERM LIABILITIES		20,190	
TOTAL LIABILITIES			$47,229
NET TANGIBLE ASSET VALUE (NTAV)			**$102,335**

Normalizing Income & Expenses

Many dentists stress production and may pay associates or employees based upon production, but the dentist cannot spend money which she/he has not yet collected and may not collect. Comparing collection to production provides an initial and meaningful way to see if the practice is operating efficiently.

In today's third-party payer systems, collections generally run around 80% to 85% of production and billing. Ideally, the collection ratio, which equals collections divided by production, is crucial to the financial health and security of the dental practice and should run in the mid to high 90% range. However, practices heavily involved and reliant upon third-party and Medicaid participation will have a much lower collection percentage. Certain write-offs and discounts are normal, but the practice must control them, for they greatly affect the bottom line and valuations. It is common today that dental practices collect a substantial pretreatment payment and make refunds when final third-party payments are collected. It is important that the appraiser question and understand these matters.

It is also important that the appraiser understands which services the practice provides and does not provide. For example, certain practices provide additional, non-routine services such as orthodontics, nutritional, temporomandibular, medical-legal/litigation support, implants and others.

Over the years, normal operating expenses in a dental practice have increased considerably, with overhead ranging from 50% to 66%. The appraiser must consider the overhead of each practice and determine if the expenses are reasonable. The appraiser must determine if other items which appear on tax returns and income statements, such as interest, other income, rent, gains, credits and losses, are practice related.

A major normalization adjustment is owner or professional compensation. Normally, all practice or professional compensation should be classified as compensation, including officers, associates, independent contractors and hygienists. Many times such professional compensation will be included as W-2 wages and salaries which the appraiser must skillfully discover and appropriately recast. A major difference between most dental practices and regular businesses is that dental practices will balance out or bonus out at the end of the year and will show little or no earnings, profit or taxable income. Authors Pratt, Reilly and Schweihs[11] have written that in professional practices, earnings are counted *before* the owner's salary, benefits and perquisites in most earnings surveys. This is because most professionals pay out most of the practice earnings in salaries, benefits and perquisites.

Although obtaining the doctors' compensation is crucial, it is also crucial that the appraiser question and determine if there are family members or others on the payroll who are non-productive, part-time or full-time employees. In such hiring matters, family education, withholding, Social Security,

11. Pratt, Shannon P., Reilly, Robert F., & Schweihs, Robert P., *Valuing Small Businesses & Practices*, McGraw-Hill, United States 1998, page 601.

Medicare, retirement contributions and other funding and benefits show up and require appropriate adjustment. The appraiser should ask whether, if the family member or other individual should leave the practice or if the practice were sold or transitioned, he or she would have to be replaced?

Promotion, marketing, advertising, meals and entertainment, travel, continuing education and vehicles are normal operating expenses in a modern general and specialty dental practice today. However, many of these expenses are personal and can run from 50% to 75% of the listed deductions. Many appraisers simply adjust and declare that 100% of such deductions are personal which is usually incorrect. Many dentists have multiple facilities, teach at various institutions, are on hospital staffs, prepare and take various specialty and other board examinations, travel to their continuing education programs and visit bankers, accountants, suppliers and consultants. I have seen practices which have a vehicle solely used for practice activities. I have also seen practices in which the practice vehicle came with a chauffeur.

A major, necessary adjustment that appears on most corporation, partnership and even sole proprietorship tax returns is contribution to pension and profit-sharing plans. The appraiser must consider the contributions that the practice makes for the doctor and the staff, which can be difficult to obtain. The appraiser, therefore, must determine a reasonable doctor-staff allocation. The doctor's contribution is a fringe benefit and adjustment to cash flow which runs around 3% of receipts. The staff's contribution is an ordinary operating expense ranging from 1% to 2% of gross receipts. Generally, the doctor's contributions are about 80% of total retirement contributions.

Rent is a major expense in most dental practices and normally runs from 3% to 6% of gross receipts. Jack Sanders of BIZCOMPS[12] writes that, generally, only exceptional businesses can afford to pay rent that is more than 10% of gross sales. Rent is a frequent adjustment, primarily when the dentist is the owner of the property. Solos frequently do not charge their practice for rent; rather, they allocate and include mortgage payments, taxes, interest, utilities, repairs and maintenance in lieu of rent. Owners of the property will charge their corporation or limited liability company excessive or above-market rent, requiring adjustments to community fair market rentals which many times are difficult to obtain. Suggested methods of determining commercial rent adjustment are: a) checking with local realtors or bankers or b) allocating about 6% of gross receipts.

The appraiser must classify and adjust depreciation, amortization and interest. Depreciation and amortization are expenses recorded to allocate the costs of certain assets over useful lives determined for tax purposes which may or may not reflect economic reality.

It is essential that the valuator be aware of one-time and nonrecurring expenses, especially in cases of divorce, employment and professional liability litigations. The appraiser must be aware of such expenses, compare them to reasonable percentages over multiple years and make appropriate adjustments.

---

12. Jack Sanders, BIZCOMPS,® P O Box 97757, Las Vegas, NV 89193.

A dental practice requires a variety of insurance policies. Most of the time, practices will lump all of the practice's insurance into one category even though some are a personal expenses. The appraiser, then, must examine the group insurance and make appropriate business, fringe and personal deductions. Generally, life and buy-out insurance is not deductible. Disability income insurance may or may not be deductible; the staff and doctor's healthcare premiums are generally deductible fringe benefits that must be separately identified.

A final adjustment is an allowance for future replacement of equipment and furniture. In modern dental practices today, equipment requires frequent expensive purchasing, updating and replacing. Therefore, it is proper to include an allocation and adjustment for such allowance in normalizing financial statements. Reviewing the depreciation and amortization schedules and being aware of the extreme costs and rapid write-offs of equipment and furnishings provide a starting point which can run from $10,000 to $30,000 per year. Figure 5 presents most common average expense items for a general dental practice.

Figure 5. Sample Expense Ratios

Expense	% of Gross
Wages	15-30
Staff fringe benefits	2-4
Supplies, clerical	1-2
Supplies, clinical	6-8
Equipment repair/maintenance	0.7-1.0
Professional fees	2-3
Laboratory	6-8
Insurance, business	0.9-1.2
Continuing education, doctor	0.3-1.2
Vehicle	0.1-2.0
Marketing/advertising	0.8-1.2
Promotion	0.2-0.5

Figure 6 lists a variety of adjustments to a dental practice income statement to normalize it for valuation purposes. The first adjustment is to take out depreciation because it is a non-cash charge. As a second adjustment, add back a $10,000 allowance for equipment replacement. The third adjustment is to take out personal expenses related to marketing, insurance, pension and profit sharing, vehicle and travel. The net result increases income by $61,249 or 23%.

Figure 6. Sample Expense Adjustments

	INCOME & EXPENSE			
Gross receipts	$771,201		$771,201	
Refunds	-5,802		-5,802	
Other income	4,405		4,405	
Total income	769,804		769,804	
EXPENSES				
Salaries & wages	211,624		211,624	
Repairs & maintenance	9,694		9,694	
Rents	40,320		40,320	
Taxes	26,910		26,910	
Depreciation	27,837	27,837	0	#1
Allowance for replacement	0	-10,000	10,000	#2
Supplies - clinical, clerical	64,754		64,754	
Advertising, marketing, promotion	16,024	8,012	8,012	#3
Employee benefits	10,066		10,066	
Insurance - doctor	10,648	10,648	0	#3
Pension, profit sharing plans	30,100	19,896	10,204	#3
Vehicle	4,308	2,154	2,154	#3
Continuing education, travel, etc.	5,404	2,702	2,702	#3
Other deductions	50,924		50,924	
Total deductions	508,613		447,364	58%
Ordinary business income	$261,191	$61,249	$322,440	42%

Notes
#1: Add non-cash charge
#2: Subtract future replacement of assets
#3: Add personal allocation

Trend Analysis

After completing the normalization, the appraiser can prepare a spreadsheet entitled Trend Analysis & Weighting. This compilation provides an overview of the practice's operations during the term of the appraisal, the most recent year being the most important.

The appraiser can see if the revenues, expenses and cash flows are increasing or decreasing and if so by how much? If the changes are in line with the Consumer Price Index and with other local practitioners? As you can see below, gross revenue increased 4% in 2008 but decreased 2% in 2009, a recession year. Notice also in the far right column that cash flow increased 1% in 2008 and 1% in 2009 despite the poor economy.

Figure 7. Trend Analysis & Weighting

YEAR	%DIFF	GROSS	WT	WEIGHTED	EXPENSES	%	NET CASH FLOW	WT	WEIGHTED	%	%DIFF
2009	-2%	769,804	3	2,309,412	447,364	58%	322,440	3	967,320	42%	1
2008	4%	784,151	2	1,568,302	464,881	59%	319,270	2	638,540	41%	1
2007		754,719	1	754,719	438,362	58%	316,357	1	350,623	42%	
	1%	769,558	6	4,632,433	450,202	58%	319,356	6	1,956,483	AVG	1
	AVG.	AVG.	SUM	SUM	AVG	AVG	AVG	SUM	SUM		AVG

WEIGHTED GROSS	WEIGHTED EXPENSES	WEIGHTED CASH FLOW
772,072	445,992	326,081
100%	58%	42%

Ratios

Ratio analysis involves establishing a relationship between specific pairs of figures found in the financial statements. Ratios reveal trends, strengths and weaknesses of a dental practice and provide an additional guide to establishing an estimate of value. There are many ratios which aid in the financial analysis of the practice. A few of the more important and applicable ones are:

Liquidity ratios indicate a practice's ability to pay its current bills or liabilities, including unexpected ones. The *current ratio*, total current assets divided by current liabilities, indicates solvency of the practice. The *quick ratio*, total current assets less inventory and supplies, indicates liquidity or the ability to pay off short-term obligations and indicates its solvency.

The *profitability ratio*, net cash flow divided by total revenues, indicates how effectively the practice has been managed, the relative amount of net cash flow which the practice generated and how much profit had been made on every dollar earned. Today, profitability ratios range from 35% for general dentists to 50% or more for specialists.

The *debt to net worth ratio*, total liabilities divided by net tangible net worth or net tangible asset value, indicates the debt structure or margin of safety and the long-term solvency of the practice. This leverage ratio indicates the practice's ability to deal with financial problems and opportunities as they arise and indicates whether or not a practice has a favorable debt structure.

Figure 8. Ratio Analysis

Current - indicates solvency		
Current Assets	$54,887	2.03
Current Liabilities	27,039	
Quick - indicates liquidity		
Current Assets - Inventory	$43,971	1.63
Current Liabilities	27,039	
Profitability - indicates efficiency of operations		
Net Cash Flow	$322,440	0.42
Revenues	769,804	
Debt to Worth - indicates debt structure or margin of safety		
Total liabilities	$47,229	0.46
Tangible net worth	102,335	

The Uniform Standards of Professional Appraisal Practice (USPAP) Standards Rule 9-4(a) states, "An appraiser must develop value opinion(s) and conclusion(s) by use of one or more approaches that are necessary for credible assignment results." Nowhere is this rule more appropriate than in the valuation of a dental practice. Proficient practice appraisers follow USPAP 9-4(a) and its multi-approach statement.

As you know, there are three approaches to valuation (Income, Asset-Based, and Market), and many acceptable, recognized, published methods in each approach which appraisers should follow and, taking this matter to another level, which courts, bankers and lenders recognize and understand. Appraisers have an excellent source of methods, material and databanks available to assist them in their noble profession. Nevertheless, there are acceptable modifications and features that an appraiser may consider and many homemade methods which are suspect. The following are examples and explanations of many acceptable and applicable methods for dental practice appraisal.

Income Approach: Capitalization of Income Method

Gross and net revenues and benefits play a large part in the valuation of a dental practice. For most appraisals in this single-period method, the appraiser reviews and analyzes three to five years' financial statements. The general outline is:

1. Gross revenues
2. Less: adjusted operational expenses
3. Less: reasonable compensation
4. Equals: profit
5. Determine capitalization rate
6. Divide profit by capitalization rate to equal practice value

Gross revenues (#1) are typically projections based upon the previous years' increases or decreases as well as trend analysis (see Figure 7). Similarly, adjusted operational expenses (#2) are based upon projections as well as trend analysis. Reasonable compensation (#3) is the amount that a dental practice would have to pay another dentist to produce the gross revenues of the practice. Data derived from the Practice Valuation Study Group, a national group of professional practice valuators originally associated with the American Dental Association, indicate that reasonable compensation for most dental practices is about 35% of gross collected revenues. This percentage can vary according to geography, type of practice and supply/demand factors.

Gross revenues minus expenses and reasonable compensation equals profit (#4). One important question is whether profit should be figured before tax or after tax. Many appraisers prefer to focus on pretax profit because of the differences in tax rates among dentists.

Determining the capitalization rate (#5) is extremely important, but can be a real challenge for many appraisers. The build-up model is most frequently used and deserves a few comments.

The first three data points of the build-up model, which are derived from Ibbotson Associates Annual Reports,[13] are the risk-free or long-term government bond rates, the equity risk premium, and the size premium or small stock premium. It is important to note that these risk premiums are figured on after-tax data of publicly traded businesses and must be converted to pretax numbers if pretax profit is used.

Other risk adjustments include industry and company-specific adjustments as well as a "management burden," which reflects an allowance for time that the new owner spends managing the practice. Finally, the capitalization rate is adjusted downward for long-term growth, usually

13. Ibbotson. Stocks, Bonds, Bill & Inflation. 2010 Yearbook. Ibbotson Associates, Chicago, IL.

around 3% to 5% to reflect population growth and inflation. Since there are many risk factors in a dental practice, these risk factors are large and can range from five to ten or more percentage points. Capitalization rates for dental practices can run anywhere from 25% to 35%.

In 1982, James A. Schilit, ASA, editor of *Business Valuation Review*,[14] listed and described guidelines for risk management premiums and classified "businesses" into categories and assigned risk premiums. His category for "small businesses of a personal service nature" indicates a risk premium (capitalization rate) of 26% to 30% which still stands up today.

Profit divided by the capitalization rate equals practice value (#6).

Figure 9. Capitalization of Cash Flow Method

Gross revenues – projected 5%	$ 808,294
Less expenses at 58%	– 468,811
Compensation – professional	– 250,000
Profit	89,483
Divided by capitalization rate (25%	÷ 25%
Practice value	**$ 357,932**

Income Approach: Discounted Future Cash Flow Method

Also called the discounted economic income method and used in the valuations of larger businesses, this method has recently become popular and applicable in the valuation of dental practices. In theory, the discounted future cash flow is the most correct method. There is virtually unanimous agreement that a dental practice is worth the future benefits it will generate for its owners, discounted to a present value by a discount rate that reflects the risk of achieving the benefits in the amounts and at the times expected. The discount rate is the previously determined capitalization rate *plus* an allowance for growth. Relying on specific projections of earnings directed into the future, this method actually states in current dollars what a willing purchaser might pay for future earnings from the practice to be realized over time. The Chancery Court of Delaware has declared that the discounted future cash flow method is the preferred method. Other courts accept this method also.

In dental practice valuations, the problems incurred with this method are: a) the determination of the annual forecasted net revenues or cash flows, b) the number of years to project the net revenues and cash flows, c) the increased or decreased annual projected rate, d) the determination of the discount rate, and e) the so-called terminal, residual or perpetuity value.

14. Schilit, James H. Relevance of Financial Analysis to Standard Appraisal Methodology. Business Valuation Review, September 1987.

However, unlike other types of businesses that are assumed to continue in perpetuity, I believe that a terminal value unrealistically increases the estimate of value of a dental practice. Five years is a reasonable projection because it is the normal time for professional practice buy-ins and payouts.

In Figure 10, gross revenues are projected to increase 5% per year. Taxes are estimated at 40% and cash flows are discounted at 30%. The sum of the discounted cash flows equals the Practice Value.

Figure 10. Discounted Cash Flow Method

Year	1	2	3	4	5
*Projected Cash Flow	$339,483	$356,457	$374,280	$392,994	$412,644
Less Taxes @ 40%	-135,793	-142,583	-149,712	-157,198	-165,057
Gross Profit	203,690	213,874	224,568	235,796	247,586
Present Values	156,685	126,553	102,216	82,559	66,682
Discounted @ 30%					
Practice Value			**$534,695**		

Discount Rate Build-Up	
Risk-free long term govt. bond rate[1]	4.0%
Risk premium[2]	6.0%
Illiquidity risk premium - small stock equity[2]	5.0%
Risk premium-unique[2]	5.0%
Management burden[3]	5.0%
Growth rate[3]	5.0%
DISCOUNT RATE	30%

1. U.S. Government 20 year bond rate
2. Stocks, Bonds, Bills & Inflation (SBBI). R. Ibbotson & R. Sinquefield, Chicago, IL
3. Appraiser's determination

Asset Approach: Adjusted Net Asset Value Method

The value of a dental practice should equal the value of all tangible and intangible assets adjusted to current fair market values less liabilities. However, the valuation of tangible assets is not simple and requires the expertise of an individual skilled in the valuation of all assets as noted in Figure 4 above. The determination of the latest balance sheet adjusted to fair market value should provide the net tangible asset value (NTAV) as a going-concern premise. In certain cases, the sole determination of the assets and liabilities of a dental practice may be indicated and necessary in divorce cases where goodwill is not a marital asset and in an orderly or forced liquidation. A drawback to this relatively simple method is that it does not explain or include a method for the valuation of the goodwill and other intangibles which normally comprise the largest aspect in the valuation of a dental practice.

Excess Earnings Method

Also called the formula or hybrid method, this method is somewhat controversial. For whatever reasons, some appraisers will not use it, while others (and I am one) find it very useful and applicable. It originated in the 1920s, and was revisited in 1968 by the IRS in Revenue Ruling 68-609. The IRS indicated that the approach may be used for determining the fair market value of intangible assets of a business *only if there is no better basis therefore available.*

The theory behind this method is that a dental practice is entitled to a return on its tangible capital including equipment and furnishings of 8% to 10%. The amount in excess of the determined percentage can be attributed to goodwill. Tangible assets, including equipment, furniture and furnishings would command a 10% investment return, while assets such as cash, accounts receivable, supplies and leasehold improvements would command somewhat less.

Since dental practices are generating large net cash flows in relation to tangible assets, it is not necessary or appropriate to capitalize the excess earnings. This removes the necessity of having to determine yet another capitalization rate, which is a subjective process at best, and leads to an unrealistic final estimate of value.

Figure 11. Excess Earnings Method

Net Adjusted Cash Flow—latest year	$322,440	a
Tangible Asset Value	89,027	
Return on Tangible Assets	10%	
	8,903	b
Excess Earnings	313,537	a – b
Plus: Net Tangible Asset Value	102,335	
Practice Value	$415,872	

Market Approach

This approach comprises the reality of the marketplace—the price at which comparable dental practices have actually changed hands—and is a direct and powerful approach. Using this approach, an appraiser tries to locate comparable practices which have exchanged ownership using arm's-length negotiations. Unlike the real estate market, there is no organized market that tabulates and maintains records of sales of dental practices.

Professional valuators, however, have knowledge of and maintain records of myriad transactions in various communities. Actual sales, transitions and transactions, buy-ins and buy-outs, equitable distributions in marital resolutions, and estate settlements are practical and useful. Over the years, the Institute of Business Appraisers in Florida, BVR, owner of Pratt's Stats, in Portland, Ore., the Goodwill Registry in Pennsylvania and BIZCOMPS in Las Vegas have gathered considerable data in their excellent databanks.

The market approach comprises a variety of methods, many of which focus on publicly traded companies. Although there are publicly traded companies that own dental practices or attach their names to the practices, the data are not that useful because such companies are too large to provide a meaningful comparison.

Direct Market Data Method (DMDM)

This method, developed, promulgated and advanced by Raymond C. Miles,[15] founder of IBA, has become a highly relevant procedure to help appraisers using the market approach with small businesses and professional practices. In the DMDM, all transactions for which market data are available are considered as a statistical ensemble that defines the market for businesses and professions of the same general type. In dentistry, the data are classified under Standard Industrial Classification (SIC) code 8021 and the North American Industry Classification System (NAICS) code 621210. Data can be obtained from the IBA, Pratt's Stats, BIZCOMPS and others.

A few of the first steps that the appraiser takes in this method are the review and analysis of the general and local economic conditions, the financial ratios and the general overall evaluation, appeal and condition of the subject practice relative to the overall market. The appraiser further determines whether the practice is or will be more or less desirable than other practices in today's modern and technological dental environment. An appraiser's first impression is important. The general review and analysis provide insight into the practice and its potential value. The appraiser, then, is getting organized to estimate the market value of the target practice from prices for which other similar practices have been sold at arm's length.

The DMDM's use of a statistical ensemble is representative of the entire market instead of a limited number of publicly traded similar practices for which there is little or no data available. This is a major difference between the direct market data method and other market valuation methods. While other market methods based upon comparisons are about practices, the DMDM is about markets.

Outline of the DMDM Method

- Gather data on dental practice sales in SIC 8021 or NAICS 621210
- Select performance measures, usually price/revenue (P/Rev) and price/earnings (P/E)
- Analyze transactional data using mean and median ratios
- Compare transactional data to the subject practice

15. Raymond C. Miles, FIBA, ASA. P. O. Box 17410, Plantation, FL 33318.

- Weight methods
- Estimate fair market value of the practice

In actual sales of dental practices, accounts receivable, accounts payable and other liabilities are typically not included in the transaction. In buy-ins, pay-outs, matrimonial matters and mergers, they may or may not be included. The appraiser must consider these relevant facts and, depending upon the purpose and function of the valuation, determine whether or not to include them. Gross revenues x (P/Rev ratio) + accounts receivable – liabilities = Practice Value.

Figure 12. DMDM Method

Gross revenues—latest year	$782,510
Price/revenue ratio	60%
Initial practice value	469,506
Plus: current assets	54,887
Less: liabilities	(47,229)
Practice value	$477,164

Other significant facts in the direct market data method are:

- The DMDM employs as many transactions as possible to assist in the determination of value while other methods use a relatively small number of transactions. The DMDM is about *ranges*; other methods are about *individual transactions.*
- DMDM data are valid for a wide range of transaction dates.
- Each dental practice is unique and most are not average. Use median, not mean.
- DMDM transactions are readily available and inexpensive to obtain.
- DMDM transactions are relatively simple to explain to clients.
- The best evidence of market value is direct observation of the marketplace.

Price To Earnings (P/E)

In the valuation of most dental practices, earnings are central and critical and the price to earnings ratio (P/E) is highly relevant. However, results gathered from the IBA transactional data bank reveals that: 1) practical problems in data gathering and interpretation limits the usefulness of the P/E ratio as a measure of market performance and 2) the most difficult and variable number from an economic perspective on the financial statements of a dental practice is net income, profit or cash flow. The number varies according to the appraiser's normalization, what may or may not be included and the appraiser's interpretation of net income, profit and cash flow. Therefore, P/E ratio data gathered through DMDM is of limited usefulness.

Price/Revenues (P/R, P/REV)

According to Ray Miles, founder of IBA, "the selling price to gross sales is a more reliable measure of market value than price to earnings." Once the appraiser selects the large number of transactions and determines the price/revenue ratio, she/he simply multiplies the ratio times the latest gross revenues of the practice. This determines the value of the practice. As of the end of 2010, data collected from the IBA and Pratt's Stats databases indicate that price to revenues are 60% for general dentistry, 62% for orthodontia and 64% for oral and maxillofacial surgery. Although the results do not mean that every practice should sell at such a ratio, the data represent significant guidelines.

Many appraisers and brokers who value dental practices maintain their own market data banks. This is an excellent practice, in that different states, areas and communities have indigenous market characteristics that deserve special and specific recognition. Unfortunately, the source and results are self-determined and unprincipled individuals use them in a self-serving manner to arrive at an unsubstantiated conclusion of value.

Revenue Multiplier Method

Another method used with the market approach is the revenue multiplier method. In this method the appraiser multiplies the latest gross revenues of the practice by an intangible factor. In most dental practice valuations, intangible asset value is important, and, generally, it is the largest or major asset in the value of a dental practice. In divorce cases in certain states, personal goodwill is not a marital asset, but commercial goodwill may be. Many appraisers have accumulated data of actual arm's length transactions while others look for reliable databases.

Figure 13. Revenue Multiplier Method

Gross revenues—latest year	$769,804
Goodwill percent—Goodwill Registry median	x 0.4632
Goodwill value	356,573
Net tangible value—see balance sheet	+ 102,335
Practice value	$458,908

For more than 20 years, the Goodwill Registry,[16] located in Plymouth Meeting, Pa., has accumulated data contributed by appraisers, practice brokers, accountants, attorneys and others for every healthcare profession. The Goodwill Registry records the reason for the valuation—sale/purchase, divorce, buy-sell arrangement and so on. It also lists practice location by state as well as by urban, suburban and rural. Interestingly, this data bank lists the methods that the appraiser used in determining the estimate of value. The methods are the comparable sales market, gross revenue multiplier, discounted future cash flow, excess earnings and capitalization of earnings/income. In its annual survey, Goodwill Registry tabulates:

- Gross revenues—the practice's cash-basis gross receipts for the past 12 months;
- Overhead percentage—the overhead rate excluding doctor compensation and benefits
- Practice price—the total sales price for 100% of the practice, normally excluding accounts receivable, accounts payable, and liabilities
- Goodwill value—including patient charts, lists, records and restrictive covenants, calculated as goodwill value/gross revenues = goodwill percentage

In its 2010 edition, the Goodwill Registry presents goodwill as a percentage of gross revenue. Endodontia has the highest goodwill; prosthodontia has the lowest.

Figure 14. Goodwill in Dentistry

Specialty	Percent of Revenues
Endodontia	53
General Dentistry	46
Oral & maxillofacial surgery	44
Orthodontia	46
Pedodontia	49
Periodontia	41
Prosthodontia	29
Average	44

The accumulation of reliable data and the sources of such data over the years has made the foremost difference in the valuation of dental practices during the past decades. Each has its major and appropriate data points and, some appraisers believe, its weaknesses. Yet each is an excellent source of valuation information and each greatly assists appraisers in their approaches to estimating the value of dental practices. Each data bank is relatively easy and inexpensive to

16. *The Goodwill Registry.*® c/o The Health Care Group, #200, 140 West Germantown Pike, Plymouth Meeting, PA 19462.

access. The data banks encourage participants to contribute data, and, by doing so, participants have free access to the data banks. Access to and proper use of the data and the application of the data from multiple data banks enhances the appraiser's reference sources and adds credibility to the appraisal report.

Summary of Values

The following is the summary of values.

Method	Value
Capitalization of Cash Flow Method	$ 357,932
Discounted Future Cash Flow Method	534,695
Excess Earnings Method	415,872
Comparable Market Data Method	477,164
Revenue Multiplier Method	458,908

Because the result of the Capitalization of Cash Flow Method was considerably less than the results of the other four methods, I felt it was an inappropriate method for this valuation and elected not to use it.

Buy-Sell Method

About 65% of specialists and 15% of general dentists are in group or multi-person practices. The relationships vary from informal office sharing to formal shareholder/corporation or member/LLC ownership. They involve buy-in and buy-out transactions. As a result, buy-sell agreements are crucial in the case of group practices.

The terms of the agreements should be reasonable, realistic and fair to all parties and, of course, committed to writing. The parties and their advisors should review, revise or update the document annually. Valuing dental practices today is common and necessary for buy-sell transactions, and the necessity for valuations is an excellent source of revenue for appraisers.

In valuing a multi-person dental practice, the appraiser must request information regarding whether there have been previous, more especially, recent transactions, and their terms. Having realistic data available from practice buy-sell transactions, in general, and the subject practice, in particular, goes a long way in the valuation process regardless of the purpose and function of the appraisal. In addition, many doctors and their advisors purposely exclude goodwill and intangible assets in their buy-sell agreements which may create a problem when the doctors or their advisors recommend a valuation and when the agreements become effective.

Funding the buy-sell agreement is crucial for the Doctors and practice which they can accomplish in many ways. Life insurance, disability buy-out and business interruption insurance are the primary methods to protect against the payouts involved in case of premature death and permanent disability. Other methods to fund a departing doctor's payout include accumulation of cash within the practice, the sale of practice assets, an installment plan agreement including a promissory note, the creation of a special profit sharing or pension plan and others. All of these methods require careful planning as well as tax considerations and are, generally long term. For example, accumulating cash within the practice could trigger an accumulated earnings tax. In any case, the appraiser must determine whether this funding mechanism is a practice asset or liability and decide whether it should be included in an appraisal.

There are three types of buy-sell agreements—equity redemption between the practice entity and owners, cross purchase among owners and a combination "wait and see" where the method is determined at the time of the triggering incident. Such incidents include death, permanent disability, voluntary and involuntary departure and divorce of the Parties. The planned steps for a cross purchase type of buy-sell agreement in anticipation of premature death and permanent disability are as follows:

- Corporation owns policies
- Tragedy occurs
- Practice entity arranges to collect benefits
- Entity collects benefits
- Entity deposits money into its bank account
- Entity pays the doctor or the estate in the event of disability or death
- Entity owns additional stock, units or interest

If the buy-sell agreement is an equity redemption type of plan, then the partners and appraisers must be aware of a flaw in the process. When the entity receives and deposits the benefits, the entity can add hundreds of thousands of dollars into its bank account and balance sheet, albeit for an anticipated short time. Two major conditions now exist: 1) If the entity owes any debts or other payables, then the lenders and creditors, normally, have first lien on the collected benefits and the practice entity cannot legally distribute the proceeds until the liabilities are satisfied or the creditors give permission to do so. 2) Heirs and their attorneys may now conclude that the value of the entity has increased considerably entitling heirs to a larger payout. A statement like the following is useful: "The benefits of a deceased or permanently disabled partner which the entity may receive shall not in any manner affect or alter the total value of the entity." Appraisers need to research these conditions and appropriately accommodate their valuation process for them.

Many times during a divorce or other litigation, the involved dentist presents a buy-sell agreement which presents a negative or unrealistic value of the doctor's interest in the practice. That's often because the value has been determined by an arbitrary formula. Courts, however, will ignore this value and look for a more reasoned one. In the fifth edition of his book, *Valuing a Business* (2008) Dr. Shannon Pratt writes that "it is highly unlikely that the price established by a formula at the time of signing a buy-sell agreement will even be close to the value of the interest at the time of the triggering event, which could be many years later. For this reason, I highly discourage the use of formulas in buy-sell agreements." He continues: "Formula approaches for setting the price in a buy-sell agreement can easily turn out to be unfair to one party or the other when the transaction eventually occurs. The valuation process should reflect a complex set of factors—usually too complex to be embodied in a formula."

Even with a proficient valuation, the seller may be disappointed because there are no buyers. Or, buyers may recognize that goodwill exists, but they don't want to pay for it. Or, they may not be interested in buying a practice if it doesn't have the latest equipment and technology.

Weighting of Values

Section 7 of RR 59-60, AVERAGE OF FACTORS, states: "No useful purpose is served by taking an average of several factors and basing the valuation on the result. Such a process excludes active consideration of other factors, and the end result cannot be supported by a realistic application of the significant facts in the case except by mere chance."

The appraisal community has interpreted this statement to mean that it is improper to take an arbitrary arithmetic average of results derived from the various methodologies. However, it is appropriate to assign mathematical weightings to the values they have developed based on judgment. Appraisers, lenders, courts and others understand this feature. However, they would like to know how much weight the appraiser gives each methodology and how the appraiser derived the assigned weight. In general, certain courts favor the income approach and the IRS favors the market approach. RR 59-60 emphasizes the market approach and so it must be considered along with the income approach. The appraiser has considerable discretion in the weighting of values.

In our example, the income approach generated a value of $534,695 using the discounted cash flow method in Figure 10. The excess earnings method (a modified asset approach) generated a value of $415,872 (Figure 11). We used two methods for the market approach and took an average: the DMDM (Figure 12, $477,164) and the revenue multiplier method (Figure 13, $458,908). We elected to weight the income approach, asset-based approach and market approach 30:30:40.

Figure 15. Reconciliation of Values

Income Approach	$534,695	30%	$160,409
Asset-Based Approach	$415,872	30%	$124,762
Market Approach	$468,036	40%	$187,214
		Rounded Value	**$470,000**

Justification of Valuation

We have completed the mechanics of valuing a dental practice. There is one additional but important procedure—justification of our efforts to see if the cash flow of the practice, at least for the first year, can substantiate the valuation result. If a buyer were to purchase the practice for this value and finance it, would the practice generate sufficient income to pay for the purchase as well as provide a reasonable lifestyle for the buyer?

Let's assume that a buyer has the option of buying this practice for $470,000 with 20% down and/or zero down and a seven year loan at 8% annual interest. The debt services are $66,870 and $83,587 per year. Assume the dentist seeks a salary of $250,000. If the practice generates collections of $808,294 as projected, after deducting expenses of $468,811, professional compensation of $250,000 and debt services of $66,870, then the dentist will have $22,613 cash flow left over. If on the other hand, the dentist were able to get a loan with zero down, then the debt payment would be higher, $83,587, and there would be a smaller, yet positive, cash flow of $5,896. This clearly shows that the practice can generate sufficient revenues so that after payment of practice expenses, professional compensation and debt service, there would be positive cash flows and that the investment in the practice would be reasonable and justifiable.

Figure 16. Justification of Valuation

	20% Down	Zero Down
Practice value	$ 470,000	$ 470,000
Down payment	94,000	Zero
Balance	76,600	470,000
Compensation	250,000	250,000
Debt service—P + I / year	66,870	83,587
Calculation		
Gross revenues	808,294	808,294
Expenses	- 468,811	- 468,811
Compensation	- 250,000	- 250,000
Debt service	- 66,870	- 83,587
Cash flow	22,613	5,896

Discounts & Premiums

It is important that the appraisal consider discounts and premiums before committing to a final estimate of value. Discounts and premiums greatly affect final estimates of value. Control of the practice and in a valuation assignment can command a premium; lack of it can command a discount. Each estimate entails ownership characteristics of each practice which inludes control and minority ownership. Control ranges from 100% to 51% and, possibly even less than 51%. State law, the practice entity's operating articles and the standard of value are important and play an important part of the control of the entity and the valuation. As in a business, control ownership is powerful and commands attention in a dental practice. Most professionals are aware of this feature and try very hard to preserve, obtain and maintain it. Control in a dental practice requires ownership and management skill, tempered judgment and delicate sensitivity and includes, but is not limited to

- Setting policies and activities of the practice
- Determining compensation for the Doctors
- Determining fringe and other benefits
- Acquiring and disposing of assets
- Declaring and paying dividends
- Determining retirement plans

The most common discounts are for lack of control and lack of marketability. Lack of control refers to the inability to make management decisions and is usually the result of owning a minority interest. Lack of marketability refers to the inability of an owner to sell his or her interest in the practice. In the case of a minority owner, lack of marketability usually refers to the inability to obtain consent from the other owners to transfer shares to an incoming dentist. For a controlling shareholder, lack of marketability usually refers to the time and effort it takes to convert a practice interest into cash which is also known as liquidity. Discounts for lack of control and marketability are frequently challenged in court because they are difficult to quantify. They also affect values and valuations in dental practices. Dental practices can end up with discounts for lack of marketability, illiquidity and control or a combination of the three which the appraiser must consider.

Practitioners treasure liquidity and solvency mentioned earlier in this chapter. Most dental practices are illiquid, that is, they cannot be converted to cash quickly. This certainly is a major deviation from the standard for marketability and liquidity in the public security market's "cash in three days." Today, an average practice sale takes between nine to twelve months. Location is a major factor, that is, rural practices require more time than to transition than urban practices as a rule.

Thus, illiquidity, lack of marketability and lack of control require adjustment which show up in valuations as "discounts." The discount shows up as a deduction or reduction of the value of the practice. Unfortunately, the reduction is not simple to determine or calculate. Over the years, there have been numerous studies performed and volumes of pragmatic data presented which address lack of marketability and control. To mention a few:

- Multi-year Restricted Stock Studies
- SEC Institutional Investory Study
- Revenue Ruling 77:287
- Valuation Advisors' Studies
- Mergerstat's Control Premium Studies & Review
- Pre-IPO Studies
- Emory Studies
- Williamette Management Associates' Studies
- The FMV Restricted Stock Study
- Silber Study
- SEC Study and
- Others

One point is major in valuations today. If the valuator decides to apply a discount or premium, she/he should explain how she/he arrived at her/his conclusion. The 1995 tax case, *Mandelbaum et al v Commissioner*[17] is a classic case relative to lack of marketability. This case lists nine representative factors which appraisers may consider in determining discounts. They are

1. Financial statement analysis
2. Dividend policy
3. Nature of the company, its history, its position in the industry and its economic outlook
4. Management

17. Mandelbaum et al v. Commissioner. T.C.Memo 1995-255.

5. Amount of control in the trasferred shares

6. Restrictions on transferability

7. Holding period for the stock

8. Company's redemption policy

9. Costs associated with a public offering

Summary

Dental practice appraisals are challenging because every practice is unique and the process is extremely complex. Reasonable minds can differ on the value of a practice. Conversely, unreasonable and unethical minds can differ and create havoc, confusion and unwarranted expense and tension. Two USPAP Standards and one Comment are applicable and sum it all up. Standards Rule 9-1: "In developing an appraisal of an interest in a business enterprise of intangible asset, the appraiser must be aware of, understand and correctly employ those recognized approaches, methods and procedures that are necessary to produce a credible appraisal." Standard Rule 9-5 (b): "In developing an appraisal of an interest in a business enterprise or intangible asset, the appraiser must reconcile the applicability and relevance of the approaches, methods and procedures used to arrive at the conclusion of value." And, finally, "The value conclusion is the result of the appraiser's judgment and not necessarily the result of a mathematical process."

Chapter 2

The Value of a Dental Practice

By L. Norton Hindley III, ASA

Surveys indicate that on a year-by-year basis, only one out of every four small business owners is actually enhancing the value of his or her business. Based on my own observations, I suspect that this is true in dentistry as well. While practice revenue levels may increase and physical assets of the practice may be enhanced, when profit margins decrease, so does practice value. Whether it's the sale of a practice, a merger with another dentist, or the hiring of an associate, earnings are critical to a successful outcome. The bottom line is that a dental practice is an investment asset, and as such, its value must be measured against earnings.

Valuation Disparity

There are probably three reasons why there is such a disparity of practice valuations in dental buy-sell transactions. First, there is a matter of perspective. Generally, a practice is worth more to the seller than to the purchaser. The seller looks at total net profit derived from the practice and doesn't typically subtract the dentist's imputed reasonable salary. It is this adjusted profit that drives practice value because the purchaser always has the opportunity to work as an associate, get paid a salary and not commit his or her assets to the practice acquisition. When an opinion of practice value is presented to a prospective seller, he or she may be shocked that the value of the practice is only 50% to 70% of current annualized revenues. The individual might complain, "I can practice for two more years and give the practice away. This will produce a greater value." In fact, the seller is right. To be sure, there are non-monetary factors. There is still the problem with the disposition of patients who have become like "family." The selling doctor is also concerned about staff and perhaps, without admitting it, a professional legacy.

A second reason for disparity in buy-sell valuations is cocktail party misinformation, usually expressed in the form of a price/revenues multiple. While a gullible dentist will state confidently that all practices are worth 100% or 150% of last year's revenues, the professional appraiser knows full well that this rule of thumb could not have come from either a competent appraiser or an experienced practice broker. The source of this distortion is frequently a peer of the selling dentist who is either expressing a "prayer" with regard to the value of his or her own practice or repeating a highly exaggerated sales result. In fact, even under the most profitable of practice scenarios, most financial institutions will refuse to fund a practice acquisition at more than 80% of annual revenues. Sadly, dental professionals, who have wrongly believed that their practice was the nest egg upon which they would retire, are then faced with the sobering reality that they should have engaged in disciplined investing through the years instead of trusting in a "windfall" when their practice sold.

The final reason for valuation disparity is the manipulation of data by a practice adviser, most commonly the broker who quotes an "appraised value" that is, in fact, a number designed to ensure that he or she will obtain the practice listing. This "valuation" is often targeted at overcoming the seller's false hopes and lost opportunities. In other words, it conforms to the desires of the seller, irrespective of marketplace realities. To manufacture such a conclusion of value, the appraiser usually undervalues the reasonable compensation paid to the professional, which results in the overstatement of the practice's value.

Fair Market Value

Any discussion of practice valuation begins by first clarifying that *fair market value* is not determined in the appraiser's mind. Rather, it is determined in the market. As stated in Section 2.02 of IRS Revenue Ruling 59-60, fair market value is defined as "the price at which the property would change hands between a willing buyer and a willing seller when the former is not under any compulsion to buy and the latter is not under any compulsion to sell, both parties having reasonable knowledge of relevant facts." In other words, a practice transaction which is consummated in the marketplace and funded by a banking institution is always a better proxy to fair market value than an appraisal completed by the most competent of practice appraisers. It must be assumed that: 1) both seller and buyer were "willing," 2) neither was under "compulsion," and 3) both had "reasonable knowledge of the relevant facts." That a financial institution blessed the acquisition by advancing money to the purchaser only corroborates the conclusion of Fair Market Value. Notwithstanding the foregoing, there are purchasers who have paid too much for a practice and sellers who have received too little.

1. "Market" should be thought of as *all* potential buyers and sellers *without regard to specific* buyers and sellers.

Even the phraseology fair market value is not reflective of just one purchaser, e.g., the in-place associate. Rather, fair market value reflects a "market" of buyers. In theory, there should be enough potential purchasers in the market to be statistically significant, e.g., the New York Stock Exchange or even houses sold and funded in a specific section of the city. While this is impractical in a small community where there may not be a practice sold for several years, the experienced appraiser will take into consideration the supply and demand for practices within a greater geographical area. If one takes Texas as an example, there is significantly more demand for practices in Austin or even the Texas Hill Country than in Beaumont, Amarillo, or the much smaller central Texas community of Brownwood in West Texas. In fact, the profit margin should be much higher in these last three locations than in the first two, although a service market discount must be taken to reflect the fact that more potential purchasers request Austin locations than anywhere else in the state of Texas. In this latter case, a service market "premium" may even be given.

In practical terms, even if an associate has been working in a particular practice for two or more years, he or she should not be required to pay a greater price for his or her partnership interest than what the owner could expect to receive in the market. Likewise, just because an individual has determined that he and his wife wanted to come home to their small country town in order to raise their children, a practice acquisition price should reflect the fact that fewer doctors elect to move to the country rather than locate in a larger metroplex. Just as this subtracting of a discount or adding a valuation premium is appropriate within a specific geographic area, the extension of such adjustments is also fitting for all oral surgery, orthodontic, or general dental practices in the various regions of the U.S. It is well known, for example, that prior to 2008 there was far less demand for practices in Pennsylvania than in California, regardless of whether the economics are justified, given the level of competition as well as the cost of living. In fact, given the budgetary challenges of California state government, these demand fundamentals may constantly shift over a period of time. However, certain national appraisers assume that these differences do not exist, and this can be most problematic in finding common ground for a purchaser or seller. It is most appropriate for a distant valuation professional to converse with a broker who is more intimately familiar with the unique characteristics of the geographic area.

As one young dentist practicing in Arizona recently told me, "Twenty percent of production is the maximum one can expect to receive working in a dental clinic in the greater Phoenix metroplex." I know of only one group practice in Texas where this would be considered appropriate. In that circumstance, the practice claims that given the level of staff support and new patient flow, the average dentist has over 1 million dollars of annual production. While, at 20%, this would generate an income of $200,000 per year, practitioners who can maintain this work level for an extended period of time are in the minority. On the other hand, a recent graduate in this environment can certainly gain hand speed confidence for an eventual practice acquisition after two or three years.

It is these geographical differences that render national rules of thumb meaningless in the hands of the inexperienced broker or selling dentist, e.g., "all practices are worth 70% of current revenues," irrespective of profit margin. Some professionals will even simplify the appraisal process by determining the in-use value of the installed dental and office equipment and then adding this conclusion to a national average for intangible value to arrive at total fair market value. This kind of biased valuation underscores the necessity of obtaining a second appraisal when the purchaser is evaluating acquisition alternatives. After all, this is probably the largest purchase that a dentist and his or her spouse will make, and they will live with the decision for 25 to 30 years.

2. "Compulsion" relates to the necessity of selling within a specific time frame, such as when a practice must be sold as a result of death or disability.

Obviously, in these cases, time is of the essence! This is especially true in those areas of high practice competitiveness. While a *locum tenens* doctor can be hired on a short-term basis, that individual usually does not have the incentive to maintain practice revenues. In circumstances related to the death of a professional, the challenge is compounded when the spouse has little idea about practice operations other than the fact that a substantial family income was always available. One of the most difficult situations I face is when our firm produces a valuation that is substantially less than the value that the deceased dentist had implied to a spouse. I strongly encourage professionals to have their practice valued while they are still healthy so that they can have a candid conversation with their spouse. Further, an objective assessment of the value of the practice for investment and/or retirement purposes can also be most helpful in one's planning for the future.

There are two ways to handle the additional risk on the part of a purchaser when he or she is purchasing the practice of a deceased dentist. The first is to arbitrarily discount the value of the practice based on the proximity of the valuation to the date of death and the fact that the seller is not available to "anoint" the purchaser with former patients. The second is to value the practice as of the month ending just prior to the date of death and then to develop terms of sale that include a substantial "contingency" or work-out agreement. Obviously the enhanced risk in this case is that the dentist is not in a position of anointing the purchaser with practice patients and/or referral sources. However, the widowed spouse can be of tremendous assistance in this transition process. If, in fact, the revenues actually generated by the purchaser subsequent to closing are equal to or greater than those assumed in the valuation, is it not true that the purchaser obtained that for which he or she had bargained? If revenues cannot be "transferred," then the purchaser will not pay as much under the contingency work-out arrangement. In this second scenario, reality has shown that the totality of revenues could not be transferred, and thus the practice had been overvalued. Remember, projections of both revenues and expenses are only "projections" and are guaranteed to be wrong—either high or low, but never right on.

Another case of compulsion would be disability. Again, a case can be made for valuing the practice as of the date of disability and utilizing the contingency work-out mechanism. Subsequent to disability onset, the profitability of the practice is greatly reduced, but if the patient base can be maintained, revenues can return to normal levels. If not, then the disabled seller must accept a lower payment. Hopefully, any difference in value will have been made up through disability income payments to the disabled doctor.

A recent example is the case of a 58-year-old dentist who had a stroke and no longer felt confident holding a handpiece. A *locum tenens* doctor was found to keep the business open. After six weeks, there were two potential purchasers, one who desired to "cram down" the appraised value and purchase price and a second who was willing to pay full value including a contingent term. The disabled dentist elected the second purchaser, even though he had to make a sacrifice with respect to the terms of sale. In fact, the seller accepted a rapid pay-down promissory note that called for payments in excess of $25,000 per month. A third alternative purchaser might have made an offer superior to the other two, but the selling dentist was under "compulsion."

3. The lack of "reasonable knowledge" may pertain to an unwary purchaser as well as to a gullible seller.

In most cases, the answers are easy, but purchasers must be sure they are asking the right questions. As the acquisition decision is a major one, an acquiring dentist should obtain counsel from a third-party adviser who has experience in dental practice purchase and sale. A full, written opinion is not usually required provided the purchaser has the appraiser's summary interpretation, especially if the verbiage adds substantially to the cost. In any case, valuation is only part of the analysis. There should also be an outline of recommended terms that are relevant both to the practice as well as to the specific marketplace. Finally, there should be an operating pro forma indicating what the net profit will be to the acquiring doctor and his or her family after practice operating expenses and debt service.

I have encountered numerous cases wherein a potential purchaser did not have reasonable knowledge of relevant facts, such as the following. Acting only on the advice of the broker, a recently graduated female African American dentist purchased the practice of a 65-year-old Caucasian male general dentist in a southern United States city. The purchase price was paid 100% in cash on the day of closing. Once the seller handed the office keys to the purchaser, he stepped on the proverbial "plane to Florida." Many patients requested records transfers, and practice revenues dropped by 50%. The purchaser ended up in bankruptcy.

In another case, where dual representation by the broker was involved, a practice producing $500,000 in revenues was only generating three new patients per month. Depending upon the type of treatment provided, at least one-half to one new patient per month should be coming forth from the practice for each $1,000 of monthly production. In other words, if practice revenues are $40,000 per month, twenty to forty new patients per month should be seen in the practice. Otherwise, a practice is probably in a state of atrophy. In this specific case, the purchaser was required to contract with several PPO plans in order to maintain practice revenues. As the resulting fee schedules were lower, the profit margin suffered, and the purchaser needed to curtail family spending in order to meet bank promissory note payments. Clearly, the purchaser had radically overpaid for the practice.

In a third case, the seller did not fully disclose that 20% of practice revenues included orthodontic treatment. The purchaser could only maintain revenues by continuing to provide such care with the ongoing assistance of the seller and by completing further advanced training himself. In each of these situations, a contingency work-out arrangement would have been optimum.

In addition to the fair market valuation and operating pro-forma, there should be an outline of terms. Critical aspects of this analysis might include: (i) facility lease terms and, possibly, an option to purchase the real property in which the dental facility is located, i) the covenant not to compete applicable to the seller, iii) the disposition of accounts receivable and patient credits after the sale, (iv) life and disability insurance requirements, if any, payable to the seller, (v) a due diligence period for the purchaser subsequent to execution of an earnest money contract, (vi) transition assistance on the part of the seller; (vii) seller letters to patients and/or referral sources, (viii) any hold-harmless provisions subsequent to closing, (ix) all compensation to seller, if any, during the "transition period," (x) asset tax allocation of the purchase price and (xi) arbitration or mediation provisions, if any, should a dispute arise between purchaser and seller. Terms of sale which are not "usual and customary" may be cause for a diminution in appraised value.

"Present Value" and the Determination of Fair Market Value

The purchase of a dental practice represents an investment—and an active investment at that. Unlike an individual who purchases stock in IBM but is not an employee of the company, the dentist purchasing a practice will be very much involved in the day-to-day operations of the practice, e.g., going into the treatment rooms every day and providing patient care. He or she is entitled to both a *return to labor* and a *return to capital.* While the IBM stockholder receives no return to labor, that individual can easily sell the stock if dissatisfied with its performance. But if the initial assumptions about projected revenues and expenses prove to have been overstated, the practice-owning dentist has no choice but to continue operations and attempt to increase revenues and/or decrease expenses. Yet unless the practice is acquired in conjunction with a practice partner, the acquiring dentist will have total control with respect to practice direction and focus. Clearly, the appraiser's goal must be to represent as accurately as possible the "present value" of the practice.

The following represent steps used to arrive at a conclusion of value.

1. Project the practice revenues
2. Project the practice expenses
3. Determine estimated gross practice net income on a year-by-year basis
4. Subtract the compensation that the dentist should be paid for providing patient treatment and care (return to labor)
5. Subtract an estimate for *capital replacement* because equipment does not last forever
6. Obtain net return on investment (return to capital)
7. Determine an adequate discount rate to compensate for the commitment of funds
8. Calculate the terminal or ending value
9. Calculate present value for the returns on investment
10. Sum the totals

Table 1 summarizes Steps 1 through 6.

Table 1. Steps 1-6 of Process Used to Arrive at a Conclusion of Value

Year	(1) Practice Revenues	(2) Practice Expenses	(3) Gross Profit	(4) Dentist Comp.	(5) Capital Replacement	(6) Return To Capital
2011	$600,000	$360,000	$240,000	$180,000	$6,000	$54,000
2012	$618,000	$370,800	$247,200	$185,400	$6,180	$55,620
2013	$636,540	$381,924	$254,616	$190,962	$6,365	$57,289
2014	$655,636	$393,382	$262,254	$196,691	$6,556	$59,007
2015	$675,305	$405,183	$270,122	$202,592	$6,753	$60,777

Some explanation of the figures in this table are in order. First, the practice revenues and expenses were grown at a constant rate of 3% per year for each of the five years. Second, practice profit margin equals 40%. Third, the dentist is being compensated (column 4) at 30% of practice revenues, a rate commensurate with a fee-for-service practice located in a moderately competitive urban environment. Thus, including consideration for a capital replacement reserve, the net pre-tax return to capital equals 9% of revenues.

For simplification purposes, as the practice being purchased in this example had a significant tangible asset base, we assumed that there were no income taxes to be paid by the purchaser as a result of asset depreciation and amortization. Thus, the last column equals the return to capital for the five years in question.

In Step 6, we cannot merely assume a 14% or 16% required rate of return. We must examine our discount rate by looking at rates of return for alternative investments and their historical rates of return. In fact, the only statistical measures that are large enough to provide actual rates of return are the publicly traded markets. Thus, we are drawn to the publicly traded bond and stock indexes which are published daily in the financial press.

This calculation is referred to as the *build-up rate* and may be somewhat complex.

Table 2. Calculation of the Build-Up Rate

Risk adjusted discount rate	18.92%
Risk-free rate of return (20-year)—June 30, 2010	3.92%
Equity risk premium	6.70%
Equity risk premium—small company	4.70%
Non C corporation tax effect to market returns	2.60%
Specific company adjustment	1.00%

We will assume that this fair market appraisal is to be calculated as of June 30, 2010. On that date, the "20-year risk-free rate of return" was 3.92%. This is the rate of return that one would earn if one invested in a 20-year Treasury bond. It is considered "risk-free" because no U.S. government Treasury bond has ever defaulted. Obviously, investing in one dental practice in a particular city in the United States is more risky than purchasing a Treasury bond. The question is, "How much riskier?"

According to the *2009 Stocks, Bonds, Bills, and Inflation Yearbook (Market Results, 1926-2009)*, published by Ibbotson and Associates (Chicago, March 2008), if one had invested in the Standard and Poor's 500 Index, one would have earned an additional 6.70 %. However, making a commitment to a single dental practice involves more risk than investing in 500 of the largest corporations in the world on a diversified basis. If one had invested in the lowest quintile of the United States stock market (NASDAQ), during the same 1926-2009 period, one would have earned an additional 4.70 %. From a comparative risk perspective, it should be noted that from April 2001 through December 2009 these results were measured by using the Dimensional Fund Advisors U.S. Micro Cap Portfolio, which at the end of the period contained 2,420 stocks with a weighted average market capitalization for each security of $515 million. The median market capitalization for each individual security was $157 million.

The next component of our build-up rate is somewhat esoteric, as it has to do with the fact that in order to be listed on the New York Stock Exchange, a company must be a Corporate Form 1120 Schedule C tax filer. Such an entity must not only pay corporate income taxes, but the shareholders must also pay income taxes on the dividends they receive. Most dental practices are non-Schedule C tax filers or are Schedule C tax filers who pay little or no corporate taxes, and, as such, they pay little or no corporate or state income tax. It is estimated that, if such public corporations did not pay federal income taxes, they could earn an additional 2.60%, which could be paid out to shareholders.

Each of these build-up components is an objective recording of actual returns or is statistically verifiable. However, the last percentage is subjective on the part of the appraiser and is drawn from a number of factors including, but not limited to, relative profit margin, position and competitiveness within the practice marketplace, depth of management, length of experience, and staff tenure. In the example referenced in Table 2, one percentage point was added to achieve a total build-up rate in our valuation cash flow present-value calculation of 18.92%. In other words, anyone buying this practice would expect to earn an 18.92% return to capital, net after taxes and a reserve for capital replacement.

Now, Step 7 must be performed in order to calculate the terminal or ending value. In investment parlance, this is called the Gordon Growth Model. The formula is as follows:

$$\text{Terminal value} = \frac{\text{Next year ending net return to capital}}{\text{Discount rate} - \text{Growth rate}}$$

$$\text{Terminal value} = \frac{\$60{,}777 \times (1 + 3\%)}{18.92\% - 3.00\%}$$

$$\text{Terminal value} = \frac{\$62{,}601}{15.92\%}$$

$$\text{Terminal value} = \$393{,}222$$

With these calculations having been concluded, Steps 8 and 9 can be completed. Please see Table 3.

Table 3. Steps 8-9 of Process Used to Arrive at a Conclusion of Value

Years	Future Value	Present Value Factor	Present Value at 19.44%
Year 1	$54,000	84.09%	$45,407
Year 2	$55,620	70.71%	$39,327
Year 3	$57,289	59.45%	$34,061
Year 4	$59,007	49.99%	$29,500
Year 5	$60,777	42.04%	$25,550
Year 5	$393,114	42.04%	$165,258
	$669,807		$339,103

In this case, no more than $339,103 should be paid for the practice. If all the projections proved to be "right on," interest rates remained the same, and there was no change in any other valuation assumption, then theoretically, the practice could be resold in five years such that the practice owner would receive an 18.92% return on initial investment. Parenthetically, if the acquiring dentist were to receive 20 years of return to capital and discount the terminal value by 20 years, we arrive at approximately the same conclusion of $339,103.

Essential Analysis and Adjustments

Obviously, there is some analytical work that needs to be done prior to making all of these calculations. Initially, the appraiser must normalize the revenues to arrive at a base from which to make the revenue projections. For example, as most dental practices are on a cash basis for accounting purposes, heavy expenses tend to occur in December with a corresponding postponement of deposits until January. Thus, the appraiser will typically average the prior two years of revenues to "flatten out" these differences and to account for the practice's recent "history" and fluctuation. In certain circumstances, other adjustments are necessary. Where there has been a reduction in revenues due to disability, for example, three years of revenues may be utilized or there could be a "normalization" of those revenues such that the disability would not be reflected. Under normal circumstances the third year prior revenues are moot in terms of the determination of value. In cases where there is a short practice operating history, i.e., a startup, a weighting of the current year in favor of the prior year may be calculated. Of course, under the circumstances, expenses need to be weighted in the same fashion. In both of these examples, there is extra risk to the purchaser.

The next step is to develop an appropriate expense structure for the practice by accounting for expenses to be assumed by the purchaser. One must make adjustments to include only normal operating overhead expenses. This would exclude such items as automobile expenses, personal insurance premiums, nonrecurring consulting fees, continuing education for the dentist, and travel and entertainment. On the other hand, an additional adjustment might be needed to reflect the value of the services of the doctor's spouse to the extent that he or she was not being compensated from the practice or was not compensated at a fair market rate. It must be presumed that the spouse will "retire" with the doctor and that someone else would be hired on either a full-time or part-time basis to assume responsibility for the practice tasks that the spouse has been performing. Under such a scenario, assumptions would be made regarding the number of weekly "family labor" hours worked in the practice as well as an hourly rate required to duplicate the services of the non-compensated or under-compensated spouse. Further, since most practice purchases or asset sales do not include liabilities, interest expense must be subtracted. And as equipment leaseholds are also retired at the time of closing, monthly lease payments are also removed from practice operating expenses.

Profitability being equal, a higher revenue stream is usually more desirable than a lesser revenue stream. Newer equipment is regarded more highly than aged equipment. However, it cannot be overemphasized that it is earnings that drive practice value. A practice generating revenues of $600,000 with a 45% profit margin utilizing old equipment is generally more valuable than a clinic with revenues of $1 million, a 25% profit margin, and brand-new equipment. The exception would be the unique purchaser who felt qualified to grow the revenue base of the practice while at the same time driving up the practice profit margin. However, this purchaser's fair market value would be approaching the definition of investment value, or what the practice is worth uniquely to him or her, as the specific purchaser.

As an example of how important the expense adjustments are as well as the accurate projection of net return to capital, suppose the operating expenses from our prior example are decreased from $360,000 per year to $350,000 per year. This increases the practice operating profit margin to 41.7% and the first-year net return to capital to $64,000, an increase of $10,000 per year or $833.33 per month. The practice fair market value increases to $401,900, an increase of $62,797 over the prior value of $339,103. It should also be noted that valuation and debt service requirements can change dramatically in a fairly short period of time. For example, as of September 1, 2010, fixed-rate seven-year practice acquisition financing could be obtained at levels under 7%. Further, if the 20-year Treasury bond rate goes down, then the risk adjusted discount rate goes down, and practice value drifts upward.

The foregoing is referred to as the discounted cash flow approach, the most academically accepted method for calculating the valuation of a business or, in this case, a dental practice. As promulgated by the Internal Revenue Service in Revenue Ruling 59-60, we will also use three additional methods in our valuation analysis. The first is the *capitalized excess earnings method*, which imbeds the value of the tangible assets in the practice. The last two methods are market forms of analyses and are titled *price-to-revenue* and *price-to-earnings*. Each of these methods and their corresponding validity will be discussed below.

As the issue of allocation was introduced, it should be noted that goodwill or intangible asset value is calculated by subtracting the tangible asset value from the practice fair market value. In the example above (Table 3), if tangible assets equal $139,000, then the goodwill would equal $200,000, i.e., $339,000 (rounded down from $339,103) minus $139,000. This is a critical calculation as dental and office supplies are depreciated over one year and equipment is depreciated over three to seven years, while goodwill is amortized over a 15-year period. Given the substantial difference, a greater allocation to tangible assets can reduce the level of income taxes for the purchaser. On the other hand, such an allocation may exacerbate the ordinary income tax liability of the seller as a result of certain depreciation recapture. The tension between seller and purchaser is obvious and illustrates the importance of their working with a qualified appraiser in the event of a tax audit by the Internal Revenue Service.

In 2006, the IRS promulgated guidelines for the definition of "qualified appraisal" and "qualified appraiser." Although focused specifically at non-cash charitable contributions for returns filed subsequent to August 17, 2006, past history indicates that this new guideline will be broadened to include other areas of estate, gift, and income taxation. In the preface to the IRS notice, it is stated that the purpose is to prevent "substantial or gross valuation misstatements." The Uniform Standards of Professional Appraisal Practice (USPAP) is recognized as a standard for completing a qualified appraisal. Qualified appraisal is defined in IRC Section 170(f)(11)(E) as ". . . appraisal that is (1) treated as a qualified appraisal under regulations or other guidance prescribed by the Secretary, and (2) conducted by a qualified appraiser in accordance with generally accepted appraisal standards. . . ." A qualified appraiser is one ". . . who (1) has earned an appraisal designation from a recognized professional appraiser organization or has otherwise met minimum education experience requirements set forth in regulations prescribed by the Secretary, (2) regularly performs appraisals for which the individual receives compensation, and (3) meets such other requirements as may be prescribed by the [Treasury] Secretary in regulations or other guidance."

Capitalized Excess Earnings

Let's examine the valuation analysis in terms of a real estate fair market appraisal. It has been said that real estate appraisal is the second oldest profession in the world. And, indeed, business appraisal is a stepchild of real estate appraisal. The major difference is that real estate is almost entirely a tangible asset, whereas a dental or specialty practice may be as much as 90% intangible asset or goodwill—or in the banker's parlance, "blue-sky" or "poof." In commercial real estate appraisal, appraisers use three approaches to their analysis: income, cost, and market. The income approach is very similar to the discounted cash flow approach. In the case of real estate, however, the net real property cash flows are a result of subtracting building operating expenses from projected rents.

The component cost approach in real estate normally comprises two calculations: (1) the fair market value of the land underneath the real property, which does not appreciate, e.g., $200,000; and (2) the depreciated amount of what it would cost to replicate the building. Let us assume it would cost $1 million to build the commercial office facility, and this new building might have a 50-year life following the completion of construction. If the subject building is 25 years old, then the cost component of the building would be $500,000 ($1,000,000 times 50%). Thus, under this approach to value, the total building value might be appraised at $700,000 ($200,000 land value plus $500,000 depreciated building value.)

In business appraisal, the cost approach is called *capitalized excess earnings*, and it actually is a combination of both an income and cost approach. If all of the tangible assets were recently acquired and subsequently installed ready for patient care, the conclusion under this theory would be very similar to the discounted cash flow approach. On the other hand, if the equipment is aged or in disrepair, the value would be lower. I use the word "theory" because this methodology is very theoretical. It is assumed that tangible assets are less risky than intangible assets. Goodwill as a part of the intangible value of a practice has a higher element of risk to its transfer. In fact, if the seller mishandles the transition to the buyer, the goodwill could be rendered valueless.

As another example of diminished value of intangible assets, let us assume that a general dentist is sued for malpractice and the case becomes widely known in the local community. To be sure, the value of the practice would be diminished. However, the tangible assets could still be sold at the same value. Because goodwill is the remainder when tangible asset value is subtracted from total practice value, intangible value would decrease. Since return on investment is reflected by the discount rate, a lower rate of return is utilized for the return on tangible assets and a higher rate of return is utilized for intangible assets.

This approach is illustrated in Table 4.

In our hypothetical appraisal (see Table 8), the tangible assets are approximately 17.5% of final practice value ($146,784 divided by $836,623). This is not unusual, and thus the excess earnings method is utilized to reflect the age of the equipment within the subject practice. The return on tangible assets is typically the seven-year bank funding rate for dental practice acquisitions. The return on intangible assets is set at a rate, e.g., 19.50%, such that the value of the practice equals the discounted cash flow method if all of the tangible assets had been recently acquired and installed. Then the percentage depreciation is assumed, which reflects the fair market value of the tangible assets. By decreasing the value of the tangible assets, a lesser amount of return is

Table 4. Capitalized Excess Earnings Approach

Office Furniture and Fixtures		$7,912		
Professional Equipment		120,468		
Tangible Assets After Economic Depreciation			128,380	
Consumable Supplies			18,404	
Total Net Tangible Assets				146,784
Historical Revenues	100%	1,219,169		
Less: Estimated Revenue Loss	0.00%	–		
2010 Projected Revenues	100%	1,219,169		
Cash-Operting Expenses-Base Costs	56.66%	690,818		
Less: Operating Retrenchment	0.00%			
Estimated Operating Expenses	56.66%	690,818		
Opportunity Cost of Labor	30.00%	365,751		
Reserve for Capital Replacement	1.00%	12,291		
Pretax (Capital) Income	12.34%	150,409		
Less: Federal Income Tax	1.53%	18,710		
Normalized Net Return To Capital	10.80%		131,699	
Return on Tangible Assets	8.00%		(11,743)	
Excess Earnings			119,956	
Capitalized Value of Excess Earnings	19.50%			615,159
Gross Value of Business/Practice				761,943
Less: Assets Excluded				–
Preliminary Fair Market Value				761,943
Plus: Adjustments for Qualitative Factors				38,097
Total Fair Market Value				$800,040

subtracted from net operating revenue and an increasing amount is subject to the higher rate of return assumed for intangible assets. Thus, the fair market value of the practice is decreased, reflecting the age and condition of the professional equipment, computer installations, office and reception furnishings, clinical and clerical supplies, and instruments.

As discussed earlier, a corollary of the cost component method, not utilized by this appraiser, is to add an intangible value amount to the value of the tangible assets. This intangible value amount is often ascertained by utilizing a study of average goodwill value in various like-kind practices throughout the United States. However, the old adage applies in this case as well: "Averages apply to everybody, but not to anybody in particular." There is no correlation in this method to the actual profit margin in the subject practice or even to the type of practice or level of new patient flow. It assumes that the purchaser can quickly adapt to the national practice average. Even if the goodwill study were adapted to a specific geographic area, dental practices can vary by 10% to 15% in profit margin depending on the types of patients seen, procedures completed, and the insurance plans with which the dentist is contracted.

Price-To-Revenue Methodology

The final approaches to value are the market approaches. The most common, and sometimes the only methodology used by some appraisers, is called the *price-to-revenue ratio*. This is the method most often used by general dental and specialty practice owners because it is the easiest to understand. A percentage is applied to current revenues to determine value, e.g., 60% of $600,000 in annualized revenues concludes a value at $360,000. In this calculation there is no regard for practice profit margin or age and condition of equipment. It is deemed to be a rule of thumb that produces an erroneous conclusion unless the practice also happens to be at the average profit margin as well as average equipment age.

Since 1987, our company has maintained a proprietary database that actually records consummated and bank-funded practice sales. Other organizations, such as the Institute of Business Appraisals, or Pratt's Stats and BIZCOMPS, have also compiled valuation statistics on a national basis. The challenge in using national statistics and the national firms that utilize such statistics in calculating an appraisal is that there can be wide disparity within various regions of the United States. The statistics in our proprietary database represent real transitions wherein we were actually involved in the sale or had intimate information with respect to the specific price and terms of sale. We have also kept a record of the profit margins for each of these practice sales. Our database indicates that for the past 23 years, the average practice has sold for 61.20% of average revenues over the past two years.

However, as we know from the study of statistics, an average is meaningless without a correlation coefficient. In fact, this 61.20% average is correlated to an average profit margin of approximately 42%. All other things being equal—and they usually aren't—a practice with a profit margin less than 42% would sell for less than 61% of revenues. Conversely, a practice with a profit margin exceeding 42% might sell at a value approaching 65% or 70% of revenues. It should also be noted that price-to-revenue ratios are not uniform throughout the United States. Not only do price-to-revenue ratios go up, but profit margins go down in areas of extreme competitiveness, e.g., the Eastern and Western United States. Obviously, this is a function of supply and demand.

This price-to-revenues approach is illustrated in Table 5.

Table 5. Price to Revenues Approach

Revenues Projected—Base Year 2010	$1,219,169
Price-Revenue Multiplier	61.20%
Specialty Profit Adjustment	0.00%
Geographical Adjustment	0.00%
	61.20%
Preliminary Fair Market Value	$746,109
Adjustments for Qualitative Factors	37,305
Total Fair Market Value	$783,414

Price-To-Earnings Methodology

The final market approach is the *price-to-earnings* method, and I believe it is the most significant. In fact, the conclusion of value under this method should closely approximate the discounted cash flow conclusion discussed previously. If you open *The Wall Street Journal* and look for information on IBM, you would have no idea what the revenues for IBM were last year or how much equipment it owned. You would find the opening and closing price of a share of the stock as well as the price/earnings ratio. In our database that tracks actual practice sales over 23 years, we have kept statistics regarding P/E for these practices.

According to our records, the 23-year average P/E ratio is 5.49 times normalized pretax earnings. We have utilized a pretax earnings level because the negotiation over tangible asset value sometimes skews the after-tax earnings for a practice sale. In my experience, the P/E ratio will also vary by geographic region. However, the skew or variance does not seem to be as dramatic as it is in price-to-revenue ratios. Practices on the East and West Coasts seem to produce more revenues as a result of higher patient volume. While these practices have lower profit margins, the total volume of earnings is higher. Given the higher levels of competition, HMO and PPO plans tend to be more prevalent in these locations, and thus reimbursement rates per procedure are somewhat lower.

In terms of additional assumptions that must be made, the current tax rate on dividends paid from a publicly traded corporation is 15%. Likewise, a 3% long-term inflation assumption has been inserted to reflect increases in both revenues and expenses. While some appraisers use higher assumptions, I believe that growth in excess of 3% is a result of the purchaser's efforts and is not inherent to the practice itself. It is possible that an increased growth assumption could be included for one or two years, but not on a long-term basis. There is a principle of physics stating that voids will be filled. In other words, extraordinary growth of a practice will stimulate additional practitioners to establish alternative practices within that community, and thus, a long-term growth assumption greater than the inflation rate, in my opinion, cannot be sustained. The price-to-earnings approach is illustrated in Table 6.

Table 6. Price to Earnings Approach

Historical Revenues	100.00%	$1,219,169	
Less: Estimated Revenue Loss	0.00%	-	
Projected Revenues	100.00%	1,219,169	
SUGGEST MOVING LINES CLOSER			
Cash Operating Expenses-Base Costs	56.66%	690,818	
Less: Operating Retrenchment	0.00%	-	
Estimated Operating Expenses	56.66%	690,818	
Net Revenues	43.34%	$528,351	$528,351
Less:			
Opportunity Cost of Labor	30.00%	$365,751	
Reserve for Capital Replacement	1.00%	12,192	
	31.00%	377,942	
Normalized Pre-Tax Earnings	12.34%		150,409
P-E Multiplier			
Base Multiplier		5.49	
Specialty Profit Adjustment		0.00	
Geographical Adjustment		0.00	
		5.49	
Preliminary Fair Market Value			$825,775
Adjustments for Qualitative Factors			41,289
Total Fair Market Value			$867,064

For comparative purposes, we have included the discounted cash flow analysis that correlates to the valuation calculations in Tables 4 through 6. This methodology is illustrated in Table 7 below.

Table 7. Discounted Cash Flow Approach

		2010	2011	2012	2013	2014
Real Revenue Increases		0.00%	3.00%	3.00%	3.00%	3.00%
(Nominal Cash Flows)						
Historical Revenues	100.0%	$1,219,169				
Less: Estimated Revenue Loss	0.0%	0				
2010-2014 Projected Revenues		1,219,169	1,255,744	1,293,416	1,332,219	1,372,185
Cash Operating Expenses-Base Costs	56.7%	690,818				
Less: Cost Retrenchment	0.0%	0				
Estimated Operating Expenses	56.7%	690,818	711,542	732,889	754,875	777,522
Normalized Net Operating Revenues	43.3%	528,351	544,201	560,528	577,343	594,664
Opportunity Cost of Labor	30.0%	(365,751)	(376,723)	(388,025)	(399,666)	(411,656)
Reserve for Capital Replacement	1.0%	(12,192)	(12,557)	(12,934)	(13,322)	(13,722)
Pre-Tax (Capital) Income	12.3%	150,409	154,921	159,569	164,356	169,286
Less: Federal Income Tax	1.5%	18,710	19,387	20,084	20,802	21,542
Net Return to Capital	10.8%	$131,699	$135,534	$139,485	$143,554	$147,745
Current Value Equivalent Returns		84.09%	70.71%	59.45%	49.99%	42.04%
Present Value-Net Return to Capital		$110,742	$95,831	$82,930	$71,768	$62,109
Total Present Value - Net Return to Capital						$423,380
Terminal Asset Value						
Beginning 6 Yr. Net Return to Capital		$152,062				
Capitalization Rate		15.92%				
Beginning 6 Yr. Terminal Asset Value			$954,896			
Present Value of Terminal Asset Value				42.04%		401,422
Preliminary Fair Market Value						$824,803
Adjustments for Qualitative Factors						41,240
Total Fair Market Value						$866,043

Qualitative Factors

As discussed previously, another assumption that can be made pertains to service market. This factor can reflect the relative health—or lack thereof—of the local economy. In addition, it is an attempt to correlate areas that are more or less in demand by potential purchasers. Unlike the residential real estate market where there is accurate sales data on numerous transactions within a given community, there are not enough dental or specialty transactions within a given community to be statistically significant. With regard to specific markets in Texas, communities such as Houston, Dallas, and San Antonio are more in demand than practices in El Paso, Texarkana, or Beaumont. Thus, discounts or "premia" must be taken into consideration to account for these differences. Unfortunately, assumptions regarding service market demand would be difficult for a layperson to ascertain.

Other qualitative factors, such as special attributes of seller—e.g., a Medicaid emphasis, lack of computerization, or high staff turnover—may be cause for a diminution of value. In other cases a discount may be taken for the size of a facility where there is no room for expansion. Conversely, a premium may be required if a facility is larger than average and has capacity for additional producers.

In some cases, for perceived or real tax reasons, a seller may require that the purchaser acquire stock as opposed to acquiring tangible and intangible assets. In such circumstances, the purchaser is disadvantaged, as he or she would not be eligible for depreciation and amortization expense deductions. *Under this requirement, we typically subtract 17.5% from practice fair market value, which represents a discount of 50% in terms of the maximum federal income tax bracket.* Albeit the purchaser would have a higher basis at practice resale, we believe that this is an appropriate discount for the purchaser being required to make payments on an after-tax basis. Occasionally in specialized cases, discounts are taken as a result a lack of marketability or the offering of a minority interest. On the other hand, a premium may be added as a result of the valuation of a majority interest.

Formulating the Fair Market Value

While my position is that the four conclusions of value must be "synthesized" to arrive at a final conclusion of practice fair market value, certain valuators take exception to this synthesis of values. Some highly respected authors have stated that one valuation methodology must be selected and all others discarded. To the contrary, we believe the weighting we have used results in a synthesis that best represents fair market value. Old equipment needs to draw down a valuation conclusion. Likewise, higher revenues are utilized by the industry in the setting of sale prices and clearly represent a greater opportunity for the purchaser to enhance value by more cost-effective financial management. Our synthesis of valuation summary can be seen in Table 8.

Table 8. Summary Table of Valuation Methods Utilized and Weightings for Conclusion

	Adjusted Valuation	%	Weighted Valuation
Cost Approaches:			
Historical Book Value	$167,863	0.00%	$0
Tangible Net Worth	$235,779	0.00%	$0
Income Approaches:			
Discounted Cash Flow	$866,043	30.00%	$259,813
Excess Earnings	$800,040	20.00%	$160,008
Market Approaches:			
Price to Revenues	$783,414	20.00%	$156,683
Price to Earnings	$867,064	30.00%	$260,119
Unweighted	$829,140		
Weighted Value			**$836,623**

I have a bias toward earnings as the foundation for the approaches used to value the subject practice. Thus, you will notice that the discounted cash flow method and the price-to-earnings ratio carry weightings of 30% to the total conclusion as opposed to 20% each for the excess earnings and price-to-revenue methodologies. As the price-to-revenues and capitalized excess approaches tend to offset one another and carry a lower weighting, there is little disparity between the weighted and the unweighted totals. If one divides the $836,623 final conclusion by the assumed $1,219,169 of annualized revenues, one arrives at a price-to-revenue ratio of 68.6%. This percentage is higher than the average of 61% because the assumed profit margin is 43.3% versus the statistical average of approximately 42%. We have already seen how a difference in operating profit can impact value, merely in terms of the additional amount of debt service capacity.

Please note that since the practice has substantive going concern value, no weight has been given to the two cost approaches. The *historical book value* method is occasionally utilized for partnership buy-sell purposes, but is, in reality, an accounting fiction. The *tangible net worth* method includes liabilities and indicates the value of the tangible assets "installed and ready to receive patients." And, in fact, the method is representative of the "salvage value" or "floor" below which the practice value should not fall.

Operating Expenses

Every practice has normal operating expenses. They include fixed expenses, semi-variable expenses, and variable expenses.

Fixed Expenses

Fixed expenses are those over which we have very little control, such as insurance costs, licenses, facility expenses, and personal property taxes. Personal property taxes are distinguished from real property taxes because most space leases include real property taxes.

It should be recognized that certain leases do not include such expenses. A "triple net lease," for example, requires that the tenant also be responsible for real property taxes, all property insurance, internal as well as external maintenance, and, if individual utility monitoring is available, all utility costs. Although these types of leases are rare, they oftentimes occur when practice owners also own their building and, to an increasing extent, in new shopping center leaseholds.

When ascertaining the true earnings level of a practice under those circumstances, it is critical to include all operating expenses. In most cases, we suggest that the owner-dentist obtain a lease rate that is a "gross lease" for the facility. Under this arrangement, the practice should pay to the landlord a rate under which the landlord assumes responsibility for building, fire, and casualty insurance, all exterior building maintenance, and real property taxes. This would be comparable to a rate wherein the dentist was leasing from a shopping center, strip mall, or professional building. Since all utility costs in a single-tenant building would be those of the practice owner, the utility expenses would be the responsibility of, and be borne by, the practice in a separate expense category.

Semi-Variable Expenses

Semi-variable expenses are those that are somewhat fixed but which can fluctuate with varying practice collection levels. They include the costs of accounting, advertising, collections, computer maintenance, janitorial services, utility charges, and telephone expenses, among others. The most important expense in this category is staff compensation, which encompasses not only actual compensation paid, but also bonuses, payroll taxes, and continuing education expense. In certain practices, the total of these categories should not be over 17% to 18% of gross practice revenues. This would include practices that are completing a significant number of cosmetic and comprehensive restorations on a limited number of patients and are incurring high laboratory expense or those specialty practices that should not require the services of a hygienist. In other cases, staffing expense could range upward to a maximum of 27%, depending on the numbers of procedures completed and patients seen. However, in these circumstances, rent, dental supplies, and laboratory expenses need to be kept at moderate levels.

Variable Expenses

The third level of expenses is variable expenses. This category includes those items of practice expense that fluctuate directly with the level of practice revenues. They include dental supplies, office supplies, laboratory expenses, office entertainment, professional continuing education and travel expense, freight and postage, and consulting expenses. In other words, if revenues are increasing, the expenses in these categories will, in all likelihood, also be increasing. Conversely, if revenues are decreasing, these expenditures should be decreasing proportionately. The exception of which might be consulting expense where "radical surgery" was required to turn the practice around, perhaps in order to enhance practice profitability.

If crown and bridge procedures are significant to a dentist's practice, then it is appropriate for laboratory expenses to also be significant. If the practice has a strong hygiene program, dental supplies will probably be a higher percentage. Neither of these circumstances is negative. In fact, both are positive. However in the first case, fees charged must be appropriate to the expenditure for laboratory services. In the second, hygiene productivity must be related to both the hygiene staff expense as well as the supply expense. In most cases, a hygienist should produce three times what he or she is being paid. Normally this productivity includes X-rays but not doctor examinations. But in order to meet this productivity level, a hygienist must, in fact, complete a certain amount of enhanced periodontal quadrant care (SRP) per day.

Just as dentists are not responsible for booking their own patients, hygienists are compensated too highly to be responsible for scheduling their own patients. The front desk should be responsible not only to book re-care but also to book quadrants of advanced therapy. In certain cases, it is most cost effective to provide the hygiene department with another assistant rather than to hire a hygienist to meet additional patient demand for prophylaxis. If this is the case, hygiene productivity expense analysis must include the compensation being paid to the hygiene assistant as well.

Dental practitioners often ask, "What is an average supply expense?" Sometimes they quote practice statistics from various consultants or even from state or national dental organizations that cite ranges from 6% to 8%. While we can sometimes discuss practice expenses on an average basis, again it is important to remember that your client's practice may not be average. And even if it is, careful consideration of all supply expense is still critical. With Internet access readily available, it is quite possible for dental professionals to check prices on all supplies and measure them against their usual and customary supplier of choice. In many cases, the latter will discount to the level that the dentist ascertained from careful research. "Bundling" of supply quantity commitment may also bring down the total amount expended over the course of the year.

Finally, certain large supply houses "commingle" their bills to include dental supplies, office supplies, computer services, small equipment, equipment maintenance, and even consulting services. Too often, the office manager or even the practice accountant, relying on expense coding by the doctor or front desk person, commingles all monies paid to a specific vendor under one expense category, e.g., dental supplies. In most cases, it is recommended that accounting software be installed, such as QuickBooks, such that the single vendor bills can be split into the various types of practice operating expenses. Only through careful delineation and understanding can expenses be managed and decisions made for a total operating margin that has become the practice target set by the owner-doctor.

Determining Margins

If a doctor wants to attain optimum practice investment value, then the entire practice operation must be managed toward a specific profit margin. That is the responsibility of the doctor as chief financial officer. It is not the responsibility of the office manager. It is not the responsibility of the practice accountant. It is not the responsibility of the practice consultant. Although each may be relied on for good counsel, the practice owner must analyze his or her profit and loss statements on a weekly and monthly basis to determine whether the dental business has been profitable. Putting one's head in the sand or assuming things will change is a game plan for less than optimal results at best—and failure at worst.

The practice owner must ask: "What is an appropriate expense margin for my practice?" Since the reciprocal of expense margin is profit margin, the first step is to identify the required profit margin for the specific practice. This is determined by both the marketplace and by the owner's personal financial objectives. And while the doctor's practice must serve him or her, and not the contrary, dealing with the reality of one's own marketplace is foundational. The first determination in establishing profit margin is to ascertain the appropriate compensation rate for the services of the doctor, i.e., *return to labor*.

Compensation-Return To Labor

As anyone completing an appraisal will tell you, one of the most difficult assumptions to make in the valuation analysis is the "normal and customary" compensation to be paid to the owner for his or her services. Obviously, this compensation is critical because it determines the *return to capital* that accrues to the business owner in addition to his or her compensation for patient treatment. And like leverage, as stated in prior pages, the impact of enhanced return to capital is dramatic to the conclusion of business value.

In every locality around the United States, associate dentists are paid a wage that is commensurate with the supply and demand for dental professionals in that marketplace. As discussed in Economics 101, when supply of available labor exceeds demand for labor, wages will be reduced. Thus, geographical areas such as California and Arizona that have a greater supply of general dental professionals compensate those dentists at both lower day rates and at lower percentages of production. Further, this also precipitates a higher prevalence of various forms of managed care, i.e., a higher percentage of dental treatment completed under PPOs and capitation/HMO reimbursement plans.

Doctors in less demanded cities and in rural communities can typically pay themselves at higher wage levels because of the lack of professional competition and the reduced levels of other practice expenses. On the other hand, rural practices don't usually see a high volume of patients except for those dominated by Medicaid. Thus, gross compensation may not be as high. Practices seeing Medicaid patients compensate producers at higher levels, not because of reimbursement levels but rather because of the customary scenario where the doctor sees in excess of 40 patients per day. Because of continuing need, certain states have increased Medicaid reimbursement rates significantly, such as Texas, where rates were increased by 50% in September 2007. On the other hand, because of state budget shortfalls, certain states have abandoned Medicaid dental plans entirely.

Finally, dental professionals who have no responsibilities other than completing treatment care with significant staff assistance and have two or three treatment rooms from which to work can be paid a lower compensation rate. In fact, those individuals working for national provider clinics can earn a maximum compensation merely because of the high volume of patients seen. There is a multi-clinic general practice in Dallas that guarantees initial annual compensation rates of $140,000 or 20% in excess of $700,000 per year. However, all financial arrangements are completed by front desk staff, dental assistance is ample, schedules are full, and all patients are of the fee-for-service or PPO type. Most dentists will find it difficult to maintain this production level for extended periods of time. For new graduate dentists, their hand speed will definitely increase!

Marketplace Compensation

Compensation rates for dental professionals can also relate to the type and complexity of dentistry being completed. Obviously doctors who are proficient at endodontic, surgical, periodontic, intravenous sedation or even Invisalign treatment deserve, and can command, higher compensation levels. It must be emphasized, however, that it is not the doctor who sets these compensation rates; it is the marketplace. Notwithstanding advanced resident training or completed courses from the Academy of General Dentistry, Pankey, or the Las Vegas Institute, an individual cannot determine his or her reimbursement rate when competition is keen. Further, in an economic downturn as observed in the fall of 2008, employment opportunities and, consequently, earnings rates can deteriorate.

Marketplace compensation rates can be observed empirically from two places. First, one can ask recent graduates about employment offers from various clinic operations. The percentage rate will typically stay the same with increased compensation earned as the level of production increases with experience. If the associate is expected to complete a significant amount of managed care, a day rate may be offered. If such a daily rate is offered, one can ask about the expected rate of daily production. Dividing the production expectation by the day rate will also yield the percentage compensation rate in the mind of the owner when the day rate was calculated. Young dentists can also be asked about offers from private offices although the responses may vary significantly based on the type of work that will be required by the hiring owner-doctor. A higher rate of compensation may be offered if the associate is "sitting on his/her hands" and seeing few patients per day, completing hygiene checks or providing patient prophylaxis. Remember that 40% of very little is still very little.

A qualified practice appraiser or dental consultant must be prepared to offer objective advice based on knowledge of the mean or average profit margin for either general or specialty practices in the area served. National profit margins cited by national consultants may or may not be applicable to the area in question. I have found that the "usual and customary" compensation rate for a specific city or locale will be approximately 10 to 13 percentage points below the average practice profit margin in that same area, e.g., a practice profit margin of 40% to 43% minus a return to labor of 30% equals 10% to 13%.

For general dentists, the "market" compensation rates will usually range from 20% (highly competitive states where managed care is prevalent) to 35% of practice revenues in low competition areas or where high technical skill is required. For the following discussion purposes, assumptions are based on the current Texas marketplace, including a median compensation rate of 30%. Keep in mind that this compensation rate is for a general dentist who is completing operative care, has a fairly full schedule, and is seeing 10 to 15 patients per day. As the objectives of the practice owner are considered, it is also assumed that 30% of the specific collection levels of the practice meet the income objectives of the doctor and the doctor's family, including long-term savings levels.

Profit Margin Impact

As mentioned earlier, the practice owner who desires maximum value from his or her practice investment needs to obtain a maximum profit margin over and above the compensation paid to the associate. In nearly 25 years of experience, I have observed that it is very difficult to move very far beyond 13 percentage points above the compensation paid to the associate. When a dentist proudly proclaimed to me recently his 48% profit margin, I inquired about the level of compensation he was paying his associate. He revealed that the agreement was at the 35% level. Hence, the true profit is 48% minus 35% or 13%. Associate periodontal compensation averages 35%, while endodontic and pediatric specialty and oral surgeon associate compensation is about 40%. Again, I remind you that averages do not necessarily apply to a specific practice. It is the responsibility of the practice owner as CEO and CFO of the practice to find out what the fair compensation rate is based on the reality of the marketplace, not on what the associate expects or what the practice owner thinks might be appropriate. And since the practice owner rarely has a grasp of marketplace realities, it becomes the appraiser's duty to understand the market and make compensation recommendations based on marketplace realities.

Excess-Return to Capital

To reiterate, the 30% paid to the associate provider is referred to as the *return to labor* or *compensation paid to professionals* (Roger K. Hill, ASA). The excess return, over and above the *return to labor*, is called the return to capital. As stated earlier, an optimum *return to capital* is 13%. It is not unreasonable to suggest that this return to capital will pay for the acquisition of a partial interest or a practice in its entirety over a seven-year period at prevailing interest rates. You may recall the term "leveraged buy-out" or LBO. In this case, an acquiring company utilizes the *excess earnings*, or amounts in excess of compensation required to keep company managers in place, for the purpose of buying the company. These excess earnings are paid to the bank for any primary or secondary financing required for business acquisition. In other words, if the practice is fairly valued, a purchaser or potential buy-in partner can continue to earn his or her fair compensation subsequent to practice or interest acquisition and concurrently retire the acquisition note utilizing the return to capital to cover principal and interest payments at the bank. If the return to capital is insufficient to retire the note over seven to 10 years, the practice is valued too highly. Please note that banks have begun to offer 15-year term notes as a way of funding practices that are overvalued, just as automobile dealerships typically offer not just a 3-year but also a 7-year loan term.

Perhaps the biggest reason that associates do not purchase the practice in which they have been working for a period of time is that they would have to take a cut in compensation in order to make the acquisition. While the seller may believe that this is appropriate, it is the market that controls this pricing decision, not the seller. This may happen because compensation paid to the associate was too high in the first place. For this reason, we encourage the senior doctor to have an appraisal completed prior to the associateship beginning if a buy-in or buy-out is contemplated in the future. In fact, the appraisal will indicate to the senior doctor the maximum that he or she can afford to pay an associate. At the same time, the valuation completed prior to the associate agreement being drafted will indicate forethought on the part of the practice owner as well as help the associate to understand the level of compensation that will be offered.

The practice owner must remember that the associate has other options. He or she can always purchase another practice at a lower price. In most cases, the potential associate/buy-in partner is also evaluating other options, in many cases with a broker who has a vested interest in seeing the associate purchase a practice that he or she represents. Parenthetically, it should also be noted that as in real estate or automobile acquisition, as discussed above, the consultant representing the seller may try to obtain a longer note amortization period in order to mitigate the cash flow on the part of the acquirer. Some banks also try this same approach under the pretense of easing cash flow for the purchaser while at the same time guaranteeing more interest income for committed loan dollars. Without complete disclosure to the naïve purchaser, I believe that this representation is inappropriate, if not deceitful.

Without further elaboration at this point, it must be added that the aging of practicing professionals is slowly creating a buyer's market. This is being offset somewhat by the number of women who are practicing fewer hours due to their dual responsibilities as mothers. Further, the economic downturn in the fall of 2008 has also caused many sellers to postpone their retirement decisions until stock portfolios can be revitalized.

As practices get larger, it appears that the most common method of practice transition will become (1) the associate buy-in, (2) an intervening partnership and (3) a final buyout. It is important then to clarify this three-step concept with all parties in order to achieve the intended conclusion. And it is absolutely critical that encapsulated within the associate agreement are (1) the details of the associate relationship; (2) the timing, price, and terms of the buy-in; and (3) the specific terms of the partnership. I cannot stress enough that the practice valuation is foundational for all of these discussions. It is truly tragic when "negotiation" has negotiated all of the "relationship" out of a relationship. This is frequently the case when the pricing and terms are not clarified at the outset of an associateship. In these situations, the associate finds an alternative practice to purchase, and the seller is left with a higher expense ratio, a stressed practice schedule, and the necessity of finding a new "partner." Unfortunately, the seller is often embittered and reluctant to begin anew. Further, he or she proclaims to all who will hear, "A partnership buy-in is rarely successful!" or "Partnerships never work!" Seldom do practice owners look at themselves and suggest that they were the ones who precipitated the failure through the lack of agreement specificity and/or not having obtained the assistance of a qualified professional.

Wage Plus Investment Value

Remember that when individuals buy into a practice or purchase a practice in its entirety, they are not buying a job; rather, they are buying the return in excess of the compensation for completing that job. Consider an example outside of dentistry. The president of IBM earns a salary. If he also owns 1 million shares of IBM, he would earn dividends on those 1 million shares. If he were fired from IBM, he would no longer receive the CEO compensation, but he would retain his dividends. On the other hand, if he retained his position but sold his stock, he would retain his annual compensation but would no longer receive his dividends. Indeed, the analogy carries over to the dental practice. The owner-dentist or acquiring interest partner earns a wage, e.g., 30%, for completing treatment on a daily basis and also a return on his or her investment from being an owner.

In order to set the stage for discussions on partnership compensation and consequent associate buy-in or buyout, it is critical to understand that when the buy-in takes place, the associate begins to receive a percentage interest in the return to capital, e.g., the 13%. If he or she buys a 10% minority interest in the practice, then he/she receives 10% of the return to capital. A junior dentist who acquires a 50% partnership interest receives 50% of the 13% return to capital. This 10% or 50% of the return to capital will be sufficient to retire the promissory note on the practice interest being acquired by the associate from the practice owner. If the associate is required to take a reduction in monthly compensation, the partnership acquisition and, consequently, the practice relationship will usually fail.

This concept is easily agreed to at the outset of the associate relationship but is oftentimes difficult to achieve one to three years after employment has commenced. An analogy that is sometimes helpful is that of looking through a kaleidoscope. Before the associate ever sets foot inside the treatment room, both the associate and the practice owner are looking through the kaleidoscope from the same end. One to three years later, they are still looking at the same "stuff," but they are looking from different ends—and seeing different pictures. The associate thinks he/she should pay the value of the practice when he/she began working. The owner thinks the associate should pay the value when the option to buy was exercised. Both are reasonable positions. However, different perspectives can cause further discussions to break down permanently. I normally recommend the position that Solomon took: "Let's split the baby." Take the two valuations—one at the outset of the relationship and one at the point of buy-in—and average the two. In effect, the owner is given the benefit of providing the base of patients and referrals while the associate is given credit for providing the "sweat" of the practice growth. Only infrequently have both parties not been able to agree on this position at the beginning of the relationship.

Managing Expenses

Let's draw some conclusions. If the market compensation or return to labor for the associate is 30% of practice revenue and the required return to capital is 13%, then the required practice profit margin is 43%. If practice revenues represent 100% and required profit margin represents 43%, then practice operating expenses must be managed to the reciprocal, or no more than 57%. Thus, national or local averages with respect to rent, dental or office supplies, laboratory expense, or staffing expense are, to a certain extent, irrelevant. What is relevant is the uniqueness of the professional's practice and how he or she delivers treatment to his or her patient base in the distinctive way to which they have grown accustomed. The responsibility of the practice owner as the chief financial officer is to manage total operating expenses so that they do not exceed, in this case, 57%.

If a new office is built and facility expense increases from 4% to 7%, two options remain: (1) reduce practice operating expenses by 3% in other areas; or (2) raise revenues such that facility expense once again returns to a 4% level. If, because of the type of procedures being completed, laboratory expense increases from 7% to 10%, there are three options: (1) decrease staff expense as a result of what may be decreased patient visits; (2) increase patient fees; or (3) reduce laboratory expenses, perhaps through alternative means, e.g., the acquisition of a Cerec type machine. I will suggest that practices utilizing a Cerec usually have laboratory expenses 2 to 4 percentage points below practices without such devices. So as not to totally endorse this unique laboratory alternative, let me add that for its high expense to be justified, (1) it must be utilized by all providers, and (2) the practice must be large enough, e.g., producing enough crown and bridge, to justify the acquisition. There have been overzealous salesmen who have oversold the product to practices that develop revenues far less than required for such a practice investment.

If you log on to www.yourpracticeasset.com, you will find a matrix for applying the principles of this chapter within your client's practice. It should be noted that a practice with a return to capital of 13% should sell for 60% to 70% of the average of the last two years of practice revenues. The range depends on certain inherent, qualitative practice factors such as the volume of patients in the community where the practice is located, new patient flow, size and quality of facility, equipment technology, and the age and experience of the staff.

For years I have encouraged practice owners to subdivide the net practice revenue they receive rather than classify all of it as personal disposable income. A practice not only will provide dentists with compensation from the "work of their hands," i.e., return to labor, but if well managed, will also provide them a return on investment and return to capital. During the course of their working careers, the typical investor reinvests the dividends from mutual funds or stocks. Yet to satisfy their current financial needs, some dentists spend not only the return to labor but also the return to capital on an annual basis. I strongly suggest that dentists, especially those who are beginning their practice careers, manage their standard of living within the 30% return to labor, which is their compensation for providing patient treatment. If a practice is purchased in its entirety, or a practice interest is acquired in a partnership, it will be necessary to utilize the 13% return to capital to retire the debt on the acquisition promissory note. However, after the "mortgage burning," it is recommended that this return to capital be saved or invested for retirement, as opposed to being spent on lifestyle enhancement. While this may sound like a sermon and probably applies to each of us within our respective businesses, if you encourage your dental clients to embrace this philosophy, I suspect their appreciation for your services will extend well beyond the specific appraisal engagement.

It has been observed that most dentists walk out of dental school with the objective of retiring by age 55. However, whether because of children's college expenses, frustrations in the stock market, or divorce, few reach that goal. Reaching that goal is not difficult, but it does take discipline. Practice investment dividends should be saved, as should the return to capital. Only in that circumstance will the dentist have the option of retiring after 25 to 30 years in practice.

Chapter 3

Dental Practice Valuations: Beyond the Numbers

By Sarah K. Lynch, Managing Partner, Jim Kasper Associates, LLC

According to the American Dental Association 2008 Survey on Dental Practice, 29.1% of all general dental practices in the U.S. had gross annual revenues over 1 million dollars. What is interesting to me as an appraiser is the variety of ways these practices achieved this economic milestone. Some of them were owned by individual doctors who possess superb managerial, communication and clinical abilities and who achieved this milestone as solo practitioners on a four-day workweek with 32 hours of clinical time. The staff mix likely comprised two registered dental hygienists, two dental assistants and one front-desk person. Other practices hitting the $1 million mark had perhaps two or more doctors working five or six days per week with the practice, offering up to 66 hours of clinical time, no registered dental hygienists, several part-time dental assistants and front-desk staff.

Which office is more valuable? It depends! Beauty is in the eye of the beholder. Location is a key driver that can amplify value significantly. Intimately knowing the marketplace and what things are selling for, I can guarantee that if both of the practices above were in "hot" markets, typically nice urban or suburban areas close to dental schools, with a strong economic base and a readily available supply of patients and potential purchasers, the values would be on the higher end of the spectrum.

That being said, when performing a dental practice appraisal, demographic research is an essential component to determine value. To capture the essence of what the general dental practice is all about, I believe a site visit is critical. The practice numbers tell one story, but the site visit tells another. Let me explain. Occasionally doctors will send me their practice tax returns and financial reports prior to my site visit. I will review them and form an impression in my mind like, "Nice cash flow! This place nets 60%!" I get there and see why! The net is so nice because the practice has not been updated in years and the practice owner's significant other doubles as the front desk/dental assistant—and is underpaid. Needless to say, there might be an adjustment or two in the final appraisal report.

Practice metrics are very telling too. Most general practices have some level of computerization. Doctors are able to produce excellent reporting information pertaining to their scope of treatment and current practice capacity. My favorite reports to glean are the production by provider (dentists and hygienists) and procedure reports. Usually those reports for the current year and previous two years are sufficient. An appraiser can decipher whether the services provided are heavily weighted in the normal ranges, with diagnostic, preventive, and restorative procedures being the most predominant in the general dental practice.

Composition of patient base is another key factor in the general practice appraisal. How large is the active patient base? Once again, many practices that are computerized have the capability of producing patient demographics reports. However, the accuracy of those reports is sometimes in question. Many practices have loaded up the computer with patients since the dawn of time and have never purged the inactive patients from the system, thus overstating the size of the patient base and skewing the other metrics tied to the reporting information, such as insurance penetration and age mix of patients.

A measure of an active patient is one who is in the hygiene recall program consistently for the past 18 months. An appraiser can manually count the active charts. If the office is paperless, the computer procedure count reports can be reviewed and cross-checked with the appointment book. The number of active patients in the hygiene recall system is a pretty reliable figure to approximate active patients. In most practices the typical full-time hygienist treats 8 to 10 patients per day worked. Most patients visit the dental practice every six months for a hygiene appointment. Annually tracking back to the production by provider and procedure reports and dividing the number of hygiene visits by two will closely approximate the active patient base.

The dental equipment and office furnishings are essentially the props on the stage. We are in an interesting era of what I like to call a technology curve. It is a mishmash of functional utility out there in the area of dental equipment and computerization. We will see dental operatories with 30-year-old dental chairs, 20-year-old cabinetry, and brand new computers in each one. Newer dental practices have embraced the digital age, with computers in every operatory, digital radiography (no more dark rooms, dip tanks, and automatic developers), and ergonomic equipment. The vast majority of dental practices have some degree of computerization, with just a handful of practices having none. It is important to note that regardless of the age of the equipment, if it is in place, functioning, and in reasonably good condition it will have some value.

The bulk of the value in an established productive full-time general practice will most always be heavily favoring goodwill. The orchestration of patient flow with provider utility is the mixture that results in revenue generation. A review of appointment book scheduling history and advance bookings is quite useful in determining if the practice has great systems and processes in place. Looking at the historical bookings shows how full the clinical schedule and broken appointment ratio was. Looking ahead indicates how strong the hygiene department is and how soon new patients can get into the doctor's schedule. The dental team and its leader have to attract patients, treat patients, bill for services, and get patients to return again for regular treatment. Capacity comes into play with office hours offered, staff mix and treatment rooms available.

When interviewing the practice owner, practice philosophy, marketing, and management style are important topics to discuss in order to understand the operational thrust of the practice.

Understanding the sources of the practice revenue stream and financial policies is important as well. Very few practices are totally fee for service, meaning payment is received from the patient on the day of treatment. Thus there will be a minuscule accounts receivable balance in those practices. Most practices accept assignment of insurance benefits as a courtesy to patients with dental insurance coverage. They will bill the patients for any unpaid insurance differential. Some practices will accept the fee paid by the insurance company as payment in full. There is usually a contract between the practice and the insurance company indicating such arrangement. The bulk of the accounts receivable is likely to represent 4 to 10 weeks of practice production. It is important for an appraiser to annotate if there is a large concentration of patients in the practice coming from a single employer's dental insurance plan or if the practice participates with a significant amount of Medicaid.

Once the practice data have been gathered, metrics reported, and financial materials analyzed, in the broadest terms, a general practice will typically have a net profitability of anywhere between 30% and 50%. There are a few exceptional practitioners who exceed the boundaries, and I have seen some as high as 60% with reasonable size staffs in place and in desirable locations.

Assigning value and checking for validity will take some forensic prowess on the part of the appraiser who does not possess intimate knowledge of what dental practices are selling for in specific geographic areas. Depending on the location and quality of the practice, some practices can sell for as much as one-and-one-half to two times annual adjusted net income. These are likely to be modern well-established practices in robust, prosperous communities with strong buyer demand. On the other hand, practices with waning patient bases, situated in declining neighborhoods or exhibiting steadily decreasing revenue trends might only sell for one year's annual adjusted net income or less.[1]

The Pediatric Dental Practice

The pediatric dental practice operates much the same as a general dental practice, and profitability ranges are similar. The key differences for this type of specialty practice are as follows: 1) the patient base is comprised of children from infant through adolescent and children with developmental disabilities; 2) the referral of the patient base is sourced largely from surrounding dental and medical communities; 3) in addition to private practice, most pediatric dentists have hospital privileges and perform a small number of procedures, usually scheduled well in advance, in a hospital operating room; 4) pediatric dentists often treat a fair number of underprivileged children with state Medicaid benefits on reduced-fee schedules; and 5) hygiene visits are much shorter in duration, and a hygienist can easily treat 12 to 16 patients per day.

It is no secret that there is a shortage of pediatric dentists in the United States, especially in rural areas. There are a total of 70 post-doctoral pediatric specialty training programs in the U.S. producing approximately 317 trained pediatric dentists every two to three years. As an appraiser, it is important to note that pediatric dental practices are in high-demand in livable areas and will always have value. The key is to look carefully at the demographics and specialist competition factor of an area when evaluating the practice. Any easy way to investigate is to visit the American Academy of Pediatric Dentistry at www.AAPD.org.

1. This appraiser defines annual adjusted net income as net profitability of the practice plus owner compensation, normalizing adjustments, and recapture of depreciation and any expenses of direct benefit to the practice owner(s).

Confidential Practice Analysis

Personal - Doctor's Name:____

Office Address:____

____ Zip code:__________

Office Telephone No: ____

Age:___ Dental School:________________________________Year:________

Special Training: ____

First Year of Private Practice:___ How long at present location: __________
Number or Treatment Rooms:________ Left Handed ____ Right Handed _____
Where did you practice before?___________________________________
How long were you there?____

Tell us about the area: ____

____

____

____

Dentists: ____

What is your philosophy of practice?______________________________

____

____

What kind of person would be the best candidate for this practice? ____________

____

____

PERSONNEL –

Position	Name	Wages	Additional Benefits	How Long Employed	Hrs/Week

Do you anticipate any changes?_______

Jim Kasper Associates, LLC –P.O. Box 369, Keene NH 03431 603-355-2260 info@jimkasper.com

Office Hours:

______ Monday Tuesday Wednesday Thursday Friday Saturday Sunday

____

Have your office hours changed within the last year?______________________
____

How many weeks out of the office last year?__________ This year?________________

APPOINTMENTS:

Average number of patients treated weekly: Doctor:__________ Hygiene:_____ Emergency:___
Appointed How far: Mornings: _____Afternoons:_____________ Evenings:_____Saturday:____

Average number of new patients per month last 6 months: _____

How does your appointment book compare to prior years? _______________________

RECALL

Describe your recall system: ______________________________________
____
Number of recall patients per month:______________________Doctor: Hygiene:
Average Fee:______ Average time between recalls: ___________________________

PATIENTS:

Number of active patient files for last two years: ___________________
Number of active patient files for last 5 years:______________________
Average age of patient: _______________________________
Number of children under 12 within the practice:_____________

FEES AND SERVICES

Approximate number of specialist referrals monthly by specialty:

ENDO: PERIO: SURGERY: ORTHO:

When did you last adjust your fees? ______________________________________
Which fees?____
What are your lab costs? C&B: Partials: Dentures:

NEW PATIENT PROCEDURES

What is your new patient procedure? ____________________________________
____

Where do your new patients come from?_______________________________
How much money did you spend on marketing last year?_______________________
Which of the following have you used? Patient newsletter _____ Yellow Pages _
Newspapers ____ TV ___ Direct Mail _______________Radio ________Other ________
Referral Plans (ie, 1-800 dentist, Welcome Wagon) _________________ Web Site:__________

Jim Kasper Associates, LLC –P.O. Box 369, Keene NH 03431 603-355-2260 info@jimkasper.com

FINANCIAL AND INSURANCE POLICY

What is your financial policy? ____

____

Do you accept credit cards? __________
Do you use a computer: ____If, yes what software are you using?_____________

Are you on-line for electronic invoicing to insurance companies? _____________
What % of your patients are covered by Dental Insurance? _____Medicaid?___________

Which dental plans do you participate in where you accept the fee as total payment? ___

____

____

Do you accept assignment of insurance benefits? ______________________________

Average number of statements per month:__________________ Amount: _______________
How are your statements prepared? ______________________________________

Total accounts receivable balance $______________________________ Over 90 days:_

INCOME

Production	Doctor(s)	Hygiene	Total	Collections
Last 6 mos:				
2009				
2008				
2007				

MAJOR EXPENSES – For Most Recent Year

Lab: ________________SUPPLIES:______________________RENT:___________________
Staff Salaries: ___________________________Associate Compensation:______________
Technology: ____

OFFICE LEASE:

Approx. Square Footage:___________
Landlord:____Tel:__________
Address:____
Dates on present lease from:______________________to:______________________
Special Provisions:____

REAL ESTATE INFORMATION:

NAME(S) OF OWNER: ____

ADDRESS OF PROPERTY: ____

____

Appraised Value: _________________________ Selling Price: ____________________

Annual Property Taxes: $__________________________ Please provide copy of property tax bill.

Jim Kasper Associates, LLC –P.O. Box 369, Keene NH 03431 603-355-2260 info@jimkasper.com

REAL ESTATE INFORMATION: (Continued)

DESCRIPTION: (Please describe your facility)

If Condo or Co-op what are monthly fees? ________________
Are there any other special assessments?________________ If yes, please explain: ______
____

Age of building:______ How long have you owned the property? __________

Square footage of dental office: ______

Utilities and provider:
Heat
Electricity
Water
Sewer
Gas

Zoning:

Are there any zoning restrictions? (if so, please describe)

Other:

COMMENTS:____
____
____
____
____
____

The description above accurately describes my practice to the best of my knowledge and belief.

Dr.____
Signature:

Dental License#____________________________

Jim Kasper Associates, LLC –P.O. Box 369, Keene NH 03431 603-355-2260 info@jimkasper.com

Chapter 4

The Orthodontic Practice Appraisal

By Thomas F. Ziegler, DDS, MS, JD

The primary difference between orthodontics and all other areas of dentistry is the length of treatment and the billing process. All other areas of dentistry perform a service or procedure that is usually completed within one or two appointments and that service is typically billed and paid for at the time the procedure is completed. Orthodontic treatment, on the other hand, usually takes 18 to 24 months to complete and the services are typically billed at the rate of 25% when the appliances are placed and the balance of the fee is billed over 18 to 24 months in equal monthly installments. This means that any buyer is due an anticipated amount of money under contract for continuing treatment.

Valuing an Orthodontic Practice

The following 12 factors should be considered when valuing an orthodontic practice:

1. One Location or Many?

Generally speaking, if an orthodontist is sufficiently successful in one location because it generates all the case starts the orthodontist wants, life will be easier for that orthodontist. If, on the other hand, the orthodontist is looking to expand by bringing in a second orthodontist, then either the primary location has to be large enough for two doctors to work efficiently or a second location will need to be found. This needs to be considered on a practice-by-practice basis.

2. Location and Longevity

It is always a good idea to consider the number of years the practice has been in its current location. Stability is good if the demographics have remained good, but an orthodontic practice trapped in a location in which the patients and referral sources have moved to another part of town is not good. Therefore, location needs to be considered in the overall desirability of a practice for sale.

3. Lease is Critical

In an outright sale, commonly referred to as an *asset sale*, in which the seller would be selling his/her practice, the existence of a lease of the premises for the buyer is critical. A bank financing the acquisition will insist that the buyer have a lease for as long as the payments are going to be made to the bank. Naturally, the buyer will need to be able to practice without having to move and incur extensive leasehold improvement costs. If the seller of the practice also owns the office real estate, the buyer must be given the opportunity to purchase that real estate. This is usually done through a lease with an option to purchase or, at least, a right of first refusal.

4. Collection Trends

It is important to look at gross collections over a period of three years when appraising an orthodontic practice to identify any upward or downward trend. Increased collections for the most recent year could be a good sign. However, if the increased collections were the result of the seller changing his or her collection procedure to have more people prepay, that would not be good for the buyer.

5. Net Income

Likewise, net income for the past three years is an important consideration. Net, too, can be manipulated by pre-collections which needs to be ruled out. Most healthy orthodontic practices are going to have an adjusted net of approximately 50% of gross collections. Adjusted net considers all benefits to the owner, not just salary reported to IRS upon which income tax is paid.

6. Phase I, Phase II and Comprehensive Patients

It is important to know the number of phase I, phase II and comprehensive orthodontic patients. In addition, find out whether the practice charges a separate phase I fee or merely deducts the phase I fee from the comprehensive fee to determine the phase II fee.

The significance of this information is that a buyer could be left with many phase II patients to treat for a greatly reduced fee. Say, for example, that the comprehensive fee is $5,000 for full braces and the phase I fee is $2,000. If the practice only charges the difference ($3,000) to place full braces on those phase I patients to do phase II treatment, then the buyer must accept a reduced fee. The appraiser should know the phase I, phase II, and comprehensive starts by month.

7. Accounts Receivable Aging

Total Contract Balances = Accounts Receivable plus Contracts Receivable (future balances to be billed). Total contract balances are extremely important to know because this represents money due the buyer after the sale. This is more critical in 100% asset sales than in buy-in fractional sales. In the case of a buy-in to a fractional interest, a lot of time will pass before the buyer has to buy out the seller.

8. Inventories

The inventory of dental equipment can be done by a local supply house, but more typically dental equipment is listed by the staff on a room-by-room basis. Then, the depreciation schedule on the tax return can be consulted to determine original cost and age. Lastly, the practice appraiser assigns a fair market value to the equipment.

Similarly, office equipment inventory is listed by staff and the depreciation schedule consulted to establish a reasonable fair market value. The usual value for dental supplies is a three-month supply as found on the prior year's income statement. Office supplies are also listed as a three-month supply as found on the prior year's P&L.

9. Office

Square footage is important to ensure that there are no limitations on future expansion or limitations on space in which an associate could work. Similarly, a sketch of the office floor plan is helpful to assess the number of rooms and number of treatment chairs. In addition, orthodontic practices need far larger reception rooms to have adequate seating for the larger amount of traffic compared to other dental practices.

10. Analysis of Referral Patterns

Since orthodontics is a referral-based profession, it is important to see where the patients are coming from. The seller needs to compile a list of top 10 referral sources and list how many patients have came from each in the past 12 months.

11. Contracts Receivable

Orthodontics is the only dental profession that has contracts receivable (CR), defined as the amount of money billed in the future for work to be completed in the future in order to complete treatment on current active patients. This is the orthodontic practice's most important asset. There is a relationship between fair market value and the amount of CR available to the buyer.

As a rule of thumb, FMV = CR/0.7 when the initial payment is 25% and the balance is spread over 24 equal monthly payments. If the initial payment is 33.3% and the monthly payments are over 18 months, then the divisor is 0.54, not 0.7.

As an illustration, here are three practices each grossing $1 million per year but having very different values. Practice #1 grosses $1 million per year and nets $500,000. It has CR of $700,000. Its value is either 1 x Gross, 2 x Net or CR/.7 = $1 million. Practice #2 also grosses $1 million per year and nets $500,000. However, CR is only $300,000 due to prepaid accounts. This practice is not worth $1 million.

Practice #3 also grosses $1 million per year and nets $500,000, but extended payment plans have created a CR of $1 million. In this case, the seller did not take out of the practice as much as he should have, leaving an excess of $300,000 behind for the buyer. Therefore, Practice #3 would be worth more than 1 x Gross or 2 x Net. As you can see, traditional approximations of practice value such as 1 x Gross or 2 x Net can be misleading.

12. Cash Flow Methods of Approximating FMV

One common approximation of value for orthodontic practices is 75% to 85% times a weighted average of a percentage of gross income, with more weight given to the most recent year. For example, let's say gross income over the past three years was $1 million (2008), $1.1 million (2009) and $1.2 million (2010). The average of the three is $1.1 million, multiplied by 75% to 85% = $825,000 to $935,000, or an average of $880,000.

Another common approximation of value is to multiply adjusted net income by a factor between one and two, with the multiplier depending on the condition of the physical facilities, the age of equipment, the staff size and compensation, the recall system and the location. Adjusted net income equals gross collections less true operating expenses such as rent, utilities, repairs, staff expenses, supplies and equipment. The balance—salary, pension, insurance, auto, travel, etc.—is the total economic benefit to the owner. For example, if adjusted net income is $500,000, then the approximate FMV ranges from $500,000 to $1 million, depending on qualitative factors. For this exercise, assume an average, or $750,000.

Yet another common approximation of FMV is 1.5 times adjusted net income plus the current value of tangible assets such as equipment, furniture and supplies. For example, if adjusted net income is $500,000 and the current value of tangible assets is $100,000, then the estimated value is $600,000 x 1.5 = $900,000.

Taking an average of the three is $843,333 or $840,000 rounded.

Tax Allocation of the Sale Price

In terms of the transaction's tax structure, buyers and sellers have competing interests. Sellers want to receive the 15% capital gains treatment on the sale's proceeds rather than the 35% tax on ordinary income. Buyers want to be able to deduct their payments as made. The problem is that there is no tax structure that permits the buyer to deduct payments as made and the seller to receive capital gain tax treatment. This conflict can generate an adversarial environment calling forth attorneys' fees. The solution is to agree to share the tax advantages/disadvantages as evenly as possible. Here is a proposed three-stage plan for achieving fairness to buyer and seller:

1. 100% Asset Sale

In a 100% asset sale, the proceeds are allocated to tangible practice assets, goodwill and the *covenant not to compete*. The tangible assets usually amount to 10% to 20% of the total price. The covenant not to compete usually has a value of $10,000. The balance is allocated to the personal goodwill of the selling doctor.

Generally, goodwill can be defined as those elements of a practice and and its Doctor(s) which cause patients to return to that practice and which may enable the practice to generate a profit in excess of that which is required for a reasonable rate of return on all of the underlying assets of the practice. For accounting purposes, this definition of goodwill is the difference between the purchase price of the professional practice and the FMV of its assets less liabilities. In two tax court decisions (*Norwalk vs. Commissioner*, TCM 1998-279; and *Martin Ice Cream Co. vs. Commissioner*, 110 TC-189), it was ruled the goodwill is personal to the individual owner rather than to the corporation provided that the shareholder does *not* have a covenant not to compete with the corporation. Therefore, covenants not to compete shall be between individuals and not an individual and the corporation.

2. Fractional Sale

In the following scenario, the junior doctor is buying into a 50% ownership over a five-year period, after which the two doctors will be partners followed by a future sale of the senior doctor's remaining 50% to the junior doctor. Usually such a buy-in to 50% ownership is structured at the rate of 10% per year for five years. The buy-in tax allocation is 10% of the purchase price for stock and 90% for "management services" payable to the senior doctor.

Assume that the total practice value is $1.5 million. The value for 50% would be $750,000—$75,000 for stock and $675,000 for the selling doctor's management services. The buyer would pay $15,000 per year to the seller on January 1 of each year for five years. Each month, $675,000/60 = $11,250 would be shifted from the buying doctor's share of net income to the selling doctor. Because this payment is deductible by the buyer and is ordinary income to the seller, the transaction favors the buyer from a tax standpoint. In this way, the buyer can purchase the practice over five years using the earnings of the practice rather than personal funds.

However, when it is time for the older doctor to sell out, the practice will be re-appraised and the transaction structured so that the seller obtains favorable capital gains treatment. The buyer gets no deduction for purchasing stock and must amortize personal goodwill over 15 years. At this point, the buying dentist will receive all of the net income from the practice.

3. Justification of Purchase Price

If the valuation is reasonable, the buyer should be able to pay off the debt service (principal and interest) on a five-year amortization schedule with no more than one-half the practice net income, and still have ample money on which to live. We do not recommend such a fast payoff, only to indicate that it is possible. We recommend a 10-year bank financing term so that the payments more closely align with their deductibility. Most of the acquisition price will be allocated to goodwill, which must be amortized over 15 years.

ORTHODONTICS

Contracts Receivable and Their Relation to Gross and Net Figures

Month	Patient Starts per Month	Total Active Patients	Individual Patient Fee	Individual Down Payment	Down Payments Collected	Individual Monthly Payments	Monthly Payments Collected	Monthly Income	Contracts Receivable
1	25	25	$4,600.00	$1,150.00	$28,750.00	$143.75	$3,593.75	$32,343.75	$82,656.25
2	25	50	$4,600.00	$1,150.00	$28,750.00	$143.75	$7,187.50	$35,937.50	$161,718.75
3	25	75	$4,600.00	$1,150.00	$28,750.00	$143.75	$10,781.25	$39,531.25	$237,187.50
4	25	100	$4,600.00	$1,150.00	$28,750.00	$143.75	$14,375.00	$43,125.00	$309,062.50
5	25	125	$4,600.00	$1,150.00	$28,750.00	$143.75	$17,968.75	$46,718.75	$377,343.75
6	25	150	$4,600.00	$1,150.00	$28,750.00	$143.75	$21,562.50	$50,312.50	$442,031.25
7	25	175	$4,600.00	$1,150.00	$28,750.00	$143.75	$25,156.25	$53,906.25	$503,125.00
8	25	200	$4,600.00	$1,150.00	$28,750.00	$143.75	$28,750.00	$57,500.00	$560,625.00
9	25	225	$4,600.00	$1,150.00	$28,750.00	$143.75	$32,343.75	$61,093.75	$614,531.25
10	25	250	$4,600.00	$1,150.00	$28,750.00	$143.75	$35,937.50	$64,687.50	$664,843.75
11	25	275	$4,600.00	$1,150.00	$28,750.00	$143.75	$39,531.25	$68,281.25	$711,562.50
12	25	300	$4,600.00	$1,150.00	$28,750.00	$143.75	$43,125.00	$71,875.00	$754,687.50
13	25	325	$4,600.00	$1,150.00	$28,750.00	$143.75	$46,718.75	$75,468.75	$794,218.75
14	25	350	$4,600.00	$1,150.00	$28,750.00	$143.75	$50,312.50	$79,062.50	$830,156.25
15	25	375	$4,600.00	$1,150.00	$28,750.00	$143.75	$53,906.25	$82,656.25	$862,500.00
16	25	400	$4,600.00	$1,150.00	$28,750.00	$143.75	$57,500.00	$86,250.00	$891,250.00
17	25	425	$4,600.00	$1,150.00	$28,750.00	$143.75	$61,093.75	$89,843.75	$916,406.25
18	25	450	$4,600.00	$1,150.00	$28,750.00	$143.75	$64,687.50	$93,437.50	$937,968.75
19	25	475	$4,600.00	$1,150.00	$28,750.00	$143.75	$68,281.25	$97,031.25	$955,937.50
20	25	500	$4,600.00	$1,150.00	$28,750.00	$143.75	$71,875.00	$100,625.00	$970,312.50
21	25	525	$4,600.00	$1,150.00	$28,750.00	$143.75	$75,468.75	$104,218.75	$981,093.75
22	25	550	$4,600.00	$1,150.00	$28,750.00	$143.75	$79,062.50	$107,812.50	$988,281.25
23	25	575	$4,600.00	$1,150.00	$28,750.00	$143.75	$82,656.25	$111,406.25	$991,875.00
24	25	600	$4,600.00	$1,150.00	$28,750.00	$143.75	$86,250.00	$115,000.00	$991,875.00

All Months After this Point Will Look Like Month 24

Gross Income	
1st Year	$625,312.50
2nd Year	$1,142,812.50
Every Year	$1,380,000.00

Net Income (52% Overhead)	
1st Year	$300,150.00
2nd Year	$548,550.00
Every Year	$662,400.00

Purchase Price (Contracts Receivable divided by .7)	
$1,416,964.29	
Purchase Price as a Percentage of Gross	
102.68%	≈ 1x Gross
Purchase Price as a Percentage of Net	
213.91%	≈ 2x Net

Figures assume there are 25 starts each month. The $4,600 fee is paid as a 25% down-payment with the balance paid over the 24 months of treatment. The first monthly payment is due with the down-payment. Practice overhead is 52%. We also assume that EVERYONE PAYS ON-TIME with NO PRE-PAYMENTS. As you can see in this ideal situation, 1x Gross, 2x Net and Contracts Receivable divided by .7 very nearly equal one another.

When determining a Purchase Price, the Contracts Receivable total is a better marker than the traditional methods (1x Gross or 2x Net) because a Purchase Price that is determined by Gross/Net figures would be raised due to pre-payment and lowered due to late-payment and, therefore, is less stable than a Purchase Price that is determined by Contracts Receivable. THE MOST IMPORTANT ASSET BEING SOLD IS THE VALUE OF THE CONTRACTS RECEIVABLE (Money available to pay down the debt).

Chapter 5

Valuing Goodwill In Dental Practices

By Robert James Cimasi, MHA, ASA, MCBA, AVA, CM&AA

Introduction

The valuation of dental practices will often confront the question of how to value the goodwill which may be attributable to the practice. Once the subject dental practice and interest to be appraised have been defined, the assets and the goodwill related to the practice will need to be appropriately classified into two categories: *tangible* and *intangible* assets. *Exhibit 1: Classification of Tangible and Intangible Assets* is an illustrative representation of the classification of tangible and intangible assets that may be present in the context of a dental practice.

Exhibit 1. Classification of Tangible and Intangible Assets

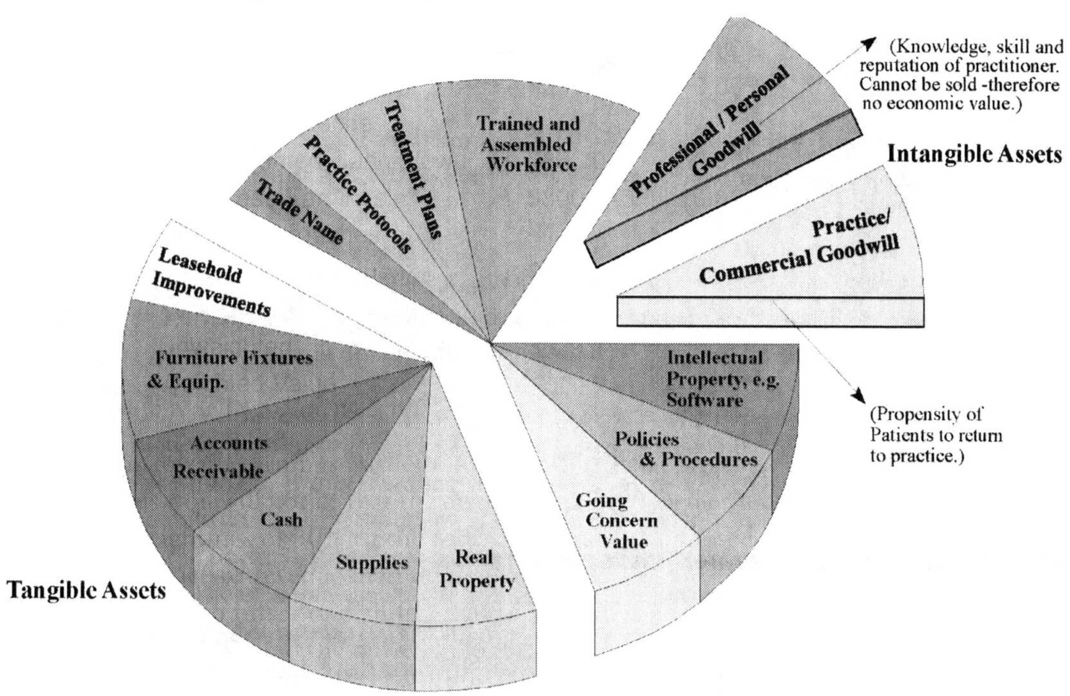

It should be noted that because this chapter focuses on the valuation of dental practice *goodwill*, the methodology related to appropriately identifying and valuing a practice's tangible and intangible assets, separate from their relationship to the valuation of a practice goodwill, will not be discussed in depth.

Dental practices are only one of a wide range of many different and unique healthcare service sector enterprises, and each dental practice will have unique and distinct attributes, *vis à vis,* the likelihood of existence of certain specific assets. Set forth in *Exhibit 2: Likelihood of Existence of Specific Assets of a Professional Practice* is an illustrative analysis of the likelihood of the existence of specific assets of a given dental practice enterprise. Exhibit 2 is a listing of the types of tangible assets and the types of intangible assets often considered, classified into 10 main categories. It should be noted that this representative listing is for illustrative purposes only.

Identification and Classification of Intangible Assets

In addition to tangible assets, there are several types of intangible assets that may be present and should be considered in the valuation of a dental professional practice, e.g., trained and assembled workforce in place, covenants not to compete, patient lists, managed care agreements, provider services agreements, practice protocols and treatment plans, and marketing plans. In making a determination as to whether some aspect of a dental practice enterprise, or factor of the operation and performance of that enterprise in the market, qualifies as an intangible asset, the aspect or factor should be endowed with several attributes, characteristic of *property*, which may be ascribed to it and that allow it to rise to the definition of *intangible asset*.

These traits, qualities, attributes, and characteristics include:

1. The item should exist and be identified in a manner that allows it to be recognized as a legal property right which can be defended in court as private property and the ownership of which can be sold or transferred;

2. The item should have some element of evidentiary support and documentation for its existence, including both the inception and the termination of its existence in relation to an action, circumstance, or event that can be legally described and identified; and,

3. The item should, despite its lack of physical substance, generate a measure of economic benefit to its owner.

Goodwill and Patient-Related Intangible Assets

As discussed above, goodwill is one type of intangible asset that may be considered in the valuation of dental practices. Goodwill is considered by some valuation professionals to be the residual amount of intangible asset value that may exist after the separately identified, separately distinguishable and separately appraised elements of intangible value have been determined.

In June 2001, the Financial Standards Accounting Board (FASB) instituted Statement of Financial Accounting Standard (SFAS) Nos. 141 and 142. Prior to these standards, companies generally reported as goodwill the entire difference between the purchase price and the book value of

Exhibit 2: Likelihood of Existence of Specific Assets of a Dental Practice

Likelihood of Existence of Specific Assets of a Dental Practice: **1**=Almost always, **2**=Often, **3**=Sometimes, **4**=Almost never, minimal	Solo	Office Based Group
Tangible		
1) Accounts Receivable	1	1
2) Cash, Investments	3	2
3) Furniture, Fixtures, and Equipment	1	1
4) Leasehold Improvements	3	1
5) Real Property	3	3
6) Supplies	1	1
7) Medical Library	4	2
Intangible		
1) Payor/Customer-Related		
a) Managed-Care Agreements	1	1
b) Provider Service Agreements/Medical Directorships	3	2
c) Direct Contracting Customer Lists	3	2
d) HMO Enrollment Lists	4	3
2) Goodwill and Patient-Related		
a) Custody of Medical Charts and Records	1	1
b) Personal/Professional Goodwill	1	1
c) Practice/Commercial Goodwill	3	2
d) Patient Lists/Recall Lists	2	2
3) Human Capital-Related		
a) Employment/Provider Contracts	4	1
b) Trained and Assembled Workforce	2	1
c) Policies and Procedures	3	2
d) Depth of Management	4	2
4) Intellectual Property-Related		
a) Practice Protocols	4	2
b) Treatment Plans/Care Mapping	3	2
c) Procedural Manuals/Laboratory Notebooks	4	2
d) Technical and Specialty Research	4	3
e) Patents and Patent Applications	4	3
f) Copyrights	4	3
g) Trade Names	3	2
h) Trade Secrets	4	3
i) Royalty Agreements	4	4

Likelihood of Existence of Specific Assets of a Dental Practice: **1**=Almost always, **2**=Often, **3**=Sometimes, **4**=Almost never, minimal	Solo	Office Based Group
5) Locations and Operations-Related		
a) Management Information / Executive Decision Systems	4	2
b) Favorable Leases-Leasehold interests	2	3
c) Going Concern Value	3	2
d) Asset Assemblage Factors	3	2
e) Historical Documents/Charts/RVU Studies	2	2
f) Supplier Contracts, e.g. Group Purchasing Orgs.	3	2
6) Governance/Legal Structure-Related		
a) Organizational Documents	4	1
b) Non-Compete Covenants	4	1
c) Income Distribution Plans	4	1
7) Marketing and Business Development-Related		
a) Print Ads, Telephone #s, Billboards, etc.	2	2
b) Franchise/License Agreements	3	3
c) Joint Ventures/Alliances, e.g. “Call-a-nurse”	3	2
d) Market Entrance Barriers/Factors	3	2
8) Regulatory/Legal-Related		
a) Facility Licenses	4	3
b) Medical Licenses	1	1
c) Permits – Real Estate Special Use	3	3
d) Litigation Awards and Liquidated Damages	4	3
e) Certificates of Need	4	3
f) Medicare Certification/UPIN	1	1
g) Certifications-e.g. NCQA, AAAHC, JCAHO	3	3
9) Financial/Revenue Stream-Related		
a) Office Share	3	3
b) Management Services Contracts	4	3
c) Financing Agreements	4	3
d) Underwriting/Private Placement Memoranda	4	3
e) Budgets/Forecasts/Projections	4	2
10) Technology-Related		
a) Computer Software/Network Integration	4	2
b) Technical/Software Documentation	4	3
c) Maintenance/Support Relationships	2	1

identified tangible assets. Intangible assets were typically capitalized as part of overall acquired goodwill and amortized over a finite period; they were *not* required to be separately identified. SFAS Nos. 141 and 142 now require that goodwill be calculated as the overall purchase price minus the value of both tangible and identifiable intangible assets that have a finite useful life.[1] Additionally, traditional accounting allocation for valuing intangible assets, such as, *replacement cost* or *book values* that fail to consider the market negotiation framework, may lead to indefensible measures of value.[2]

Accounting v. Appraisal Definition of Goodwill

In the accounting world, intangible asset values are most often viewed and characterized in a different manner than the valuation profession. For example, the term *goodwill* is still often referred to by accountants as "the difference between the book value of assets on the healthcare entity's balance sheet and what the entity would sell for"; or as "the going concern value which results from an organized assemblage of revenue-producing assets."

It should be noted that, in economic fact, goodwill is only one of many identifiable and quantifiable intangible assets related to healthcare service sector entities. In healthcare service sector entities, e.g., professional practices, the term goodwill should be more appropriately defined as "the propensity of patients and customers (and the revenue stream thereof) to return to the entity in the future." Specifically, this term may appropriately be considered as "the propensity of patients (and the revenue stream thereof) to return to the practice" incremental to that which is quantified as the contribution of the other tangible and intangible assets in the assemblage of assets which comprises the subject practice enterprise. Since goodwill is only one of the several intangible assets that may be found to exist in a dental professional practice, it is not a catch-all moniker for all intangible assets in the aggregate.

Intangible assets that are sometimes considered as part of goodwill and patient-related include custodial rights to medical charts and records; electronic medical records; patient recall lists; and both personal/professional and/or practice/commercial goodwill. The custody of medical charts, electronic medical records, and patient recall lists may be separately identified and quantified as a distinct intangible asset apart from goodwill; however, they are often considered together with goodwill as they create the background that supports the propensity for the continued patient-provider relationship.

Sources for guidance as to the definition of goodwill can be found in IRS Revenue Ruling 59-60 and established judicial opinions from valuation related case law. In the event that the valuator determines, first, the existence of intangible asset value in the subject practice enterprise and, second, the existence of goodwill as one of the intangible assets existing, the next step is to identify, distinguish, disaggregate, and allocate the relevant portion of the existing goodwill to either *professional/personal goodwill* or *practice/commercial goodwill*.

1. "Grasping the Value of Intangible Assets," By Phillip A. Beutel & Bryan Ray, *International Tax Journal*, Vol. 30, No. 1, Winter 2004, p. 35-36.
2. *Ibid.*, p. 37.

Professional/Personal Goodwill

Professional/personal goodwill results from the charisma, education, knowledge, skill, board certification and reputation of a specific dental practitioner. Professional/personal goodwill is generated by the reputation and personal attributes of the dentist which accrue to that individual dentist. Since these attributes "go to the grave" with that specific individual dentist and, therefore, can not be sold, they have no economic value.

Professional/personal goodwill is not transferable. Even with long transition periods of introduction for a new acquiring dentist owner, the charisma, skills, reputation and personal attributes of the seller cannot, by definition, be transferred. It is often stated that with assisted transfer (i.e., extended transition period) a large portion of professional goodwill may be transferred. The transferability violates the definition of professional/personal goodwill. That portion of goodwill that may be transferred is defined as practice (or commercial) goodwill as described below.

Practice/Commercial Goodwill

Practice/commercial goodwill, as distinguished from professional/personal goodwill, is transferred frequently. Practice/commercial goodwill may be described as the unidentified, unspecified, residual attributes of the practice as an operating enterprise that contribute to the propensity of patients (and the revenue stream thereof) to return to the practice in the future. There are several significant factors to consider in determining the existence and quantity of practice/commercial goodwill-related value.

It must be determined whether patients return to the dental practice because of attributes of the practice or because they are mandated to do so by their managed care insurance coverage. The practice's participation on a given managed care panel of providers may be subject to rapid and unexpected change. In that circumstance, the valuator needs to decide whether the value of the practice that may be attributable to managed care organization relationships should perhaps be considered as an identifiable, specific contract-related asset, and separately valued, as opposed to being treated as practice/commercial goodwill.

Goodwill in Divorce Proceedings

The treatment of goodwill that may be attributable to a given dental professional practitioner or dental practice enterprise, for purposes of classifying it as part of the marital estate to be divided in divorce proceedings, varies by state.[3] A minority of states holds that neither practice/commercial goodwill nor personal/professional goodwill is part of the marital estate. Another small group of states holds that both practice/commercial goodwill and professional/personal goodwill are part of the marital estate. Lastly, a majority of states draw a distinction between practice/ commercial

3. "When the Marriage is Over, What Is the Practice Worth?" By Stacy D. Udell, *BVR's Guide to Healthcare Valuation*, 2009, p. 16-1.

goodwill and professional/personal goodwill with practice/commercial goodwill considered part of the marital estate to be separately valued in divorce proceedings. *Exhibit 3: Dental Practice Goodwill as a Martial Asset—Selected Case Law by State* provides a representative guideline of selected states' treatment of dental practice goodwill in divorce proceedings.

Conclusion

The value attributed to the goodwill associated with a given dental practice enterprise should first be discretely identified and measured. In the event that there is a residual intangible asset value over and above the other identifiable and distinguishable intangible assets of the practice, the valuator may be led to the conclusion that a residual amount of intangible asset value exists that may be attributed to *goodwill.*

Exhibit 3: Dental Practice Goodwill as a Marital Asset—Selected Case Law by State

State	Case Name	Practice Type	Treatment of Goodwill
Arkansas	*Tortorich v Tortorich*, 902 S.W. 2d 247 (Ark. App. 1995)	Dental Practice	Practice goodwill is a marital asset; personal goodwill is not a marital asset
Colorado	*In re Marriage of Nichols*, 606 P2d 1314 (Colo. App., 1979)	Dental Practice	Practice goodwill and personal goodwill are marital assets
Delaware	*Wright v Wright*, 469 A.2d 803 (Del.Fam.Ct. 1983)	Dental Practice	Practice goodwill is a marital asset; personal goodwill is not a marital asset
Florida	*Weinstock v Weinstock*, 634 So.2d 775 (Fla.App. 5 Dist. 1994)	Dental Practice	Practice goodwill is a marital asset; personal goodwill is not a marital asset
Illinois	*In re Marriage of Schnieder*, 824 N.E.2d 177 (Ill. 2005)	Dental Practice	Practice goodwill is a marital asset; personal goodwill is not a marital asset
Iowa	*In re Marriage of Hogeland*, 448N.W.2d 678 (Iowa App. 1989)	Dental Practice	Goodwill depends on the professional continuing in practice, and is a factor bearing on his/her future earning potential
Kentucky	*Gaskill v Robbins*, Ky., 282 S.W.3d 306	Oral Surgery Practice	Practice goodwill is a marital asset; personal goodwill is not a marital asset
Maine	*Ahern v. Ahern*, 938 A.2d 35 (Me. 2008)	Dental Practice	Practice goodwill is a marital asset; personal goodwill is not a marital asset
Maryland	*Hollander v Hollander*, 597 A2d 1012 (Md. App. 1991)	Dental Practice	Practice goodwill is a marital asset; personal goodwill is not a marital asset

State	Case Name	Practice Type	Treatment of Goodwill
Michigan	*Kowalesky v Kowalesky*, 384 N.W.2d 112 (Mich. App. 1986)	Dental Practice	Practice goodwill and personal goodwill are marital assets
Minnesota	*In re Marriage of Rolfe*, 2000 WL 1146132	Dental Practice	Practice goodwill is a marital asset; personal goodwill is not a marital asset
Mississippi	*Singley v Singley*, 846 So.2d 1004 (Miss. 2002)	Dental Practice	Neither practice goodwill nor personal goodwill is a marital asset
Missouri	*Hanson v Hanson*, 738 S.W.2d 429 (Mo.banc 1987)	Oral Surgery Practice	Practice goodwill is a marital asset; personal goodwill is not a marital asset
New Hampshire	*In re Watterworth*, 821 A.2d 1107 (N.H. 2003)	Dental Practice (orthodontia)	Practice goodwill is a marital asset; personal goodwill is not a marital asset
North Carolina	*Poore v Poore*, 331 S.E.2d 266 (N.C. App. 1985)	Dental Practice	Practice goodwill and personal goodwill are marital assets
North Dakota	*Sommers v Sommers*, 660 N.W.2d 586 (N.D. 2003)	Dental Practice (orthodontia)	Practice goodwill and personal goodwill are marital assets
Ohio	*Reichert v Reichert*, 1992 WL 6660	Dental Practice	Practice goodwill and personal goodwill are marital assets
Pennsylvania	*Gaydos v Gaydos*, 693 A.2d 1368 (Pa.Super. 1997)	Dental Practice	Practice goodwill is a marital asset; personal goodwill is not a marital asset
South Carolina	*Dickert v Dickert*, Supreme Court of South Carolina Opinion No. 26757 (March 29, 2010)	Dental Practice	Neither practice goodwill nor personal goodwill is a marital asset
Tennessee	*McKee v McKee*, 2010 WL 3245246	Dental Practice	Neither practice goodwill nor personal goodwill is a marital asset
Texas	*Geaccone v Geaccone*, 2005 WL 1774964	Dental Practice	Practice goodwill is a marital asset; personal goodwill is not a marital asset
Utah	*Sorensen v Sorensen*, 839 P.2d 774 (Utah 1992)	Dental Practice	Practice goodwill is a marital asset; personal goodwill is not a marital asset
West Virginia	*May v May*, 589 S.E.2d 536 (W. Va. 2003)	Dental Practice	Practice goodwill is a marital asset; personal goodwill is not a marital asset
Wisconsin	*McReath v McReath*, 2010 WL 2943198	Dental Practice	Practice goodwill is a marital asset; personal goodwill is not a marital asset

Chapter 6

Recent Cases on Dental Valuation

Rhodes v. Rhodes

Mississippi Gets Two Chances to Value Business Goodwill

Citation: 2011 WL 80222 (Miss. App.)
Date of decision: Jan. 11, 2011
Country: US
State or Federal: State
State/Jurisdiction: Mississippi
Court: Court of Appeals
Type of action: Marital Dissolution
Experts: James Angle (wife)
Judge: Maxwell

Mississippi is one of only two states that still decline to assign any value to the goodwill of a marital business in divorce. (Kansas is the other; see "Goodwill Hunting," the free state-by-state summary of valuing goodwill in marital dissolution cases, available at BVResources.com.) Three cases establish the Mississippi precedent:

1. In *Singley v. Singley*, 846 So.2d 1004 (Miss. 2002), the state Supreme Court considered the value of a solo dental practice and ruled that "goodwill is simply not property; thus it cannot be deemed a divisible marital asset in a divorce." Fair market appraisals should exclude goodwill, because it leads to inaccurate and unreliable values. Trying to distinguish and determine "enterprise goodwill" from "personal goodwill" is just as objectionable, the court said, because the two concepts "are simply too interwoven."

Notably, in making its decision of "first impression," the court cited several of its "sister states" that also precluded any goodwill from the valuation of marital businesses, including Kansas, Texas, and Wisconsin. Since then, both Texas and Wisconsin have adopted the majority rule recognizing the distinction between enterprise goodwill (divisible) and personal goodwill (non-divisible). Kansas relies on precedent that goes back 30 years.

2. In *Watson v. Watson*, 882 So.2d 95 (Miss. 2004), the Supreme Court confirmed and clarified *Singley*. In precluding goodwill value from the appraisal of a solo veterinary practice, it found that goodwill "is a nebulous term" that depends on the continued presence of the particular professional as a personal asset. In particular:

In a furniture or appliance business with several owners, it would be difficult to assess the value . . . attributable to one of the owners. Customers go to the business looking for furniture or appliances. However, in the context of a single-owner professional practice, it becomes less difficult. Patients (including pet owners) go there looking for their doctors.

By precluding any goodwill value from the appraisal, courts will avoid the "glaring inequity" that results from using the professional's income to calculate spousal support and also to calculate the value of the "business," the court explained.

3. In *Yelverton v. Yelverton*, 961 So.2d 19 (Miss. 2007), the court revisited the issue in valuing a car dealership. It remanded the case with the instruction to the lower court that "'goodwill,' whether 'personal goodwill' or 'business enterprise goodwill' shall not be included in the value" of the dealership. In a footnote, the court expressly found that *Watson* applied, even though "*Watson* involved a 'solo professional practice' as opposed to [the auto dealership], which involves two shareholders."

Husband owns 100% of a flooring store. Now come two recent Mississippi cases to muddy the goodwill waters. In the first, which recalls the distinction by the *Watson* decision between a solo professional practice and a "furniture or appliance business," the husband was the sole shareholder of his family's carpet and drapery business. His parents had gifted him (and his brother) equal shares just after the parties' marriage, in 2003. Just one week later, the husband bought out his brother for cash.

The parties' marriage started to deteriorate within a year, and at their divorce, the husband argued the business was his separate property. He presented a valuation, prepared by a business valuation expert in connection with the redemption of his brother's shares, showing the business was worth approximately $1.6 million. The husband claimed the business had not appreciated in the five years since then.

The wife also presented a BV expert, but the husband challenged his report under the state's analogue to Rule 702 of the Federal Rules of Evidence and *Daubert*. The expert failed to distinguish the tangible assets of the business from its intangible assets, including goodwill. The analyst had also never appeared as an expert in court, the husband asserted, and had not performed a business valuation "other than what was required for one of his certifications." The court ultimately precluded the expert on both grounds, finding that he lacked sufficient qualifications and his methodology was unreliable because it considered the goodwill value of the business.

After losing her expert evidence, the wife attempted to show the appreciation of the business during the marriage by way of financial statements, which showed income increasing substantially in 2006. The husband countered by saying that his flooring business received a surge of orders after Hurricane Katrina, due to the many flood-damaged homes in the area, but that its income "plummeted" the following year, due to general market factors. Based on this evidence, the court found that the business value had not appreciated during the "fairly short" marriage and the wife appealed both rulings, the exclusion of her expert and the finding of no increased value.

The Mississippi Court of Appeals first found that that the lower court erred by excluding the wife's expert based on his lack of testifying experience. "We have no qualms with [his] qualification as an expert in business valuation," it said. The test is whether the expert possesses particular knowledge that will help the trier-of-fact. "Every expert witness has a first time," one of the justices noted in a concurring opinion. To hold otherwise would establish an insurmountable "Catch-22," in which "no witness could ever qualify as an expert for the first time because that would require being retained previously as an expert."

At the same time, the court also found the expert had neither excluded goodwill, nor assigned a separate value to it. Although he "may have performed calculations under other methods that did not include goodwill," the expert failed to use these methods as the basis for his opinion, the court said, and sustained his exclusion for failing to follow state precedent. "Our Supreme Court recently made clear that, in a divorce action, goodwill should not be utilized in performing a valuation of a business," the court held, citing *Yelverton*. It repeated the rule in both *Singley* and *Watson* that "goodwill is simply not property; thus it cannot be deemed a divisible marital asset."

Accordingly, the court also confirmed the lower court's finding that the business had not appreciated in value during the marriage, based largely on the \$1.6 million redemption valuation at the beginning and the financial statements that showed overall flat income levels at the end.

A strong dissent says the Supreme Court got it wrong. The decision on the exclusion of the wife's expert was split among the justices, with six agreeing with the result, one disagreeing but calling it "harmless error," and three registering a strong dissent. In particular, the dissent disputed the majority's assertion that "there is no Mississippi case that excludes 'goodwill' to a 'service business.'" Even if there were such authority, the husband's business in this case was not a professional service firm but a retail sales business that installs its products. "We must carefully examine the Supreme Court precedent," the dissent said.

In *Singley*, the court considered the value of a small dental practice; in *Watson*, it considered a solo veterinary practice. In particular, the dissent called attention to the language the court used in *Watson* to differentiate a business that sold furniture or appliances from a firm that offered professional services. The dissent also highlighted the footnote in *Yelverton*, where the court specifically said *Watson* applied even though it involved a "solo professional practice" as opposed to the car dealership, "which involve[d] two shareholders."

The dissent concluded, "It appears that the Supreme Court mistakenly considered [the car dealership] a professional practice" when it made its ruling prohibiting the consideration of goodwill. (*Note:* In the majority opinion, the court found no mistake or inconsistencies in the precedent. "We fail to see how [the husband's] flooring business, wholly owned by him, should be treated differently than the car-dealership interest involved in *Yelverton*.) The three-judge dissent would have reversed the decision to exclude the wife's expert and remand the case for a new trial on valuation—a strong enough vote to perhaps encourage the wife to appeal. It is not yet known whether the wife in *Rhodes* decided to petition the state Supreme Court. However, less than a month later, the court decided *Lewis v. Lewis* (113 Wis. 2d 172, 336 N.W.2d 171, 1983 Wisc. App. LEXIS 3546).

In *Lewis*, the husband and wife owned a residential real estate development company in equal shares. As part of the operations, they bought and sold property together, with one or the other taking title to the property. During the parties' difficult divorce, however, the husband diverted corporate assets for his own use, including setting himself up in a separate building company. He refused to respond to the wife's discovery demands concerning the value of the various assets and told the trial court the real estate company was "worthless."

The wife did not retain a business valuation expert. Instead, she submitted financial documentation that was admittedly incomplete and out of date, but was the best she could find. After the close of evidence, the trial court complained that each side had given him "way too much" in this "complicated matter financially." Nevertheless, it valued the business at roughly $1.2 million and the husband appealed.

The Court of Appeals agreed, finding "manifest errors" in the trial court's valuation. It remanded the case with the specific instruction to value the real estate business using all relevant data, including "any goodwill equity." This time, the wife appealed to the state Supreme Court.

Precedent rules. The Supreme Court reversed the appellate instruction. Citing *Singley*, *Watson*, and *Yelverton*, it confirmed the hard and fast rule that, in Mississippi, the goodwill value of any business is not marital property. Despite the dissents in those decisions, the law of the state was "clear and comprehensive," the court said. "*Stare decisis* demands this result." It remanded the case for a valuation of the business, with the exception of considering goodwill equity.

The issue may yet be fully settled in the state, however. Two justices on the *Lewis* panel dissented, arguing that *Watson* limited "the blanket rule in *Singley* to those cases either involving a solo professional practice" or close analogues. In support, the dissent also cited the current majority rule among states, which recognizes the distinction between personal goodwill and enterprise goodwill. "This rule is in line with the principle that a professional license held by a spouse is not itself marital property, even where the practice dependent on that license may be . . . a marital asset subject to equitable distribution."

General accounting principles also support valuing of goodwill along with other intangibles, the dissent pointed out, citing FAS 142 (issued in 2001). "Furthermore, goodwill is treated alongside other intangible assets such as patents, customer lists, or licenses under the Internal Revenue Code as a depreciable asset subject to taxation or as a deductible and amortizable cost," it observed. "Goodwill, at its core, represents the excess value of a business enterprise after subtraction of the value of all other assets from its fair market value, and, despite its seeming nebulousness as a term of art, is well recognized as an intangible business asset."

In this case, the parties jointly owned and operated the business, at least until the husband began diverting its assets. Applying the "blanket rule" inappropriately restricts a trial court's discretion to assign a fair value to the parties' actual assets, the dissent said, particularly when the enterprise is not a professional practice and is not dependent on just one of the spouses' efforts. For these reasons, the dissent would have affirmed the appellate court's instructions and remanded the case to the trial court for "a full determination of the market value of [the marital business], including an evaluation of [its] enterprise goodwill, as well as whatever personal goodwill, if any, is attributable to either or both of the parties.

In re Marriage of Bruns

Broker and BV Expert Battle Goodwill Value of Dental Practice in Divorce

Citation: 2011 WL 237969 (Iowa App.)(unpublished)
Date of decision: Jan. 20, 2011
Country: US
State or Federal: State
State/Jurisdiction: Iowa
Court: Court of Appeals
Type of action: Marital Dissolution
Experts: John Trask (husband); Cyril Mandelbaum (wife)
Judge: Tabor

Thirty years ago, an Iowa dentist bought his practice for roughly $75,000. By the end of his 40-year marriage, he employed a staff of three and was earning $150,000 per year working only three days a week.

At the parties' divorce trial, the husband presented a management consultant and business broker who'd been selling dental practices for over three decades and had performed over 500 related appraisals. He valued the tangible assets of the husband's practice at $77,000, including equipment, supplies, and accounts receivable. If he included the goodwill value of the practice, it was worth just over $198,000.

The wife retained a CPA and accredited senior appraiser who had more than 20 years of business valuation experience, including appraising several dental practices. In her opinion, the total value of the practice amounted to $241,000. This included a normalizing adjustment to the salary of the receptionist (with whom the dentist was having a romantic relationship), asserting her wages were higher than market value.

Dentist wouldn't sell for stated value. The trial court remarked the "dueling experts" and conceded that it could not determine the precise fair market value of the practice without a sale. At the same time, it noted that the husband bought the practice 30 years before for more or less the same value that his broker said it was worth at trial. Moreover, the husband testified that he would not sell his practice for $77,000. After reviewing all the evidence, the trial court valued the practice, excluding goodwill, at $115,450.

Both parties appealed. The husband claimed the trial court's value "must have" included goodwill, and the wife argued that the value was too low, brought down by the broker's "questionable" methodology. The appellate court acknowledged the difficulty of valuing professional practices, "because their income flows almost exclusively from the efforts of the professional who owns the business."

At the same time, it found the trial court had correctly followed longstanding state precedent, which holds that the "goodwill of a professional practice bears on the professional's earning capacity (for the purposes of determining alimony), but should not be additionally listed as an asset in the valuation of a professional practice." Further, the trial court had the discretion to discount the value placed on the practice by the wife's expert, "based on her more limited experience in appraising dental practices and her opinion that a non-compete agreement would make no difference in valuation," the appellate court held. Because the $115,450 valuation fell within the range of permissible evidence, the appellate court confirmed the same.

Banchefsky v. Banchefsky

Divorce Court Limits Professional Goodwill to Value of Non-Compete

Citation: 2010 WL 3527578 (Ohio App.)
Date of decision: Sept. 9, 2010
Country: US
State or Federal: State
State/Jurisdiction: Ohio
Court: Court of Appeals
Type of action: Marital Dissolution
Experts: Brian Russell (husband)
Judge: Sadler
SIC: 8021 Offices and Clinics of Dentists

This is the third case in as many months to decide the value of a dental practice in divorce. First came *McReath v. McReath*, 2010 WL 2943198 (Wis. App.)(July 29, 2010), in which the Wisconsin Court of Appeals ruled that all *salable* goodwill is a marital asset and subject to division, whether it is corporate or professional. Key to the court's ruling was its finding that both parties (and their valuation experts) agreed that a non-compete agreement would effectively transfer a "lion's share" of the spouse-practitioner's professional goodwill to a prospective buyer, thereby evidencing its salable nature.

By contrast, in *McKee v. McKee*, 2010 WL 3245246 (Tenn. Ct. App.)(Aug. 17, 2010), the Tennessee Court of Appeals valued the wife's one-third interest in her longstanding dental practice at only $97,000 (net asset value), despite evidence that one of her partners had recently bought into the practice at $749,000. In that particular sale, the parties had allocated 45% of the buy-in price to the professional goodwill of the wife and her partner and 34% to the patient files and records. Nevertheless, the court found the patient records "had no value" in the wife's divorce—that is, they constituted professional goodwill and were non-divisible.

Dentist sells his practice during divorce. In the *Banchefsky* case—and for reasons the Ohio Court of Appeal's opinion does not reveal, the husband sold his solo cosmetic dentistry practice for $580,000 during the proceedings. In the purchase agreement, the parties allocated specific amounts to the tangible assets ($126K), patient records ($20K), agreement not to compete ($15K), and unspecified "goodwill" ($416K). The husband and wife agreed the sale was arm's length and the price reflected the current fair market value for the dental practice.

For purposes of divorce, however, the husband's valuation expert said that the value attributed to the non-compete in the purchase agreement was "arbitrary." To find its appropriate value, he subtracted the tangible asset value from the total sale price and allocated the remainder ($431,000) to professional and enterprise goodwill. Specifically, the husband's expert defined "professional goodwill" as a direct function of earnings from patients who patronized the husband for his individual and personal attributes. He characterized enterprise goodwill as "goodwill that would go along with the business practice itself and could be sold with or without" the husband. To distinguish the components in this case, he applied the Multiattribute Utility Model (MUM), developed by valuation and forensic analyst David Wood, CPA/ABV, CVA (Mt. Vernon, IL). Using MUM, the expert found that the appropriate value for the husband's willingness not to compete was $215,000 and constituted professional, non-divisible goodwill. *Note*: For more on MUM, see "'Multiattribute Utility Model' Accepted in Allocating Enterprise/Personal Goodwill," in the Dec. 2006 *BVU*; "'MUM's the Word': A Formal Method to Allocate Blue Sky Value in Divorce," by David Wood in the March 2007 *BVU*; and "Still Hunting: In Search of Consistent, Functional Definition for Personal Goodwill," by David Wood in the April 2010 *BVU*.

The trial court expressly acknowledged MUM's utility in determining the fair market value of a professional practice, but in this case, it found the model was neither necessary nor appropriate due to the arm's length sale of the business. Accordingly, it determined the husband's personal goodwill was worth no more than the value assigned to the non-compete in the purchase agreement ($15K), and it divided the remainder of the sale proceeds ($565,000) equally between the parties.

The husband appealed, arguing that the trial court should have deferred to his expert's opinion and his application of MUM. The appellate court confirmed the utility of MUM in "determining the impact an individual's departure might have on the fair market value of a business." However, like the trial court, it also found that "it was simply unnecessary to determine the value of the covenant-not-to-compete through the use of a business model pertaining to the hypothetical case of a hypothetical business" when there was evidence of an actual sale. It also found, based on prior case law, that a covenant not-to-compete is a non-marital asset. Accordingly, the $15K non-compete constituted the husband's personal goodwill and his separate, non-divisible property, the court held, and confirmed the trial court's allocation of value in all respects.

McReath v. McReath

Wisconsin Appellate Court Articulates New Standard on Division of Goodwill in Divorce

Citation: 2010 WL 2943198 (Wis. App.)
Date of decision: July 29, 2010
Country: US
State or Federal: State
State/Jurisdiction: Wisconsin
Court: Court of Appeals
Type of action: Marital Dissolution
Experts: unnamed
Judge: Lundsten
SIC: 8021 Offices and Clinics of Dentists

Are corporate goodwill and professional goodwill truly distinct, or do they overlap? How does a monopoly in a geographic area . . . affect determinations of corporate goodwill and professional goodwill? Is such a monopoly a component of corporate goodwill or professional goodwill? If [the former] . . . how does one go about differentiating the business value attributable to monopoly status from the business value owing to [the professional's] . . . skills and reputation?

These are the questions the Wisconsin Court of Appeals addressed when it recently considered the "hotly debated" issue of dividing the value of professional practice goodwill in divorce cases, a topic that still creates a "quagmire for courts." "We do not, in this decision, pull Wisconsin out of this quagmire," the court conceded. Rather, it aimed to clarify the issues by considering whether to adopt a per se rule excluding "salable professional goodwill" from divisible marital property.

The only orthodontist around. In 1996, during the parties' marriage, the husband bought an orthodontic practice from another sole practitioner for approximately $930,000. Over the next 15 years or so, he practiced in two offices located in south central Wisconsin, enjoying a conversion ratio (percentage of new patients who stay with the practice) of 75%, compared with an industry average of about 50%. At their divorce trial, the parties disputed the value of the practice. The husband's expert said it was worth only $415,000, but the court rejected this value, based largely on the husband's buy-in price two decades earlier and the practice's consistently high earnings.

Using an income approach, the wife's expert said the practice would be worth just over $1 million to a potential buyer, consisting of $247,000 for the tangible assets and the remaining $811,000 of goodwill value. Although the expert did not identify the components of value as either professional or corporate goodwill, when the trial court adopted his valuation, it expressly assumed that a substantial portion consisted of professional goodwill. It also found that a buyer would insist on a non-compete agreement, similar to the one the husband received when he bought the practice from its former owner. In fact, the husband estimated that 89% of his purchase price was for profession goodwill and the rest for the tangible assets and "corporate goodwill."

The court divided the value of the practice equally (50/50) between the parties. It then calculated the husband's practice earnings by looking at his average net cash flow over the five years prior to divorce. On this basis, the court awarded the wife $16,000 in monthly maintenance for the next 20 years, and the husband appealed.

On appeal, although the husband admitted he could sell his practice for approximately $1 million, most of that value was attributable to professional goodwill. Under controlling case law, professional goodwill is not a divisible asset, he argued. Further, because professional goodwill is so inextricably linked to earnings, it would be unfair to divide the value of his professional goodwill and then also base maintenance payments, in part, on the earnings that flow from that same professional goodwill (what the case law referred to as "double counting" or "double dipping").

The wife's argument was simple: In this case, because the husband's professional goodwill was all *salable*, it was divisible marital property.

No good definition of goodwill. The court began by noting that neither party provided a clear definition of "corporate goodwill" or "professional goodwill." This was not surprising, due to the lack of clarity in the case law and commentary, which also failed to provide a consistent, working definition of the components of goodwill. The confusion is compounded by some courts making an incorrect assumption—"namely . . . that professional goodwill, by definition, is not salable. This is plainly not true," the Wisconsin court observed, "as the record before us demonstrates."

For example, although the husband tried to argue that professional goodwill was never divisible because it is not salable, he ultimately admitted that when he bought the practice, the "lion's share" of the purchase price was for professional goodwill, as evidenced in part by the non-compete. In this case, both parties (and experts) agreed that a non-compete agreement would effectively transfer a substantial portion of the husband's professional goodwill to the buyer. Accordingly, "there is no serious dispute that a significant, but unspecified, portion of [the practice value] is attributable to salable professional goodwill," the court held. (It also noted the overlap with corporate goodwill; for example, the husband's high conversion rate could be due to his particular skills—or that his practice enjoyed a near monopoly in the area, an attribute belonging to the business.)

Based on this analysis, the husband's true contention was that salable *professional* goodwill should never be included in marital property. This would require the court to remand the case to determine the value and exclude the salable professional goodwill—but first, it examined the husband's legal arguments in support.

In particular, a 1981 Wisconsin case considered a lawyer's share in the goodwill value of his law firm and found, like a professional license or degree, it could not be sold on an open market and thus was not an "asset" subject to division. However, that case addressed only "non-salable" professional goodwill, the court pointed out, as opposed to this one, in which the evidence clearly showed salable professional goodwill.

A subsequent decision concerning the value of a dental practice remanded the case for a finding on whether the goodwill value was "*merely* a measure of earning capacity" or whether it was marketable and had a value "over and above *the professional's skills and services*." (emphasis added by the court) Thus it could be distinguished on the same grounds as the 1981 case. "There is no hint in either [case] that we considered whether *salable* professional goodwill should be divisible property," the court said, preserving both cases as precedent while moving to the husband's main argument against the inclusion of salable professional goodwill: the double-dip.

Three alternate proposals. The husband claimed his proposed rule prohibiting the inclusion of all professional goodwill from marital property would solve the problem presented by double-counting. The wife declined to recognize any problem; she simply wanted all salable goodwill, regardless of its label, to be included in the divisible value of a professional's practice. On its own, the court proposed a third alternative: include salable professional goodwill as divisible property, but then deal with the double-counting issue by adjusting the maintenance determination.

The court agreed with the husband that if he continued his practice, there would be some double-counting of earnings, but it rejected his proposal for fairness reasons. For example, what if a practicing orthodontist plans to retire a year after divorce and sell his practice? Under the husband's per se rule, the wife couldn't share in the full value of the business, and yet a court would have to set maintenance knowing that retirement was imminent. Similarly, what if a practicing dentist dies unexpectedly after divorce; if the court had been precluded from dividing the full value of the practice, the non-dentist spouse would have lost that value—and then lose maintenance (which typically terminates on the payer's death). Finally, a per se rule against including any salable professional goodwill would apply even when maintenance was not an issue; there would be no problem of double-counting—but the non-professional spouse "would still lose out," the court said.

The court also failed to see that a per se rule made much "economic sense." Using the parties' case as an example, acknowledging the existence of double-counting was not the same as "understanding the dollar relationship between the amount [the wife] received in the property division attributable to salable professional goodwill and the portion of her maintenance payments attributable to professional goodwill." In other words, assuming (as the husband's expert surmised) that 95% of the total salable goodwill of the $1 million practice was attributable to professional goodwill, then under a per se rule the wife's share would drop from over $500,000 to just under $144,000.

"We have no idea whether this $385,225 reduction . . . constitutes a reasonable offset for the benefit [the wife] will receive by including all of [the husband's] earnings when calculating maintenance," the court said. Perhaps if the husband had presented an expert to explain or propose an offset, the trial court could have considered this approach—but without such evidence in the record, neither it nor the appellate court could make such a determination. Moreover, double-counting is only a problem if the husband does not sell his practice; if he sells after the divorce and his earnings decline (because of a non-compete), the wife would have received her share of the business and the husband could petition to modify maintenance.

The appellate court also questioned the assumption that dividing the value of corporate goodwill, alone, did not lead to double-counting. As with salable professional goodwill, a business owner's ongoing earning capacity is enhanced by salable corporate goodwill, the court explained. Since Wisconsin law clearly permits the division of salable corporate goodwill, a blanket prohibition against dividing salable professional goodwill might conflict with this well-settled rule.

Finally, the court noted that non-compete agreements are not (as the husband argued) the only mechanism for transferring professional goodwill. For example, the husband's purchase agreement with the former owner of the practice required the latter to introduce the husband to his existing patients. "What reason would [the husband] give for excluding the value of professional goodwill transferred in this manner?" the court asked. Indeed, even if non-competes were the only means to transfer the value of professional goodwill, "why . . . does this . . . suggest that the professional goodwill is not divisible? [The husband] does not explain," the court said.

An opportunity for divorce experts? The court's alternative proposal, to include salable goodwill in the property division and then adjust maintenance, would avoid the double-counting problem and its potential unfairness. But despite the proposal's theoretical appeal, the husband did not make an argument for it, and the parties did not brief the issue. Thus the court could not adequately determine its legal support. Nor could it give the family court sufficient guidance on remand. As before, without the benefit of expert testimony or evidence, the court didn't know how "or even if" the trial court could calculate a reduction in maintenance "to *appropriately* offset the amount the wife received in the property division attributable to salable professional goodwill" (emphasis by the court):

> For example, we do not know what expert testimony [the husband] might have been able to provide if he had, as an alternative argument, accepted the proposition that salable professional goodwill is divisible, and sought a compensating downward adjustment in maintenance.

None of the case law or legal authorities shed light on the issue, the court observed. It could not reverse the trial court's determination and remand for further findings based on "mere speculation" that the maintenance award was unfair. Further, the husband failed to argue on appeal that the trial court erred in setting the maintenance award, and thus the appellate court was barred from reviewing the same. For all these reasons, it adopted the wife's approach (effectively the same one adopted by the trial court): "include all salable goodwill, both corporate and professional, as a divisible asset and then, essentially, ignore . . . that [the husband's] earnings are intertwined." Because no existing rule precluded this approach, and because the court declined to adopt a per se rule against including all salable professional goodwill, it affirmed the lower court's division of property and maintenance award.

Dissent wants a fairness analysis. A single judge dissented from the majority opinion, disagreeing that the problem was a "lack of expert testimony" to resolve the double-counting issue. The dissent also saw no need for "an exact finding" regarding what portion of the value of the husband's practice was divisible and what was not. Instead, the real problem may have been the lack of any clear rule against double-counting. The only Wisconsin case that considered the issue (*Cook v. Cook*, 560 N.W.2d 246 (1977)), simply directs trial courts to consider fairness when dividing income-producing marital property and determining maintenance. Thus, the dissent would have posited a rule requiring family courts to conduct "a *Cook* analysis" (essentially, a fairness analysis) when double-counting is an issue, and would have remanded this case accordingly. Whether this legal question provides grounds for further appeal remains to be seen.

McKee v. McKee

Tennessee Court Excludes Patient Files as Professional Goodwill in Dental Practice Valuation

Citation: 2010 WL 3245246 (Tenn. Ct. App.)
Date of decision: Aug. 17, 2010
Country: US
State or Federal: State
State/Jurisdiction: Tennessee
Court: Court of Appeals
Type of action: Marital Dissolution
Experts: Tom Price (wife); Mike Hallum (husband)
Judge: Bennett
SIC: 8021 Offices and Clinics of Dentists

The Tennessee Court of Appeals' decision in *McKee* makes an interesting contrast to the Wisconsin appellate court's findings in *McReath*. Both cases concerned the valuation of a longstanding dental practice developed during an equally long marriage, except that in the case of *McKee*, the wife owned the practice and earned significantly more than the husband. Both courts considered expert valuations based on the income approach—and both purported to apply the majority rule concerning the disposition of goodwill value on divorce, but with very different results.

A three-partner practice. Much of the McKees' divorce trial focused on the valuation of the wife's dental practice, which she started in 1983 as a sole proprietor, adding another dentist in 2000 and a third in 2005 as equal partners. The wife relied on a CPA and financial planning firm to determine the buy-in price of both transactions. In 2005, for example, the incoming dentist purchased his one-third interest in the ongoing practice for $749,000, of which 45% was allocated to the personal goodwill of the wife and her co-partner, and 34% to patient files and records.

The wife did not call these consultants as divorce experts. Instead, she called a valuation expert, who appraised her 33% interest at just over $97,000. The expert distinguished his valuation method from the financial consultants' by its context. In a buy-sell transaction, he said, "value is based on tangible assets like cash, accounts receivable, fixed assets, and pre-paid expenses, as well as intangible assets in the form of goodwill," which is allocated into "identifiable and unidentifiable goodwill." In a divorce setting, however, "the distinction is between personal goodwill and business goodwill," he said, because the applicable law considers only the latter to be a marital asset. (Notably, both parties agreed that it was appropriate under Tennessee law to include practice/business goodwill in valuing a professional services firm for divorce purposes, but not personal/professional goodwill.)

The wife's expert further testified that her financial consultants used the capitalization of earnings method to value her dental practice for the buy-in transactions but did not have a specific formula to value the patient records. In the context of divorce, the wife's expert attributed no value to the patient records, because it equated to personal/professional goodwill. In reaching this conclusion, he relied on a checklist developed by an accredited business valuation expert for use in professional education courses. The wife's expert cited the checklist in his report, in particular its "rubric" that "the customer components are all factors of personal goodwill." The relationship between dentist and patient is highly personal, the expert explained, based on the reputation, trust, and skill of the professional. "That relationship is what [a prospective buyer] hopes to purchase from the seller," he said.

At the same time, the wife's expert testified that patient records are not capable of earning money "without a professional providing the service." The presence of a non-compete is "proof," in his opinion, "of the existence of goodwill. Although the 2000 and 2005 partnership buy-ins provided a reasonable basis for the fair market value of the wife's interest "*outside* of a divorce proceeding," the wife's expert said (his original emphasis), for purposes of a marital dissolution, the inclusion of personal goodwill values was not appropriate, and he did not consider the two prior transactions in his valuation of the wife's interest.

Patient records: personal or practice goodwill? By contrast, the husband's expert classified the patient files as a separate asset from professional goodwill. This view was consistent with the two prior valuations of the dental practice for the partnership buy-ins. The husband's expert relied heavily on these two prior transactions, because in their absence, "it would have been difficult" for him to calculate how much of the intangible goodwill value attached to the business and how much to the professionals. He also said that "valuation literature" requires consideration of transactions occurring within five years of the valuation date. Although he admitted having "no idea" how the financial consultants arrived at the roughly 33% or $255,000 value for the patient records in the 2005 purchase price, this amount appeared "reasonable based on the general makeup of the practice," its makeup and its reputation. Allocating goodwill value between the professional and the practice firm is "subject to argument and difficult to define," he also admitted, but ultimately valued the wife's one-third interest at approximately $460,000.

The trial court ultimately adopted the valuation by the wife's expert ($97,000). If the wife's one-third interest was sold, the court said, "the only assets which would be marketable would be the equipment and accounts receivable." It also found, based on testimony by the husband's expert, the patient records "had no value" without a non-compete. (*Note*: It's unclear from the opinion whether either expert testified to the likelihood that a prospective buyer would insist on a non-compete clause in the purchase agreement.) Based on the husband's lack of financial and other contributions as a "homemaker" in the marriage, the court also awarded an unequal division of marital property, 75% to the wife and 25% to the husband, and denied his claims for alimony—and the husband appealed.

The Tennessee Court of Appeals examined all the evidence, including the testimony from both experts and the legal as well as factual findings by the family court. "On appeal, there is a presumption that the trial court's valuation, a question of fact, is correct," the court said. "Because [Tennessee] courts have consistently held that personal goodwill cannot be a component in the valuation of a professional practice in an equitable distribution of a marital estate," the valuation by the wife's expert was "reasonable," the court said. Finding the trial court's reliance was also reasonable and its valuation within the range presented by the evidence, the appellate court confirmed the $97,000 value of the wife's interest in her dental practice and its unequal disposition of marital assets, including the denial of alimony to the husband.

Howard v. United States

Non-Compete Is a Corporate Asset for Income Tax Purposes

Citation: 2010 WL 3061626 (E.D.Wash.)
Date of decision: July 30, 2010
Country: US
State or Federal: Federal
State/Jurisdiction: Federal Circuit
Court: United States District Court
Type of action: Federal Taxation
Judge: Peterson
SIC: 8021 Offices and Clinics of Dentists

This case, focusing on a dental practice in the context of federal income tax, considers whether professional goodwill, as evidenced by the value of a non-compete agreement, belongs to the practitioner or the business.

Doctor agrees not to compete against himself. In 1980, Larry Howard, DDS, incorporated his practice, becoming the sole shareholder, officer, and director of the Howard Corp. Dr. Howard entered an agreement not to compete with the Howard Corp. (in effect, protecting the company from himself). The non-compete provided that Dr. Howard would not practice dentistry for three years and within 50 miles so long as he continued to be an employee and stockholder of the corporation. The agreement did not address whether the doctor or the business owned the related professional goodwill.

When Dr. Howard retired in 2002, he sold his practice to another dentist and his personal service corporation. The parties' asset purchase agreement expressly allocated nearly $549,900 to Dr. Howard for his personal goodwill and $16,000 for a consideration not to compete with the buyer (plus approximately $47,000 for the tangible assets). In filing his joint federal tax returns that year, Dr. Howard reported just over $320,000 as long-term capital gain income resulting from the sale of goodwill. The IRS re-characterized the goodwill as a corporate asset, however, and treated the dentist's receipt of $320,000 as a dividend. After the IRS assessed a deficiency of just over $61,000 plus interest, the dentist and his wife claimed a refund in district court.

The Howards argued that the goodwill was personal to Dr. Howard and that he was entitled to claim the goodwill sale proceeds as long term capital gain. In support, the Howards pointed to state divorce law, which holds that professional goodwill "has value to the professional" and is included among the divisible assets. (*Note:* Washington, a community property state, follows the minority rule, finding no distinction between professional and enterprise goodwill; both are assets subject to disposition in divorce.)

In particular, the Howards quoted a 1979 divorce decision by the Washington Supreme Court (also concerning a dental practice), which found that professionals "can expect a large number, if not most, of [their] patients to accept as their dentist a person to whom [they] sell the practice." Although the case excerpt does not specifically mention whether a non-compete accomplishes the patient transfer, it clearly finds the patients of the selling dentist are "a part of goodwill, and they have a real pecuniary value" to the buyer.

The Howards also argued that the parties' asset purchase agreement controlled the characterization of goodwill—in particular, its classification of the Howard Corp. goodwill as a personal, non-corporate asset. They also claimed that the purchase agreement effectively terminated the original, 1980 non-compete agreement, thereby rendering its terms inapplicable to the present case.

Covenant not to compete is the controlling factor. The government relied on federal income tax law to argue that the goodwill of Dr. Howard's dental practice was a corporate rather than personal asset. One case, in particular (*Martin Ice Cream Company v. Commissioner*, 110 T.C. 189 (1998), available at *BVLaw*), held that "the goodwill of a corporation was an individual asset when the employer had not obtained exclusive rights to either the employee's future services or a continuing call on the business generated by the employee's personal relationships."

Alternatively, a second case, *Norwalk v. Commissioner*, T.C. Memo. 1998-279 (also available at *BVLaw*), holds that if a professional/employee works for a corporation under a contract with a covenant not to compete, then the corporation—and not the individual—owns the goodwill generated from the professional's work. "Even when a corporation is dependent upon a key employee," the district court explained, in discussing *Norwalk*, "the employee may not own the goodwill if the employee enters into a covenant not to compete . . . whereby the employee's personal relationships with clients may become the property of the corporation."

The IRS also argued that the parties' asset purchase agreement was not dispositive of the issue and that, even if the agreement somehow terminated the 1980 covenant not to compete, it would not have changed the character of the goodwill that the dentist generated from 1980 through the sale of his practice in 2002. Finally, the government claimed the "economic reality" of the transaction should control the outcome of the case. Dr. Howard testified that he simply accepted the proposed price for the practice without significant negotiation or discussion of how to allocate the proceeds.

The court found that the parties' asset purchase agreement did not control the ownership of goodwill, nor was it a valid reflection of the relationship between Dr. Howard and the Howard Corp. There was no dispute that Dr. Howard was bound by a contractual covenant not to compete until he sold his practice in 2002. Further, the tax cases clearly distinguished between personal and corporate ownership of goodwill by the existence of a non-compete. Finally, the Howard Corp. was the entity that earned, controlled (and reported) the practice income from the time of incorporation (1980) through the sale.

"The covenant not to compete . . . reinforces the conclusion that the Howard Corporation controlled the assets, earned the income from Dr. Howard's services, and barred Dr. Howard from competing with Howard Corporation," the court held. Accordingly, it found that the goodwill is a corporate asset, belonging to the Howard Corp., and the taxpayers were not entitled to a refund.

On review by the federal district court (E.D. Wash.), the taxpayer relied on state divorce law to argue that professional goodwill was a personal asset. Moreover, the purchase agreement had classified it as such, and the sale of the company effectively terminated the non-compete. By contrast, the IRS cited Tax Court cases to show that if an employee works under a covenant not to compete, then the company owns the goodwill generated from the professional's work—and the court ultimately agreed. "The covenant not to compete reinforces the conclusion that Howard Corporation controlled the assets, earned the income from Dr. Howard's services, and barred Dr. Howard from competing with Howard Corporation."

In re Marriage of Theurer

Valuation of Orthodontic Practice Includes Goodwill, Excludes Patient Prepays

Citation: 2009 WL 3823648 (Cal. App. 2 Dist.)
Date of decision: Nov. 17, 2009
Country: US
State or Federal: State
State/Jurisdiction: California
Court: Court of Appeals
Type of action: Marital Dissolution
Experts: Edward Lieberman (wife); Mark Kohn and Thomas Fitterer (husband)
Judge: Perluss
SIC: 8072 Dental Laboratories

This divorce case offers a lesson in listening to clients, or at least enough to know what they'll say about their own business in court. After hearing the husband describe his orthodontic practice and then hearing from three valuation experts, the trial court found that the husband was "one of the best orthodontists in the world," with "no competitors whatsoever," providing services at a higher standard than any other orthodontic practice in Lancaster, California (the eighth largest city in Los Angeles County).

Nearly 1,000 new patients per year. The husband began his orthodontic practice in 1988. Fifteen years later he was still the only licensed orthodontist, but he had 14 people on staff, including eight dental assistants. His staff permitted him to see, on average, 100 to 150 patients per day (225 patients on one or two days per month). The practice also used the most advanced computer and lab technology. In 2002, it grossed over $2.5 million and the husband earned $1.2 million before tax.

Further, compared to most sole orthodontic practices, which typically generate 250 new patients per year ("new starts"), the husband's annual new starts averaged 921 during the four years prior to divorce. To maintain this "extraordinary" level of new patients, the husband spent substantial time marketing and promoting his practice by sponsoring local youth programs, beauty pageants, and academic events.

At trial, the wife called a forensic accountant to value the husband's practice. The accountant applied an investment standard of value (value to the owner), assuming the business would continue in the future as it had in the past, with the same historical revenues and expenses. He also valued goodwill under the excess earnings approach, estimating the husband's reasonable compensation as $500,000 per year and applying a multiple of four. The relatively high cap rate was justified by the practice's low degree of risk, he said, including its five-year increase in gross revenues and the husband's consistent net income. He valued goodwill at $2.5 million and the overall practice at $3.0 million.

The husband called two expert witnesses. The first—a forensic accountant specializing in family law matters—also applied the investment value standard. Like the wife's expert, he used a capitalization of earnings method to value goodwill, but he applied a multiplier of 2.5 to reflect his opinion of higher risk and the ease with which a competitor could enter the market. He also concluded reasonable compensation at $776,000 per year. (The court does not cite either expert's source for the reasonable comp figures.) In addition, he calculated goodwill using the market method and three months of gross income to determine a weighted average of $980,000.

Notably, the husband's first expert deducted patient prepayments—which amounted to over $1.1 million—as a liability. His reasoning: If the husband stopped working, he would have to hire another orthodontist or refund patients' money. The practice also accounted for patient prepays as a liability, he said. As a final risk factor, the husband's income and his new starts had been decreasing in recent years, and overall, the husband's first expert valued the orthodontic practice at $126,905.

Husband's second expert 'visibly shaken.' Curiously, the husband's second expert had originally been retained by the wife. (The court does not address the conflict of interest or its possible waiver.) This expert, a broker with over 40 years' experience selling private practices, testified that the excess earnings approach (used by the wife's expert and the husband's first expert, in part) is not normally used to value goodwill in connection with the sale of professional firms.

Instead, this second expert applied the fair market value standard (i.e., what a buyer would be willing to pay for the practice assuming that the husband no longer provided his services but past earnings ($1.6 million) would continue into the future). He used two different methods to determine FMV. First, he calculated a net asset value, finding $300,000 of tangible assets plus $1.3 million in goodwill. To determine the latter, he multiplied the husband's $1 million net income times 1.3 percent (130%), because, based on his experience, the goodwill component of a professional practice sells for between 50% and 300% of net income. Although he admitted this figure was arbitrary, he believed 130% of net income was appropriate in this case.

Under his second method, the expert multiplied the practice's gross revenue ($2.6 million) by 60%—the multiple commonly used by banks and buyers to value an orthodontic practice, he said. Notwithstanding his characterization of the facility as "one of the best I've ever seen," the expert believed the majority of buyers would want a location closer to the ocean. For example, he'd apply an 80% or 90% multiplier to a Santa Monica practice.

The husband's second expert did not reduce his valuation by prepays, because the patient contracts did not provide for refunds. Further, he'd already factored modest patient refunds (e.g., $30,000 in 2002) into his goodwill calculations. Finally, the expert testified that the number of new starts is relevant to a practice valuation but that he'd not received that information from the husband. (The court provided no explanation for why the husband's expert failed to get the data from the wife's expert's report.)

The expert was surprised to learn that the husband received 866 new starts in 2002. In fact, he appeared "visibly shaken" on the stand. In response to his attorney's repeated attempts to establish that a buyer would pay less for so many new patients due to the extra work and staffing, the husband's expert replied: "I would think [it] would be wonderful to have 866 starts. Great Scott, that's a lot. You sure it's 866 new starts? . . . The buyer would clap his hands . . . I think it would be positive. The more the merrier."

Trial court arrives at a mid-value. The trial court credited the wife's expert's investment valuation but reduced his multiple from 4 to 3 to reflect its finding that the practice was "substantially dependent on [the husband's] exceptional orthodontic and managerial skills." This led to a goodwill value of $1.9 million, or roughly the midpoint of the experts' three numbers ($2.5 million by the wife's expert, $1 million by the husband's first expert, and $1.3 million by his second).

The court rejected the husband's argument, which was raised and briefed at trial, claiming that it was compelled by California case law to apply the fair market value standard. Although the husband's second expert was "credible and unbiased," his evident surprise at the new start numbers persuaded the court to reject his FMV valuation as well. Lastly, the court rejected the inclusion of patient prepays by the husband's first expert, because, unlike future taxes, for instance, the liability was neither immediate nor specific. It also found that the husband's second expert effectively impeached the first by concluding that prepays were not a liability, and that one year's modest repayment ($30,000) was based largely on insurance reimbursements.

The husband appealed these two points—both the court's failure to apply the FMV standard (specifically in its determination of goodwill), and its failure to treat patient prepays as a liability. He also claimed that the wife's expert used an inappropriate method (excess earnings) to value the goodwill of a professional practice. The California Court of Appeal considered both arguments in light of the evidence and applicable law.

A question of fact, not law. "There is no absolute rule specifying how goodwill of a particular practice should be valued, and any reliable method is acceptable if warranted by the facts," the court held, stating the broad rule, which was similar to the standard found in most state jurisdictions that valuation is not a legal but factual determination. Nothing in the applicable case law precluded a court from applying the capitalization of earnings calculation of goodwill in the appropriate circumstances, the court added. Indeed, the excess earnings approach, discredited by the husband's second expert but utilized by his first (and the wife's expert), "is a method that is commonly used to determine the value of goodwill in a professional practice," the court said.

Thus, the sole issue before the trial court was in determining which expert's approach (or combination of approaches) best approximated the value of the practice. In this case, the evidence amply supported the trial court's primary reliance on the wife's expert, including its downward adjustment of the cap rate and its calculation of goodwill as roughly midway between all of the experts' numbers. It was also appropriate for the court to discredit the husband's second expert, due to his visible surprise at learning the new starts data and his inappropriate reduction in value due to location (especially since he admitted the practice was not "typical" because it was more profitable than most).

Likewise, the trial court's treatment of patient prepays as a liability was appropriate, because (unlike tax contingencies) they were speculative, uncertain, and remote. There was no evidence that any patients would leave the practice; moreover, just because the practice accounted for prepays as a liability on its balance sheets did not require the court to do the same. In addition, every year the substantial number of new starts together with their prepayments for services exceeded the prior year's starts and payments.

"The premise for the goodwill valuation of a professional practice and its goodwill is that it will continue into the future in essentially the same form as in the past," the appellate court held, and confirmed the $2.4 million valuation.

Schneider v. Schneider

Personal Goodwill Excluded, Accounts Receivable Included in Professional Practice in Illinois Marital Dissolution Case

Citation: 2005 Ill. LEXIS 7
Date of decision: January 21, 2005
Country: US
State or Federal: State
State/Jurisdiction: Illinois
Court: Supreme Court
Type of action: Marital Dissolution
Experts: Stephen Mareta (for husband)
Bruce Richman (for wife)
Judge: Thomas
SIC: 8021 Offices and Clinics of Dentists
Key words: Marital dissolution, Accounts receivable, Personal goodwill, Tangible assets, Intangible assets

The issue in this marital dissolution was the value of husband's dental practice and whether personal goodwill and accounts receivable should be included in that value.

The trial court concluded that personal goodwill and accounts receivable should be excluded from the valuation. Wife appealed and the appeals court reversed. The appeal to the state's highest court was granted to settle this issue before the case was remanded back to the trial level for final determination.

Valuation evidence. Both parties presented expert testimony as to the value of husband's dental practice. Stephen Mareta, testifying for husband, concluded that the fair market value of the practice was $346,300. Mareta attributed the majority of the value ($311,300) to personal goodwill and attributed $35,000 to fixed assets. Mareta defined fixed assets as "property and equipment, but [fixed assets] did not include cash on hand, accounts receivable, cash surrender value of life insurance, and loans due from officers." He explained that "the accounts receivable were merely a reflection of future income," and thus not properly included in the valuation.

Bruce Richman testified for wife and concluded that the fair market value of the dental practice was $481,000. Richman attributed $336,587 of the practices value to "intangible assets." Richman described those assets as, "dental records, the leasehold interest, a trained work force, intellectual property, trade names and enterprise goodwill." However, he specifically excluded personal goodwill from that definition. Richman also attributed $144,413 of the value to tangible assets, "including accounts receivable, furniture and equipment, cash surrender value of insurance, and inventory."

Holding and rationale. The Supreme Court noted in its opinion, "The goodwill in a professional practice is generally personal in nature, while the goodwill in a corporation might include both personal and enterprise goodwill." The court concluded that it is not proper to include personal goodwill in the value of a professional practice:

> In *Zells* we noted that adequate attention to the preceding factors would result in an appropriate consideration of professional goodwill as an aspect of income potential that would then be reflected in the maintenance and support awards. We therefore held that any additional consideration of goodwill value is duplicative and improper. However, as this court made clear in *Talty*, the basis for our holding in *Zells* was not simply the fact that maintenance and support were awarded. Rather, the basis for our holding in *Zells* was the fact that personal goodwill "is already reflected in a number of the circumstances that must be considered by a judge in making an equitable division of property under the [Dissolution] Act."
>
> Specifically we stated: "A workable definition of goodwill is that 'goodwill is the value of a business or practice that exceeds the combined value of the physical assets.' . . . 'Goodwill represents merely the ability to acquire future income.' . . . To the extent that the goodwill of the car dealership depends on [the husband's] personal efforts, the same elements that underlie that calculation were also considered by the court in its assessment of the criteria contained in *section 503(d)*."

The Supreme Court also concluded that the inclusion of accounts receivables into the value of the practice was proper. It therefore affirmed the appeals court's conclusion on this issue. The court stated:

> Although accounts receivable have not been collected, they are assets that have been earned and have a known value and, thus, are distinguishable from future earnings or income-generating ability. Because accounts receivable have a known value, a court can properly consider accounts receivable as assets of the business. As the *Tietz* court correctly observed, accounts receivable are future income only in the sense that they will be collected in the future. Accounts receivable are not future income in the sense that they are assets considered by a circuit court in determining a party's income-generating ability for purposes of maintenance or child support awards. The fact that the accounts receivable may not be collected until a future date does not transform those assets into speculative or future income.

Daniela David v. Dr. Aurel David

Canadian Dental Practice Valued

Citation: 2004 CanLII 46652 (ON S.C.)
Date of decision: December 8, 2004
Country: Canada
Type of action: Marital Dissolution

In *Daniela David v. Dr. Aurel David*, 2004 CanLII 46652 (ON S.C.), decided December 8, 2004, the Ontario Supreme Court considered several issues surrounding the valuation of a dental practice. The husband is a Romanian immigrant, practicing dentistry in Thornhill. He employs several dentists in his practice, who are paid 50% of their net receipts (where 40% is the norm) and who are not subject to restrictive employment agreements. The practice's clientele is disproportionately drawn from the local Romanian community. The practice had been established for four years prior to the February 2002 date of separation.

This was not the husband's only practice during the marriage. In 1998, he sold a similar practice for $365,000. The sale price included $212,500 in goodwill. It had been established six years prior to the date of sale. Additionally, the husband established two offices in other Ontario cities post-separation.

Both parties presented the Supreme Court with valuation evidence from business brokers as to the value of the practice on the valuation date. Each expert considered comparable transactions of local practices in addition to their income and asset valuations. The experts also considered allegations of underreported cash.

The husband's expert, a certified accountant, performed a full appraisal of the practice. He conducted a site visit and interviewed the husband and his associates. He further sampled the patent records to investigate the underreported cash charge. He also performed an analysis of the practice's repeat clientele. He concluded that there was no underreported cash. This expert then valued the practice using an asset approach. The goodwill portion was valued using a capitalization method. He applied a 19% capitalization rate, which considered the ethnic makeup of the clientele and the above-market pay of the associates. He concluded that the practice had a value of $212,000, including a goodwill component of $65,000.

The wife's expert prepared a two-page limited scope letter of opinion, in which he relied on information from the husband's expert's appraisal. This expert concluded that the practice was growing on the date of separation and had underreported cash, but suffered from potential competition from its associates. He measured the goodwill component using a capitalization method, which included a 15 percent capitalization rate. He concluded that the practice had goodwill of $115,000, or $139,500 if the underreported cash was considered. Notably, he did not conduct a site visit or perform any management interviews. On cross-examination this expert admitted, "A letter of opinion is not a satisfactory valuation of a dental practice."

The Supreme Court found the testimony of the husband's expert preferable because of its "thoroughness and completeness." However, after considering the pre-valuation date sale of the husband's similar practice, it determined that neither party accurately determined the value of the practice's goodwill. Thus, it valued the goodwill at $102,500, the midpoint between the experts' opinions, for a total value of $249,500.

To that value, the court added an amount for the accounts receivable in existence on the valuation date, which the husband's expert indicated were not considered in his valuation. The practice had accounts receivable of $39,000. It then considered the percentage of accounts receivable paid to the associates using year-end 2002 data. It concluded that the practice retained 51.4% of the gross billings. It then applied that percentage to the total accounts receivable and determined that $20,046 should be added to the practice's value to account for this asset.

This abstract originally appeared in *Valuation Case Canada*, authored by John J. Stockdale, Jr. Link to full text court case: http://www.canlii.org/on/cas/onsc/2004/2004onsc12716.html

In re the Marriage of Davis

Income Estimate Based on Industry Norms Alone Rejected

Citation: 2003 Cal. App. Unpub. LEXIS 3405
Date of decision: April 7, 2003
Country: US
State or Federal: State
State/Jurisdiction: California
Court: Court of Appeals
Type of action: Marital Dissolution
Experts: Mark Luttrell (for wife)
Judge: Yegan
SIC: 8021 Offices and Clinics of Dentists
Key words: Marital dissolution

Wife filed a motion to set aside the parties' 1997 marital dissolution judgment on the grounds that husband had concealed income from his dental practice, which materially affected the valuation of the dental practice. Wife argued that husband's concealment was fraudulent and a breach of his fiduciary duty to her. The trial court found that she had failed to prove actual fraud by husband or that she would benefit from having the judgment set aside. The court of appeals affirmed.

Evidence of concealed income. At the hearing to set aside the judgment, wife presented the expert testimony of Mark Luttrell, a forensic accountant. Luttrell was not an expert at the 1997 dissolution trial where the value of husband's dental practice was established. Rather, Luttrell was hired by wife two years later in response to husband's motion to reduce spousal support. At the spousal support hearing, Luttrell determined that husband's 1999 earnings were $431,071 per year, not $206,000 as husband contended. The court agreed and found husband's income to be $431,071.

Wife then filed this motion to set aside the 1997 judgment. At the hearing, Luttrell testified that he could not determine husband's 1996 precise income because general ledgers and checks had been destroyed, and that the only way to determine husband's true income was analytically. Luttrell estimated husband's annual income based on the following factors:

- Husband's reported income was "substantially below industry norms."
- There were no material operational changes in the practice between 1996 and 1999.
- Husband's practice was in a "very mature phase" and very stable over the years.
- Husband's 1999 profit margin of 27.4%, adjusted for items discovered at the 1999 modification hearing, should be equally applicable to 1996.

Trial court findings and appeal. The trial court found that wife did not prove that husband engaged in actual fraud. Husband testified that he had provided her original trial expert with all of the financial information and documents that she and her counsel requested. "Wife failed to prove that husband prevented her access to the documents needed to prepare an accurate appraisal." In addition, wife was aware of husband's bartering practices, and could have inquired further as to the extent of those practices at trial.

In addition, the trial court found that wife had failed to prove that she would materially benefit from having the judgment set aside. The record indicated that the trial court at the dissolution trial had taken into account husband's bartering practices, and that wife's expert had access to all business records. There was no evidence to support wife's argument that the dental practice would have been assigned a higher value if husband had not concealed income as she alleged. Luttrell's estimate, without access to the records of the dental practice, was insufficient to prove a higher value.

The court of appeals found that the trial court did not abuse its discretion in denying wife's motion to set aside the judgment.

Editor's note: There is a lesson to be learned from this case. Significant to the court was that wife could not prove that husband prevented her from reviewing the necessary documents at the dissolution trial. Rather, in the absence of reliable written evidence on the issue, the court found husband's testimony persuasive that he provided wife and her counsel what they requested.

This case accents the need for appraisers to be thorough in requests for information, and to document these requests in writing. Moreover, if an appraiser is suspicious about an account, he or she should document this concern. It is clear from this case that parties may be held to a high standard when represented by counsel and experts.

Expert Testimony Based on Estimates Insufficient to Prove Actual Fraud in Connection With a Divorce Judgment

In *In re the Marriage of Davis*, No. B156636 (Cal. App. 2 Dist. April 7, 2003), unpublished, the California Court of Appeals, Second District considered whether a marital property judgment should be set aside. The husband was a dentist engaged in private practice. In addition to providing dental services for money, he also bartered his services for goods and services. Additionally, some personal expenses were paid by the practice. The husband testified that he accurately reported his income on his federal tax returns. At the time of the divorce, the wife was aware of the above situation. The wife was represented by counsel and engaged expert testimony to value the husband's practice. During discovery, the husband provided the wife with all the documents she requested. At that time the husband earned approximately $200,000 annually, and the family court determined that his practice had a value of $399,679 in 1996. The divorce was finalized in 1997. Two years later, the wife discovered that the husband's annual income had increased to $431,071 by 1999. She then brought a motion to set aside the property division based on fraud in connection with the valuation of the practice.

At trial, the wife presented testimony from a forensic accountant regarding the husband's income at the time of trial. This expert determined that the husband's dental practice was in "a very mature phase" and its income was expected to remain relatively stable over the years. He then considered the industry norms at the time of the divorce and determined that the husband's practice was operating substantially below those norms. Using the practice's 1999 profit margin (27.4%) and applying it to the practice's 1996 figure, he concluded that the husband had concealed approximately $182,559 in income. However, he also testified that he had never valued a dental practice in San Luis Obispo County before this engagement.

The trial court rejected the wife's plea to set aside the judgment. It found that she was aware of the bartering and personal expenses run through the business at the time of the divorce. It further found that she was not denied access to the records of the business at that time. Moreover, it found that she did not prove that she would materially benefit from setting aside the judgment relating to the valuation. She appealed.

On appeal, she renewed her plea to set aside the judgment on the grounds of actual fraud. The appellate court also rejected her argument. It noted that at the time of the divorce, the wife, her attorney and her experts had access to all the financial information and utilized that financial information in appraising the practice. It stated, "Wife failed to prove that husband prevented her access to the documents needed to prepare an accurate appraisal. As a result, the trial court factually found that she did not establish grounds for setting aside the judgment." Moreover, it noted that the wife's only evidence regarding the "true" amount of the husband's income at the time of the trial came from her expert witness. However, it noted that this witness "admitted that he had never before appraised a dental practice in San Luis Obispo County, that he could only estimate the personal expenses husband paid through the practice and his bartering income, and that his opinion that husband concealed such income was based on the assumption that husband's earning from the practice were 'very substantially below industry norms. . . .'" The appellate court determined, "Under these circumstances, the trial court was not required to rely on . . . [the expert]'s estimate of husband's 'true' income." Thus, it affirmed the lower court's decision not to set aside the judgment because the wife failed to show that the husband committed actual fraud.

Chapter 7

The Art of the Appraisal

By Timothy A. Brown, President & CEO, ROI Corporation

The appraisal document is the factual presentation for numerous financial and legal issues. The appraisal defines what the dentist has built for him- or herself—a statement of fact about what it is worth in today's market. It is not a management report for suggestions for future growth.

When performed by professional appraisers, their accreditations and standards, with absolutely no conflict of interest, will assure the client of quality work and complete confidentiality. Their objectivity ensures that readers of the appraisal (accountants, lawyers, bankers, insurers, and potential buyers) can do so with confidence.

The appraisal can be used for many purposes: insurance, estate planning, marital and partnership dissolution, borrowing or refinancing of funds, buying and selling a practice and merger of practices. Sometimes a parent and child will consider or perform a family practice transition. They all need the appraisal statement to document the value of the practice.

The author's philosophy of the appraisal has always been that it is designed, written and formatted for the intended reader. The intended reader is a specific dentist. Lawyers and accountants, bankers, consultants and family members also read appraisals but the intended reader is the dentist.

Thirty or forty years ago the appraisal was not necessary because dental practices were not worth anything. Why would you pay a thousand dollars in 1972 to have your practice appraised if it was only going to sell for five thousand dollars? As the market has developed, the need for appraisal has grown simply because the value of the business has increased sharply. In late 2008, certain practices were even selling for a million or two million or more dollars. It is understandable that a bank, a lawyer, an accountant and a purchaser would want and need a proper appraisal.

Owners are sometimes reluctant to invest in the appraisal because they have a pretty good idea what their business is worth. Their accountant may have given them some advice. They've heard about other transactions of classmates. "His practice is just like mine so it is probably worth $500,000," for example. A buyer will not accept that.

When someone sells their house, the first thing they do is interview two or three real estate agents. A part of that process is not only interviewing them and hearing their marketing plan but also finding out what the house is worth. In effect, they are getting two or three appraisals before they list the house. Why would professionals, if they are thinking of transitioning their practice (the "baby" they have built from scratch over 40 years), not invest in a proper appraisal so that they know where they stand?

Appraisals are also becoming a mid-career planning tool. "If my business is worth half a million today, what will it be worth in 10 years? Will I be able to retire at age 57 or 66 or whatever my retirement plan might be?" Appraisals are also becoming an elective product that dentists are pursuing in mid or later career to explore the question, "What are my options?"

The Process

In our experience, it takes about a month for a professional appraisal firm to cmplete a proper appraisal. It is necessary to identify, document and give value to the various goodwill factors involved in the practice as well as accurately record the details of all major company assets: that is, model, manufacturer, value, serial number, age, condition and color.

An appraisal usually remains valid for about one to three years. This depends on major market fluctuations, which are not that common in dentistry, or on whether the practice goes through rapid changes such as expanding, bringing on new staff, buying new equipment, taking over the suite next door or moving across the road to buy their own building.

Experience dictates that the appraisal should not be free, even though some firms do offer it as part of their sale package. The fee normally charged is about $5,000 for the appraisal and a separate fee for the sale. Appraisal fees, normally butnot always, are 100% tax deductible. A reputable professional appraisal will save the dentist both time and money since it is far more likely to be accurate and serve as a usable document.

Essentially, the appraisal fee and the sale fee can be likened to how dentists run their practices. A patient who goes to a dentist for teeth cleaning does not expect a rebate if he or she comes back a few weeks later for a couple of crowns. These are separate services even though they are performed at the same office.

Current Users of Appraisals

Years of observation reveal that there are two groups of dentists. There is the age 65-plus club which might be referred to as the traditional generation of dentists. That is a "do-it-yourself" generation. Their thinking has been forged by a post-depression belief in frugal self-reliance. They fix their own equipment. They repair their own dental chair. They mow their own lawn. They change the oil in their car.

These dentists will do their own appraisals, often to their peril. Such appraisals are likely to be inaccurate and unacceptable to purchasers. They will try to sell their own practice using a FSBO (for sale by owner) sign. This same activity often occurs in real estate markets which enhances the same skepticism about the need for professional help and guidance.

Then there is the baby boomer generation. The boomers are the quintessential planners and consumers of professional services. They hire investment advisers, appraisers, brokers, accountants and consultants. They are prudent and also recognize that they cannot leave their practice to their family in case of death. Martin Houser, a lawyer with Harris, Sheaffer in Toronto, suggests that 50% of Canadian business owners do not have a will. The appraisal *is* the will of the dentist's business. With an appraisal, dentists or their estate can sell the practice.

Seven Uses of Professional Appraisal

1. The appraisal may be reviewed with an accountant or other practice adviser to identify any opportunities for improvement or change.

2. The appraiser can meet with the dentist or his or her advisers to explain her/his methodology and to assist the dentist in preparing a "critical path" plan.

3. The appraisal provides an opinion of the full replacement cost of the practice leaseholds and equipment. The dentist can use it to review the office contents insurance to be certain the practice is not under or overly insured.

4. The "minus" adjustments portion of an appraisal is found on the calculation of the goodwill page. These are the "negative" aspects of the practice as purchasers will view them. Some of these problems can be solved to increase practice value at little or no cost.

5. A copy of the appraisal should be stored with a dentist's other valuable documents when steps 1, 2, 3 and 4 are complete. The dentist should attach a letter of direction which can be prepared as part of the appraisal that will help in the event of his or her sudden death or disability. A last will and testament should also be included.

6. To increase the practice income, appraiser and major appraisal companies can recommend companies and individuals that teach fundamental business techniques to help dentists achieve this goal.

7. Years of service in the appraisal business generates a national list of accountants, lawyers, bankers, insurance professionals and practice management consultants who can help with the next phase of the dentist's career, whatever it may be.

Additional Notes

Determining Specific Company Risk

According to the American Dental Association, the capitalization rate of a practice typically ranges between 20% and 35%. At least half of this cap rate is dependent upon specific practice factors, many of which are qualitative in nature. The appraiser should consider these factors and rank them on a scale of 1 to 5, where 1 represents a problem area and 5 represents an excellent feature of the practice.

1. Patient lists. List patients by specific dentist. How many patients are assigned to dentists who are leaving the practice? How far away do patients live from the practice?
2. New patients per month over the past three years.
3. Practice location. How many dentists in the area?
4. Fees. Are they higher or lower than average or competitive?
5. Reputation of selling dentist.
6. Quality of management information systems.
7. Condition of office and equipment.
8. Demographic profile of patients. Age, income levels, how many have insurance?
9. Contractual relationships with insurance companies of any kind and when they expire.
10. Types of services—recurring versus one-time.
11. Length of time each dentist is booked ahead.
12. Staff members, longevity with the practice. Will they stay?
13. Length of time dentist has practiced in the community and at current location.
14. Demonstrated compliance with OSHA, HIPAA and other regulations.
15. Selling dentist's intentions in terms of helping with transition.
16. Has the selling dentist signed a covenant not to compete?

Source: American Dental Association

How Much Should the Associate Pay to Buy Into the Practice?

Assume that Dr. Taft joined a successful two-person dental practice on January 1, 2010. His starting salary was $125,000. After a trial or break-in year, the partners offered him a buy-in opportunity over three years. On January 1, 2011, an appraiser valued the practice at $600,000. Dr. Taft would work as an employee for an additional three years and buy a one-third interest in the practice for $200,000. He would pay $20,000 in cash to the practice and agree to reduce his salary by $60,000 per year below the market compensation for three years.

The selling doctors also agreed to reduce the $60,000 by an interest rate factor of 10%, the amount the local bank would charge for a loan to buy the practice. Assuming that interest begins on January 1 of each year, the $60,000 was reduced to $45,078, $49,587 and $54,545 in years 1, 2 and 3, respectively. The 10% interest rate is significantly higher than the risk-free U.S. Treasury rates on two-year securities, but significantly lower than the discount rate used to generate a capitalization rate to calculate the value of the practice. In addition, the selling dentists agreed to use the valuation date in 2011 rather than 2014 when Dr. Taft would become a shareholder. In doing so, there would be no question as to whether Dr. Taft created the value that he was buying.

Source: American Dental Association

Appraisal of a Dental Practice—Sample Valuation Report

DR. ALLAN BROWN
DENTAL SURGEON

30 Corporate Way
Vancouver, British Columbia
V5L 6J4

SAMPLE ONLY

APPRAISAL OF THE DENTAL PRACTICE

AND CERTAIN ASSETS OF

DR. ALLAN BROWN
555 BC PROFESSIONAL LIMITED

Prepared For

DR. ALLAN BROWN
DENTAL SURGEON

30 Corporate Way
Vancouver, British Columbia
V5L 6J4

SAMPLE ONLY

(604) 555 - 4145

AS OF

May 31, 20XX

At market value, tangible assets installed
and working at present location,
and present condition.

ROI CORPORATION

JUNE 1, 20XX

ROI CORPORATION IS 100% PRIVATELY OWNED AND HAS OPERATED IN CANADA SINCE 1974.

ROI CORPORATION

June 1, 20XX

Dr. Allan Brown
30 Corporate Way
Vancouver, British Columbia V5L 6J4

RE: APPRAISAL OF DENTAL PRACTICE

Dear Dr. Brown:

In accordance with your request for an Appraisal of your practice and related assets known as the dental practice of Dr. Allan Brown, 30 Corporate Way, Vancouver, BC we submit the following report.

We have inspected the practice assets and facility and as a result of the investigation and analysis of the pertinent data, it is our opinion that the market value as of May 31, 20XX is:

	MARKET VALUE	REPLACEMENT VALUE
Leasehold Improvements & Fixtures	84,830	121,030
Clinical Equipment & Fixtures	187,280	364,820
Administrative Furniture & Fixtures	12,430	29,790
Computer Software	10,170	11,780
Computer Hardware	12,870	18,350
Instruments & Materials	27,200	36,450
Subtotal	**334,780**	**582,220**
Goodwill	356,160	Not Replaceable
APPRAISED MARKET VALUE	**$690,940**	

SIX HUNDRED NINETY THOUSAND NINE HUNDRED FORTY DOLLARS

This value is for the assets as stated herein and does not include accounts receivable, cash or other assets or the deduction of liabilities of the practice. This document is an opinion of the fair market value of the practice and is not intended for any other purpose in total or in part, or intended to be a narrative or presentation of the practice.

To the best of our knowledge, the data contained in this Appraisal report and related information is correct. Please do not hesitate to make further inquiries.

Respectfully submitted,

Roi Corporation

ROI CORPORATION

1155 Indian Road, Mississauga, Ontario L5H 1R8 Tel (905) 278-4145 Fax (905) 278-4705 www.roicorp.com roi@roicorp.com
Vancouver • Edmonton • Toronto • Ottawa • Montreal • Halifax

TABLE OF CONTENTS

PREFACE

PURPOSE

The purpose of this Appraisal is to determine from a qualified, independent Practice Appraiser and Business Valuator, the current fair market value of the practice goodwill and the market value and replacement costs of the tangible assets of this practice, supported by recent sales comparisons of similar practices based on factual, historical, legal records.

Fair market value is based upon the assumption that the Owner (Vendor) would offer the practice for sale over a reasonable period of time with full co-operation to transfer the practice goodwill and assets to the Purchaser for their benefit.

A complete Appraisal will identify and reveal the pertinent financial and other such information, as well as provide a proper legal description of the assets.

APPROACH

The opinion of the value of goodwill and the assets appraised of this practice has been determined by the Earnings Method, supported by the DIRECT MARKET SALES COMPARISON APPROACH.

Other approaches to determine investment value such as capitalization rates, multiple of earnings, discounted cash flow, replacement costs and rule of thumb are not as reliable for a Personal Service Professional Practice.

The Direct Market Sales Comparison approach, which is based on the factual current market place of supply and demand for certain geographic areas and types of practices, is the most accurate method. Sellers, buyers, financial institutions and the courts give the most weight and consideration to this approach.

LIMITING CONDITIONS

This Appraisal is made expressly subject to the conditions and assumptions as follows:

1. That the legal documents, leases, statements, letters, contracts, patient count, opinions and information supplied by all sources for the preparation of this report are assumed to be correct. We assume no responsibility for their accuracy.

2. That no responsibility is assumed for matters legal or clinical in nature or patient records, count or retention.

3. That possession of this report or a copy thereof does not carry with it the right of distribution, publication or reproduction in part or total in any manner without the consent of ROI Corporation.

4. That this Company, or its representatives, is not required to give testimony unless satisfactory arrangements are mutually agreed upon.

5. That the assignment of leased assets, premises or computer software programmes, which require written permission by the owners, will not be unreasonably withheld.

6. The opinion of goodwill has been determined by financial records and specific adjustment for this particular practice using the earnings method supported by market sales.

7. This report has been prepared for Dr. Brown in order to assist him in determining the fair market value of the practice. It is not to be relied upon by any other party for other matters.

8. This Appraisal has been determined as of May 31, 20XX. Consequently, we reserve the right to change our estimates as considered necessary, if any new information existing prior to or at the valuation date becomes known to us subsequent to the date of this report.

Certification and Qualifying Conditions

We hereby certify that a qualified Associate of ROI Corporation has inspected the practice records and assets adequately for the purpose of this Appraisal.

We are a qualified Appraiser of professional practices. We have knowledge of the fair market value of goodwill and assets based on historical documented sales.

We are familiar with this practice and will support our opinions and values as stated, E. & O. E.

ROI CORPORATION:

Roi Corporati

FUNCTION OF A PRACTICE APPRAISAL

Transfer of ownership involves buying, selling and trading of assets. Each transaction requires an opinion or estimate of value.

In order to represent assets, tangible or intangible, an asking price in terms of dollar value is necessary. To obtain credit, loans, leases or mortgages, a value is required.

The actual legal transfer of assets, the allocation of values for taxation for capital gains, and various provincial and federal taxes, all require that realistic values be determined prior to transfer or sale.

VALUE CONCEPTS

The term "value" is a difficult concept and one that is hard to define in specific terms. Down through the years, many schools of economic thought have dealt with and developed value concepts. Those schools of thought seem to have had two main themes:

Value Is Objective

The word "objective" means - being, or regarded as being, independent of the mind, real (Webster). Thus, in arguing for objectivity, it is said that it is the quantity of an object, which has value in exchange, and, therefore, the cost of its creation is the primary measure of value.

Value Is Subjective

The word "subjective" means - have or resulting from the feelings of the subject, or person thinking, rather than the attributes of the object thought of (Webster). An object has the power to give satisfaction and its value may be created and exist in the mind of the individual.

The subjective value concept is dominated in real property (land, building, etc.); however, a practice (business) is both subjective and objective. The costs to replace or recreate a practice and its viability are key factors.

From an economical sense, viability means to live, survive and develop under normal conditions. The value of income earned from the assets is a major consideration.

ELEMENTS OF VALUE

From the many schools of economic thought, three important elements of value have emerged. These are: utility, scarcity and demand. In order to have value, an object must satisfy all three.

Objects having a high degree of utility are air and water. Scarcity, on the other hand, must also be involved because air and water, although very useful, could hardly be considered as scarce. The object must be present in limited amounts in order to have value. Examples of this are: diamonds and gold. "Demand" as the name implies, means that people must want the object and have the ability to buy it.

Present worth or value means the price someone will pay today for the privilege of enjoying all the future benefits or rights of ownership. It is the rights, which are the main subject matter of valuation, not just the physical assets and the facility.

The most important value concept in practice appraising is the term "market value" which is the Appraiser's instrument in almost every valuation.

Many special factors enter into the value of both practice goodwill and assets, such as age, location, condition, replacement costs and technological changes.

The overriding factor is the market data approach using the actual price of recent "open market" sales of similar practices, whereupon ownership and title were legally transferred at arms length. This is commonly referred to as "direct sales comparison", and is the approach to which buyers give the most credence and to which the courts and Canada Revenue Agency give the most consideration.

INTERPRETATION OF VALUES

Book Value	Original costs on owner's books minus the total taken or allowed recorded depreciation. No direct relationship to present condition, value or use.
Trade In	Allowance as partial payment on a purchase.
Market	Prevailing price under certain circumstances: A. Separate individual sale. B. System in place or part of a group. C. Total value, greater than the sum of the individual components.
Fair Market Value	Highest price expressed in money obtainable in an open and unrestricted market between knowledgeable, prudent and fully informed parties dealing at arm's length.
Replacement	Return to former place, condition or performance; similar equivalent substitute.
Value In Use	Versus "Value In Exchange". The value of assets, which are being put to profitable use, is usually higher than assets not in use and offered in exchange for cash.
Liquidation Value	An orderly liquidation of tangible assets (excluding goodwill, i.e. not in use) as a complete facility with right-of-use (e.g. premise lease), the assets in-place, "as is" and offered for sale over a reasonable period of time.
Break-up Value	The sale of assets as individual components, "as is" (piecemeal), to be removed at purchaser's expenses once offered for sale over a short period of time.
Condition	Stipulated requirement of performance to be proper or fit.
As Is Where Is	Purchaser examines, acknowledges and accepts at that time.
In Good Working Order	Purchaser to receive in a certain condition at a certain time.

DESCRIPTION

DESCRIPTION OF THE PRACTICE

Dr. Allan Brown graduated from the University of British Columbia, Faculty of Dentistry, in 19XX.

Immediately following graduation, Dr. Brown associated with Dr. Evans in Kelowna for two years. In November, she moved to Vancouver and purchased this existing practice from a retiring dentist. As her practice was growing she required a larger facility therefore in April 20XX she relocated her practice to the current location.

The location, community and area of Vancouver, British Columbia were selected because Dr. Brown grew up in this area and enjoys the city.

This is a general dental practice.

The Associate, Dr. E. Lee, has been with the practice since July 2007. She is currently working three days per week upon returning from maternity leave.

The Associate, Dr. S. Sandhu, will start with the practice in September 2008. Dr. Sandhu will be working five days per week.

Three hygienists are employed with the practice. Hygiene assistance has been employed since 1982. Please refer to the appendices for a copy of the standard employment contract.

INCORPORATION

This dental practice appraisal was performed using the tangible assets basis. Shares of the Professional Corporation or Hygiene Corporation (Technical Services), if applicable, are not included in this report.

PHILOSOPHY OF PRACTICE

PREVENTIVE

The goal of the practice is to develop a strong partnership with each of the patients. To help them understand the importance of oral health. To work closely with all of the patients to achieve optimum dental health. As well, to address the cause of problems rather than just treat the symptoms. To stress the importance of regular home and professional care for a lifetime of trouble-free periodontal and masticatory health. Full head and neck examinations have been the standard of care since 1980 with over 80 undiagnosed life-threatening diseases being discovered.

PATIENT ORIENTED

To place the patient's needs first; providing full explanations of treatment procedures and pertinent office policies; keeping patients abreast of current options and techniques providing the patient the ability to choose the appropriate treatment plan.

PROGRESSIVE

To provide a broad spectrum of treatment. Further, to provide all treatment required for the patients' long-term benefit while keeping abreast of beneficial changes in treatment and technique through continuing education.

SERVICES AND TREATMENT RENDERED

Description	~% of Gross
01000 – 09999 Diagnostic	12.98
10000 – 19999 Preventive	12.52
20000 – 29999 Restorative	48.02
30000 – 39999 Endodontics	10.05
40000 – 49999 Periodontics	3.20
50000 – 59999 Prosthetics – Removable	4.99
60000 – 69999 Prosthetics – Fixed	0.96
70000 – 79999 Oral Surgery	6.10
80000 – 89999 Orthodontics	0.03
90000 – 99999 Other Services	1.15
TOTAL	**100%**

Sedation – I.V. or Oral	Yes
Analgesia – N_20	No
Composites only	No

Services Referred Out	#/Month
Emergencies	-
New Patients	-
Endodontic – Anterior	-
– Molar	0-1
Periodontic	1-2
Prosthodontics – Specialists	0-1
– Denture Therapists	-
Oral Surgery	0-1
Paediatric	1-2
Orthodontic	1-2
Implantology	-

APPOINTMENT PROCEDURES

Usual appointment and treatment procedures are booked in 10-minute units.

Appointment		**Treatment**
First	Adults	Length: 60 minutes with hygienist. 40 minutes with Dr. Brown.
	Children	Length: 30 minutes with hygienist (CDA). 20 minutes with Dr. Brown.

- Exchange of dental experiences with patient.
- Dental and medical history.
- Complete oral examination.
- Radiographs.
- Treatment of immediate need and rebook NPE.
- Complete head and neck, cancer/or significant medical disorder, exam.

Recall	Adults Children	Length: 60 minutes. Length: 30 minutes.

- The hygienist performs 90% of recalls and reports the periodontal status to the doctor. A periodontal program is then assigned for each patient.
- Recall examination by the doctor
- Complete head and neck exam.
- Prophylaxis and scaling, if necessary.
- Oral hygiene instructions at every visit.
- Radiographs, if necessary.
- Treatment of immediate need.
- Updated medical history.

Rubber Dam	Endo & Resins.
Infection Control	Universal Sterilization Technique. (masks, gloves, glasses, sterilized handpieces)

OFFICE HOURS

DAILY	**DR. BROWN**	**DR. LEE**	**DR. SANDHU** (Will start in September)	**HYGIENE**	**# OF HYG.**
Monday	8:30-3:00	-	8:30-5:00	8:00-4:30*	1
Tuesday	8:30-3:00	-	8:30-5:00	8:00-4:30	2
Wednesday	8:30-5:00	-	8:30-5:00	8:00-4:30	1
Thursday	8:30-3:00	8:00-5:00	8:30-5:00	8:00-4:30	2
Friday	-	8:00-5:00	8:30-5:00	8:00-4:30	2
Saturday	Once monthly	8:00-12:30	-	8:00-4:30*	1

* Every 2 weeks.

Lunch:	Usual lunch break on full days is 1 hour.			
Weekly	24-32 hours 4-5 days	20½ hours 2½ days	37½ hours 5 days	60 hours 8 days
Annually **As per Doctor	38 weeks** 984 hours 161 days	47 weeks** 936½ hours 117½ days	47 weeks** 1,762½ hours 235 days	46 weeks** 2,760 hours 368 days
Continuing Education	17-18 days	12-14 days	-	3 days
Holidays	All statutory			

Note: *The number of weeks worked annually is calculated by deducting statutory holidays (2 weeks) and continuing education from the total of 52 weeks per year.*

After Hours Service

- Telephone answering machine.

PERSONNEL

POSITION		NAME	PAID HOURS PER WEEK	SALARY PER HOUR
OWNER		Dr. Allan Brown 20+ years service at this practice	24-32	-
ASSOCIATES	#1	Dr. Lee <1 year service at this practice	20½	40%percentage of collections
	#2	Dr. Sandhu Will start at this practice in September	37½	40% percentage of collections
HYGIENISTS	#1	1 year service at this practice	35	$42.00
	#2	3 months service at this practice	20-24	$40.00
	#3	4 years service at this practice	8/month	$40.00
RECEPTIONISTS	#1	8 years service at this practice	35	$23.00
	#2	4 years service at this practice (Returning from maternity leave)	8	-
	#3	5 months service at this practice	35	$17.50
	#4	>1 month service at this practice (recall and charts audits only)	30	$16.00
	#5	2 years service at this practice (part-time evenings)	8	-
CHAIRSIDE ASSISTANTS	#1	2 years service at this practice	35	-
	#2	3 months service at this practice	35	$17.50
	#3	Part-time service at this practice	16	$17.50

Full time staff is paid for 50 weeks per year. Annual pay increase for staff is given on an individual basis and is based on performance.

BENEFITS

- Uniform allowance ($150.00 for full-time staff, paid in 2 installments $75.00 in January and in July).
- Employee's wage/salary is paid while attending courses/convention.
- Vacation/Holiday pay.
- Dental care (excluding lab fees and family members) covered on those amounts not covered by employees insurance company.

Note: **In the event of the sale of a practice, the owner and purchaser should seek legal and accounting advice with regard to employment standards well in advance of the closing of the sale.**

PATIENT INFORMATION

as of May 31, 20XX per Dr. Brown

*(ROI Corporation **does not audit or count** patient charts. In the event of a sale of the practice, a purchaser is responsible for performing his/her own audit of charts.)*

The approximate number of patients who are attending the practice on a recall programme is 2,000.

The practice performs an average of 7-12 recalls per day, 35-60 per week, 120 per month and 1,440 per year.

The files are culled for inactive patients on an ongoing basis.

Average Numbers	Dr. Brown	Associates	Hygienist (each)	Total
Patients seen /day	10	10	10	-
New patients /month	-	-	-	40
Emergencies /month (non-active patients)	-	-	-	25-30

Patient Profile

Age Breakdown	%	Patient Location	%	Referral Sources	%
0-12	20	Live nearby	80	Patients	60
13-25	20	Work nearby	12	Professional	10
26-50	40	Travel 5+ km	5	Advertising	30
51-65	20	Travel long distances	3		
66+					

Approximately 98% of the patients are able to speak English. The patients of this practice are predominantly Canadian with 8% being of Asian descent.

Semi or Inactive Patients

The estimated percentage of semi-active or inactive patients, who occasionally return for treatment is 5%.

FEES, INSURANCE, PAYMENTS

Fees

The practice follows the current British Columbia Dental Fee Guide with the exception of dentures which are higher.

Insurance

80% of the patients are covered by a type of dental insurance plan which includes approximately 20% of social service patients.

The practice does accept assignment.

The difference between the amount received from the insurance company and the fee is collected at the time of appointment.

The practice is using the EDI/CDA Service.

Treatment Planning

The policy of the practice is to submit the treatment plan to the insurance company. The receptionist follows up the treatment plan. An appointment is pre-booked just after the estimated approval time.

Financial

For large cases, the patient, for payments over a period of time, signs a financial agreement.

Payment & Credit Policy

- 23% cash or cheque.
- 30% credit/debit card.
- 1% postdated cheques.
- 46% from government and/or insurance company.

SYSTEMS & RECORDS

Appointments

All appointments are entered on the computer with a daily and weekly screen available.

The notation NP identifies new patients and each new patient must have a complete extended exam.

The practice is currently booked ahead 3 weeks for Dr. Brown, 2 weeks for Dr. Lee and 1½ months for Hygiene. The estimated backlog of work is 20-30% for Dr. Brown and 30% for Dr. Lee. The estimated backlog of work for Hygiene is due to a shortage of hygienists.

Recall System

The hygienist/chairside assistant books appointments on an operatory terminal.

The receptionist/assistant does a final check of appointments before each patient leaves the office.

The patient also fills out a postcard that is mailed to them three weeks before their appointment, as a reminder. On the postcard is a reminder sticker that can be placed on a calendar.

All recall patients are usually telephoned 2 days in advance to remind them of their appointment.

Accounts Receivable

Fee charges, payments and balances are recorded and controlled through use of a computer using the current version of Exan Power Practice software for Windows. The maintenance support is ongoing.

The computer is used to track the fees, payments, number of patients, hours attended and insurance patients per day on a summary basis for any time period. In addition, some monthly reports such as an A/R aging report and an expense analysis report is generated, ie. salaries to production, supplies to production.

Accounts Payable

The method of accounting and recording all disbursements is by use of a computerized one-write system by Simply Accounting.

SYSTEMS & RECORDS – Continued

Financial Statements

Statements are prepared from the office records by ABC & Company, Chartered Accountants, on a regular annual basis.

Clinical Records

Clinical records, charts, x-rays, and other related treatment records are stored and filed alphabetically in Safeguard envelopes. The file folders are colour coded.

The ledger information is kept off-site on a computer.

Policy & Procedures

- Staff meetings are held monthly and participation is good.
- A list of duties is available.
- An office manual has been prepared.

Marketing

- Advertising
    - Yellow pages
- Promotional
    - Thank you notes/card for new patient referrals
    - Birthday and Christmas cards
    - Free toothbrush
- Systems
    - The doctor and hygienist use a Spectraview intra–oral camera in all of the operatories.

FACILITY

DESCRIPTION OF FACILITIES

Area:	Retail/residential and high density.
Transportation:	Private vehicle and public transit.
Parking:	Ample and free in a parking lot.
Signage:	On the road, on the office and building fascia.
Building:	30 – 40 year old strip mall.
Improvements:	Some have been completed with plans for more.
Tenants:	Coffee House, Dollar Store, hairdresser, optician, bakery, medical office, Royal Bank, Liquor Store, video store, dry cleaner, supermarket and pharmacy.
Heating/Air:	Central air with controls.
Ceiling Height:	8 to 9 feet.

DESCRIPTION OF FACILITIES – Continued

The following items have been considered in the Location/Draw and Facility adjustments found in the calculation of goodwill.

Advantages

- Central location
- Ground floor
- Main street
- Established location
- High density residential
- Exclusive in plaza/building
- Ample parking
- High traffic mall/plaza
- Retail plaza setting
- High growth area
- Store-front office
- High visibility
- Wheelchair access
- Stable community
- Northern exposure

Disadvantages

- Lack of natural lighting

Office Layout

- Basic centre corridor
- Open concept
- Good in-office traffic flow
- Good privacy requirements
- Good patient comfort

Office Décor

- Modern décor
- Very bright/clean
- Warm neutral colours

X-ray Inspection Certificate

- Available upon request

VALUE OF PREMISE LEASE

See appendices for a copy of the lease renewal agreement, statement of monthly rent and the complete and existing lease.

Landlord: Vancouver Canada Inc.

Tenant: Dr. Allan Brown.

Current Term: 10 years, December 1st, 20XX to November 30th, 20XX (lease renewal agreement).

Renewal Option: It is assumed a renewal could be negotiated.

Assignment or Sublet: With the prior written consent of the Landlord, such consent shall **not** be unreasonably withheld. Tenant shall **first offer** to assign the premises to the Landlord with Landlord's option to terminate lease and Tenant's option to withdraw the request (lease, Article 12.00).

Demolition: Landlord may terminate this lease upon giving the Tenant 12 months' notice if it is Landlord's intention to demolish or substantially renovate the building (lease, 15.17)

Relocation: Landlord reserves the right to change the location of the premises within the project. If the Tenant does not accept relocation, Tenant may, within 30 days, terminate this lease (lease, Article 6.00).

Signage: As existing.

Total Area: Approximately 1,550 sq. ft. (statement of monthly rent).

Rental Rates:

Annually*	Per Sq. Ft.
$48,837	$31.51

*As per January 31, 20XX Financial Statement.

Extra and Escalation Costs: Proportionate share of operating costs and taxes (lease, Articles 7.00 & 8.00).

VALUE OF PREMISE LEASE – Continued

Summary

The value of a premise lease is based upon the legal right-of-use of the existing leasehold improvements by the assignment of the existing premise lease, or the ability of the Vendor to provide the Purchaser with a lease (if building owned by the Vendor) or a new premise lease (with a renewal option) in place for the tenant.

Providing that the assignment is obtained, the major factors affecting the value of the existing lease are the rental rate, the terms of the lease and the stability of the location. It is expected and assumed that the existing lease could be renewed or extended to a minimum of ten (10) years of use. These factors are considered in the goodwill value of the practice.

DEMOGRAPHICS

Location: In central Vancouver near two major intersections.

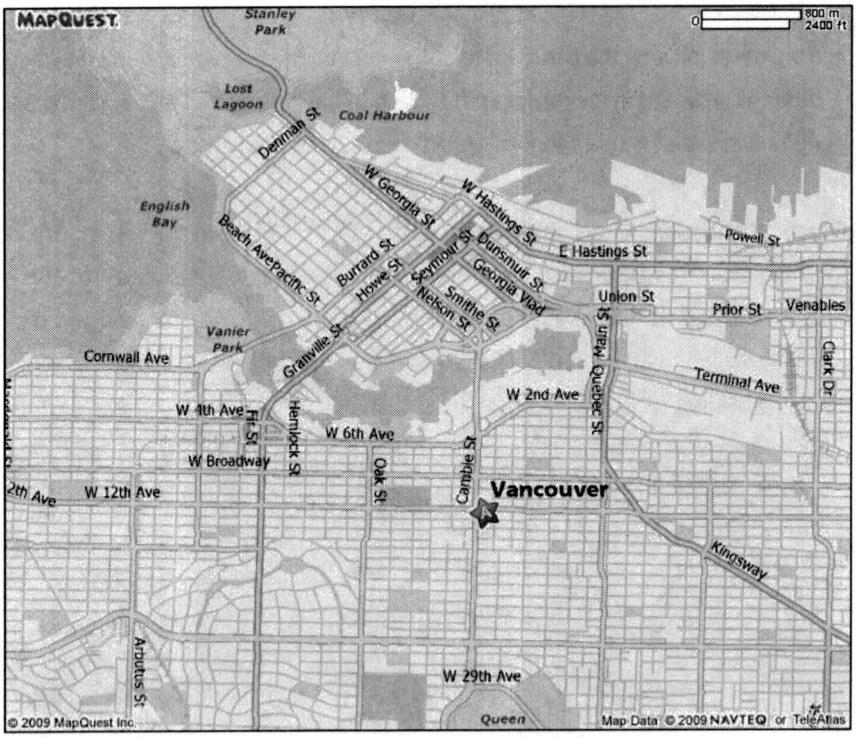

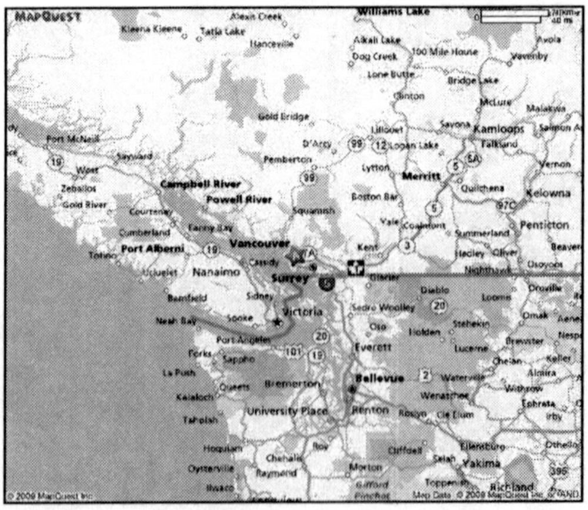

DEMOGRAPHICS – Continued

Trading Area: There is a freeway between Greater Vancouver and the United States, linking it to Washington state at the Canada-U.S. border. There is about a 3-hour drive between Seattle and Vancouver. The Trans-Canada Highway runs through the province connecting the city westward to Victoria by ferry routes and eastward to the rest of Canada.

Community Profile: Vancouver is located in the southwest corner of Canada in the province of British Columbia. It is a city with quite a cosmopolitan mix of many multicultural groups. The city is surrounded by water on three sides and its climate is one of the mildest in Canada. Vancouver is the third largest city in Canada and it offers a wide range of services and opportunities. It has a beautiful scenic location and is a major tourist destination.

Schools: The Vancouver School Board provides education programmes for 60,000 elementary, secondary and adult students in 109 schools and six adult education centres. There are opportunities for post-secondary education within the province at many renowned colleges and universities.

Industry, Commerce: As one of the nation's largest industrial centres, Vancouver is a major port. It is the main western terminus of Canada's transcontinental highway and rail routes. Around 1,800 acres of industrial land provide an important range of support services, manufacturing and wholesale premises for businesses throughout the city and region. Downtown Vancouver continues to be the prime location for business and major institutions.

Potential Growth of Community: Vancouver has expanded as a centre for software development and biotechnology, while film studios and the streets provide a backdrop for the developing film industry. The commercial services sector continues to grow to encompass services to businesses, restaurants, accommodation, travel agents and many others.

Fluoridated Water: No.

DEMOGRAPHICS – Continued

Statistics taken from the FP Markets – Canadian Demographics 200X	Vancouver	British Columbia	Canada
POPULATION			
July 1, 200X estimate	620,270	4,399,200	33,327,758
Change 200X – 200X	2.69%	2.45%	1.92%
Average Growth Rate per Year	1.33%	1.22%	0.95%
LABOUR FORCE			
White collar occupations	86%	77%	74%
Blue collar occupations	14%	23%	26%
AVERAGE HOUSEHOLD INCOME	$75,854	$72,642	$73,392
EDUCATION (Post Secondary)			
Population over 20 years	72%	60%	54%
HOUSING – No. of Dwellings	274,742	1,777,026	13,247,902
Owned	48%	70%	68%
Rented	52%	30%	32%
Average No. Per Household	2.2	2.4	2.5
HOME LANGUAGE	%	%	%
English	54.13	78.00	62.03
French	0.26	0.16	19.15
Arabic	0.05	0	0.19
Chinese	14.19	4.20	1.57
German	0.06	0.11	0.15
Hindi	0.21	0.15	0.05
Italian	0.24	0.09	0.38
Japanese	0.43	0.15	0.04
Korean	0.52	0.43	0.15
Persian (Farsi)	0.28	0.24	0.14
Polish	0.10	0.08	0.19
Portuguese	0.15	0.06	0.21
Punjabi	1.13	1.64	0.48
Russian	0.18	0.10	0.13
Serbian	0.14	0.05	0.05
Spanish	0.39	0.17	0.24
Tagalog (Pilipino)	0.51	0.16	0.13
Tamil	0.09	0	0.15
Vietnamese	1.16	0.31	0.21
Multiple & Other	25.78	13.9	14.36

DEMOGRAPHICS – Continued

Dental/Population Ratios

While population ratios do not account for differences in population demands or needs or differences in productivity, there is a lack of criteria to establish an adequate alternative. In our opinion, this measure is a suitable guide for describing the average level of need for dental services.

Additionally, the current listings of dentists are often outdated and do not reflect those who are licensed, yet not active in full-time practice. In order to more accurately reflect the equivalent full-time (E.F.T.) dental manpower ratios, the number of DDS, as per note (1), could be reduced by 5 – 15% for most cities, towns and communities.

	Vancouver	British Columbia
No. of General Dentists (1)	522	2,412
Population (2)	620,270	4,399,200
Ratio per General Dentist	1: 1,188	1: 1,824

Summary

Vancouver sees an annual average growth in population that is higher than that for British Columbia. The labour force is strong. It also shows a greater percentage of white-collar occupations than the province although the average household income is slightly lower. The number of those who choose post-secondary education is more than the rest of Canada. Figures show the proportion of residents who own their dwelling is lower than those renting. Many report to be English speaking. There is a high representation of the populace who speak Chinese and a multiple of other home languages.

Demographics Reference Sources

1) The Canadian Dental Directory 200X
2) FP Markets – Canadian Demographics 200X
3) The Internet

ASSETS

EQUIPMENT & OFFICE MACHINES

The assets listed on the following pages have been appraised under the following assumptions:

1) Unless readily identifiable or otherwise advised, the items have received "average" servicing.
2) All items are in "normal working condition" according to their age (as supplied by the owner) as of date of appraisal.
3) All x-ray units and protection meet standard safety requirements for the present location and use.
4) Assets are appraised as installed and in current use.
5) Leasehold Improvements and Fixtures do not include millwork and cabinetry; these are priced separately in each operatory/ room.

SUMMARY

		VALUE	
		MARKET	**REPLACEMENT**
Leasehold Improvements & Fixtures (Tenant's Right of Use)		84,830	121,030
Clinical Equipment & Fixtures		187,280	364,820
Administrative Furniture & Fixtures		12,430	29,790
Computer System:	Software	10,170	11,780
	Hardware	12,870	18,350
Instruments & Materials (ROI Formula)		27,200	36,450
Excluded Assets		–	–
Liabilities		–	–
	TOTAL	**334,780**	**582,220**

Note: For evaluating U.S.A. and foreign manufactured goods, the current Canadian dollar exchange rates and duties were taken into consideration.

LEASEHOLD IMPROVEMENTS AND FIXTURES - ESTIMATE - (Units in place method)

The leasehold improvements included are the normal and standard improvements for dental offices. The value of the building is separate and would not include these specific leaseholds.

The basic building includes retaining and demising walls, stairs, windows, ceilings, bare floors, basic heating and air conditioning, washroom facilities, all of which are not considered as part of leasehold improvements and fixtures. Removable cabinetry and desks are listed as equipment and also not included in the leaseholds.

Retail shopping plazas differ from general office or medical buildings and do not supply the tenant with the traditional finished office area. The tenants usually must supply all the improvements at their own expense, (i.e. demising walls, ceiling, floors, store front entrances, all plumbing, air conditioning and heating equipment).

The position a landlord should take is that of the owner and a prudent investor. The tenant and their special leasehold improvements for the business or practice needs should be an investment cost of that special tenant.

The leasehold improvements are extensive and for the benefit of the tenant only. Their value is in direct relationship to the legal right of use.

The original specifications and plans were prepared by Ash Temple in 1987.

General and Architectural		**Replacement Costs**
155	- linear feet of interior (demising walls excluded) standard floor to ceiling stud partitions with 1/2" gyproc each side or equivalent	
E	- necessary x-ray radiation protection within the area to meet provincial standards **as required at time of installation**	
4	- interior standard doors including bi-fold with frames and required hardware (demising doors excluded)	
4	- supports for ceiling-mounted dental lights	
6	- linear feet of wall supports for wall-mounted cabinets and x-ray heads	
		$36,620
Plumbing and Mechanical		
1	- washroom, 2 piece, staff and patients	
6	- unit/control rough-ins with cold water, drain, air line, vacuum suction line	
10	- rough-ins for stainless steel sinks, hot and cold water, drains, traps and vents including x-ray tank (washroom sinks excluded)	
6	- hook-ups for air compressor	
6	- hook-ups for vacuum/suction pump	
		$29,980

LEASEHOLD IMPROVEMENTS AND FIXTURES - ESTIMATE - Continued
(Units in place method)

Electrical	**Replacement Costs**
55 - duplex wall electrical outlets	
17 - wall switches	
45 - fluorescent fixtures 2's & 4's	
12 - incandescent fixtures	
1 - wall clock outlet	
4 - wiring sets for ceiling-mounted dental lights	
6 - wiring sets for x-ray machine with remote timers each separate control, separate circuits per x-ray head	
6 - wiring for central air compressor	
6 - wiring for central vacuum/suction pump	
1 - main breaker panel for suite with extra power service and power feeder line	
5 - music speakers with volume controls	
8 - telephone outlets	
E - computer outlets	
6 - rough-ins for power to dental units	
E - miscellaneous wiring for fixtures	
9 - signals, wiring and hook-up (buzzer, chimes)	
1 - exhaust fan	
2 - illuminated signs including outlet and wiring	
2 - emergency lights	
E - cable outlets	
	$39,310

LEASEHOLD IMPROVEMENTS AND FIXTURES - ESTIMATE - Continued
(Units in place method)

Interior Finishes and Materials		**Replacement Costs**
5%	painting both sides interior walls, doors and cupboards including demising wall	
92%	vinyl wall coverings	
45%	ceramic tile flooring	
50%	vinyl flooring	
5%	hardwood flooring	
E	miscellaneous decor, related fixtures, children's toys, books, plants, planters, wall hangings, pictures, kitchen items, work tools, soap and paper dispensers, film dispensers, towel racks and holders, waste baskets, murals, fire extinguishers and bulletin boards	
E	venetian blinds	
		$15,120

NB "E" represents "Existing".

Total estimated replacement costs for similar utility, not including any leasehold inducements (if applicable) (not exact reproduction costs) ($78.08 per sq. ft.)............. **$121,030**

Less accrued depreciation (i.e. diminished utility), physical deterioration (curable and incurable), functional obsolescence and deficiencies **$36,200**

Market value based on legal right-of-use by tenants of existing leasehold improvements by the existing premise lease and assuming renewal options exercised and extended to a minimum of ten (10) years of use.

Present market value, based upon the assignment of Premise Lease, is **$84,830**

www.roicorp.com 27

EQUIPMENT & FIXTURES

OPERATORY # 1

Approximate year equipped - 1989
Ownership interest - 100%

QTY	DESCRIPTION	VALUE MARKET	VALUE REPLACEMENT
1	A-dec chair, motor, lounge, model Priority, fabric & vinyl, tan	1,150	7,150
1	Custom stool, doctor's, vinyl, tan	120	680
1	A-dec stool, assistant's, model 1620, serial # E865496, rose	260	940
1	Belmont light, operating, ceiling mtd., model HLT, serial # 7358, white, 1997	1,720	2,750
1	A-dec delivery unit, wall mtd., w/3 handpiece controls, fibre optics & 1 syringe, model 3042, serial # E718043, grey	1,530	3,630
1	Custom vacuum kit, wall mtd., w/1 HVE, 1 SE & 1 syringe, w/articulating tray, stnls.	150	1,090
1	Vivadent amalgamator, model Silamat C, serial # 1358, tan	120	490
2	Caulk curing lights, model The Max 100, serial #'s 53111 & 60037, beige	360	1,420
1	Custom cabinet, lower, w/1 sink unit & 3 doors, 122" x 18" x 34", lam. ext. & int., rose	370	1,240
1	Custom cabinet, upper, w/4 doors, 30" x 11" x 52", lam. ext. & int., rose, (1997)	500	840
1	Custom cabinet, lower & upper, including 1 sink unit, 15 drawers & 3 doors, w/2-sided sliding glass doors, 84" x 28" x 70", rose, (between Ops. # 1 & # 2) lam. ext. & int.	2,050	6,860
1	Siemens x-ray, tube, head & arm, w/control in hall, model 3724861, serial # 17344, brown, (1987)	1,910	6,370
1	Cling Shield x-ray apron, vinyl, blue	80	130
1	Custom glove container, new	20	20
	TOTAL	**10,340**	**33,610**

www.roicorp.com 28

EQUIPMENT & FIXTURES

OPERATORY # 2

Approximate year equipped - 1989
Ownership interest - 100%

QTY	DESCRIPTION	VALUE MARKET	VALUE REPLACEMENT
1	Takara chair, motor, lounge, model AXIS 90, serial # 83020129, rust	1,580	6,350
1	Custom stool, doctor's, vinyl, tan	120	680
1	A-dec stool, assistant's, model 1620, serial # B852437, rose	260	940
1	Belmont light, operating, ceiling mtd., model HLC, serial # 5223, rose, 1997	1,720	2,750
1	A-dec delivery unit, cabinet mtd., w/3 handpiece controls, fibre optics & 1 syringe, model 172, serial # 43109549	1,530	3,630
1	A-dec vacuum kit, mtd. on mobile cart, w/1 HVE, 1 SE & 1 syringe, w/2 drawers, model TRAY ZAR, 32" X 18" X 29", lam. ext. & int.	140	860
1	Ambu bag, model Mark III, serial # 209440	110	220
2	Life Support mask resuscitators, model 239, serial # 14107	240	480
1	Custom IV drug kit	260	450
2	Custom stethoscopes	20	180
1	JVC television, 21", ceiling mtd., w/brackets, white	340	570
1	Degussa amalgamator, model Mixomat, serial # 2548	190	680
1	Kerr/Demetron curing light, cordless, w/rechargeable battery, model 952251, serial # 71017162, white, new	1,760	1,850
1	Custom cabinet, lower, including 1 sink unit, w/8 doors, 122" x 18" x 34", lam. ext. & int., rose	620	2,480
1	Custom cabinet, upper, corner, w/2 doors, 19" x 19" x 52", lam. ext. & int., rose, 1997	550	840
2	Almedic blood pressure cuffs	130	220
1	Siemens x-ray tube, head & arm, w/control in hall, model 5938, serial # 733D3195 09130, white, 1990	3,210	5,250
1	Flow x-ray viewer, desk, plastic, white	70	120
1	Hudson emergency life saver kit, model 1173	190	250

.../Continued

EQUIPMENT & FIXTURES

OPERATORY # 2

Approximate year equipped - 1989
Ownership interest - 100%

QTY	DESCRIPTION	VALUE MARKET	VALUE REPLACEMENT
1	A-dec cart, assistant's, w/control box, new	1,370	1,500
1	Gendex x-ray unit, new	4,010	4,500
1	Custom glove container, new	20	20
	TOTAL	**18,440**	**34,820**

EQUIPMENT & FIXTURES

OPERATORY # 3- HYGIENE

Approximate year equipped - 1989
Ownership interest - 100%

QTY	DESCRIPTION	VALUE MARKET	VALUE REPLACEMENT
1	Belmont chair, motor, lounge, model BEL 7, serial # 03005262, beige & rose	1,560	6,250
1	Custom stool, doctor's, vinyl, tan	120	680
1	A-dec light, operating, ceiling mtd., model 6300, serial # J075490, 1997	2,050	3,150
1	A-dec delivery unit, wall mtd., w/3 handpiece controls & 1 syringe, model 3010, serial # L521014	1,430	4,790
1	Custom vacuum kit, wall mtd., w/1 HVE & 1 SE	130	810
1	Custom chair, child's, wood	10	60
1	JVC television, 21", ceiling mtd., w/brackets, white	340	570
1	Dentsply dual select unit, Cavitron, model DISP 118, serial # 118-03504, white	560	2,790
1	Dentsply scaler, Cavitron, model SPS, serial # 11935318, white	2,870	3,550
1	Custom cabinet, lower, w/6 doors, w/mobile drawer, 120" x 19" x 34", lam. ext. & int., rose	870	3,460
1	Custom cabinet, upper, w/4 doors, 54" x 12" x 20", lam. ext. & int., rose	220	880
1	Custom cabinet, upper, w/open shelves, 24" x 12" x 16", lam. ext. & int., white	60	240
1	Trophy x-ray, tube, head & arm, w/control on extendable cord, model AD332, serial # E402125, white, 1994	2,090	4,370
1	Clive Craig x-ray viewer, desk, plastic, beige	60	120
	TOTAL	**12,370**	**31,720**

EQUIPMENT & FIXTURES

OPERATORY # 4

Approximate year equipped - 1989
Ownership interest - 100%

QTY	DESCRIPTION	VALUE MARKET	VALUE REPLACEMENT
1	Belmont chair, motor, lounge, model BEL 7, serial # 03005162, beige & rose	1,560	6,250
1	Custom stool, doctor's, vinyl, tan	120	680
1	Belmont light, operating, ceiling mtd., model HLT, serial # 7357, white, 1999	2,150	2,750
1	A-dec delivery unit, wall mtd., w/2 handpiece controls & 1 syringe, model 3010, serial # L64112	1,430	4,790
1	Custom vacuum kit, wall mtd., w/1 HVE & 1 SE	130	810
2	Custom desktop lighted magnifying glasses	250	410
1	Custom chair, fabric & wood, tan	40	120
2	Knowell Therapeutic Tech chlorzoin therapy incubators, model APO1, serial #'s 0401 & 1731, beige, 1993	60	250
1	Dentsply scaler, Cavitron, model 3000, serial # 110-24220, ivory	1,890	2,790
1	Custom cabinet, lower, including 1 sink unit & 4 doors, 121" x 18" x 34", lam. ext. & int., rose	480	1,660
1	Custom cabinet, upper, w/4 doors, 30" x 11" x 52", lam. ext. & int., rose, 1997	500	840
1	Custom cabinet, lower & upper, including 1 sink unit, 15 drawers & 3 doors, w/2-sided sliding glass doors, 84" x 28" x 70", lam. ext. & int., rose, (between Ops. # 3 & # 4)	2,050	6,860
1	General Electric x-ray, tube, head & arm, w/control in hall, model 700, serial # 286780DN2, beige, 1980	370	4,910
	TOTAL	**11,030**	**33,120**

www.roicorp.com 32

EQUIPMENT & FIXTURES

OPERATORY # 5

Approximate year equipped - 1997
Ownership interest - 100%

QTY	DESCRIPTION	VALUE MARKET	VALUE REPLACEMENT
1	Healthco chair, motor, lounge, serial # 22039194, rose	3,730	7,310
1	Custom stool, doctor's, vinyl, rose	340	620
1	Custom stool, assistant's, vinyl, rose	360	680
1	Belmont light, operating, cabinet mtd., serial # 7251	1,710	2,630
1	Dentech delivery unit, cabinet mtd., w/3 handpiece controls, fibre optics, 1 syringe & articulating tray arm, model Ultima 2, serial # 58139, white	2,980	4,310
1	Custom vacuum kit, cabinet mtd., w/1 HVE, 1 SE & 1 syringe, white	670	1,020
1	Custom chair, fabric & wood, tan	40	120
1	Kerr/Demetron curing light, cordless, w/rechargeable battery, model 952251, white, (new)	1,760	1,850
1	Triangle cabinet, lower, including 1 sink unit, 2 sliding glass doors, 69" x 20" x 72", lam. ext. & int., white	4,340	6,380
1	Triangle cabinet, lower, w/8 doors, including 6 glass doors, 39" x 20" x 72", lam. ext. & int., white	4,940	7,260
1	Triangle cabinet, lower, including 1 sink unit, 4 doors & 6 drawers, 98" x 20" x 72", lam. ext. & int., white, (between Ops. # 5 & # 6)	5,760	8,480
1	JVC television, 21", ceiling mtd., w/brackets	340	570
1	Trophy x-ray, tube, head & arm, w/control in operatory on ext. cord., model FU47, serial # S5076, white, 1994	2,090	4,370
1	Star x-ray viewer, plastic, beige	60	120
1	Spectra Vu intra-oral camera system, w/multiple docking stations & accessories, model 2100, serial # 9000907	4,710	16,360
	TOTAL	**33,830**	**62,080**

www.roicorp.com 33

EQUIPMENT & FIXTURES

OPERATORY # 6

Approximate year equipped - 1997
Ownership interest - 100%

QTY	DESCRIPTION	VALUE MARKET	VALUE REPLACEMENT
1	Healthco chair, motor, lounge, serial # 22041094, rose	3,730	7,310
1	Custom stool, doctor's, vinyl, rose	340	620
1	Custom stool, assistant's, vinyl, rose	360	680
1	Belmont light, operating, cabinet mtd., serial # 13166, white	1,710	2,630
1	Dentech delivery unit, cabinet mtd., w/3 handpiece controls, 1 syringe & articulating tray arm, model Ultima 2, serial # 58137, white	2,580	4,310
1	Custom vacuum kit, cabinet mtd., w/1 HVE, 1 SE & 1 syringe, white	670	1,020
1	Custom chair, fabric & wood, tan	40	120
1	Custom chair, wood, child's	10	60
1	Triangle cabinet, lower, w/8 doors, including 6 glass doors	4,940	7,260
1	Triangle cabinet, including 1 sink unit, w/4 doors including 2 glass doors & 2 drawers, 57" x 20" x 72", lam. ext. & int., white	4,340	6,380
1	Clive Craig x-ray apron, vinyl, grey	80	110
1	ADO x-ray apron, w/collar, vinyl, blue & white	90	130
1	Kerr/Demetron curing light, cordless, w/rechargeable battery, model 952251, white, (new)	1,760	1,850
	TOTAL	**20,650**	**32,480**

EQUIPMENT & FIXTURES

HANDPIECES/ATTACHMENTS

Ownership interest - 100%

QTY	DESCRIPTION	VALUE MARKET	VALUE REPLACEMENT
1	NSK straight, model EX6, serial # 1633350	60	220
1	NSK contra angle, model Phatelus II, serial # 43129	70	340
1	NSK handpiece motor, model TN203, serial # 2999	220	760
5	W & H high speeds, fibre optic, 1 - model TA96LW, 4 - model TA98LW, serial #s 03260, 05027, 05028, 05037, E1239	5,370	5,650
1	NSK high speed, fibre optic, model Phatelus II, serial # 43127	420	730
1	Schein high speed, model Master, serial # Y5469	160	310
2	KaVo straights, models 10A, 10B	610	1,080
1	NSK straight, Pallas, model SH-E	120	260
1	Midwest high speed, fibre optic, model Tradition	660	1,270
7	Midwest high speeds, model Quiet Air, serial #s 40984, 148663, 160732, 509326, 517559, 529738, 529746	2,550	4,910
1	NSK high speed, model Pana Air, serial # AD32141	100	210
1	NSK high speed, surgical, 2004	1,040	1,100
2	NSK high speeds, surgical, new	1,730	2,080
	TOTAL	**13,110**	**18,920**

EQUIPMENT & FIXTURES

STERILIZATION

Approximate year equipped - 1997
Ownership interest - 100%

QTY	DESCRIPTION	VALUE MARKET	VALUE REPLACEMENT
1	Triangle cabinet, lower, including 1 sink unit, 7 drawers & 1 door, w/built-in baths, 67" x 24" x 36", serial # 1187 9000X2, white	13,210	19,420
1	Triangle cabinet, upper, w/4 doors, 67" x 12" x 25", white		
1	Triangle Cabinet, lower, w/3 drawers & 4 doors, 27" x 24" x 82", white		
1	SciCan sterilizer, cassette, Autoclave, model Statim L, white	4,060	6,250
1	L & R ultrasonic cleaner, model Quantrex 310H, stnls.	1,370	2,110
1	Analytic Technology vitality scanner, model 2006, serial # 2612193, white	490	830
1	W & H handpiece cleaner, Assistina, model 301 Plus, white	1,520	2,340
1	Tuttnauer sterilizer, steam, w/full cassette, new	910	1,000
1	BioSonic cleaner, ultrasonic, new	1,620	1,800
	TOTAL	**23,180**	**33,750**

EQUIPMENT & FIXTURES

MAKE READY

Approximate year equipped - 1989
Ownership interest - 100%

QTY	DESCRIPTION	VALUE MARKET	VALUE REPLACEMENT
1	Custom cabinet, lower, L-shape, w/1 sink unit & 6 doors, 126" x 24" x 36", lam. ext. & int., rose	1,060	4,240
1	Custom cabinet, upper, w/7 doors, 126" x 14" x 34", lam. ext. & int., rose	330	1,640
1	Custom cabinet, upper, lam. ext. & int., 1997	500	840
1	Custom cabinet, lower, w/2 sink units, 4 doors & 2 drawers, 63" x 18" x 36", lam. ext. & int.	840	3,220
1	Custom cabinet, upper, w/sliding glass doors & adj. shelves, 63" x 12" x 32", lam. ext. & int.		
1	Buffalo sterilizer, glass bead, model 62, serial # 42307	110	360
1	L & R ultrasonic cleaner, serial # 62090	400	1,330
1	Analytic Technology vitality scanner, model 2006, serial # 2621635, ivory	490	830
1	Buffalo Dental vibrator	20	160
1	Custom vacuum former, black, new	510	540
1	Hanau articulators, serial # 24669	230	450
1	Instrument & Technology surveyor, serial #s 2108980, 2168540	280	540
1	Yen Sun wet towel dispenser, hot/cold, 20" x 9" x 18", serial # YS701TM, white	100	180
1	Dentsply amalgamator, model Varimix III VMD	150	490
1	Dentsply Cavitron, model GEN 103, serial # 10311558, gold	830	2,780
1	Harvey instrument sharpener, serial # 3350	190	630
1	Almore bleaching instrument, model Monarch II	60	280
1	Danville micro etcher, sandblaster, model er	150	280
1	Custom refrigerator, w/freezer section, white, (bar type)	60	190
1	DentalEz dental suction, w/2 pumps, model MC201, serial # V8931, blue	1,290	4,330

...../Continued

EQUIPMENT & FIXTURES

MAKE READY

Approximate year equipped - 1989
Ownership interest - 100%

QTY	DESCRIPTION	VALUE MARKET	VALUE REPLACEMENT
1	MDT McKesson compressor, w/2 new heads, model 3408-1000-3D, serial # GI1996, blue	2,790	4,150
1	Zipp TT plaster trap, (under sink)	110	210
2	Custom compressor heads, new	1,750	2,000
	TOTAL	**12,250**	**29,670**

X-RAY AREA

Approximate year equipped - 1997
Ownership interest - 100%

QTY	DESCRIPTION	MARKET	REPLACEMENT
1	Planmeca panoramic x-ray, w/control, w/autoprint, model Proline PM2002CC, serial # 949258	17,940	29,900
	TOTAL	**17,940**	**29,900**

EQUIPMENT & FIXTURES

DARK ROOM

Ownership interest - 100%

QTY	DESCRIPTION	VALUE MARKET	VALUE REPLACEMENT
1	Custom shelf, L-shape, lower, 62" x 18" x 4", lam. ext. & int., white	40	160
1	Apollo compressor, teal	2,760	4,240
1	Kodak x-ray safelight, model GBX2, grey	30	90
1	Dent-X x-ray processor, model 810 Basic, serial # 24021 2660, beige	660	4,750
1	Inst-A mini tank, Microcopy	60	190
1	Hoover model trimmer, w/2 chucks & spray pans	150	520
1	Harvey Autoclave	470	2,150
1	Solmetex amalgam separator, new	1,760	2,000
1	Dentsply dental suction, new	2,700	3,000
	TOTAL	**8,630**	**17,100**

EQUIPMENT & FIXTURES

HALL

Approximate year equipped - 1997
Ownership interest - 100%

QTY	DESCRIPTION	VALUE MARKET	VALUE REPLACEMENT
1	Custom treasure chest, 30" x 20" x 21", wood & steel, black & brown	110	260
1	Custom mirror, oval-shape, 34" x 24", wood	70	120
1	Cling Shield x-ray apron, vinyl, beige	80	130
1	Custom desk, 48" x 30" x 30", lam. ext. & int., rose	150	240
1	Custom cabinet, lower, w/2 doors, 30" x 15" x 54", lam. ext. & int., white	230	360
1	Custom cabinet, upper, w/11 doors, 172" x 15" x 48", lam. ext. & int., white	590	920
2	Mardan cabinets, chart, w/6 drawers (3 rows 12 x 6 charts), 42" x 22" x 50", lam. ext. & int., wood	2,030	2,980
1	Vivadent amalgamator, model Silamat C, serial # 1355, tan	300	480
1	Omega telephone, model IV	190	310
1	Kerr/Demetron curing light, cordless, w/rechargeable battery, white, (new)	1,760	1,850
	TOTAL	**5,510**	**7,650**

www.roicorp.com 40

FURNITURE & FIXTURES

RECEPTION AREA

Approximate year equipped - 1989
Ownership interest - 100%

QTY	DESCRIPTION	VALUE MARKET	VALUE REPLACEMENT
4	Custom chairs	160	480
3	Custom chairs, w/arms, fabric, flower patterned	120	360
2	Custom tables, end, 24" x 18" x 20", wood	40	140
1	Custom bookcase, w/3 levels, 36" x 10" x 36", wood, (1997)	80	220
1	Custom picnic table, children's, 26" x 29" x 18", plastic, red & blue	40	70
1	Custom aquarium, 72" x 24" x 18", w/stand, 74" x 26" x 30", black	1,500	2,500
1	Custom cabinet, lower, w/2 doors, 31" x 19" x 30", lam. ext. & int., rose	70	280
2	Custom chairs, new	310	400
	TOTAL	**2,320**	**4,450**

FURNITURE & FIXTURES

BUSINESS OFFICE

Approximate year equipped - 1989
Ownership interest - 100%

QTY	DESCRIPTION	VALUE MARKET	VALUE REPLACEMENT
1	Custom desk, reception, C-shape, w/2 sections, 8 pigeon-holes, 1 pedestal & 3 drawers, 150" x 26" x 47", lam. ext. & int., rose	1,220	4,880
1	Custom chair, mobile, w/arms, fabric, green	40	170
1	Custom chair, mobile, w/o arms, fabric, grey	40	140
1	Custom cabinet, chart, w/6 drawers, w/4 filing drawers, legal size, 60" x 22" x 52", lam. ext. & int., rose	420	1,680
1	Custom cabinet, filing, w/4 drawers, legal size, lateral, 15" x 22" x 52", lam. ext. & int., rose		
1	Custom cabinet, mobile, w/2 drawers, 21" x 21" x 18", lam. ext. & int., rose	50	180
2	Plantronics handsets/headsets, (new)	900	920
1	Royal paper folder, auto., model APF300	110	360
1	Custom telephone system, w/4 handsets & 2 headsets	1,150	2,750
	TOTAL	**3,930**	**11,080**

www.roicorp.com 42

FURNITURE & FIXTURES

PRIVATE OFFICE

Approximate year equipped - 1989
Ownership interest - 100%

QTY	DESCRIPTION	VALUE MARKET	VALUE REPLACEMENT
1	Custom desk, C-shape, w/3 drawers, 74" x 24" x 29", lam. ext. & int., rose, w/Star x-ray viewer, built-in	130	540
1	Custom chair, mobile, w/arms, Executive, black	120	260
1	Custom cabinet, filing, w/4 drawers, letter size, 21" x 25" x 55", wood	90	280
1	Custom cabinet, upper, 72" x 15" x 52", lam. ext. & int., rose	410	1,640
1	Canon telephone/facsimile machine, model L75, serial # Y2W 02154, (new)	370	390
	TOTAL	**1,120**	**3,110**

MANAGER'S OFFICE

Approximate year equipped - 1989
Ownership interest - 100%

QTY	DESCRIPTION	MARKET	REPLACEMENT
1	Custom desk, w/3 drawers, 90" x 24" x 6", lam. ext. & int., rose	150	580
1	Custom chair, mobile, w/o arms, fabric, green	60	180
1	Custom cabinet, filing, w/2 drawers, letter size, 14" x 18" x 27", steel, green	40	160
1	AT & T telephone answering machine, model 74S1, white	30	90
1	Canon photocopier, w/1 tray, model NP6412, serial # NUN15384, w/stand, 17" x 19" x 29", w/1 door, beige, (new)	120	270
1	Hitachi video printer, colour, model VV190, serial # 71102936, wł	240	1,510
1	Custom cabinet, upper, w/10 doors, 90" x 15" x 52", lam. ext. & int., rose	740	2,480
1	Polaroid camera, model Spectra System	30	110
2	Custom chairs	80	240
1	Minolta photocopier, sorting, new	1,710	2,000
	TOTAL	**3,200**	**7,620**

FURNITURE & FIXTURES

STAFF ROOM/KITCHEN

Approximate year equipped - 1997
Ownership interest - 100%

QTY	DESCRIPTION	VALUE MARKET	REPLACEMENT
1	Custom cabinet, lower, L-shape, w/1 sink unit, 3 doors & 1 drawer, 64" x 25" x 36", lam. ext. & int., white	790	1,220
1	Custom cabinet, upper, w/4 doors & open shelves, 64" x 10" x 52", lam. ext. & int., white	410	640
1	Danby refrigerator, w/freezer section, white, (bar type)	130	210
1	Superior kettle, 2 litre	10	30
1	Panasonic microwave oven, w/turntable, 18" x 15" x 10", stnls., (new)	110	120
1	Braun coffee maker, 10-cup, w/auto. shut-off, white, (new)	40	60
1	Black & Decker toaster oven, 6-slice, white	30	70
1	Pioneer synthesizer, digital	240	840
1	Pioneer cassette deck, stereo/receiver		
1	Pioneer CD player, 3-disc		
1	Pioneer cassette deck, double		
	TOTAL	**1,760**	**3,190**

WASHROOM

Approximate year equipped - 1989
Ownership interest - 100%

QTY	DESCRIPTION	MARKET	REPLACEMENT
1	Custom cabinet, lower, w/1 sink unit, w/2 doors, 24" x 21" x 30", lam. ext. & int., rose	100	340
	TOTAL	**100**	**340**

FURNITURE & FIXTURES

COMPUTER SYSTEM

Ownership interest - 100%

QTY	DESCRIPTION	VALUE MARKET	VALUE REPLACEMENT
	Software:	10,170	11,780
	Exan Power Practice (current version)		
	PC Anywhere		
	MS Win 2000		
	TOTAL	**10,170**	**11,780**

Note: The above software programmes have been valued with the assumption that the author's/licensor's consent, if required to transfer the said software licence(s), will not be unreasonably withheld.

QTY	DESCRIPTION	VALUE MARKET	VALUE REPLACEMENT
	Hardware:	12,870	18,350
6	Custom CPUs, (2 are servers)		
4	IBM PCs, 2008		
3	Custom monitors, flat screens, 2008		
1	Hewlett Packard printer, model LaserJet 4 Plus		
1	Hewlett Packard printer, laser, new		
1	Fax modem		
1	UPS back-up		
1	Custom Scanner		
	TOTAL	**12,870**	**18,350**

SUMMARY

Equipment, Furniture and Fixtures

			Market Value $	Replacement Costs $
CLINICAL				
	Operatory # 1		10,340	33,610
	Operatory # 2		18,440	34,820
	Operatory # 3 - Hygiene		12,370	31,720
	Operatory # 4		11,030	33,120
	Operatory # 5		33,830	62,080
	Operatory # 6		20,650	32,480
	Handpieces/Attachments		13,110	18,920
	Sterilization		23,180	33,750
	Make Ready		12,250	29,670
	X-ray Area		17,940	29,900
	Dark Room		8,630	17,100
	Hall		5,510	7,650
		TOTAL	**187,280**	**364,820**
ADMINISTRATIVE				
	Reception Area		2,320	4,450
	Business Office		3,930	11,080
	Private Office		1,120	3,110
	Manager's Office		3,200	7,620
	Staff Room/Kitchen		1,760	3,190
	Washroom		100	340
		TOTAL	**12,430**	**29,790**
COMPUTER SYSTEM				
	Software		10,170	11,780
	Hardware		12,870	18,350
		TOTAL	**23,040**	**30,130**

INSTRUMENTS AND MATERIALS (INVENTORY) - ROI Formula - ESTIMATE

A list may be prepared by the Vendor, before the close of sale, of the current in-use instruments and materials to be included in the sale of the practice. The list will contain the count, type, price, extension and total of the final inventory to be purchased.

The pricing will be at current replacement prices for like or similar items for the approximate price rounded to the nearest dollar, less the stated discount.

Instruments: Items and material not usable due to rust, disrepair or obsolescence will not be included.

Materials: Sundries, with the package, box or container opened will not be included.

Categories, Description and Discount

1. Used Instruments and Items

Non-consumable re-use items including hand and surgical instruments, lead aprons, retainers, clamps, punches, frames, dispensers, slabs, syringes, clips, carriers, impression trays, specialized instruments, inlay, perio, endodontic and orthodontic including contra and straight angles, and handpiece attachments that are not listed under major equipment.

Also includes laboratory instruments such as pliers, spatulas, burners, bowls, impression and sterilizing trays, articulators, flasks and laboratory chucks and tools.

To be priced at current replacement less 50% discount for use or unsuitability to the Purchaser.

Estimated at **$9,250**
(after the above discount)

2. New Instruments and Items - Unused

Carbide and steel burs, diamonds, discs, pins, mandrels, wheels, stones, brushes, endo instruments. Also including bands, attachments, crowns, stainless and others, regardless if package broken.

To be priced at current replacement costs.

Estimated at **$8,100**

INSTRUMENTS AND MATERIALS (INVENTORY) - ROI Formula - ESTIMATE

3. New and Unopened Materials

Consumable supplies in-dated that are currently of a type in use by the Vendor, such as: alloy, alginates, anaesthetics, acrylic, liners, cements, composites, films, impression materials, drugs and medicaments, mercury, needles, ejectors, solutions, waxes, etc. Estimated amount of alloy, if applicable, is normal.

To be priced at current replacement costs.

Estimated at **$9,150**

4. Opened Materials

Spent items and consumables; all packages of open consumable materials, sundries, drugs and supplies will not be included in the sale, including used brushes, wheels, stones, discs, strips, burs, diamonds, endo instruments, drills and polishers, excepting dispensed drugs and medicaments.

5. Stationery

Forms, charts, mounts, filing supplies, office items, accounting forms, and stationery not personally imprinted.

To be priced at current replacement costs.

Estimated at **$700**

TOTAL ESTIMATED INVENTORY ON DAY OF CLOSE $27,200
(Four categories)

Note: Inventory may vary considerably by closing date due to increases and decreases in quantities and prices.

The Owner should not purchase or sell large quantities of any inventory items between date of acceptance of an offer and the closing date.

EXCLUDED ASSETS

Accounts Receivable - Not included

Outstanding and due accounts receivable are not included. In the event of a sale, the balance owing by the patient or insurance provider, and due the Vendor on day of close, will remain the Vendor's assets for collection.

The Vendor will prepare a list of all accounts receivable at close, and supply, either a copy of the list or photocopies of the ledger cards, to the Purchaser.

The Purchaser agrees to forward all payments (cheques, cash, money orders) to the Vendor promptly for receivables collected for the Vendor.

Payments made by patients will be first applied to the oldest outstanding balance on the Vendor's receivables unless patients specify otherwise.

Other Assets - Not Included

Personal items such as:

Textbooks	Photographs
Professional publications	Visual aid demonstrators
Membership materials	Personal mementos
Gowns	Precious metals (excluding alloy)
Diplomas	Scrap amalgam

And specifically:

Custom mirror in Washroom
Workforce tool chest in Hall
Paintings, prints and personal photos
All implant kits, implant supplies, grafting materials, Osseo set and implant surgical cassette and equipment

Doctor to provide a list of items not included, if applicable.

Rental or Service Contracts:

Arrangements would be made to assume leases, contracts, or return rental items for the following, **if applicable**:

Telephone systems	Coffee machines
Water heaters & softeners	Postage meters
Nitrous, oxygen & propane gas tanks	**Alarm systems**
Photocopiers	Professional signs
Waste removal contract	**Water coolers**
Computer maintenance agreements	Towel service
Credit card authorization devices	**Debit card machines**

LIABILITIES

The practice and assets will be clear of all financial liabilities. All accounts payable and payroll will be fully paid including laboratory, supply and equipment accounts.

All loans, leases, chattels and mortgages will be paid off.

GROSS INCOME

Fiscal Year Ends - January 31

Year			% Change
20XX Actual	723,135		-
20XX Actual	866,102		19.77%
20XX Actual	834,609		-3.64%
20XX Actual	747,762	(1)	-10.41%
20XX Actual	920,484		23.10%
20XX Actual	916,711		-0.41%
20XX Actual	990,578		8.06%
20XX Actual	939,924		-5.11%
20XX Actual	1,078,791	(2)	14.77%
20XX Estimated	1,150,000	(3)	6.60%

(1) Decrease attributed to an associate leaving the practice and a hygienist being on maternity leave.

(2) After accountant's year-end adjustments.

(3) As per Appraiser.

Note: Revenues shown are after accountant's year-end adjustments and do not include interest income and professional fees related to prior years as it is not directly related to the annual income of the practice.

FISCAL YEAR 20XX

	Charges (1)
February 1, 20XX to January 31, 20XX	
Total for year:	**1,078,339**
Average per month:	89,862

(1) As per January 31, 20XX producer production analysis report provided by Dr. Brown.

GROSS INCOME - Continued

	FISCAL YEAR 20XX	
	Charges	**Collections**
February 20XX	70,888	77,074
March	76,925	86,427
April	87,716	75,890
May	79,587	83,863
Total for year:	**315,116**	**323,254**
Average per month:	78,779	80,814

INCOME, EXPENSES AND EARNINGS

Fiscal Year Ends - January 31

		20XX Actual	%	20XX Actual	%	20XX (1) Estimated	%
PROFESSIONAL FEES		**939,924**		**1,078,791**		**1,150,000**	
EXPENSES							
Wages & Benefits		225,248	*24.0%*	293,334	*27.2%*	325,170	*28.3*
Dental Supplies		51,315	*5.5%*	94,643	*8.8%*	42,900	*3.7*
Laboratory Fees		92,022	*9.8%*	80,412	*7.5%*	79,050	*6.9*
Rent		48,542	*5.2%*	48,837	*4.5%*	49,870	*4.3*
Telephone		12,975	*1.4%*	9,840	*0.9%*	10,070	*0.9*
Dues & Licenses		5,046	*0.5%*	4,975	*0.5%*	4,800	*0.4*
Insurance		6,876	*0.7%*	6,569	*0.6%*	6,600	*0.6*
Amortization		9,522	*1.0%*	8,557	*0.8%*	7,700	*0.7*
Accounting & Legal		6,062	*0.6%*	5,439	*0.5%*	7,790	*0.7*
Associate Fees		151,991	*16.2%*	121,860	*11.3%*	108,240	*9.4*
Automotive Expenses		7,044	*0.7%*	7,068	*0.7%*	6,920	*0.6*
Bank Charges & Interest		6,319	*0.7%*	8,520	*0.8%*	7,090	*0.6*
Bookkeeping		9,892	*1.1%*	7,927	*0.7%*	8,620	*0.7*
Computer Costs		4,902	*0.5%*	5,069	*0.5%*	5,200	*0.5*
Management Salaries		136,698	*14.5%*	132,708	*12.3%*	132,700	*11.5*
Office, Postage & Stationery		28,197	*3.0%*	30,921	*2.9%*	28,430	*2.5*
Professional Development		14,687	*1.6%*	4,665	*0.4%*	4,700	*0.4*
Promotion & Business Develop.		14,956	*1.6%*	11,647	*1.1%*	15,820	*1.4*
Repairs & Cleaning		17,488	*1.9%*	15,429	*1.4%*	17,060	*1.5*
Utilities		5,041	*0.5%*	5,184	*0.5%*	5,020	*0.4*
TOTAL EXPENSES		**854,823**	*90.9%*	**903,604**	*83.8%*	**873,750**	*76.0*
NET INCOME PRE-TAX		**85,101**	*9.1%*	**175,187**	*16.2%*	**276,250**	*24.0*
AMORTIZATION	(2)	9,522	*1.0%*	8,557	*0.8%*	7,700	*0.7*
NON-PRACTICE EXPENSES	(3)	42,600	*4.5%*	34,315	*3.2%*	35,740	*3.1*
ASSOCIATE FEES	(4)	145,900	*15.5%*	117,000	*10.8%*	103,900	*9.0*
MANAGEMENT SALARIES	(5)	120,874	*12.9%*	116,884	*10.8%*	116,876	*10.2*
TOTAL PROFESSIONAL CASH EARNINGS		**403,997**	*43.0%*	**451,943**	*41.9%*	**540,466**	*47.0*

INCOME, EXPENSES AND EARNINGS - Continued

(1) Gross and expenses are estimated.

(2) Amortization expense.

(3) Adjustment to normalize expenses not directly related to the annual income of the practice or are one-time non-reoccurring.

	20XX	20XX	20XX
Automotive Expenses	7,044	7,068	6,920
Professional Development	7,600	2,600	0
Promotion & Business Develop.	14,956	11,647	15,820
Repairs & Cleaning	13,000	13,000	13,000
Total	**42,600**	**34,315**	**35,740**

(4) Associate fees paid less 4% for estimate of Associate's own expenses.

(5) Cost of management adjustment.

Management Salaries	136,698	132,708	132,700
Spouse*	(27,984)	(27,984)	(27,984)
Spouse**	12,160	12,160	12,160
Total	**120,874**	**116,884**	**116,876**

*Earned wages which were expensed in management salaries.
**Expensed in wages.

FINANCIAL ANALYSIS

True Operating Expenses and Cash Earnings as a Percentage of Gross Billings. Overhead values on financial statements may or may not be indicative of the true costs of the practice due to owners minimizing tax incidence.

	20XX	20XX	20XX	Averages
Wages & Benefits (1)	25.6%	28.7%	29.7%	24% - 26%
Dental Supplies	5.5%	8.8%	3.7%	5% - 8%
Laboratory	9.8%	7.5%	6.9%	4% - 7%
Rent	5.2%	4.5%	4.3%	5% - 8%
Other & Administration	10.9%	8.6%	8.4%	4% - 8%
Total Expenses	**57.0%**	**58.1%**	**53.0%**	**42% - 57%**
Total Professional Cash Earnings (2)	**43.0%**	**41.9%**	**47.0%**	**58% - 43%**

(1) Excluding management salaries.
(2) Excluding depreciation, leasing and interest expense and including Associate's fees paid.
* Based upon review of database available to Appraiser.

CASH FLOW

The cash flow pro forma statement or budget, on the next page, is based on:

"A") 20XX Actual Gross.
"B") 10% Increase on the 20XX Actual Gross.

The cash for repayment of both principal and interest of the capital invested by a new owner is included.

Amount of investment:	$690,000
Rate:	2.50%
Term:	8 years
Monthly Payment:	$7,938

	Monthly	Annually	Term
Principal	$7,188	$86,250	$690,000
Interest	750	9,000	72,000
Total	$7,938	$95,250	$762,000

CASH FLOW - Continued

GROSS	"A" 20XX Estimated		"B" 10% Increase	
Per Year	1,150,000		1,265,000	
Per Month	95,833		105,416	
Per Week (4.3 weeks)	22,287		24,516	
Per Day (5.0 Days)	4,457		4,903	
PROFESSIONAL FEES	**1,150,000**	**100%**	**1,265,000**	**100%**
EXPENSES				
Fixed		**%**		**%**
Rent	49,870	4.3%	49,870	3.9%
Insurance	6,600	0.6%	6,600	0.5%
Telephone	10,070	0.9%	10,070	0.8%
Dues & Licences	4,800	0.4%	4,800	0.4%
Principal	86,250	7.5%	86,250	6.8%
Interest	9,000	0.8%	9,000	0.7%
Sub-Total	166,590	14.5%	166,590	13.1%
Variable				
Wages & Benefits	340,994	29.7%	375,705	29.7%
Dental Supplies	42,900	3.7%	46,800	3.7%
Laboratory	79,050	6.9%	87,300	6.9%
All Other	74,800	6.5%	82,200	6.5%
Sub-Total	537,744	46.8%	592,005	46.8%
TOTAL EXPENSES	**704,334**	61.3%	**758,595**	59.9%
NET CASH (1)	**445,666**	38.7%	**506,405**	40.1%
AFTER REPAYMENT OF INVESTMENT LOAN (2)	540,916	47.0%	601,655	47.6%

(1) Actual earnings (accrual method) would be higher - add principal less depreciation.

(2) Assuming constant dollars and including Associate's fees paid.

GOODWILL

Goodwill values can vary considerably from practice to practice and from one specialty to another. Actual fair market sales confirm this, with goodwill ranging from 18% to 74% of the total value of a practice.

Experience indicates that, where the ratio of practitioners to population is average, the value of an established location with patient flow is now being recognized as a prudent investment.

Goodwill is usually greater than the sum of many intangible factors over a period of time, such as net income, gross, fixed and variable expenses, fees and services rendered, patient flow, demographics, market economics, relationship of gross and net to assets, location, leases, systems, records and other key considerations.

Our experience with many unique practice sales since 1974 supports our methods, formulas and judgement of value and worth.

The goodwill of an active practice sold in the open market, with the seller willing and able to recommend the buyer and also to assist in turning over the patients, is of more value when compared to a practice which, due to death or other circumstances, was unattended for a period of time.

The location of the practice geographically, the ratio of population to practitioners and the dental I.Q. of the patients are other important factors.

The ability of a new practitioner to identify, communicate, and serve the patients' needs within the practice, is totally dependent on the individual. If this ability exists and is applied in an established practice versus a new practice with few patients, there would be a vastly different result in the amount of treatment performed and the fees received.

The costs to search out and investigate a location to establish a practice (especially a rental location with protection to the lessee for continual use over a long period of time, at controlled costs), negotiate the lease, choose designers, order leasehold improvements, supervise contractors, arrange credit, acquire and install equipment, supplies, furniture and set up record keeping, office and clinical procedures and systems all add up to a considerable cost.

The following is our opinion of how these factors determine the value of the goodwill of this practice.

PRACTICE SALES COMPARISON AND MARKET FACTORS

Professional practice historic sales records are difficult to locate and practices are highly individual by nature, however, the following comparables and non-comparables have been selected to illustrate and determine the appropriate market factor. The market value of general and specialty practices, and their locations, vary considerably. The market factor is based on over 1,000 actual sales controlled exclusively by this firm that have ranged from .30 to 1.00 since 1974.

	Subject	**A**	**B**	**C**	**D**
LOCATION	Vancouver	Kamloops	Kamloops	Vancouver	Vancouver
Age	29 years	20 years	17 years	10 years	28 years
Gross	1,150,000	~1,159,008	717,379	553,020	~636,912
Date	Jan/XX	Jan/01	Nov/05	Dec/06	Jan/99
Net	540,466	~540,808	245,087	223,000	~332,212
% of Gross	47%	47%	34%	40%	52%
Size (sq. ft.)	1,550	2,535	1,460	1,300	2,115
APPRAISED VALUE	690,940	695,610	385,560	599,800	351,760
Date	Jan/XX	Oct/2000	Feb/06	Aug/06	Nov/98
Goodwill %	52%	68%	58%	41%	64%
Asset %	48%	32%	42%	59%	36%
ASKING PRICE		695,000	385,560	595,050(s)	350,000
Date		June/01	Mar/06	Nov/06	Jan/99
Selling Price		615,000	340,000	450,000(s)	320,000(s)
Closing Date		June/01	Mar/07	Nov/07	Mar/99
MARKET FACTOR	.65	.65	.65	.75	.70
Details					

s = share purchase

RECONCILIATION

Following careful consideration comparisons of these and numerous other practices, practices "A" and "B" were determined to be the most comparable due to size and area and practices "C" and "D" the least due to location and type.

The market factor for the subject practice is, in my opinion, .65.

(Total practice & professional earnings)					Weighted Market Factors		Amount $
Gross Income							
Last Full Years	20XX	939,924					
	20XX	1,078,791					
Estimate Fiscal	20XX	1,150,000					
	Weighted Average		1,091,251	x	0.325	=	354,657
Total Professional Cash Earnings							
(Cash flow pre-tax)							
Last 2 Full Years	20XX	403,997					
	20XX	451,943					
Estimate Fiscal	20XX	540,466					
	Weighted Average		488,214	x	0.650	=	317,339
					Sub-total		$671,996
					Divide / 2 (major total)		$335,998

Adjustments "+" or "-"

	Plus	Minus
1) Associate	-	7.0
2) Partnership/Cost Share	-	-
3) Sub-specialty	-	2.5
4) Services Referred Out	2.5	-
5) Attendance/Hours	-	-
6) Fees/Payments	12.5	-
7) Insurance	-	25.5
8) Business Systems	5.0	-
9) Records Management	-	-
10) Patient Flow	5.0	-
11) Patient Location	-	5.0
12) Patient Profile	-	-
13) Location/Draw	15.0	-
14) Facility	7.5	-
15) Lease Right Of Use	-	7.5
16) Area Demographics	-	2.5
17) Population Ratios	2.5	-
18) Overall Trend	6.0	-
Total	**56.0**	**- 50.0**

Net Factor 6.0	**$20,160**
Major Total x +106.0	**$356,158**
Rounded to (nearest $10)	**$356,160**

Market factor of 0.65 based on recent market data of legal sales and arms length transfers of professional practices. The factor is weighted at one-half for gross income as cash earnings are a more meaningful indicator of value than gross income.

www.roicorp.com 58

SUMMARY

An existing practice offers:

a) Income - thereby providing cash flow

b) Patient flow - thereby providing busyness

c) A facility - thereby providing a place to <u>immediately</u> treat patients and realize income.

Based on the financial statements and the information and facts as represented to me and taking into consideration all the foregoing information and including all patients' charts, records, x-rays, and the necessary accounting records to continue the practice, but excluding the work in progress performed and charged to-date ....

And in recognition of the following assumptions:

a) The owner of the practice is willing to sign a mutually agreeable letter of introduction.

b) The owner agrees to do everything reasonable to ensure that the existing telephone number of the practice is transferred to a new owner.

c) The owner agrees not to carry on or be engaged in a practice within a reasonable radius of this practice and further not to solicit any patient known to be a patient of this practice as arranged by a legal covenant.

The value of the practice goodwill and organizational costs, in my opinion, is **$356,160.**

FINANCIAL DATA

FOR SAMPLE APPRAISAL PURPOSES ONLY

FIGURES MAY NOT MATCH THE FINANCIAL SECTION OF THIS APPRAISAL

DR. ALLAN BROWN

UNAUDITED FINANCIAL STATEMENTS

FOR THE YEAR ENDED
JANUARY 31ST, 20XX

FOR SAMPLE APPRAISAL PURPOSES ONLY

FIGURES MAY NOT MATCH THE FINANCIAL SECTION OF THIS APPRAISAL

NOTICE TO READER

I have compiled the balance sheet of Dr. Allan Brown as at January 31st, 20XX and the statements of income and capital for the year then ended from information provided by management. I have not audited, reviewed or otherwise attempted to verify the accuracy or completeness of such information. Readers are cautioned that these statements may not be appropriate for their purposes.

Vancouver, Ontario
January 31st, 20XX

CHARTERED ACCOUNTANTS

BALANCE SHEET
(Unaudited - See Notice To Reader)
as at January 31, 20XX

	20XX	20XX
LIABILITIES AND SHAREHOLDERS' EQUITY		
Current Liabilities		
Accounts payable and accrued liabilities	$ 38,025	$ 63,040
Wages payable	9,270	3,941
Due to government agencies	37,726	37,089
Shareholders' loans (Note 4)	75,754	37,655
	160,775	141,725
Future Income Taxes (Note 5)	3,200	3,900
Shareholders' Equity		
Share Capital (Note 6)		
Class A common	100	100
Class B common	100	100
Preferred (redeemable at the option of the holder for a total of $96,377)	10	10
	210	210
Contributed Surplus	96,367	96,367
Retained Earnings	133,412	3,234
	229,989	99,811
	$ 393,964	$ 245,436

The attached notes are an integral part of these financial statements

STATEMENT OF INCOME AND RETAINED EARNINGS
(Unaudited - See Notice To Reader)
for the year ended January 31, 20XX

	20XX	20XX
Revenue		
Professional fees	$1,078,791	$ 939,924
Interest income	3,829	5,233
	1,082,620	945,157
Expenses		
Accounting and legal	5,439	6,062
Amortization	8,557	9,522
Associate fees	121,860	151,991
Automotive expenses	7,068	7,044
Bank charges, interest and credit card discounts	8,520	6,319
Bookkeeping	7,927	9,892
Computer costs	5,069	4,902
Dental supplies	94,643	51,315
Insurance	6,569	6,876
Laboratory fees	80,412	92,022
Licences and dues	4,975	5,046
Management salaries	132,708	136,698
Office, postage and stationery	30,921	28,197
Professional development	4,665	14,687
Promotion and business development	11,647	14,956
Rent	48,837	48,542
Repairs and cleaning	15,429	17,488
Telephone	9,840	12,975
Utilities	5,184	5,041
Wages and benefits	293,334	225,248
	903,604	854,823
Income Before Income Taxes	179,016	90,334
Corporation Income Taxes		
Current	31,538	16,251
Future	(700)	200
	30,838	16,451
Net Income For The Year - Carried Forward	148,178	73,883

The attached notes are an integral part of these financial statements

Cont.../

STATEMENT OF INCOME AND RETAINED EARNINGS
(Unaudited - See Notice To Reader)
for the year ended January 31, 20XX

	20XX	20XX
Net Income For The Year - Brought Forward	$ 148,178	$ 73,883
Retained Earnings, Beginning Of Year	3,234	97,351
	151,412	171,234
Dividends	18,000	168,000
Retained Earnings, End Of Year	$ 133,412	$ 3,234

The attached notes are an integral part of these financial statements

NOTES TO THE FINANCIAL STATEMENTS
(Unaudited - See Notice To Reader)
January 31, 20XX

Note 1. Marketable Securities

The marketable securities consist of the following investments:

	20XX	20XX
Cash held with broker	$ 171,678	$ ---
Money market funds	---	21,100
Shares of a public corporation	8	8
	$ 171,686	$ 21,108

Investment in marketable securities is recorded at cost or written down to market value where there is a material decline in value. Investments have a book value of $2,777 lower than original cost at January 31, 20XX.

Note 2. Property And Equipment

	Cost	Accumulated Amortization	Net Book Value 20XX	Net Book Value 20XX
Equipment	$ 254,805	$ 236,028	$ 18,777	$ 20,248
Computers	80,551	73,467	7,084	12,009
Leasehold improvements	106,156	106,156	---	---
	$ 441,512	$ 415,651	$ 25,861	$ 32,257

Property and equipment are recorded at cost. Amortization is being recorded on a declining balance basis at the following annual rates:

Equipment	20%
Computers	30%/45%

In the year of acquisition, one half of the rate is used.

Cont.../

NOTES TO THE FINANCIAL STATEMENTS
(Unaudited - See Notice To Reader)
January 31, 20XX

Note 3. Bank Indebtedness

The company has entered into an Overdraft Line of Credit Agreement to a maximum of $50,000 with the Canadian Imperial Bank of Commerce, bearing interest at prime, secured to assets of the company.

Note 4. Shareholders' Loans

The shareholders' loans are non-interest bearing and have no specific terms of repayment.

Note 5. Future Income Taxes

The company follows the tax allocation basis of accounting for corporation income taxes, whereby tax provisions based on temporary differences between the tax basis of an asset or liability and its carrying amount on the balance sheet are recorded as future income taxes.

Cont.../

NOTES TO THE FINANCIAL STATEMENTS
(Unaudited - See Notice To Reader)
January 31, 20XX

Note 6. Share Capital

	20XX	20XX
Authorized:		
200 class A common shares, par value $1 each		
200 class B common shares, par value $1 each		
1,000 preferred shares, par value $.01 each		
Issued and fully paid:		
100 class A shares	$ 100	$ 100
100 class B shares	100	100
1,000 preferred shares, redeemable and retractable for $96 each	10	10
	$ 210	$ 210

Note 7. Incorporation and Nature of Business

The company was incorporated under the laws of the Province of British Columbia on January 30, 20XX. The main business activity is dentistry.

Note 8. Lease Commitment

The company occupies premises leased by until November 20XX.

STATEMENT OF INCOME AND RETAINED EARNINGS
(Unaudited - See Notice To Reader)
for the year ended January 31, 20XX

	20XX	20XX
Revenue		
Professional fees	$ 939,924	$ 990,578
Professional fees related to prior years	---	10,851
Interest income	5,233	1,710
	945,157	1,003,139
Expenses		
Accounting, legal and appraisal costs	6,062	14,830
Amortization	9,522	8,614
Associate fees	151,991	96,108
Automotive expenses	7,044	6,384
Bank charges, interest and credit card discounts	6,319	6,969
Bookkeeping	9,892	7,866
Computer costs	4,902	3,143
Dental supplies	51,315	77,091
Insurance	6,876	7,895
Laboratory fees	92,022	91,188
Licences and dues	5,046	4,633
Management salaries	136,698	133,568
Office, postage and stationery	28,197	43,240
Professional development	14,687	7,080
Promotion and business development	14,956	13,622
Rent	48,542	50,561
Repairs and cleaning	17,488	13,252
Telephone	12,975	8,103
Utilities	5,041	4,134
Wages and benefits	225,248	244,864
	854,823	843,145
Income Before Income Taxes	90,334	159,994
Corporation Income Taxes		
Current	16,251	29,877
Future	200	200
	16,451	30,077
Net Income For The Year - Carried Forward	73,883	129,917

The attached notes are an integral part of these financial statements

Cont.../

STATEMENT OF INCOME AND RETAINED EARNINGS
(Unaudited - See Notice To Reader)
for the year ended January 31, 20XX

	20XX	20XX
Revenue		
Professional fees	$ 990,817	$ 916,711
Professional fees related to prior years	10,851	---
Interest income	1,710	676
Insurance recoveries	---	9,454
	1,003,378	926,841
Expenses		
Accounting and legal and appraisal costs	14,830	5,299
Amortization	8,614	9,463
Associate fees	96,108	105,258
Automotive expenses	6,384	5,928
Bank charges, interest and credit card discounts	6,969	6,818
Bookkeeping	7,866	7,340
Collection costs	239	665
Computer costs	3,143	3,312
Dental supplies	77,091	52,261
Insurance	7,895	8,193
Laboratory fees	91,188	89,456
Licences and dues	4,633	5,393
Management salaries	133,568	131,582
Office, postage and stationery	43,240	30,397
Professional development	7,080	14,733
Promotion and business development	13,622	11,011
Rent	50,561	45,252
Repairs and cleaning	13,252	17,946
Telephone	8,103	11,805
Utilities	4,134	4,828
Wages and benefits	244,864	222,175
	843,384	789,115
Income Before Income Taxes	159,994	137,726
Corporation Income Taxes		
Current	29,877	24,370
Future	200	500
	30,077	24,870
Net Income For The Year - Carried Forward	129,917	112,856

The attached notes are an integral part of these financial statements

Cont.../

STATEMENT OF INCOME AND RETAINED EARNINGS
(Unaudited - See Notice to Reader)
for the year ended January 31, 20XX

	20XX	20XX
Revenue		
Professional fees	$ 916,711	$ 920,300
Interest income	676	888
Insurance recoveries	9,454	---
	926,841	921,188
Expenses		
Accounting and legal	5,299	4,857
Amortization	9,463	11,250
Associate fees	105,258	125,155
Automotive expenses	5,928	5,892
Bank charges, interest and credit card discounts	6,818	5,906
Bookkeeping	7,340	6,619
Collection costs	665	1,068
Computer costs	3,312	3,160
Dental supplies	52,261	64,681
Insurance	8,193	6,300
Laboratory fees	89,456	107,178
Licences and dues	5,393	4,611
Management salaries	131,582	130,874
Office, postage and stationery	30,397	29,940
Professional development	14,733	8,553
Promotion and business development	11,011	19,347
Rent	45,252	45,462
Repairs and cleaning	17,946	17,770
Telephone	11,805	10,359
Utilities	4,828	4,838
Wages and benefits	222,175	195,504
	789,115	809,324
Income Before Income Taxes	137,726	111,864
Corporation Income Taxes		
Current	24,370	19,675
Future	500	300
	24,870	19,975
Net Income For The Year - Carried Forward	112,856	91,889

See accompanying notes

Cont.../

STATEMENT OF INCOME AND RETAINED EARNINGS
for the year ended January 31, 20XX

	20XX	20XX
Revenue		
Professional fees	$ 747,762	$ 834,609
Interest income	586	1,089
Write down in carrying value of marketable securities	(87)	(2,690)
	748,261	833,008
Expenses		
Accounting and legal	5,083	5,448
Amortization	19,137	23,996
Associate fees	96,940	84,772
Automotive expenses	5,760	5,748
Bank charges, interest and credit card discounts	4,553	3,510
Bookkeeping	4,598	---
Collection costs	976	---
Computer costs	2,300	2,618
Dental supplies	68,520	43,358
Insurance	7,061	6,693
Laboratory fees	75,065	76,144
Licences and dues	3,510	2,298
Management salaries	129,786	129,393
Office, postage and stationery	31,712	31,806
Professional development	13,414	4,232
Promotion and business development	21,030	28,145
Rent	45,342	45,240
Repairs and cleaning	11,678	1,567
Telephone	9,533	8,885
Utilities	4,481	3,851
Wages and benefits	175,171	216,262
	735,650	723,966
Income Before Income Taxes	12,611	109,042
Corporation Income Taxes		
Current	3,364	21,371
Future	700	---
	4,064	21,371
Net Income For The Year - Carried Forward	8,547	87,671

Prepared without audit

Cont…/

STATEMENT OF INCOME AND RETAINED EARNINGS
for the year ended January 31, 20XX

	20XX	20XX
Revenue		
Professional fees	$ 866,102	$ 723,135
Interest income	2,162	833
	868,264	723,968
Expenses		
Accounting and legal	7,866	4,104
Amortization	31,060	36,799
Associate fees	60,668	37,093
Automotive expenses	5,220	4,908
Bank charges, interest and credit card discounts	4,500	4,498
Computer costs	3,540	5,397
Dental supplies	47,794	42,861
Insurance	6,528	6,007
Laboratory fees	84,006	62,890
Licences and dues	5,337	957
Management salaries	129,744	130,464
Office, postage and stationery	30,779	23,155
Professional development	8,862	1,909
Promotion	12,638	14,530
Rent	44,571	42,753
Repairs and cleaning	7,096	7,085
Telephone	5,733	6,440
Utilities	3,872	3,880
Wages and benefits	225,452	210,328
	725,266	646,058
Income Before Income Taxes	142,998	77,910
Corporation Income Taxes	27,744	17,273
Net Income For The Year	115,254	60,637
Retained Earnings, Beginning Of Year	21,207	15,570
	136,461	76,207
Dividends	60,000	55,000
Retained Earnings, End Of Year	$ 76,461	$ 21,207

See accompanying notes

Prepared without audit

LEASE/FLOOR PLAN

LEASE
(COMMERCIAL)

Made the 15th day of MARCH,

BETWEEN

(the "Landlord")

- and -

(the "Tenant" in a personal capacity)

In consideration of the rents, covenants and obligations stipulated herein the Landlord and the Tenant have agreed to enter into a Lease of the premises known municipally as
Plan 1685, and more particularly described in Schedule "A" attached (the "Premises").

1. GRANT OF LEASE

1. The Landlord leases the Premises to the Tenant:

(a) at the Rent set forth in Section 2;

(b) for the Term set forth in Section 3; and

(c) subject to the conditions and in accordance with the covenants, obligations and agreements herein.

2. The Landlord covenants that he has the right to grant the leasehold interest in the Premises free from encumbrances except as disclosed on title.

2. RENT

1. Rent means the amounts payable by the Tenant to the Landlord pursuant to this Section and includes Additional Rent.

2. The Tenant covenants to pay to the Landlord, during the Term of this Lease rent as follows:

(a) The sum of ELEVEN THOUSAND AND FORTY DOLLARS ($11,040.00) plus GST per annum, payable monthly in advance in equal installments of NINE HUNDRED AND TWENTY DOLLARS ($920.00) plus GST on the 1st day of each and every month, commencing on the first day of the Term; Where the commencement date is not on the first day of the calendar month, the installment due shall be prorated accordingly.

3. The Tenant further covenants to pay all other sums required by this Lease to be paid by him and agrees that all amounts payable by the Tenant to the Landlord or to any other party pursuant to the provisions of this Lease shall be deemed to be additional rent ("Additional Rent") whether or not specifically designated as such in this Lease.

LANDLORD	TENANT

2

4. The Landlord and the Tenant agree that it is their mutual intention that this Lease shall be a completely carefree net lease for the Landlord and that the Landlord shall not, during the Term of this Lease, be required to make any payments in respect of the Premises other than charges of a kind personal to the Landlord (such as income and estate taxes and mortgage payments):

(a) and to effect the said intention of the parties the Tenant promises to pay the following expenses related to the Premises as Additional Rent;

i) utilities (including but not limited to gas, electricity, water, heat, air conditioning);
ii) services supplied to the Premises, provided that this does not in any way oblige the Landlord to provide any services, unless otherwise agreed in this Lease;
iii) maintenance;
iv) insurance premiums;
v) any tax or duty imposed upon, or collectable by the Landlord which is measured by or based in whole or in part directly upon the Rent including, without limitation, the goods and services tax, value added tax, business transfer tax, retail sales tax, federal sales tax, excise tax or duty or any tax similar to any of the foregoing;
vi) the Landlord's reasonable administration and supervisory management fee; and
vii) real property taxes, rates, duties and assessments including such portion of real property taxes formerly known as business taxes. The Landlord shall have the right to determine the assessment value of the Premises acting reasonably, bearing in mind, current principles of assessment, previous assessments and the proportionate share that the rentable area of the Premises is to the total rentable area of all premises in the building of which the Premises forms a part (if applicable). The assessment value of the Premises as determined aforesaid shall be multiplied by the current tax rate of the Premises to determine the real property taxes payable as Additional Rent;
viii) all other charges, impositions, costs and expenses of every nature and kind whatsoever relating to the Tenants' use and operation of the premises save for those which are the Landlord's responsibility as specifically provided for herein.

(b) and if any of the foregoing charges are invoiced directly to the Tenant, the Tenant shall pay same as and when they become due and produce proof of payment to the Landlord immediately if requested to do so, but the Tenant may contest or appeal any such charges at the Tenant's own expense;

(c) and the Tenant hereby agrees to indemnify and protect the Landlord from any liability accruing to the Landlord in respect of the expenses payable by the Tenant as provided herein;

(d) and if the Tenant fails to make any of the payments required by this Lease then the Landlord may make such payments and charge to the Tenant as Additional Rent the amounts paid by the Landlord, and if such charges are not paid by the Tenant on demand the Landlord shall be entitled to the same remedies and may take the same steps for recovery of the unpaid charges as in the event of Rent in arrears;

LANDLORD	TENANT

3

(e) and if the Tenant enjoys the use of any common areas and facilities not included in the Premises, the Tenant shall pay his proportionate share of the foregoing expenses relating to such common areas and facilities.

5. Prior to the commencement of each lease year, the Landlord shall notify the Tenant of its reasonable and bona fide estimate of Additional Rent for that lease year. The Tenant shall pay such estimated amount in equal monthly installments in advance on the same dates stipulated for payment of Rent in Section 2(2). From time to time during a lease year the Landlord may, acting reasonably, re-estimate the amount of the Additional Rent and shall fix monthly installments for the then remaining balance of the lease year so that the Landlord's estimate, original or revised, of Additional Rent will have been entirely paid during that lease year. The Landlord shall make a final determination of Additional Rent for the relevant lease year within 120 days of the Landlord's financial year end, which shall be binding upon both parties and shall provide the Tenant with a statement of the Additional Rent for the relevant lease year. The Landlord and the Tenant shall expeditiously make any necessary readjusting payment; provided that the Tenant may not claim a re-adjustment based solely upon any error of estimation, determination or calculation unless claimed in writing within six months after the lease year to which the claim relates.

6. All payments to be made by the Tenant pursuant to this lease shall be delivered to the Landlord at the Landlord's address for service set out in Section 15 or to such other place as the Landlord may from time to time direct in writing.

7. The Tenant agrees to pay in advance to the Landlord at the commencement of the Term the first and last months' net and additional Rentals payable under Section 2(2) of this Lease.

8. All Rent in arrears and all sums paid by the Landlord for expenses incurred which should have been paid by the Tenant shall bear interest from the date payment was due, or made, or expense incurred at a rate per annum equal to Eighteen (18) per cent.

9. The Tenant acknowledges and agrees that the payments of Rent and Additional Rent provided for in this Lease shall be made without any deductions for any reason whatsoever unless expressly allowed by the terms of this Lease or agreed to by the Landlord in writing; and

(a) no partial payment by the Tenant which is accepted by the Landlord shall be considered as other than a partial payment on account of Rent owing and shall not prejudice the Landlord's right to recover any rent owing.

3. TERM AND POSSESSION

1. The Tenant shall have possession of the Premises for a period of Five (5) years, commencing on the 1st day of April, 1999 (the "Commencement Date") and ending on the 31st day of March, 2004, (the "Termination Date").

2. Subject to the Landlord's rights under this Lease, and as long as the Lease is in good standing the Landlord covenants that the Tenant shall have quiet enjoyment of the Premises during the Term of this Lease without any interruption or disturbance from the Landlord or any other persons or persons lawfully claiming through the Landlord.

LANDLORD	TENANT

3. If the Tenant fails to take possession of the Premises or to open for business on or before the date specified for commencement of the Term of this Lease, the Landlord shall, in addition to any other remedies, have the right to terminate this Lease upon 24 hours written notice to the Tenant, and to recover from the Tenant the cost of all work done by the Landlord on behalf of the Tenant.

4. ASSIGNMENT

1. The Tenant shall not assign this Lease or sublet the whole or any part of the Premises unless he first obtains the consent of the Landlord in writing, which consent shall not unreasonably be withheld, and the Tenant hereby waives his right to the benefit of any present or future Act of the Legislature of Ontario which would allow the Tenant to assign this Lease or sublet the Premises without the Landlord's consent.

2. The consent of the Landlord to any assignment or subletting shall not operate as a waiver of the necessity for consent to any subsequent assignment or subletting.

3. Any consent granted by the Landlord shall be conditional upon the assignee, sublessee or occupant executing a written agreement directly with the Landlord agreeing to be bound by all the terms of this Lease as if the assignee, sublessee or occupant had originally executed this Lease as Tenant.

4. Any consent given by the Landlord to any assignment or other disposition of the Tenant's interest in this Lease or in the Premises shall not relieve the Tenant from his obligations under this Lease, including the obligation to pay Rent and Additional Rent as provided for herein.

5. If the party originally entering into this Lease as Tenant, or any party who subsequently becomes the Tenant by way of assignment or sublease or otherwise as provided for in this Lease, is a corporation then:

(a) the Tenant shall not be entitled to deal with its authorized or issued capital or that of an affiliated company in any way that results in a change in the effective voting control of the Tenant unless the Landlord first consents in writing to the proposed change;

(b) if any change is made in the control of the Tenant corporation without the written consent of the Landlord then the Landlord shall be entitled to treat the Tenant as being in default and to exercise the remedies stipulated in Section 10(2) of this Lease and any other remedies available in law;

(c) the Tenant agrees to make available to the Landlord or his authorized representatives the corporate books and records of the Tenant for inspection at reasonable times.

5. USE

1. During the Term of this Lease the Premises shall not be used for any purpose other than a Dentistry Office without the express consent of the Landlord given in writing. The Landlord covenants and agrees with the Tenant that, during the Term of the Lease, including any renewals thereof, provided the Tenant is not in default, not to lease premises within the plaza in which the Premises are located for use as a family dental practice. For greater certainty, this restriction shall not preclude the Landlord from leasing space for use for specialty practices within the area of dentistry.

2. The Tenant shall not do or permit to be done at the Premises anything which may:

(a) constitute a nuisance;

(b) cause damage to the Premises;

LANDLORD	TENANT

5

(c) cause injury or annoyance to occupants of neighbouring premises;

(d) make void or voidable any insurance upon the Premises; or

(e) constitute a breach of any by-law, statute, order or regulation of any municipal, provincial or other competent authority relating to the Premises.

6. REPAIR AND MAINTENANCE

1. The Tenant covenants that during the term of this Lease and any renewal thereof the Tenant shall keep in good condition the Premises including all alterations and additions made thereto, and shall, with or without notice, promptly make all needed repairs and all necessary replacements as would a prudent owner, but the Tenant shall not be liable to effect repairs attributable to reasonable wear and tear, or to damage caused by fire, lightning or storm.

2. The Tenant shall permit the Landlord or a person authorized by the Landlord to enter the Premises to examine the condition thereof and view the state of repair at reasonable times:

(a) and if upon such examination repairs are found to be necessary, written notice of the repairs required shall be given to the Tenant by or on behalf of the Landlord and the Tenant shall make the necessary repairs within the time specified in the notice;

(b) and if the Tenant refuses or neglects to keep the Premises in good repair the Landlord may, but shall not be obliged to, make any necessary repairs, and shall be permitted to enter the Premises, by himself or his servants or agents, for the purpose of effecting the repairs without being liable to the Tenant for any loss, damage or inconvenience to the Tenant in connection with the Landlords' entry and repairs, and if the Landlord makes repairs the Tenant shall pay the cost of them immediately as Additional Rent.

3. Upon the expiry of the Term or other determination of this Lease the Tenant agrees peaceably to surrender the Premises, including any alterations or additions made thereto, to the Landlord in a state of good repair, reasonable wear and tear and damage by fire, lightning and storm only excepted.

4. The Tenant shall immediately give written notice to the Landlord of any substantial damage that occurs to the Premises from any cause.

7. ALTERATION AND ADDITIONS

1. If the Tenant, during the Term of this Lease or any renewal of it, desires to make any alterations or additions to the Premises, including but not limited to: erecting partitions, attaching equipment, and installing necessary furnishings or additional equipment of the Tenant's business, the Tenant may do so at his own expense, at any time and from time to time, if the following conditions are met:

(a) before undertaking any alteration or addition the Tenant shall submit to the Landlord a plan showing the proposed alterations or additions and items included in the plan which are regarded by the Tenant as "Trade Fixtures" shall be designated as such on the plan, and the Tenant shall not proceed to make any alteration or addition unless the Landlord has approved the plan, in writing, and the Landlord shall not unreasonably or arbitrarily withhold his approval;

LANDLORD	TENANT

6

(b) any and all alterations or additions to the Premises made by the Tenant must comply with all applicable building code standards and by-laws of the municipality in which the Premises are located. Such work shall be performed by competent workers in a good workmanlike manner.

2. The Tenant shall be responsible for and pay the cost of any alterations, additions, installations or improvements that any governing authority, municipal, provincial or otherwise, may require to be made in, on or to the Premises.

3. No sign, advertisement or notice shall be inscribed, painted or affixed by the Tenant, or any other person on the Tenant's behalf, on any part of the inside or outside of the building in which the Premises are located unless the sign, advertisement or notice has been approved, in writing, in every respect by the Landlord, which approval shall not be unreasonably withheld. The sign must comply with all municipal by-laws.

4. All alterations and additions to the Premises made by or on behalf of the Tenant, other than the Tenant's Trade Fixtures, shall immediately become the property of the Landlord without compensation to the Tenant.

5. The Tenant agrees, at his own expense and by whatever means may be necessary, immediately to obtain the release or discharge of any encumbrance that may be registered against the Landlord's property in connection with any additions or alterations to the Premises made by the Tenant or in connection with any other activity of the Tenant.

6. If the Tenant has complied with his obligations according to the provisions of this Lease, the Tenant may remove his Trade Fixtures at the end of the Term or other termination of this Lease and the Tenant covenants that he will make good and repair or replace as necessary any damage caused to the Premises by the removal of the Tenant's Trade Fixtures.

7. Other than as provided in paragraph 7 (6) above, the Tenant shall not, during the Term of this Lease or anytime thereafter remove from the Premises any Trade Fixtures or other goods and chattels of the Tenant except in the following circumstances:

(a) the removal is in the ordinary course of business;

(b) the Trade Fixtures has become unnecessary for the Tenant's business or is being replaced by a new or similar Trade Fixture; or

(c) the Landlord has consented in writing to the removal;

but in any case the Tenant shall make good any damage caused to the Premises by the installation or removal of any Trade Fixtures, equipment, partitions, furnishings and any other objects whatsoever brought onto the Premises by the Tenant.

8. The Tenant shall, at his own expense, if requested by the Landlord, remove any or all additions or improvements made by the Tenant to the Premises during the Term and shall repair all damage caused by the installation or the removal or both.

9. The Tenant shall not bring onto the Premises or any part of the Premises any machinery, equipment or any other thing that might in the opinion the Landlord, by reason of its weight, size or use, damage the Premises or overload the floors of the Premises, and if the Premises are damaged or overloaded the Tenant shall restore the Premises immediately or pay to the Landlord the cost of restoring the Premises.

LANDLORD	TENANT

8. **INSURANCE**

1. During the Term of this Lease and any renewal thereof the Landlord shall maintain with respect to the Premises, insurance coverage insuring against:

(a) loss or damage by fire, lightning, storm and other perils that may cause damage to the Premises or the property of the Landlord in which the Premises are located as are commonly provided for as extended perils coverage or as may be reasonably required and obtained by the Landlord, and the insurance policy shall provide coverage on a replacement cost basis in an amount sufficient to cover the cost of all signs and leasehold improvements;

(b) liability for bodily injury or death or property damage sustained by third parties up to such limits as the Landlord in his sole discretion deems advisable;

(c) rental income protection insurance with respect to fire and other perils to the extent of one year's Rent payable under this Lease;

(d) insurance covering plate glass forming part of the Leased Premises;

but such insurance and any payment of the proceeds thereof to the Landlord shall not relieve the Tenant of its obligations to continue to pay rent during any period of rebuilding, replacement, repairing or restoration of the Premises except as provided in Section 9.

2. The Tenant covenants to keep the Landlord indemnified against all claims and demands whatsoever by any person, whether in respect of damage to person or property, arising out of or occasioned by the maintenance, use or occupancy of the Premises or the subletting or assignment of same or any part thereof. And the Tenant further covenants to indemnify the Landlord with respect to any encumbrance on or damage to the Premises occasioned by or arising from the act, default, or negligence of the Tenant, its officers, agents, servants, employees, contractors, customers, invitees or licensees and the Tenant agrees that the foregoing indemnity shall survive the termination of this Lease notwithstanding any provisions of this Lease to the contrary.

3. The Tenant shall carry insurance in his own name to provide coverage with respect to the risk of business interruption to an extent sufficient to allow the Tenant to meet his ongoing obligations to the Landlord and to protect the Tenant against loss of revenues.

4. The Tenant shall carry insurance in his own name insuring against the risk of damage to the Tenant's property within the Premises caused by fire or other perils and the policy shall provide for coverage on a replacement cost basis to protect the Tenant's stock-in-trade, equipment, Trade Fixtures, decorations and improvements.

5. The Tenant shall carry public liability and property damage insurance in which policy the Landlord shall be a named insured and the policy shall include a cross-liability endorsement. Such insurance shall not be less than Three Million Dollars ($3,000,000.00) per occurrence and Five Million Dollars ($5,000,000.00) in the aggregate for all occurrences within each policy year.

6. The Tenant shall provide the Landlord with a copy of the above policies.

LANDLORD	TENANT

9. DAMAGE TO THE PREMISES

1. If the Premises or the building in which the Premises are located, are damaged or destroyed, in whole or in part, by fire or other peril, then the following provisions shall apply:

(a) if the damage or destruction renders the Premises unfit for occupancy and impossible to repair or rebuild using reasonable diligence within 120 clear days from the happening of such damage or destruction, then the Term hereby granted shall cease from the date the damage or destruction occurred, and the Tenant shall immediately surrender the remainder of the Term and give possession of the Premises to the Landlord, and the Rent from the time of the surrender shall abate;

(b) if the Premises can with reasonable diligence be repaired and rendered fit for occupancy within 120 days from the happening of the damage or destruction, but the damage renders the Premises wholly unfit for occupancy, then the rent hereby reserved shall not accrue after the day that such damage occurred, or while the process of repair is going on, and the Landlord shall repair the Premises with all reasonable speed, and the Tenant's obligation to pay Rent shall resume immediately after the necessary repairs have been completed;

(c) if the leased Premises can be repaired within 120 days as aforesaid, but the damage is such that the leased Premises are capable of being partially used, then until such damage has been repaired, the Tenant shall continue in possession and the Rent shall abate proportionately.

2. Any question as to the degree of damage or destruction or the period of time required to repair or rebuild shall be determined by an architect retained by the Landlord.

3. Apart from the provisions of Section 9(1) there shall be no abatement from or reduction of the Rent payable by the Tenant, nor shall the Tenant be entitled to claim against the Landlord for any damages, general or special, caused by fire, water, sprinkler systems, partial or temporary failure or stoppage of services or utilities which the Landlord is obliged to provide according to this Lease, from any cause whatsoever.

10. ACTS OF DEFAULT AND LANDLORD'S REMEDIES

1. An act of Default has occurred when:

(a) the Tenant has failed to pay Rent for a period of 15 consecutive days, regardless of whether demand for payment has been made or not;

(b) The Tenant has breached his covenants or failed to perform any of his obligations under this Lease; and

i) the Landlord has given notice specifying the nature of the default and the steps required to correct it; and
ii) the Tenant has failed to correct the default as required by the notice;

LANDLORD	TENANT

9

(c) the Tenant has;

i) become bankrupt or insolvent or made an assignment for the benefit of Creditors;
ii) had its property seized or attached in satisfaction of a judgment;
iii) had a receiver appointed;
iv) committed any act or neglected to do anything with the result that a Construction Lien or other encumbrance is registered against the Landlord's property;
v) without the consent of the Landlord, made or entered into an agreement to make a sale of its assets to which the Bulk Sales Act applies;
vi) taken action if the Tenant is a corporation, with a view to winding up, dissolution or liquidation;

(d) any insurance policy is cancelled or not renewed by reason of the use or occupation of the Premises, or by reason of non-payment of premiums;

(e) the Premises;

i) become vacant or remain unoccupied for a period of Fifteen (15) consecutive days; or
ii) are not open for business on more than thirty (30) business days in any twelve (12) month period or on any twelve (12) consecutive business days;
iii) are used by any other person or persons, or for any other purpose than as provided for in this Lease without the written consent of the Landlord.

2. When an Act of Default on the part of the Tenant has occurred:

(a) the current month's rent together with the next three month's rent shall become due and payable immediately; and

(b) the Landlord shall have the right to terminate this Lease and to re-enter the Premises and deal with them as he may choose;

3. If, because an Act of Default has occurred, the Landlord exercises his right to terminate this Lease and re-enter the Premises prior to the end of the Term, the Tenant shall nevertheless be liable for payment of Rent and all other amounts payable by the Tenant in accordance with the provisions of this Lease until the Landlord has re-let the Premises or otherwise dealt with the Premises in such manner that the cessation of payments by the Tenant will not result in loss to the Landlord, and the Tenant agrees to be liable to the Landlord, until the end of the Term of this Lease for payment of any difference between the amount of Rent hereby agreed to be paid for the Term hereby granted and the Rent any new tenant pays to the Landlord.

4. The Tenant covenants that notwithstanding any present or future Act of the Legislature of the Province of Ontario, the personal property of the Tenant during the term of this Lease shall not be exempt from levy by distress for Rent in arrears:

(a) and the Tenant acknowledges that it is upon the express understanding that there should be no such exemption that this Lease is entered into, and by executing this Lease:

i) the Tenant waives the benefit of any such legislative provisions which might otherwise be available to the Tenant in the absence of this agreement; and

LANDLORD	TENANT

ii) the Tenant agrees that the Landlord may plead this covenant as an estoppel against the Tenant if an action is brought to test the Landlord's right to levy distress against the Tenant's property.

5. If, when an Act of Default has occurred, the Landlord chooses not to terminate the Lease and re-enter the Premises, the Landlord shall have the right to take any and all necessary steps to rectify any or all Acts of Default of the Tenant and to charge the costs of such rectification to the Tenant and to recover the costs as Rent.

6. If, when an Act of Default has occurred, the Landlord chooses to waive his right to exercise the remedies available to him under this Lease or at law the waiver shall not constitute condonation of the Act of Default, nor shall the waiver be pleaded as an estoppel against the Landlord to prevent his exercising his remedies with respect to a subsequent Act of Default. No covenant, term, or condition of this Lease shall be deemed to have been waived by the Landlord unless the waiver is in writing and signed by the Landlord.

LANDLORD	TENANT

11. TERMINATION UPON NOTICE AND AT END OF TERM

~~1. If the Landlord desires at any time to remodel or demolish the Premises or any part thereof, to an extent that renders continued possession by the Tenant impracticable, the Tenant shall, upon receiving one hundred and eighty (180) clear days written notice from the Landlord:~~

~~(a) surrender this Lease, including any unexpired remainder of the Term; and~~

(b) ~~vacate the Premises and give the Landlord possession.~~

2. If the Premises are expropriated or condemned by any competent authority:

(a) the Landlord shall have the right to terminate this Lease by giving ninety (90) clear days notice in writing to the Tenant; or

(b) the Landlord may require the Tenant to vacate the Premises within thirty (30) days from payment by the Landlord to the Tenant of a bonus equal to three months' rent, but payment of the said bonus shall be accompanied or preceded by written notice from the Landlord to the Tenant advising of the Landlord's intent to exercise this option.

3. The Tenant agrees to permit the Landlord during the last Twelve months (12) of the Term of this Lease to display "For Rent" or "For Sale" signs or both at the Premises and to show the Premises to prospective new tenants or purchasers and to permit anyone having written authority of the Landlord to view the Premises at reasonable hours.

4. If the Tenant remains in possession of the Premises after termination of this Lease as aforesaid and if the Landlord then accepts rent for the Premises from the Tenant, it is agreed that such overholding by the Tenant and acceptance of Rent by the Landlord shall create a monthly tenancy only but the tenancy shall remain subject to all the terms and conditions of this Lease except those regarding the Term. The Rent Payable for the over-holding period shall be equal to the last full month of the Term plus Twenty-five percent (25%).

LANDLORD	TENANT

11

12. ACKNOWLEDGEMENT BY TENANT

The Tenant agrees that he will at any time or times during the Term, upon being given at least forty-eight (48) hours prior written notice, execute and deliver to the Landlord a statement in writing certifying:

(a) that this Lease is unmodified and is in full force and effect (or if modified stating the modifications and confirming that the Lease is in full force and effect as modified);

(b) the amount of Rent being paid;

(c) the dates to which Rent has been paid;

(d) other charges payable under this Lease which have been paid;

(e) particulars of any prepayment of Rent or security deposits; and

(f) particulars of any subtenancies.

13. SUBORDINATION AND POSTPONEMENT

1. This Lease and all the rights of the Tenant under this Lease are subject and subordinate to any and all charges against the land, buildings or improvements of which the Premises form part, whether the charge is in the nature of a mortgage, trust deed, lien or any other form of charge arising from the financing or re-financing, including extensions or renewals, of the Landlord's interest in the property.

2. Upon the request of the Landlord the Tenant will execute any form required to subordinate this Lease and the Tenant's rights to any such charge, and will, if required, attorn to the holder of the charge.

3. No subordination by the Tenant shall have the effect of permitting the holder of any charge to disturb the occupation and possession of the Premises by the Tenant as long as the Tenant performs his obligations under this Lease.

14. RULES AND REGULATIONS

The Tenant agrees on behalf of itself and all persons entering the Premises with the Tenant's authority or permission to abide by such reasonable rules and regulations that form part of this Lease and as the Landlord may make from time to time.

LANDLORD	TENANT

12

15. NOTICE

1. Any notice required or permitted to be given by one party to the other pursuant to the terms of this Lease may be given

To the Landlord at:

To the Tenant and Guarantors at the Premises or at:

2. The above addresses may be changed at any time by giving ten (10) days written notice.

3. Any notice given by one party to the other in accordance with the provisions of this Lease shall be deemed conclusively to have been received on the date delivered if the notice is served personally or seventy-two (72) hours after mailing if the notice is mailed.

16. REGISTRATION

The Tenant shall not at any time register notice of or a copy of this Lease on title to the property of which the premises form part without consent of the Landlord.

17. INTERPRETATION

1. The words importing the singular number only shall include the plural, and vice versa, and words importing the masculine gender shall include the feminine gender, and words importing persons shall include firms and corporations and vice versa.

2. Unless the context otherwise requires, the word "Landlord" and the word "Tenant" wherever used herein shall be construed to include the executors, administrators, successors and assigns of the Landlord and Tenant, respectively.

3. When there are two or more Tenants bound by the same covenants herein contained, their obligations shall be joint and several.

18. RENEWAL

The Tenant, when not in default, shall have the right to renew its Lease for One (1) further term of Five (5) years, provided that written notice is given to the Landlord not less than One (1) year prior to the expiry of the Term, on the same terms and conditions as herein contained save for the rental rate and save for any further Right to Renew and save for any free rent, allowances, credits, Landlord's Work or other inducements provided to the Tenant. The rental for the renewal shall be determined based upon fair market rent for premises of similar size, type and location. If the parties are unable to agree as to the base rent for the renewal term within two-hundred and seventy (270) days after the exercise of the option herein by the Tenant, then this Lease shall become void and the Landlord shall have the right to re-lease the Premises.

LANDLORD	TENANT

If the Tenant fails to exercise its Right to Renew within the period provided the Right to Renew shall be forever extinguished.

19. POST-DATED CHEQUES

The Tenant will, at the option of the Landlord, on the execution of the Lease, provide the Landlord with post-dated cheques to cover Basic Rent and Additional Rent inclusive of G.S.T. for the first year of the Term of the Lease. Thereafter the Tenant shall, upon the anniversary date of the Lease Term, provide post-dated cheques for the monthly said rents due in that year.

20. SECURITY RENTAL DEPOSIT

The Tenant shall submit to the Landlord the sum of ONE THOUSAND FOUR HUNDRED AND SEVENTY-NINE DOLLARS and EIGHTY-SEVEN CENTS ($1,479.87) representing Basic Rent, Additional Rent and G.S.T. to be credited towards the last month of the Term.

In Witness of the foregoing covenants the Landlord, Tenant have executed this Lease.

SIGN, SEALED AND DELIVERED in the presence of) LANDLORD

Per:____________________ Date

____________________ Witness

Per:____________________ Date

14

SCHEDULE "A"

To Lease made between

(the "Landlord")

- and -

DESCRIPTION OF THE LEASED PREMISES

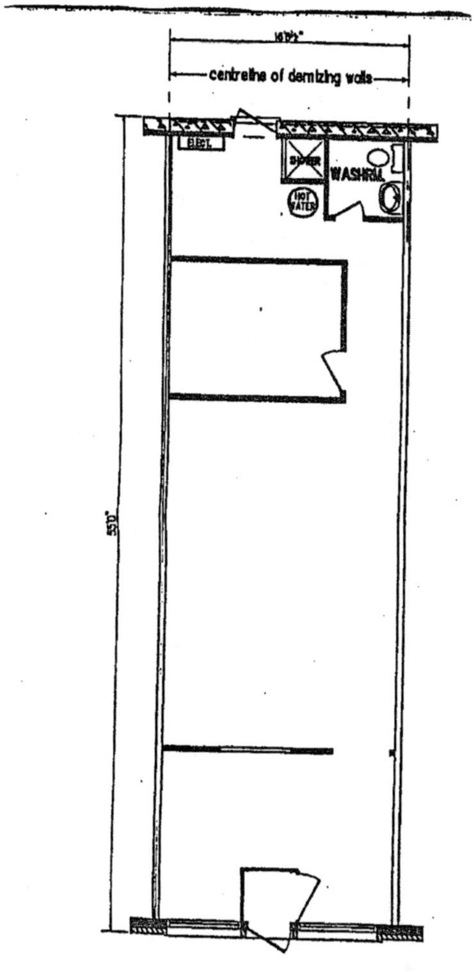

RENTABLE AREA = 55' x 16'–8 1/2" = 920 S.F.

LANDLORD	TENANT

15

SCHEDULE "B"

LANDLORD'S WORK

NONE

TENANT'S WORK

All further work necessary to make the premises suitable for the use and purpose for which the premises were leased, including the following responsibilities of the Tenant:

1. Plans and Specifications

The Tenant shall submit to the Landlord, for the Landlord's approval, plans and specifications of all the Tenant's work and improvements.

The Tenant shall not proceed with its work until the Landlord shall have given the written approval thereof.

2. Compliance with Governmental Authorities

The Tenant shall apply for and secure all Permits/Inspections and passing of work and shall in all respects comply with Building, Fire Codes, and with orders of those having jurisdiction. Such permits will include "building Permit" and "Occupancy Permit".

The Tenant shall submit copies of all permits to the Landlord before commencement of work or occupancy, as the case may be.

In no case shall work commence before issuance of a Building Permit and the submission of a copy thereof to the Landlord.

The Landlord shall not be liable for damages due to delays encountered by the Tenant in compliance with the requirements herein.

NOTE

Any cutting through the roof deck and roof membrane must be arranged through the Landlord, to be arranged by and supervised by the Landlord's representative.

LANDLORD	TENANT

16

SCHEDULE "C"

ACKNOWLEDGEMENT OF COMMENCEMENT DATE OF LEASE

I/We hereby acknowledge that I/We took possession of the Leased Premises, . .
on the 15th March, 1999 and the commencement date of the Lease was on the 1st day of April, 1999 as herein set out.

AT THIS 15th DAY OF MARCH, 1999

TENANT

LANDLORD	TENANT

SCHEDULE "D"

RULES AND REGULATIONS

1. Loading and Unloading

The Tenant agrees that all loading and unloading of supplies, materials, fixtures and other chattels shall be made only through or by means of such doorways and corridors and during such days and hours as the Landlord shall designate in writing from time to time.

2. Delivery of Merchandise

The delivery and shipping of supplies, materials, fixtures and other chattels to and from the Leased Premises shall be subject to such rules and regulations as in the judgement of the Landlord are necessary for the property operation of the Leased Premises and the Property.

3. Care of Interior of Leased Premises

The Tenant agrees to keep the interior of the Leased Premises orderly and tidy and to keep the Leased Premises reasonably clean and free from debris, garbage, trash and refuse. The Tenant shall only contract for janitorial service with a janitorial contractor approved by the Landlord in writing.

4. Defacing Leased Premises

The Tenant shall not mark, paint, drill or in any way deface any walls, ceilings, partitions, floors, wood, stone or iron, of or in the Leased Premises, without the written consent of the Landlord.

5. Annoyance To Other Tenants

The Tenant shall not permit the Leased Premises to be used in such a manner as will cause annoyance to other tenants of the Property.

6. Restrictions on Locks

(1) The Tenant shall not install or permit the installation of any additional lock, bolt, fastening or other security device on any door of the Leased Premises without the written consent of the Landlord.

(2) The Tenant shall not change or permit the change of any lock, bolt, fastening, or other security device on any door of the Leased Premises without the written consent of the Landlord.

7. Surrender of Keys on Termination of Lease

Upon the termination of this Lease, the Tenant shall surrender forthwith to the Landlord all keys with respect to the Leased Premises.

8. Overloading of Floors

The Tenant shall not permit any floor of the Leased Premises to be overloaded.

9. Safes and Other Heavy Objects

The Tenant shall not permit any safe, other heavy object, or anything liable to injure or destroy any part of the Leased Premises or the building in which the Leased Premises are situated, to be moved therein or taken therefrom without the written consent of the Landlord. Any permitted moving shall be done under the Landlord's direction, and at such times, by such means, and by such persons as the Landlord shall have approved.

10. Obstruction of Plumbing and Washroom Facilities

The Tenant agrees that it will not use or permit its employees, agents or invitees to use the plumbing or washroom facilities of the Leased Premises or the building in which the Leased Premises are situated, for any purpose other than that for which they were constructed and no foreign substance of any kind shall be thrown therein, and the expense of any breakage, stoppage or damage resulting from a violation of this provision shall be borne by the Tenant.

LANDLORD	TENANT

11. Radio and Television

(1) The Tenant shall not erect or cause to be erected any aerial on the roof or exterior walls of the Leased Premises without the Landlord's prior written approval.

12. Advertising Displays and Devices

The Landlord shall have the right to rule on all advertising displays and devices of the Tenant which may b seen or heard outside the Leased Premises, and any such display or device which is deemed objectionable by the Landlord in its sole discretion shall be forthwith discontinued and removed by the Tenant at the request of the Landlord or the Landlord's Manager of the Property.

13. Telephone Connections and Wiring

The Tenant shall not permit the installation of any telephone or telegraphic connections or electric wiring in the Leased Premises in places other than those designated by the Landlord, unless the Tenant first obtains the written consent of the Landlord. Where such consent is obtained the connections or writing, or both, shall be installed in accordance with the Landlord's direction as to location and manner of installation.

14. Overloading of Electrical Facilities

If the Tenant installs any electrical equipment in or about the Leased Premises which overloads the electrical facilities thereof or of the Property, the Tenant shall forthwith at its expense make whatever changes are necessary to comply with the requirements of the insurance underwriters or government authorities having jurisdiction, but no changes shall be made by the Tenant until the Tenant first submits to the Landlord plans and specifications for such changes and obtains the Landlords' written approval to make the same.

15. Tenant to Permit Service Installations

The Tenant shall permit any person authorised by the Landlord to use, install, maintain, and/or repair, pipes, wires, ducts, or other installations in, under, over, or through the Leased Premises for or in connection with the supply of any services to the Leased Premises or any other premises or building in the Property. Such services shall include, without limiting the generality of the foregoing, gas, electricity, water, sanitation, telephone, music, heat, ventilation and air-conditioning.

16. Maintenance of Temperature in Leased Premises

The Tenant shall keep the Leased Premises at a temperature sufficiently high to prevent freezing in the pipes and fixtures therein.

17. Noises, Vibrations and Odours

The Tenant shall not use or permit any part of the Leased Premises to be used in such manner as to cause or permit objectionable noises or vibrations or offensive odours. The Tenant agrees that the Landlord shall have the right to determine in its sole discretion if any such state or condition exists.

18. Pest Extermination

The Tenant shall, at its expense, use such pest-extermination contractors for the Leased Premises as the Landlord may direct and at such intervals as the Landlord may require.

19. Restriction on Use of Leased Premises

The Tenant shall not use the Leased Premises for cooking (except with the Landlord's prior written consent), or for sleeping or other residential purposes, or for the storage of personal effects or articles other than those it requires in connection with its business.

20. Restrictions on Dangerous Materials

The Tenant shall not keep or use, in or upon the Leased Premises anything of a dangerous, inflammable or explosive nature.

LANDLORD	TENANT

19

21. Notices by Tenant in Case of Fire or Accident

The Tenant shall give immediate notice to the Landlord or to the Landlord's representative in case of fire or accident in the Leased Premises or in the building in which the Leased Premises are situated, or in case of defects therein or in any fixtures or equipment thereof, notwithstanding that the Landlord may have no obligations with respect thereto.

22. Debris, Garbage, Trash and Refuse

(1) No debris, garbage, trash or refuse shall be placed or left, or be permitted to be placed or left, in, on or upon any part of the property outside of the Leased Premises, but shall be removed daily by the Tenant or as often as the Landlord deems necessary. If any of such items are of a perishable nature, they shall be kept property refrigerated in equipment provided by the Tenant at its expense. If the Landlord provides garbage facilities and removal service then the Tenant shall pay such charges or, it's proportionate share of such charges.

(2) The Tenant shall not burn any debris, garbage, trash, or refuse of any kind in or about the Leased Premises.

23. Parking

The Tenant shall furnish the Landlord with the licence numbers of the Tenant's car or cars and cars of the Tenant's employees within five (5) days after the date of commencement of this Lease and shall thereafter notify the Landlord of any changes within three (3) days after such changes occur.

24. Restrictions on Vending Machines, Etc.

The Tenant shall not without the prior written consent of the Landlord,

(a) permit in the Leased Premises any machine vending or dispensing food or beverages, or any coin-operated telephone, or

(b) permit food or beverages to be brought to the Leased Premises except by such means, at such times and by such persons as the Landlord may authorise from time to time.

25. Shared H.V.A.C. Service (where applicable)

Tenant acknowledges and agrees that where a Tenant shares a zone of air-conditioning and heating with one or more tenants and that the zone is controlled by only one thermostat which has been set by the Landlord an may be re-set by the Landlord in its sole discretion from time to time during the term of the Lease. Tenant agrees to co-operate with other tenants within the zone to maximize the comfort levels of all who share the zone. Tenant will direct any problems with the temperature setting directly to the Landlord or its representative.

Landlord shall determine the setting of all zones as nearly as possible within a range of 68 to 74 degrees and Tenant agrees to abide by that setting. Tenant will not adjust, tamper with, or otherwise handle the thermostat or any other part of the air-conditioning and heating system, and will indemnify Landlord from loss, liability and expense (including attorney's fees and court costs) if it does. Any disagreement with regard to temperature set as nearly as possible within the above range will not entitle the tenant to withhold rent or to void or terminate the lease or to assert any claim of any kind against Landlord.

26. Interpretation

In these Rules and Regulations the word "Tenant" shall include, where the context allows, the employees, agents, invitees, concessionaires, licensees and sub-tenants of the Tenant, and all others over whom the Tenant might reasonably be expected to exercise control.

27. Pets

Tenant shall not bring into the Premises any pets or animals, nor shall the Tenant permit or allow any person, invitee, customer to bring into the Premises any pet or animal.

LANDLORD	TENANT

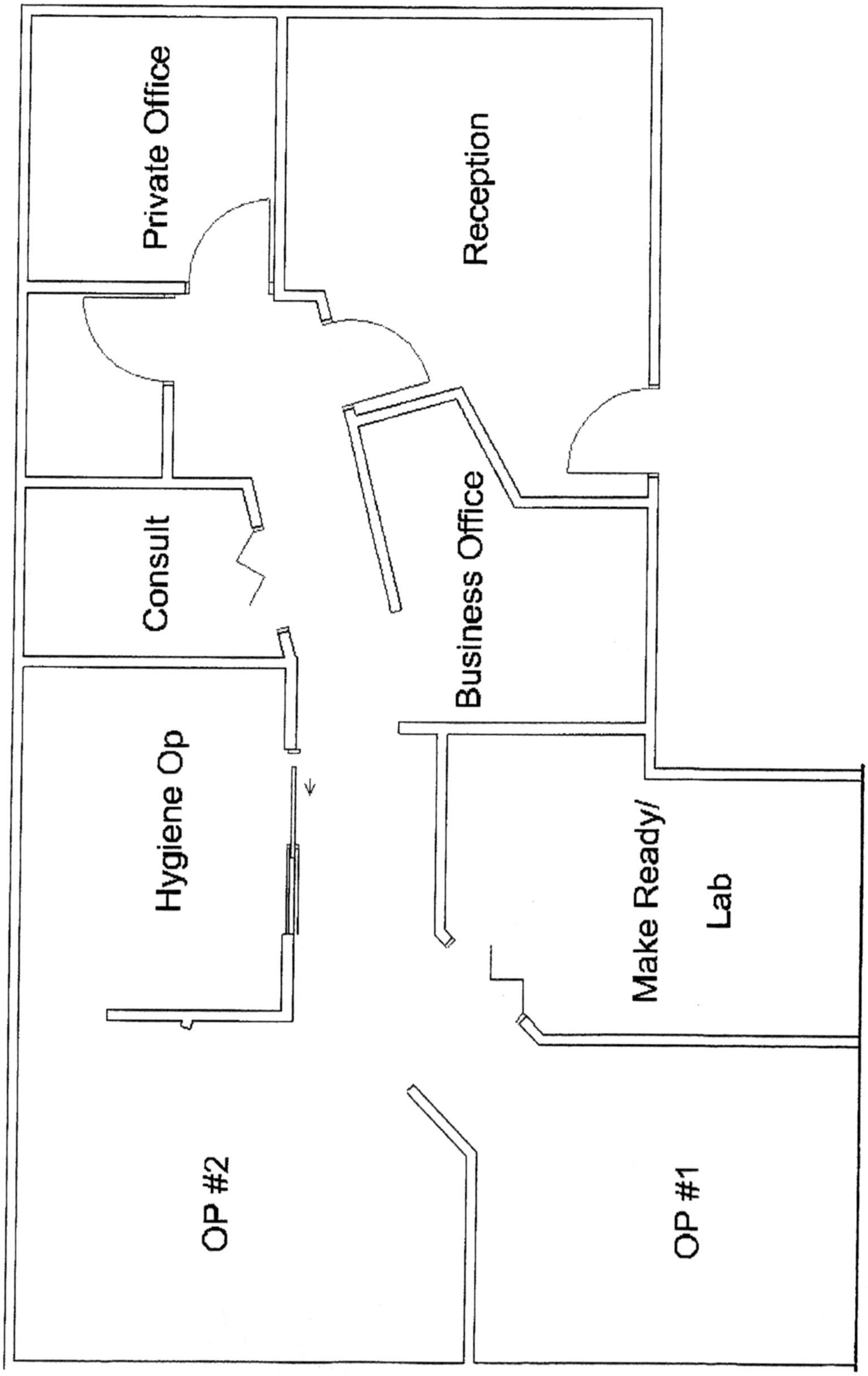
Private Office
Reception
Consult
Business Office
Hygiene Op
Make Ready/
Lab
OP #2
OP #1

PHOTOGRAPHS

Scanned Photographs are for Sample Purposes Only
They do not reflect the equipment & furniture listed in this appraisal

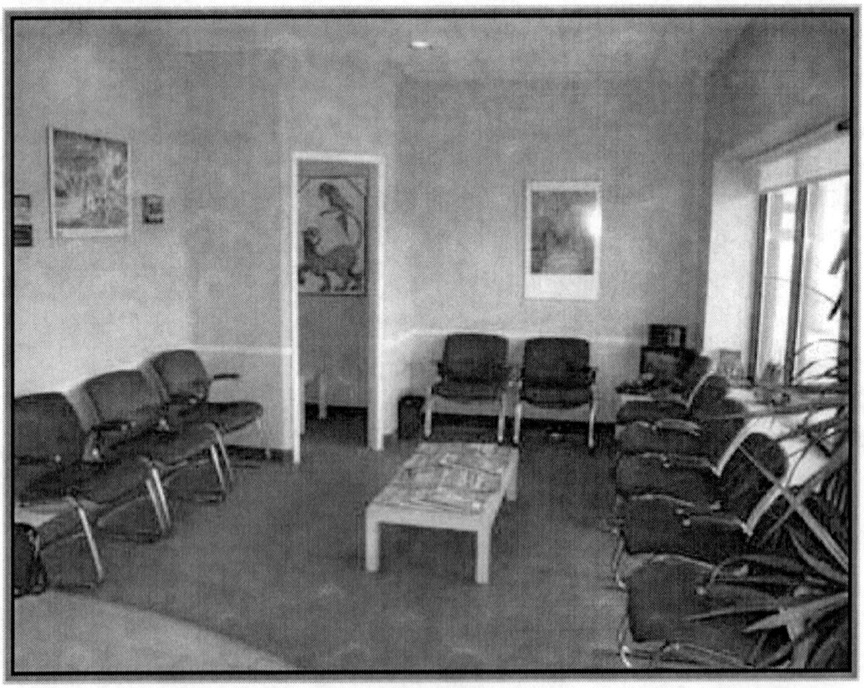

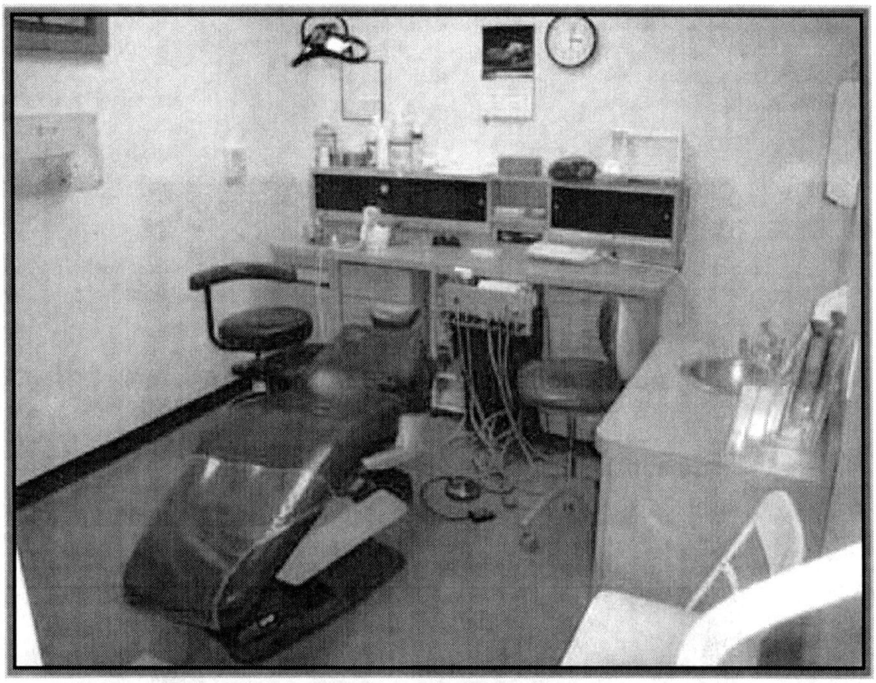

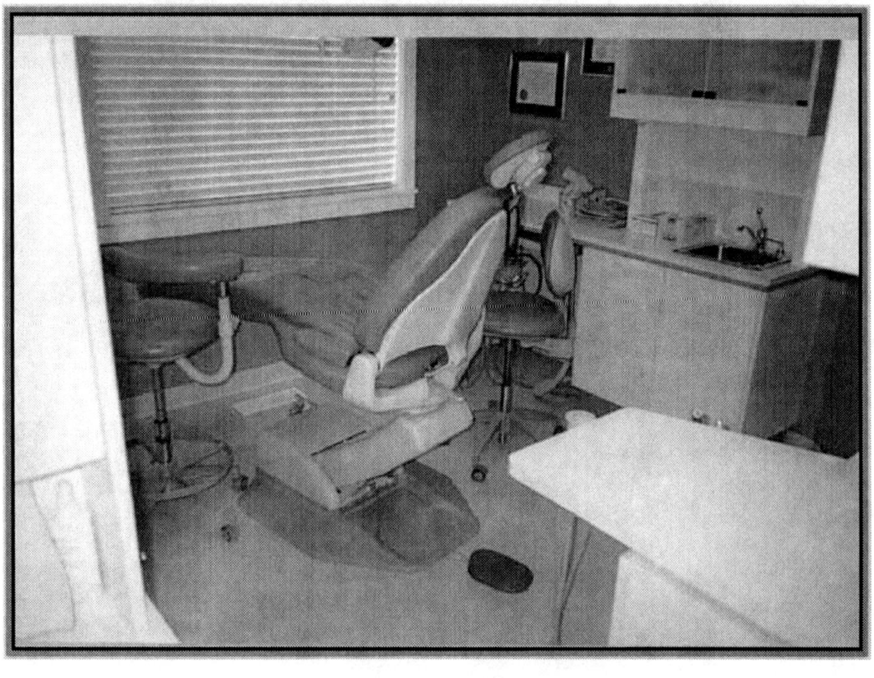

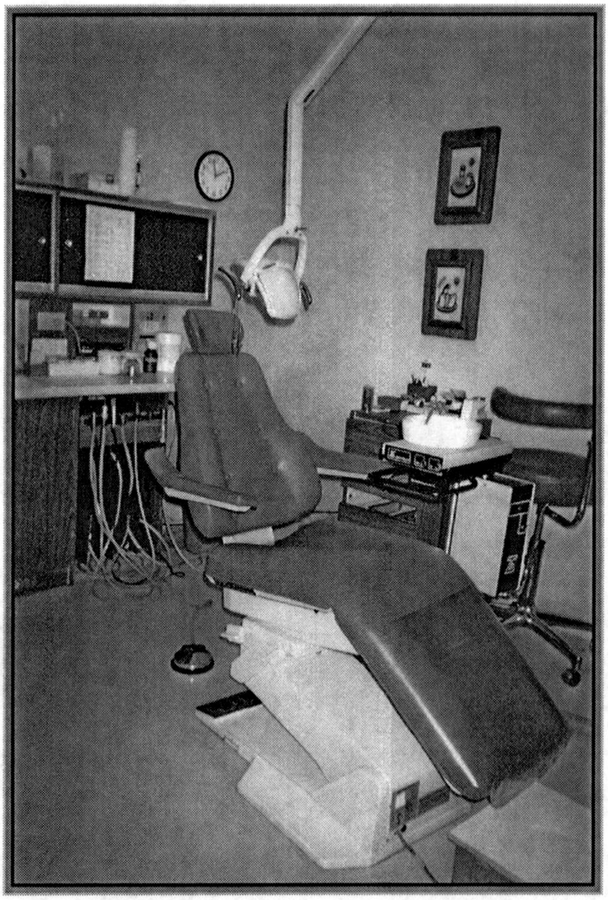

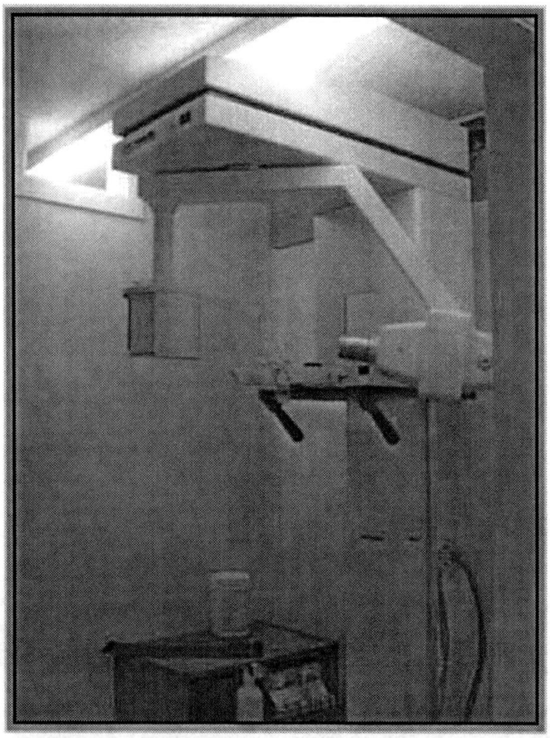

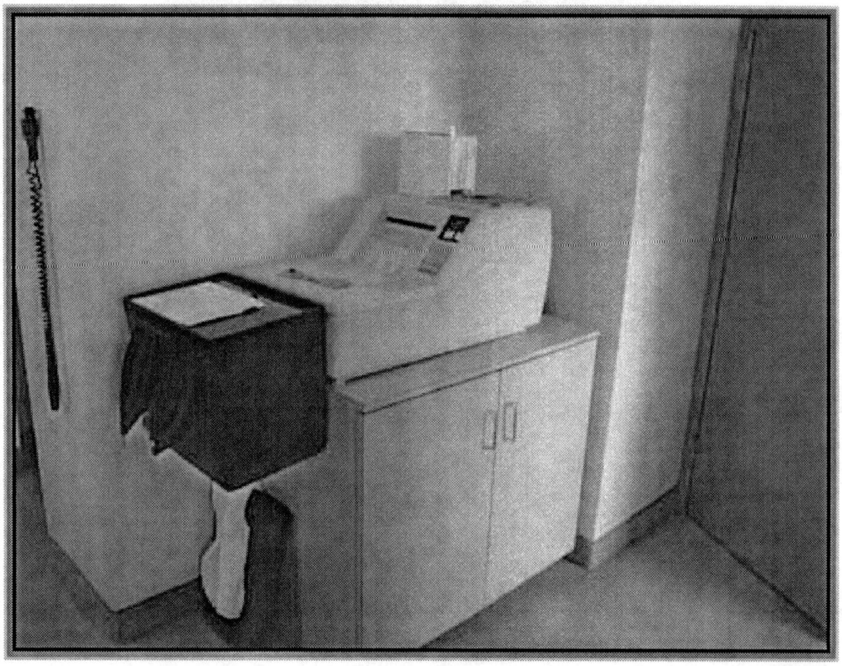

DEMOGRAPHICS

The Demographics do not correspond to this Appraisal

(City)
Vancouver CMA

In Greater Vancouver Regional District.

Population

July 1, 2007 Estimate	607,151
% Cdn. Total	1.85
% Change, '01 -'07	6.81
Avg. Annual Growth Rate, '01-'07, %	1.10
2009 Projected Population	617,837
2012 Projected Population	633,875
2007 Households Estimate	269,036
2009 Projected Households	277,374
2012 Projected Households	289,896

Income

% Above/Below National Average	+12
2007 Total Income Estimate $	19,566,420,000
% Cdn. Total	2.07
2007 Average Hhld. Income $	72,700
2007 Per Capita $	32,200
% 2007 Hhlds., Income $100,000+	16.87
2009 Projected Total Income $	21,686,430,000
2012 Projected Total Income $	25,052,120,000

Retail Sales

% Above/Below National Average	+11
2007 Retail Sales Estimate $	8,294,350,000
% Cdn. Total	2.05
2007 per Household $	30,800
2007 per Capita $	13,700
2007 No. of Establishments	5,238
2009 Projected Retail Sales $	9,212,400,000
2012 Projected Retail Sales $	10,932,340,000

Population

2007 Estimates:

Total	607,151
Male	301,048
Female	306,103

Age Groups	*Male*	*Female*
0-4	11,681	11,073
5-9	12,661	12,267
10-14	14,902	14,317
15-19	17,575	16,932
20-24	23,460	22,545
25-29	26,601	25,999
30-34	26,391	26,102
35-39	27,282	26,933
40-44	26,386	25,526
45-49	25,093	24,578
50-54	21,787	22,039
55-59	19,076	19,155
60-64	14,389	14,520
65-69	10,268	10,771
70+	23,496	33,346

Daytime Population

2007 Estimates:

Working Population	399,908
At Home Population	259,254
Total	659,162

Income

2007 Estimates:

Avg. Household Income $	72,728
Avg. Family Income $	86,759
Per Capita Income $	32,227
Avg. Employment Income Male $	49,506
Avg. Employment Income Male (Full Time) $	66,490
Avg. Employment Income Female $	35,290
Avg. Employment Income Female (Full Time) $	48,634

Disposable & Discretionary Income

2007 Estimates:

Disposable Income per Hhld. $	53,200
Discretionary Income per Hhld. $	16,269

2005 Estimates:

Equity Investments per Hhld. $	106,989
Interest Bearing Investments per Hhld. $	84,678
Total Liquid Assets per Hhld. $	191,667
Total Liabilities per Hhld. $	109,160

Labour Force

2007 Estimates:	*Male*	*Female*
In the Labour Force	182,010	165,887
Participation Rate	70.5	62.8
Employed	171,879	156,578
Unemployed	10,131	9,309
Unemployment Rate	5.6	5.6
Not in Labour Force	76,219	98,463

Occupations by Major Groups

2007 Estimates:	*Male*	*Female*
Management	25,091	14,528
Business, Finance & Admin.	21,523	41,951
Natural & Applied Sci. & Rel'd.	22,281	6,060
Health	6,016	13,273
Social Sci., Gov't Serv's & Relig'n	7,770	10,427
Education	6,034	8,970
Arts, Culture, Recr'n & Sport	11,327	10,359
Sales & Service	41,164	45,896
Trades, Transp. & Equip. Ops. etc.	25,304	2,668
Primary Industries	2,599	677
Processing, Mfg. & Utilities	8,183	7,206

Level of Schooling

2007 Estimates:

Population 20 years +	488,072
Less than Grade 9	44,459
Grades 9-13 w/o Certif.	59,867
Grade 9-13 with Certif.	46,929
Trade Certif. /Dip.	36,530
Non-Univ. w/o Certif./Dip.	30,595
Non-Univ. with Certif./Dip.	71,564
Univ. w/o Degree	51,518
Univ. w/o Degree/Certif.	33,148
Univ. with Certif.	18,370
Univ. with Degree	146,610

Average Household Expenditures

2007 Estimates:

Food $	8,258
Shelter $	13,832
Clothing $	3,013
Transportation $	8,312
Health & Personal Care $	2,841
Recr'n, Read'g & Education $	6,117
Taxes & Securities $	18,309
Other $	8,853
Total Expenditures $	69,536

Private Households

2007 Estimates:

Private Households, Total	269,036
Pop. in Private Households	599,480
Avg. No. per Household	2.2

Families

2007 Estimates:

Families in Private Households	141,815
Husband-Wife Families	117,566
Lone-Parent Families	24,249
Avg. No. Persons per Family	2.9
Avg. No. Sons/Daughters at Home	1.1

Housing

2007 Estimates:

Occupied Private Dwellings	269,036
Owned	117,759
Rented	151,277
Single-Detached House	74,513
Semi-Detached House	4,456
Row Houses	8,312
Apartment, 5+ Storeys	58,544
Owned Apartment, 5+ Storeys	15,258
Apartment, Fewer than 5 Storeys	90,882
Apartment, Detached Duplex	31,509
Other Single-Attached	564
Movable Dwellings	256

Financial Post

(City)

Vehicles

2005 NVR ('05 YE)	21,370
'03-'05 Model Yrs VOR (July '04)	39,895
% '03-'05 Total VOR (July '04)	14.69
'81-'02 Model Yrs VOR (July '04)	231,662
% '81-'02 Total VOR (July '04)	85.31
Total VOR (July '04)	271,557

NVR = New Vehicles Registered.
VOR = Vehicles on the Road.

Marital Status

2007 Estimates (Age 15+):

Single (never married)	174,473
Married (legal & common-law)	275,631
Separated (legally married)	15,717
Widowed	30,191
Divorced	34,238

PSYTE Categories

2007 Estimates:

	No. of Hhlds.	% Total	Index
Canadian Elite	1,996	0.74	102
Professional Duets	244	0.09	13
Asian Heights	22,847	8.49	899
Urban Gentry	84	0.03	2
Young Technocrats	16,276	6.05	587
Family Crossroads	10,678	3.97	262
Row House Streets	3,002	1.12	185
University Enclaves	12,950	4.81	215
Town and Country	547	0.20	9
Urban Promise	3,678	1.37	62
South Asian Corners	2,039	0.76	223
Workers' Landing	4,886	1.82	326
Pacific Fusion	63,312	23.53	3,285
Sushi and Shiraz	70,284	26.12	1,497
Hi-Rise Sunsets	5,776	2.15	130
New Canada Neighbours	186	0.07	13
Senior Town	1,192	0.44	90
Urban Vibe	326	0.12	18
Blue Collar Stride	6,738	2.50	107
Elder Harbour	1,071	0.40	13
Hi-Rise Melting Pot	662	0.25	30
Service Crew	26,682	9.92	404
Blues in Motion	12,434	4.62	181
Quebec Seniors	315	0.12	15
Metro Medley	831	0.31	39

Financ¢ial P$YTE

2007 Estimates:

	No. of Hhlds.	% Total	Index
Platinum Domain	9,664	3.59	498
Savvy Investors	1,183	0.44	29
Upper Middle Amenities	9,654	3.59	160
Kids and Credit	32,805	12.19	311
Frugal Families	1,192	0.44	15
Cautious Consumer	67,474	25.08	694
Quiet Neighbours	326	0.12	0
High Rise Low Liquidity	84,879	31.55	590
Just Checking	4,837	1.80	11
New Beginnings	57,022	21.19	157

2007 Estimates:

English	323,254	53.92
French	1,549	0.26
Chinese	86,292	14.39
Croatian	335	0.06
German	366	0.06
Greek	397	0.07
Gujarati	444	0.07
Hindi	1,284	0.21
Italian	1,501	0.25
Japanese	2,357	0.39
Korean	2,850	0.48
Persian (Farsi)	1,478	0.25
Polish	632	0.11
Portuguese	929	0.15
Punjabi	6,961	1.16
Romanian	383	0.06
Russian	1,074	0.18
Serbian	784	0.13
Serbo-Croatian	440	0.07
Spanish	2,422	0.40
Tagalog (Pilipino)	3,148	0.53
Tamil	575	0.10
Vietnamese	7,157	1.19
Other languages	9,056	1.51
Multiple responses	143,812	23.99
Total	599,480	100.00

Building Permits

	2005	2004	2003
Value $000	1,589,593	1,603,022	1,011,136

Housing Starts

	2005	2004	2003
No.	4,155	5,715	4,571

Vital Statistics

	2005	2004	2003	2002
Births	n.a.	n.a.	5,621	5,553
Deaths	n.a.	n.a.	3,671	3,844
Natural Increase	n.a.	n.a.	1,950	1,709
Marriages	n.a.	n.a.	n.a.	3,479

Note: Latest available data.

MEDIA INFO

see Vancouver, CMA

FP Markets - Canadian Demographics 2007 565

British Columbia

Population

July 1, 2007 Estimate	4,357,521
% Cdn. Total	13.27
% Change, '01 -'07	7.04
Avg. Annual Growth Rate, '01-'07, %	1.14
2009 Projected Population	4,451,165
2012 Projected Population	4,591,677
2007 Households Estimate	1,767,977
2009 Projected Households	1,823,818
2012 Projected Households	1,907,482

Income

% Above/Below National Average	-1
2007 Total Income Estimate $	123,702,310,000
% Cdn. Total	13.08
2007 Average Hhld. Income $	70,000
2007 Per Capita $	28,400
% 2007 Hhlds., Income $100,000+	18.29
2009 Projected Total Income $	135,857,200,000
2012 Projected Total Income $	155,092,270,000

Retail Sales

% Above/Below National Average	+3
2007 Retail Sales Estimate $	55,506,500,000
% Cdn. Total	13.73
2007 per Household $	31,400
2007 per Capita $	12,700
2007 No. of Establishments	32,434
2009 Projected Retail Sales $	61,027,200,000
2012 Projected Retail Sales $	71,595,970,000

Population

2007 Estimates:

Total		4,357,521
Male		2,160,224
Female		2,197,297
Age Groups	*Male*	*Female*
0-4	108,140	102,737
5-9	113,931	107,752
10-14	131,004	123,683
15-19	142,711	135,855
20-24	158,695	150,457
25-29	151,950	147,394
30-34	144,227	145,737
35-39	157,371	160,378
40-44	170,302	172,608
45-49	177,304	180,681
50-54	165,035	169,475
55-59	146,558	148,246
60-64	114,200	116,968
65-69	84,661	88,171
70+	194,135	247,155

Daytime Population

2007 Estimates:

Working Population	2,212,987
At Home Population	1,983,454
Total	4,196,441

Income

2007 Estimates:

Avg. Household Income $	69,968
Avg. Family Income $	78,470
Per Capita Income $	28,388
Avg. Employment Income Male $	46,218
Avg. Employment Income Male (Full Time) $	60,781
Avg. Employment Income Female $	29,582
Avg. Employment Income Female (Full Time) $	43,174

Disposable & Discretionary Income

2007 Estimates:

Disposable Income per Hhld. $	51,536
Discretionary Income per Hhld. $	15,519

Liquid Assets

2005 Estimates:

Equity Investments per Hhld. $	105,964
Interest Bearing Investments per Hhld. $	91,819
Total Liquid Assets per Hhld. $	197,783
Total Liabilities per Hhld. $	105,144

In the Labour Force	1,260,798	1,113,269
Participation Rate	70.8	60.6
Employed	1,187,271	1,048,318
Unemployed	73,527	64,951
Unemployment Rate	5.8	5.8
Not in Labour Force	520,388	723,655

Average Weekly Earnings

(Including overtime, industrial aggregate)

	British Columbia	*Canada*
Apr 2006 $	746.83	748.94
Apr 2005 $	709.80	721.66
Apr 2004 $	698.85	707.12
Apr 2003 $	681.93	686.04
Apr 2002 $	672.41	677.47

Number of Employees

(Industrial aggregate)

Apr 2006	1,765,700
Apr 2005	1,718,216
Apr 2004	1,672,153
Apr 2003	1,644,231
Apr 2002	1,596,016

Manufacturing Industries

	2004	*2003*
Employees	149,449	151,930
Salaries, Wages $000	6,998,574	6,830,617
Materials & Supplies $000	21,901,760	20,823,193
Total Revenue $000	42,807,983	39,064,612

Occupations by Major Groups

2007 Estimates:	*Male*	*Female*
Management	164,544	89,279
Business, Finance & Admin.	106,959	302,922
Natural & Applied Sci. & Rel'd	115,743	26,644
Health	28,202	92,758
Social Sci., Gov't Serv's & Relig'n	33,100	65,251
Education	30,751	54,128
Arts, Culture, Recr'n & Sport	37,032	39,573
Sales & Service	251,237	342,806
Trades, Transp. & Equip. Ops. etc.	314,119	20,156
Primary Industries	72,231	24,867
Processing, Mfg. & Utilities	82,405	27,908

Level of Schooling

2007 Estimates:

Population 20 years +	3,339,798
Less than Grade 9	215,842
Grades 9-13 w/o Certif.	588,397
Grade 9-13 with Certif.	411,108
Trade Certif. /Dip.	428,494
Non-Univ. w/o Certif./Dip.	240,633
Non-Univ. with Certif./Dip.	560,113
Univ. w/o Degree	306,460
Univ. w/o Degree/Certif.	194,835
Univ. with Certif.	111,625
Univ. with Degree	588,751

Retail Sales

	2005	*2004*
New Car Dealers $m	9,309	8,875
Used & Recreational Motor Vehicle & Parts $m	1,698	1,797
Gasoline Stations $m	5,555	4,759
Furniture $m	1,130	1,042
Home Furnishings $m	754	669
Computer & Software $m	224	221
Home Electronics & Appliance $m	1,657	1,554
Home Centres & Hardware $m	2,232	2,014
Specialized Building Materials & Garden $m	707	747
Supermarkets $m	9,227	8,941
Convenience & Specialty Food $m	1,012	875
Beer, Wine & Liquor $m	2,412	2,282
Pharmacies & Personal Care $m	2,806	2,753
Clothing $m	2,097	1,993
Shoe, Clothing Accessories & Jewellery $m	635	624
General Merchandise $m	5,415	5,117
Sporting Goods, Hobby, Music & Book $m	1,550	1,487
Miscellaneous Store Retailers $m	1,496	1,467
Total $m	49,915	47,217

Food $	7,510
Shelter $	13,425
Clothing $	2,684
Transportation $	8,916
Health & Personal Care $	2,816
Recr'n, Read'g & Education $	5,561
Taxes & Securities $	17,258
Other $	9,402
Total Expenditures $	67,579

Private Households

2007 Estimates:

Private Households, Total	1,767,977
Pop. in Private Households	4,305,051
Avg. No. per Household	2.4

Families

2007 Estimates:

Families in Private Households	1,136,770
Husband-Wife Families	958,835
Lone-Parent Families	177,935
Avg. No. Persons per Family	2.9
Avg. No. Sons/Daughters at Home	1.1

Housing

2007 Estimates:

Occupied Private Dwellings	1,767,977
Owned	1,171,600
Rented	588,521
Band Housing	7,856
Single-Detached House	966,841
Semi-Detached House	53,536
Row Houses	114,069
Apartment, 5+ Storeys	116,749
Owned Apartment, 5+ Storeys	41,109
Apartment, Fewer than 5 Storeys	349,394
Apartment, Detached Duplex	113,702
Other Single-Attached	4,089
Movable Dwellings	49,597

Vehicles

2005 NVR ('05 YE)	185,488
'03-'05 Model Yrs VOR (July '04)	283,808
% '03-'05 Total VOR (July '04)	12.11
'81-'02 Model Yrs VOR (July '04)	2,059,384
% '81-'02 Total VOR (July '04)	87.89
Total VOR (July '04)	2,343,192

NVR = New Vehicles Registered.
VOR = Vehicles on the Road.

Marital Status

2007 Estimates (Age 15+):

Single (never married)	1,049,975
Married (legal & common-law)	2,066,674
Separated (legally married)	108,947
Widowed	208,738
Divorced	235,940

PSYTE Categories

2007 Estimates:

	No. of Hhlds.	*% Total*	*Index*
Canadian Elite	8,333	0.47	65
Suburban Affluence	1,874	0.11	19
Exurban Estates	6,922	0.39	97
Professional Duets	244	0.01	2
Family Comfort	14,151	0.80	47
Commuter Homesteads	18,796	1.06	108
Euro Traditionals	783	0.04	6
Primary Pursuits	9,714	0.55	62
Towns with Tempo	1,175	0.07	5
Suburban Growth	12,897	0.73	52
Asian Heights	72,262	4.09	433
Urban Gentry	10,817	0.61	30
Cruising Commuters	13,270	0.75	44
Bicycles and Bookbags	13,488	0.76	57
Young Technocrats	16,526	0.93	91
Exurban Wave	23,669	1.34	74
Family Crossroads	115,395	6.53	431
Row House Streets	22,288	1.26	209
University Enclaves	90,309	5.11	228
Upbeat Blues	482	0.03	3
Town and Country	276,761	15.65	660
Satellite Suburbs	12,635	0.71	38
Urban Promise	32,227	1.82	82
South Asian Corners	22,142	1.25	368
Conservative Homebodies	2,859	0.16	8
Agrarian Heartland	17,922	1.0	55

518 Financial Post

PSYTE Categories *(Continued)*

2007 Estimates:

	No. of Hhlds.	*% Total*	*Index*
\orthern Lights	11,623	0.66	134
/illage Views	6,862	0.39	20
Norkers' Landing	21,473	1.21	218
\lew Frontier Families	21,207	1.20	70
²acific Fusion	93,639	5.30	739
/illage Blues	8,607	0.49	13
Sushi and Shiraz	71,474	4.04	232
⁴i-Rise Sunsets	67,984	3.85	232
\lew Canada Neighbours	186	0.01	2
Senior Town	11,184	0.63	129
Suburban Hi-Rise	5,756	0.33	42
⁴ighland Havens	232,205	13.13	568
Jrban Vibe	6,457	0.37	53
)pen Country	2,151	0.12	14
Middletown Mix	5,963	0.34	14
Cabins and Cottages	24,790	1.40	77
3lue Collar Stride	15,181	0.86	37
²eaceful Pastures	2,838	0.16	5
Elder Harbour	90,014	5.09	170
⁴i-Rise Melting Pot	11,160	0.63	77
Second City Renters	69,919	3.95	209
Service Crew	104,665	5.92	241
First Peoples	5,440	0.31	42
3lues in Motion	54,380	3.08	121
Quebec Seniors	4,047	0.23	30
Metro Medley	831	0.05	6

Financial P$YTE

2007 Estimates:

	No. of Hhlds.	*% Total*	*Index*
Platinum Domain	17,788	1.01	139
Savvy Investors	5,236	0.30	20
3lue Chip Commuters	35,252	1.99	61
Jpper Middle Amenities	49,324	2.79	124
Monster Mortgage	13,027	0.74	25
Kids and Credit	316,807	17.92	457
rugal Families	35,249	1.99	69
Cautious Consumer	184,560	10.44	289
3aby Bills	26,892	1.52	46
Quiet Neighbours	560,872	31.72	124
⁴igh Rise Low Liquidity	190,276	10.76	201
Rent-to-Own	11,935	0.68	5
ust Checking	105,248	5.95	37
New Beginnings	215,414	12.18	91
Not Classified	97	0.01	6

Home Language

2007 Estimates:

		% Total
nglish	3,355,380	77.94
rench	7,029	0.16
Chinese	183,368	4.26
German	4,895	0.11
lindi	6,393	0.15
alian	3,892	0.09
apanese	6,201	0.14
orean	18,269	0.42
ersian (Farsi)	10,821	0.25
olish	3,597	0.08
ortuguese	2,760	0.06
unjabi	68,632	1.59
ussian	4,195	0.10
erbian	2,174	0.05
panish	7,489	0.17
agalog (Pilipino)	6,969	0.16
ietnamese	13,779	0.32
ther languages	42,433	0.99
Multiple responses	556,775	12.93
otal	4,305,051	100.00

Building Permits

	2005	*2004*	*2003*
alue $000	10,191,099	7,938,727	6,394,238

Housing Starts

	2005	*2004*	*2003*
o.	34,667	32,925	26,174

Total Expends. $m	n.a.	n.a.	37,424.9
Capital Expends. $m	34,344.1	32,256.7	29,664.7
Construction $m	24,194.9	22,551.7	20,741.9
Machinery & Equip. $m	10,149.2	9,705.1	8,922.8
Repair Expends. $m	n.a.	n.a.	7,760.2
Repair Construction $m	n.a.	n.a.	3,336.8
Repair Machinery & Equip. $m	n.a.	n.a.	4,423.4

Vital Statistics

	2005	*2004*	*2003*	*2002*
Births	40,680	40,489	40,496	40,065
Deaths	30,047	29,681	29,320	28,884
Natural Increase	10,633	10,808	11,176	11,181
Marriages	21,773	18,892	18,937	21,247

Travel Statistics

	2005	*2004*
Automobile-Tourists Entering from U.S.	3,663,840	3,982,714
Bus-Tourists Entering from U.S.	110,304	75,476
Rail-Tourists Entering from U.S.	33,486	33,556
Air-Tourists Entering from U.S.	1,022,735	1,053,851
Marine-Tourists Entering from U.S.	681,670	620,940
Other Methods-Tourists Entering from U.S.	238,920	272,558
Total-Tourists Entering from U.S.	5,750,955	6,039,095
Land (via U.S.)-Entering from Other Countries	194,611	182,748
Air-Tourists Entering from Other Countries	1,180,327	1,134,717
Marine-Tourists Entering from Other Countries	98,895	91,189
Total-Tourists Entering from Other Countries	1,473,833	1,408,654
Automobile-Cdns. Returning from U.S.	5,943,596	5,640,831
Bus-Cdns. Returning from U.S.	154,421	114,876
Rail-Cdns. Returning from U.S.	4,703	3,571
Air-Cdns. Returning from U.S.	922,450	815,642
Marine-Cdns. Returning from U.S.	87,467	94,399
Other Methods-Cdns. Returning from U.S.	112,188	137,061
Total-Cdns. Returning from U.S.	7,224,825	6,806,380
Land (via U.S.)-Cdns. Returning from Other Countries	6,661	16
Air-Cdns. Returning from Other Countries	1,124,158	1,040,135
Marine-Cdns. Returning from Other Countries	4	5
Total-Cdns. Returning from Other Countries	1,130,823	1,040,156

Population

July 1, 2007 Estimate	32,849,008
% Cdn. Total	100.00
% Change, '01 -'07	5.94
Avg. Annual Growth Rate, '01-'07, %	0.97
2009 Projected Population	33,325,329
2012 Projected Population	34,041,102
2007 Households Estimate	13,128,548
2009 Projected Households	13,416,851
2012 Projected Households	13,848,507

Income

2007 Total Income Estimate $	945,454,090,000
% Cdn. Total	100.00
2007 Average Hhld. Income $	72,000
2007 Per Capita $	28,800
% 2007 Hhlds., Income $100,000+	19.23
2009 Projected Total Income $	1,034,732,810,000
2012 Projected Total Income $	1,175,023,260,000

Retail Sales

2007 Retail Sales Estimate $	404,301,570,000
% Cdn. Total	100.00
2007 per Household $	30,800
2007 per Capita $	12,300
2007 No. of Establishments	231,513
2009 Projected Retail Sales $	442,191,640,000
2012 Projected Retail Sales $	510,029,650,000

Population

2007 Estimates:

Total	32,849,008
Male	16,271,653
Female	16,577,355

Age Groups	*Male*	*Female*
0-4	881,686	842,451
5-9	923,315	883,391
10-14	1,051,094	1,000,874
15-19	1,113,037	1,060,760
20-24	1,157,415	1,100,005
25-29	1,154,102	1,118,723
30-34	1,124,414	1,107,298
35-39	1,178,667	1,163,695
40-44	1,321,457	1,309,243
45-49	1,356,168	1,355,319
50-54	1,209,554	1,232,198
55-59	1,041,068	1,067,774
60-64	833,505	862,528
65-69	611,260	657,763
70+	1,314,911	1,815,333

Daytime Population

2007 Estimates:

Working Population	16,624,404
At Home Population	14,863,212
Total	31,487,616

Income

2007 Estimates:

Avg. Household Income $	72,015
Avg. Family Income $	81,104
Per Capita Income $	28,782
Avg. Employment Income Male $	47,382
Avg. Employment Income Male (Full Time) $	60,548
Avg. Employment Income Female $	29,858
Avg. Employment Income Female (Full Time) $	42,303

Disposable & Discretionary Income

2007 Estimates:

Disposable Income per Hhld. $	52,671
Discretionary Income per Hhld. $	16,696

Liquid Assets

2005 Estimates:

Equity Investments per Hhld. $	88,385
Interest Bearing Investments per Hhld. $	80,438
Total Liquid Assets per Hhld. $	168,823
Total Liabilities per Hhld. $	76,653

2007 Estimates:	*Male*	*Female*
In the Labour Force	9,582,973	8,402,823
Participation Rate	72.8	61.8
Employed	8,908,017	7,860,346
Unemployed	674,956	542,477
Unemployment Rate	7.0	6.5
Not in Labour Force	3,574,364	5,192,086

Average Weekly Earnings

(Including overtime, industrial aggregate)

Apr 2006 $	748.94
Apr 2005 $	721.66
Apr 2004 $	707.12
Apr 2003 $	686.04
Apr 2002 $	677.47

Number of Employees

(Industrial aggregate)

Apr 2006	13,835,770
Apr 2005	13,604,431
Apr 2004	13,380,111
Apr 2003	13,230,865
Apr 2002	12,872,410

Manufacturing Industries

	2004	*2003*
Employees	1,751,563	1,842,798
Salaries, Wages $000	81,005,551	81,105,425
Materials & Supplies $000	345,667,354	322,870,637
Total Revenue $000	611,961,265	581,184,539

Occupations by Major Groups

2007 Estimates:	*Male*	*Female*
Management	1,211,167	654,535
Business, Finance & Admin.	860,413	2,307,925
Natural & Applied Sci. & Rel'd	906,177	244,062
Health	190,231	722,619
Social Sci., Gov't Serv's & Relig'n	224,760	478,560
Education	233,591	423,289
Arts, Culture, Recr'n & Sport	222,809	261,321
Sales & Service	1,778,538	2,371,638
Trades, Transp. & Equip. Ops. etc.	2,423,301	184,569
Primary Industries	552,511	175,756
Processing, Mfg. & Utilities	822,633	407,224

Level of Schooling

2007 Estimates:

Population 20 years +	24,580,766
Less than Grade 9	2,485,651
Grades 9-13 w/o Certif.	4,238,188
Grade 9-13 with Certif.	3,424,770
Trade Certif. /Dip.	2,899,493
Non-Univ. w/o Certif./Dip.	1,573,422
Non-Univ. with Certif./Dip.	4,025,496
Univ. w/o Degree	1,741,547
Univ. w/o Degree/Certif.	1,065,278
Univ. with Certif.	676,269
Univ. with Degree	4,192,199

Retail Sales

	2005	*2004*
New Car Dealers $m	71,968	68,141
Used & Recreational Motor Vehicle & Parts $m	15,331	14,559
Gasoline Stations $m	38,408	33,364
Furniture $m	8,953	8,507
Home Furnishings $m	4,768	4,439
Computer & Software $m	1,593	1,582
Home Electronics & Appliance $m	10,211	9,443
Home Centres & Hardware $m	18,206	16,598
Specialized Building Materials & Garden $m	4,500	4,373
Supermarkets $m	62,746	59,761
Convenience & Specialty Food $m	9,124	8,807
Beer, Wine & Liquor $m	14,443	13,790
Pharmacies & Personal Care $m	23,951	22,769
Clothing $m	16,116	15,312
Shoe, Clothing Accessories & Jewellery $m	4,963	4,877
General Merchandise $m	43,686	42,124
Sporting Goods, Hobby, Music & Book $m	9,464	8,831
Miscellaneous Store Retailers $m	9,398	9,446
Total $m	367,828	346,721

2007 Estimates:

Food $	7,718
Shelter $	12,914
Clothing $	2,877
Transportation $	9,085
Health & Personal Care $	2,848
Recr'n, Read'g & Education $	5,587
Taxes & Securities $	18,439
Other $	9,557
Total Expenditures $	69,025

Private Households

2007 Estimates:

Private Households, Total	13,128,548
Pop. in Private Households	32,332,105
Avg. No. per Household	2.5

Families

2007 Estimates:

Families in Private Households	8,857,294
Husband-Wife Families	7,460,006
Lone-Parent Families	1,397,288
Avg. No. Persons per Family	3.0
Avg. No. Sons/Daughters at Home	1.2

Housing

2007 Estimates:

Occupied Private Dwellings	13,128,548
Owned	8,670,986
Rented	4,387,946
Band Housing	69,616
Single-Detached House	7,528,942
Semi-Detached House	644,531
Row Houses	719,245
Apartment, 5+ Storeys	1,198,726
Owned Apartment, 5+ Storeys	247,171
Apartment, Fewer than 5 Storeys	2,344,502
Apartment, Detached Duplex	471,867
Other Single-Attached	45,973
Movable Dwellings	174,762

Vehicles

2005 NVR ('05 YE)	1,625,102
'03-'05 Model Yrs VOR (July '04)	2,666,663
% '03-'05 Total VOR (July '04)	14.07
'81-'02 Model Yrs VOR (July '04)	16,286,806
% '81-'02 Total VOR (July '04)	85.93
Total VOR (July '04)	18,953,469

NVR = New Vehicles Registered.
VOR = Vehicles on the Road.

Marital Status

2007 Estimates (Age 15+):

Single (never married)	7,805,697
Married (legal & common-law)	15,582,176
Separated (legally married)	696,293
Widowed	1,603,339
Divorced	1,578,692

PSYTE Categories

2007 Estimates:

	No. of Hhlds.	*% Total*	*Index*
Canadian Elite	95,853	0.73	100
Suburban Affluence	72,510	0.55	100
Exurban Estates	53,042	0.40	100
Professional Duets	95,231	0.73	100
Family Comfort	223,126	1.70	100
Commuter Homesteads	128,695	0.98	100
Euro Traditionals	94,125	0.72	100
Primary Pursuits	116,240	0.89	100
Towns with Tempo	168,899	1.29	100
Suburban Growth	185,315	1.41	100
Asian Heights	124,056	0.94	100
Urban Gentry	271,084	2.06	100
Kindergarten Boom	95,585	0.73	100
Cruising Commuters	225,091	1.71	100
Quebec Upscale	246,549	1.88	100
Bicycles and Bookbags	175,892	1.34	100
Young Technocrats	135,226	1.03	100
Exurban Wave	238,848	1.82	100
Family Crossroads	198,620	1.51	100
Row House Streets	79,301	0.60	100
University Enclaves	293,655	2.24	100

60 Financial Post

'SYTE Categories *(Continued)*

'007 Estimates:

	No. of Hhlds.	% Total	Index
'pbeat Blues	115,801	0.88	100
ɔwn and Country	311,472	2.37	100
atellite Suburbs	250,031	1.90	100
rban Promise	291,235	2.22	100
outh Asian Corners	44,650	0.34	100
uebec Melange	227,777	1.73	100
onservative Homebodies	256,263	1.95	100
grarian Heartland	243,491	1.85	100
orthern Lights	64,422	0.49	100
uebec Rows	279,764	2.13	100
uebec Urbanites	130,749	1.00	100
llagê Views	254,566	1.94	100
'orkers' Landing	73,041	0.56	100
ew Frontier Families	224,188	1.71	100
ıcific Fusion	94,049	0.72	100
llage Blues	501,263	3.82	100
ıshi and Shiraz	229,066	1.74	100
-Rise Sunsets	217,473	1.66	100
ıebec Farm Families	496,701	3.78	100
ɜw Canada Neighbours	72,329	0.55	100
ɜnior Town	64,417	0.49	100
ıburban Hi-Rise	101,953	0.78	100
ghland Havens	303,609	2.31	100
ban Vibe	90,823	0.69	100
ıen Country	113,273	0.86	100
iddletown Mix	324,205	2.47	100
bins and Cottages	238,251	1.81	100
ıe Collar Stride	308,313	2.35	100
ro Quebec	142,755	1.09	100
aceful Pastures	452,152	3.44	100
ler Harbour	393,961	3.00	100
ɔan Bohemia	125,992	0.96	100
ebec Rural Blues	525,668	4.00	100
ian Mosaic	68,044	0.52	100
ebec Walk-Ups	256,806	1.96	100
Rise Melting Pot	107,294	0.82	100
ɔond City Renters	248,126	1.89	100
rvice Crew	321,917	2.45	100
ebec Town Elders	320,456	2.44	100
ɜt Peoples	95,123	0.72	100
es in Motion	334,597	2.55	100
ɜbec Seniors	99,232	0.76	100
ɜtro Medley	105,260	0.80	100
ɜbec Urban Stress	289,211	2.20	100
t Classified	1,836	0.01	100

ıan¢ial P$YTE

)7 Estimates:

	No. of Hhlds.	% Total	Index
ɜinum Domain	94,774	0.72	100
ɤy Investors	198,786	1.51	100
ɜ Chip Commuters	426,798	3.25	100
ɪer Middle Amenities	294,393	2.24	100
ıster Mortgage	391,479	2.98	100
; and Credit	514,393	3.92	100
ɟal Families	377,348	2.87	100
tious Consumer	474,491	3.61	100
y Bills	433,445	3.30	100
ɜt Neighbours	3,360,206	25.59	100
ı Rise Low Liquidity	701,709	5.34	100
t-to-Own	1,968,471	14.99	100
: Checking	2,112,117	16.09	100
ɤ Beginnings	1,767,343	13.46	100
Classified	12,795	0.10	100

2007 Estimates:

		% Total
English	20,024,061	61.93
French	6,191,418	19.15
Arabic	64,004	0.20
Armenian	11,553	0.04
Bengali	13,843	0.04
Blackfoot	705	0.00
Bulgarian	3,480	0.01
Chinese	507,285	1.57
Chipewyan	72	0.00
Cree	24,159	0.07
Creoles	8,328	0.03
Croatian	12,158	0.04
Czech	3,024	0.01
Dakota/Sioux	2,218	0.01
Danish	349	0.00
Dogrib	678	0.00
Dutch	4,036	0.01
Estonian	1,531	0.00
Finnish	2,419	0.01
Flemish	161	0.00
Gaelic languages	44	0.00
German	49,092	0.15
Greek	36,056	0.11
Gujarati	20,752	0.06
Hebrew	2,713	0.01
Hindi	16,003	0.05
Hungarian	12,800	0.04
Inuktitut (Eskimo)	16,545	0.05
Italian	121,331	0.38
Japanese	11,925	0.04
Khmer (Cambodian)	6,712	0.02
Korean	50,338	0.16
Kurdish	2,171	0.01
Kutchin-Gwich'in (Loucheux)	11	0.00
Lao	5,727	0.02
Latvian (Lettish)	1,100	0.00
Lithuanian	1,708	0.01
Macedonian	3,947	0.01
Malayalam	1,368	0.00
Malay-Bahasa	1,342	0.00
Maltese	757	0.00
Micmac	2,524	0.01
Montagnais-Naskapi	8,582	0.03
Norwegian	151	0.00
Ojibway	5,625	0.02
Pashto	2,885	0.01
Persian (Farsi)	47,100	0.15
Polish	60,406	0.19
Portuguese	69,262	0.21
Punjabi	156,701	0.48
Romanian	18,443	0.06
Russian	42,026	0.13
Serbian	18,219	0.06
Serbo-Croatian	10,615	0.03
Slovak	2,592	0.01
Slovenian	1;587	0.00
South Slave	272	0.00
Spanish	77,159	0.24
Swedish	327	0.00
Tagalog (Pilipino)	40,886	0.13
Tamil	50,560	0.16
Thai	665	0.00
Tlingit	13	0.00
Turkish	6,299	0.02
Ukrainian	15,583	0.05
Urdu	34,801	0.11
Vietnamese	70,699	0.22
Yiddish	4,409	0.01
Other languages	130,801	0.40
Multiple responses	4,214,989	13.04
Total	32,332,105	100.00

	2005	2004	2003
Value $000	60,755,671	55,578,581	50,771,985

Housing Starts

	2005	2004	2003
No.	225,481	233,431	218,426

Capital Expenditures

(Public & Private)	2006	2005	2004
Total Expends. $m.	n.a.	n.a.	301,362.5
Capital Expends. $m.	281,633.2	265,511.7	247,881.7
Construction $m	179,590.5	167,838.4	154,125.2
Machinery & Equip. $m	102,042.7	97,673.2	93,756.5
Repair Expends. $m	n.a.	n.a.	53,480.8
Repair Construction $m	n.a.	n.a.	23,120.1
Repair Machinery & Equip. $m	n.a.	n.a.	30,360.7

Vital Statistics

	2005	2004	2003	2002
Births	340,368	337,072	335,202	328,802
Deaths	235,329	231,200	226,169	223,603
Natural Increase	105,039	105,872	109,033	105,199
Marriages	151,334	146,093	145,048	146,738

Travel Statistics

	2005	2004
Automobile-Tourists Entering from U.S.	24,486,323	27,254,823
Bus-Tourists Entering from U.S.	1,264,523	1,346,553
Rail-Tourists Entering from U.S	109,273	108,993
Air-Tourists Entering from U.S.	4,279,389	4,328,939
Marine-Tourists Entering from U.S.	996,018	959,640
Other Methods-Tourists Entering from U.S.	519,486	627,166
Total-Tourists Entering from U.S.	31,655,012	34,626,114
Land (via U.S.)-Entering from Other Countries	547,894	537,734
Air-Tourists Entering from Other Countries	3,831,169	3,565,560
Marine-Tourists Entering from Other Countries	126,031	115,258
Total-Tourists Entering from Other Countries	4,505,094	4,218,552
Automobile-Cdns. Returning from U.S.	30,874,097	29,649,404
Bus-Cdns. Returning from U.S.	1,130,830	1,090,402
Rail-Cdns. Returning from U.S.	22,803	24,128
Air-Cdns. Returning from U.S.	5,189,358	4,640,006
Marine-Cdns. Returning from U.S.	133,932	141,573
Other Methods-Cdns. Returning from U.S.	442,974	501,784
Total-Cdns. Returning from U.S.	37,793,994	36,047,297
Land (via U.S.)-Cdns. Returning from Other Countries	6,682	28
Air-Cdns. Returning from Other Countries	6,221,609	5,729,439
Marine-Cdns. Returning from Other Countries	8,660	9,529
Total-Cdns. Returning from Other Countries	6,236,951	5,738,996

MISCELLANEOUS

Associate,Hygienist,Partnership or Cost-Share Agreements

would be here as well as

Office Policies or Information

Valuation of a Sole Proprietor Dental Practice: Sample Report

VALUATION OF

100.00% OF THE SOLE PROPRIETORSHIP OF

____________________ DDS Dental Care Clinics, PLC____________________

DATE OF VALUATION: September 30, 2010
REPORT DATE: December 1, 2010

PERFORMED BY

BILL SIPES CPA/ABV/PFS/ASA/CBA/CFF/BVAL/ABAR

Certified Public Accountant
Accredited in Business Valuation, American Institute of CPAs
Personal Financial Specialist, American Institute of CPAs
Accredited Senior Appraiser, American Society of Appraisers
Certified Business Appraiser, Institute of Business Appraisers
Certified Financial Forensics, American Institute of CPAs
Business Valuator Accredited in Litigation, Institute of Business Appraisers
Accredited in Business and Appraisal Review, Institute of Business Appraisals
Of
Sipes and Seaton CPA PC
Business Valuator & Advisors
www.sipescpa.com

SIPES & SEATON
CPAs, Business Advisers & Appraisers
Minimizing Taxes™ - Protecting Assets - Building Wealth

FOR FURTHER INFORMATION CONTACT:

BILL SIPES CPA/ABV/PFS/CFF/ASA/CBA /BVAL/ABAR

SIPES AND SEATON CPA PC

166B West University Pkwy
Vernonia, OR 38305
731-664-7777

REPRINTED BY BVR WITH PERMISSION
NOTE: THIS REPORT IS PROVIDED AS AN EXAMPLE ONLY

VALUATION OF 100.00% OF THE SOLE PROPRIETORSHIP
OF
DDS Dental Care Clinics, PLC A Oregon
Sole Proprietorship

OPINION OF VALUE

In the opinion of the undersigned valuator, using accepted methods of valuation, and subject to the assumptions and limiting conditions herein, the fair market value of **100.00%** of the sole proprietorship of DDS Dental Care Clinics, PLC, at September 30, 2010 is:

$869,000

Valuator's Certification

1. The statements of fact, opinions and conclusions expressed herein are correct to the best of the valuator's knowledge and belief, and subject only to the assumptions and limiting conditions stated herein.
2. Neither William H Sipes, Jr. nor any employee of Sipes and Associates has any present or prospective interest in the subject; nor any interest or bias, which would impair a fair and unbiased valuation. Compensation paid to the valuator for this valuation is independent of the value reported and is not contingent on any action or event resulting from the valuation.
3. The Valuator has made a personal inspection of the subject property.
4. This valuation has been conducted and this report issued pursuant to the Business Appraisal Standards and Code of Ethics of the Institute of Business Appraisers; the Principles of the Appraisal and Code of Ethics of the American Society of Appraisers, the Code of Professional Conduct and Business Appraisal Standards of the American Institute of Certified Public Accountants and applicable standards of the Uniform Standards of Professional appraisal Practice.
5. Only the person whose name appears below materially participated in the preparation of this report.

Authorized reports will be signed in blue ink by the William H. Sipes, Jr. Copies not signed in blue ink are not valid, unauthorized, inDDS, not approved for distribution and may cause harm.

William H. Sipes, Jr., ASA CPA/ABV/PFS/CFF CBA/BVAL/ABAR

Foreword

A valuation is defined as:

> *"The act or process of determining the value of a business, a business ownership interest, a security, or an intangible asset."*

A Business can have many values. This seemingly odd and interesting statement seems to defy logic. But to a Business Valuator, it is quite understandable. Often, the purpose of the valuation as well as the facts and circumstances will dictate the path the business valuator is to follow and which value is appropriate.

Some aspects of Business Value are:

1. The business value is equal to the present value of the future benefits to the owner, or the prospective investor.
2. Business Valuation is often subjective and full of judgments and estimates.
3. Value is dynamic and changing, so value must be captured as of a single date, i.e. the valuation date.
4. Value can be a single number or a range.

Business Valuation Methods are based on three principles:

- **The Principle of Alternatives** which relates that to any transaction there are a number of alternatives to the prospective investor.
- **The Principle of Substitution** which means that an investor will not invest in a particular asset if there is a more attractive substitute.
- **The Principle of Future Benefits** which states that the value of an investment is equal to the future benefit discounted to present value at the most suitable and appropriate rate of return.

VALUATION OF 100.00% OF THE SOLE PROPRIETORSHIP
OF
DDS Dental Care Clinics, PLC A Oregon
Sole Proprietorship

EXECUTIVE SUMMARY

Overview. DDS Dental Care Clinics, PLC, is a multispecialty dental practice, headquartered in Plains, OR 97204. The dental practice is managed by 1 sole proprietor, Dr. Wilcox. This individual owns 100% of the member units in the practice. Our assignment is to value **100.00%** of the membership units in the Company. This valuation arose from a Marital Dissolution and Dr. Wilcox is our client.

Analysis. At valuation the Company presents 5 years of mixed revenue, as well as mixed results in operating profit and net income. The performance of the PLC is presented in summary form below:

Exhibit 1
DDS Dental Care Clinics, PLC
Historical Performance, as reported

Historic Summary Income Statements

	Period Ending September 30, 2010	Year Ending December 31, 2009	Year Ending December 31, 2008	Year Ending December 31, 2007	Year Ending December 31, 2006
Revenue	2,935,001	4,705,627	3,935,559	4,115,755	2,447,885
Operating Expenses	2,629,922	4,239,869	4,121,862	3,094,970	2,079,556
Operating Profit	305,079	465,758	-186,303	1,020,785	368,329
Other Income/(Expense)	-70,871	-112,054	-75,537	-59,173	-34,388
Income Before Taxes	234,208	353,704	-261,840	961,612	333,941
Income Taxes	0	0	0	0	0
Net Income	234,208	353,704	-261,840	961,612	333,941

The subject's past operating strategy has shown to produce profitable results. The Company is solvent but has a very large debt balance that will impact further operations, perhaps dramatically.

Valuation: I elected to value the practice directly. The primary indicator of value was developed using the Asset Approach, which is a method that relies heavily on the recasting of the Assets and Liabilities to their Fair Market Value. The Capitalization of Cash Flow Method was considered but not used. I also considered a market transaction method, but rejected it due to the lack of additional information about the transactions that were not available. Accordingly, my final approach of value reflects only the value derived from the Adjusted Asset Method.

VALUATION OF 100.00% OF THE SOLE PROPRIETORSHIP
OF
DDS Dental Care Clinics, PLC A Oregon
Sole Proprietorship

Table of Contents

SUMMARY OF IMPORTANT FACTS AND DATES

Governing Standard:	AICPA SSVS 1
Purpose/Intended Use:	Marital Dissolution
Scope:	No Limitation
Restriction on Transfer of Ownership:	No, Except by Operation of Law
Standard Definition of Value:	Fair Market Value
Premise of Value:	Value as a Going Concern
Level of Value:	Control
Client Name:	Dr. Wilcox
Relationship of Client to Subject:	Sole Proprietor (Owner)
Subject's Name:	DDS Dental Care Clinics, PLC
State of Incorporation of Organization:	Oregon
Type of Entity:	Sole Proprietorship
Business % Interest Valued:	100.00% of the Equity of the Practice
Valuation Date:	September 30, 2010
Report Date:	December 1. 2010
Site Visit Date:	July 29, 2010
Management Interview Date:	July 29, 2010
Valuator Name:	William H. Sipes, Jr.
Valuator's Firm:	Sipes and Seaton PC, CPAs and Business Appraisers
Conclusion of Value:	$869,000

ASSIGNMENT DESCRIPTION AND DISCLOSURES

The initial part of this report has as its purpose to inform the reader of the cogent issues as they relate to the valuation. The information in this section is necessary for a good understanding of the nature of the valuation, the process followed as well as the final conclusion of value

Subject of the Valuation

The Subject of this valuation is 100.00% of DDS Dental Care Clinics, PLC; a Oregon Sole Proprietorship as of September 30, 2010. A picture of the Columbia Springs clinic at 21 Columbia Springs Dr., Vernonia, OR 97201 is shown below:

SITE PHOTO HERE

Purpose of the Valuation

Our client, Dr. Wilcox, engaged us to perform this valuation for the sole purpose of Marital Dissolution. The opinion of value expressed in this report is valid for that purpose only.

Dr. Wilcox, the legal and tax professional that is advising our client, and any regulatory agencies whereby reporting is required, will use this valuation for the sole and exclusive purpose of determining the value of the company upon the marital dissolution of Dr. Wilcox. Any other use of this report is unauthorized and the information included in the report should not be relied upon for any other purposes.

The valuation report is based on the data, analysis, and information available to the date of the valuation.

Restrictions to Transfer of Ownership

Sections 11 of The Articles Of Organization

11. No members of the professional limited liability company nor parties to any contribution agreement or contribution allowance agreement shall have preemptive rights.

The equity is transferable, except as prohibited by state law to someone that holds a license to practice dentistry.

Brief Description of the Company

DDS Dental Care Clinics, PLC ("the Company" or "the Subject Company" or "the subject") offers professional dentistry services and services ancillary to the practice of dentistry in the Plains, Oregon area and is located at 382 Oregon Avenue North. The subject also has two other operating dental clinics, which are based in Hermiston, OR (Hermiston Dental) and Vernonia, OR (Columbia Springs).

Use of this Valuation is Restricted

The use of this report is restricted to the use set forth above under "Purpose of the Valuation," and any other use of this report is unauthorized and not valid. William H. Sipes Jr. and Sipes and Seaton have copyrighted this report. Any reproduction of this report without our express written consent is not authorized.

Summary Report

The appraisal result is reported in summary form. [1] This reporting form is limited in narrative discussion of the description of the company and its operating environment, and presents the discussion of the valuation of the company in less detailed fashion. This report form is appropriate where, as in the case, the intended readers of the report are already familiar with the pertinent features of the company, its markets, financial performance and the industry environment in which the Company operates.

The Standard of Value

The appraisal assignment specifies that the subject be appraised at Fair Market Value. This is the standard of value applied here.

[1] This is the form contemplated by Uniform Standards of Professional Practice, Standards Rule 10-2 (a).

The following definition of Fair Market Value was jointly developed by representatives of the American Institute of CPAs, the American Society of Appraisers, the Canadian Institute of Business Valuers, the Institute of Business Appraisers, and the National Association of Certified Valuation Analysts and is as follows:

> *Fair Market Value, is defined as the price that a buyer might reasonably except to receive for the subject property, assuming that the subject property is held for sale on the open market for a reasonable period, and that both buyer and seller are in possession of all pertinent facts and under no unreasonable compulsion to act.*

This definition can also be found within Appendix D of the glossary to this report.

As used here this definition of *Fair Market Value* incorporates the following assumptions:

1. The prospective purchaser is prudent and profit seeking, and without synergistic benefit,[2]
2. The business will continue as a going concern and not be liquidated;
3. The business would be sold for cash or cash equivalent; and
4. The business would be held on the market for a reasonable period of time.

Hypothetical Buyer. The prospective purchaser under the fair market value standard is a hypothetical. The prospective purchaser is anonymous, represents a composite of all arms-length purchasers, and is usually presumed to be a *financial purchaser* as opposed to a *strategic purchaser*.[3] This assumption excludes the buyer who by virtue of some other business relationship will benefit from some "value added" effect on the respective value of some other business and the subject.

This standard of value also usually excludes from consideration the value of the business to specific existing parORers, creditors, or a related or controlled entity, which may be willing to acquire the subject at an artificially high or low price because of motivations not typical of an arm's length financial buyer.

Hypothetical Seller. The seller under fair market value standard is anonymous, and is assumed to know all relevant facts regarding the effect of market forces on the value of the subject, the effect of risk on value, the return available from alternative investments, the effect of control characteristics on value, and the effect of liquidity on value.

[2] As distinguished from a synergistic purchaser who will benefit in his own enterprise from the purchase of the subject.

[3] A *strategic* purchaser is inherent in the *investment value* standard of value. If the identity of the prospective purchaser is known, the *investment value* standard is sometime more appropriate.

Levels of Value

Although valuation is a range concept, current valuation theory suggests that there are five basic "levels" of value applicable to a business or business interest. The levels of value are respectively:

Control Strategic Value (Public or Private Company): This is a synergistic, acquisition or investment value which would include the amount of an acquisition premium.

Controlling Interest: The value of the control shares in the enterprise as a whole.

As if Freely Tradable Minority Interest: The value of a minority interest, lacking control, but enjoying the benefit of market liquidity. This is often referred to as "stock market value".

Restricted Stock: This is the value of "impaired" stock in a public company.

Non-marketable Minority Interest: The value of a minority interest, lacking both control and market liquidity. Minority shares in private companies attract the largest discounts.

This valuation is prepared on a controlling interest basis.

Ownership and Control

At September 30, 2010 the date of the valuation, the management questionnaire informed us that the ownership of the PLC Member units of the subject practice is held as follows:

Mark Wilcox-100% Ownership

Scope of the Assignment

Real Estate Appraisal Report: During the process of completing this valuation we received a real estate appraisal report from a well-known real estate appraiser by the name of David Smith (License #452). The entire real estate appraisal report was furnished to us by Smith and Associates Inc., and contained separate reports for the Pendleton, OR (Dated: 10/28/2010), Hermiston, OR (Dated: 11/04/10), and Vernonia, OR (Dated: 10/22/2010) clinics. We used these real estate appraisal reports in our valuation to determine the amount of rental expense adjustment necessary for each clinic of DDS Dental Care Clinics, PLC. In order to arrive at the appropriate rental expense adjustment we used the potential gross income of each clinic that was reported in David Smith's real estate appraisal report. However, we did not independently verify the information and we assume no liability for its accuracy.

Forensic Accounting Excluded: This scope of the appraisal assignment is limited to the development of a good-faith estimate or opinion of value based on the standard of value and assumptions set forth herein. The scope of this appraisal precludes forensic accounting, and more than a reasonable inquiry into the quality of management.

Reliance on Management Representations: We have relied on the representation of management and counsel without independent investigation or corroboration as though they fairly and accurately represent the financial condition and performance of the proprietorship.

Neither our engagement nor this report can be relied upon to disclose any misrepresentation, fraud, deviations from Generally Accepted Accounting Principles (GAAP), or other errors or irregularities. We have absolutely no knowledge of issues related to litigation, regulatory compliance, or environmental hazards, which would have a negative material impact on the value or transferability of the interest being valued.

Primary Sources of Information

Principle sources of information used by the appraiser include one or more of the following:

- Financial Statements, income tax returns, and/or other financial information for the years 2003-2010 prepared by Horne's accountants, whom operate in Vernonia, OR, or by the client's internal accounting staff.
- Information provided by Dr. Wilcox, counsel and/or management, either in writing or verbally.
- Economic statistics published by the government such as, the Bureau of Labor and Statistics, the U.S. Census, the Bureau of Economic Analysis, the Oregon Business and Economic Outlook, as well as others.
- Information provided to us regarding the real estate appraised values for DDS Dental Care Real Estate Holding Group. These real estate appraisal reports were dated on October 22, 2010 (Columbia Springs Clinic), October 28, 2010 (Plains Clinic), and November 4, 2010 (Hermiston Clinic), and were provided to us by a well-known real estate appraiser; David Smith (License #452). This report, along with the potential gross income of each individual clinic, was used to determine the adjusted rental expense of DDS Dental Care Clinics, PLC.
- Industry statistics, studies, and/or forecasts, which were provided by First Industry Research, the American Academy of Dentistry, Medicaid or other sources specified through out this valuation report.
- Interviews with the client regarding the business operations, financial structure, and marketing techniques.
- Other sources specified herein.

Assumptions and Limiting Conditions

There are several key assumptions and limiting conditions that this report relies on.

The business valuation process requires that the appraiser rely on certain assumptions and limited conditions. These assumptions and limiting conditions may have significant influence on the conclusion of value. This appraisal is subject to the following assumptions and limiting conditions:

- This report is for the sole purpose set forth in the section entitled "Purpose of the Valuation". Because the purpose of a valuation points the valuator toward certain specific approaches and methods, its use for any other reason is not appropriate and may cause harm.

- The valuation process is a good faith opinion of value. The opinion is supported by a reasonable amount of analysis, research and thought but is, in the end, only the unbiased and informed judgment of the valuator.

- In addition to being business valuators we are a CPA firm. In this regard, we have not audited, reviewed, or compiled the financial information included in this report and we express no assurance on it.

- Information, estimates, and opinions contained in this report are obtained from sources we considered reliable.

- The value estimate provided with this report may rely on estimated values for some assets of the subject company if an independent valuation for these assets was not available. No warranty or guarantee is made with respect to these values where such values are used in this report. If these values are inaccurate, the resulting estimate of value of the subject company may be affected.

- This report is copyrighted and Sipes and Seaton CPA and the valuator claim all rights of publication. This valuation report and the information contained within the report may not be used for any purpose by anyone other than the client without the previous written consent of Sipes and Seaton CPA and the valuator. In all events proper attribution is demanded.

- We relied upon the real estate appraisal reports provided to us by David Smith, License #452, of Vernonia, OR. These reports were dated on October 22, 2010 (Columbia Springs Clinic), October 28, 2010 (Plains Clinic), and November 4, 2010 (Hermiston Clinic).

Definitions

As with any profession, definition of terms is important to the understanding of the process and the work product. Because of this, the Appendix has a glossary of terms that is helpful to understanding the valuation process and some are applicable to this engagement.

OVERVIEW OF THE SUBJECT COMPANY

This section discussed the company being valued from a historical and operational perspective. Its purpose is to allow the reader to more fully understand the nature of the company. The information in this section was obtained from management through a written questionnaire and in person and telephonic interviews.

Description of the Subject Company

DDS Dental Care Clinics, PLC operates as a Oregon Sole Proprietorship organized under the Internal Revenue Code. The company is owned by sole proprietor: Dr. Mark Wilcox. The Company may pursue the business endeavors set forth in the Agreement, and lawful under the laws of the State of Oregon or other appropriate jurisdiction.

The subject company's mission and goal, as quoted by DDS Dental Care Clinics, PLC Business Plan, which is dated January 31, 2005 is as follows:

> *"The mission of DDS Dental Care Clinics is to provide the highest quality comprehensive dental care to patients of all ages in an atmosphere that is caring and respectful to the patients, staff and health professionals."*
>
> *"The objectives of the DDS Dental Care Clinics, PLC (CDCC) are to develop dental offices beginning in West Oregon in predominately underserved areas bringing the multi disciplines of dentistry where patients would normally have to travel long distances to obtain these services."*

The clinics of DDS Care Dental Clinics, PLC are currently operating in three different geographic areas, which include Vernonia, OR, Hermiston, OR, and Plains, OR. The clinic that is located in Plains, OR is 6,186 square feet and was opened in 2000. The next clinic, which is located in Hermiston, OR, was opened by DDS Dental Care Clinics, PLC during 2006. This clinic is currently 7,778 square feet. The most recent dental clinic of the subject was opened during 2008 in Vernonia, OR, and is 14,115 square feet.

Brief History

According to the subject's Business Plan, Plains Dental Clinic, which is the starting foundation for CDCC was founded in July 1990 when Dr. Wilcox purchased an existing part-time practice that rented space from a local physician. In 1991, Dr. Wilcox purchased a building on Main St., which is located in Plains OR, which had a total of five dental operations. He hired his first associate in 1998 and moved to his current office on Feb. 1, 2000. The office has three full-time General Dentists, an Oral Surgeon on Tuesday and an Orthodontist on Thursday.

A Professional Limited Liability Corporation (PLC) was formed Dec. 2004, which will facilitate the additional or acquisition of future dental clinics.

The DDS Dental Clinics have gained recent success by building new dental practices in areas that are underserved and in need of those dental services. The subject's plans to continue growth now lie within recruiting and training its professional healthcare staff and other employees so that these individuals will continue to care for the clinic patients in a "caring, tender, and professional manner."

Form of Organization

- Entity Designation: Professional Liability Company
- Date of Formation: December 2004
- Domicile: Oregon

Subsidiaries & Affiliates

Dr. Wilcox reported DDS Dental Care Real Estate Holding Group as a current affiliate.

This partnership, owned by Dr. Mark Wilcox and his wife Michelle, provides the real estate to the practice to house its dental clinics. The appraised values of their three dental properties were determined by Mr. David Smith in his reports dated October 22, 2010 (Columbia Springs Clinic), October 28, 2010 (Plains Clinic), and November 4, 2010 (Hermiston Clinic). These appraisals revealed that the debt of the partnership exceeds the Fair Market Value of the Real Estate and Other Assets.

Prior Transactions in the Subject Interest

Dr. Wilcox reported no transactions in the subject company interest prior to the date of valuation, other than the original distribution of member interest.

Management

The PLC is managed by Dr. Mark Wilcox, Sole Proprietor, with the help of the following team members:

- Michele Wilcox, Business Manager;
- Dr. Jennifer M., Hermiston Dentist;
- Dr. Joe W., Vernonia Dentist;
- Dr. Rusty A., Plains Dentist; and
- Dr. Jo D., Hermiston Dentist (part-time).

In addition to these managers, other individuals were brought to our attention by management as being key people:

- Lianne B. – Office Manager (All three clinics)
- April T. – Office Manager (All three clinics)
- Jana T. – Office Manager (All three clinics)
- Margie R. – Office Manager (Plains Dental)

Site Tour and Management Interview(s)

On July 29, 2010, the valuator traveled for a site tour and management interview at the physical location of Columbia Springs Dental., which is located in Vernonia, OR. During the site visit the valuator spoke personally with multiple individuals, and discussed the business operations, financial structure, marketing techniques, and conducted a thorough review of the subject's facility at Columbia Springs in Vernonia, OR. I did a walk through in order to review the assets and building layout.

Environmental and Regulatory Issues

Dr. Mark Wilcox informed us that there are no environmental or regulatory issues within the practice.

Production by Dentist

Exhibit 2
DDS Dental Care Clinics, PLC
2009 Production by Dentist

2009 Production by Dentist

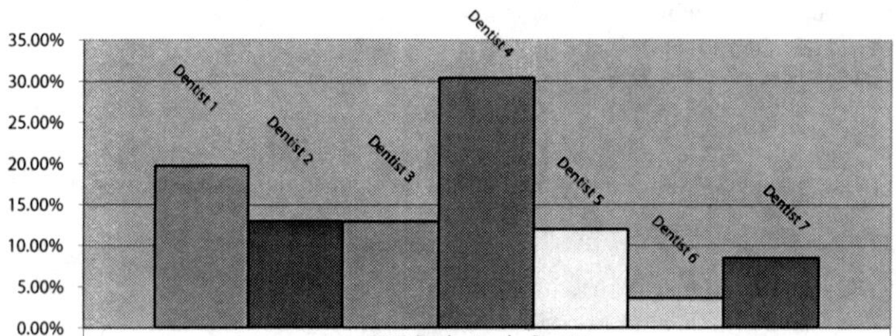

	2009 Production by Dentist
Dentist 1	19.71%
Dentist 2	12.98%
Dentist 3	12.89%
Dentist 4	30.38%
Dentist 5	11.98%
Dentist 6	3.62%
Dentist 7	8.47%

Nathan Nash, D.D.S.	11.98%
Stefanie Whitmer, D.D.S.	3.62%
Victoria S. Rice, D.D.S	8.47%

The above graph shows the production for the year ended December 31, 2009 for each individual dentist. Of all the dentists 30.38% of total production for the subject is due from Dr. Wilcox's contributions to the practice. Obviously, Dr. Wilcox is a key person to the practice and his loss would be difficult to overcome.

Treatments and Services

DDS Dental Care Clinics, PLC provides a variety of services such as general dentistry, children dentistry, hospital dentistry, orthodontics, and oral surgery to special need patients, hospital patients, children, and general patients. These services are provided by the following clinics on the following days: general dentistry, full-time at all locations; children's dentistry, 1 day a week; special needs patients, 1 day a week; hospital dentistry, 1 day a week; orthodontics, 2 days a month at the Plains and Hermiston locations; and oral surgery, 1 day a month at the Plains and Hermiston locations. An example of a dental room in which the services are provided by DDS Dental Care Clinics, PLC is displayed below:

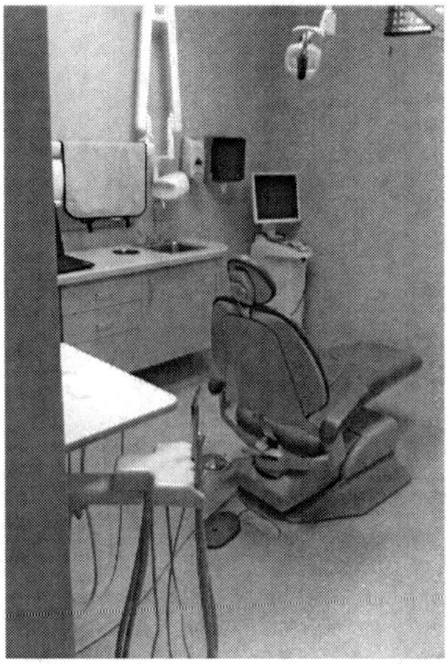

Source: Site Visit

Seasonality

Below is a line graph of the month to month production levels of the dental practice for the entire years of 2008 and 2009.

Exhibit 3
DDS Dental Care Clinics, PLC
Line Graph of Monthly Production (2008 & 2009)

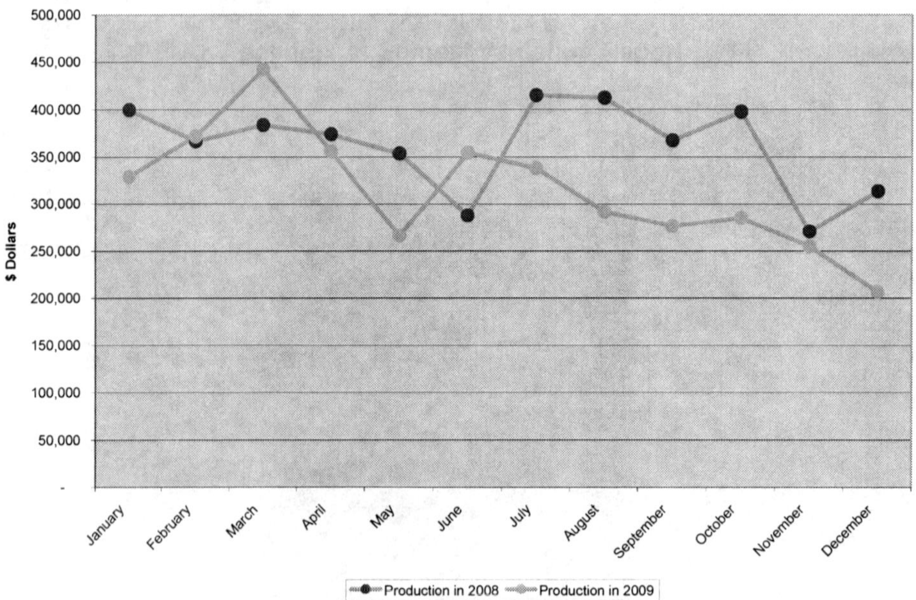

This above graph gives a detailed explanation of the production amounts (in dollars) per month for the years of 2008 and 2009. The amounts of production that are displayed in the graph above are generated from the dental services provided by DDS Dental Care Clinics, PLC. Since the subject operates in the client dependent industry production amounts are frequently expected to change from month to month, which is illustrated by the graph above.

The most notable feature of the production line graph is that production for the year of 2009 has been in a continuous downward trend since June.

As opposed to contrasting one another, as in the graph on the previous page, the production data on a month-by-month basis for a two year consecutive period is displayed below:

Exhibit 4
DDS Dental Care Clinics, PLC
Line Graph of Monthly Production (2008 & 2009)

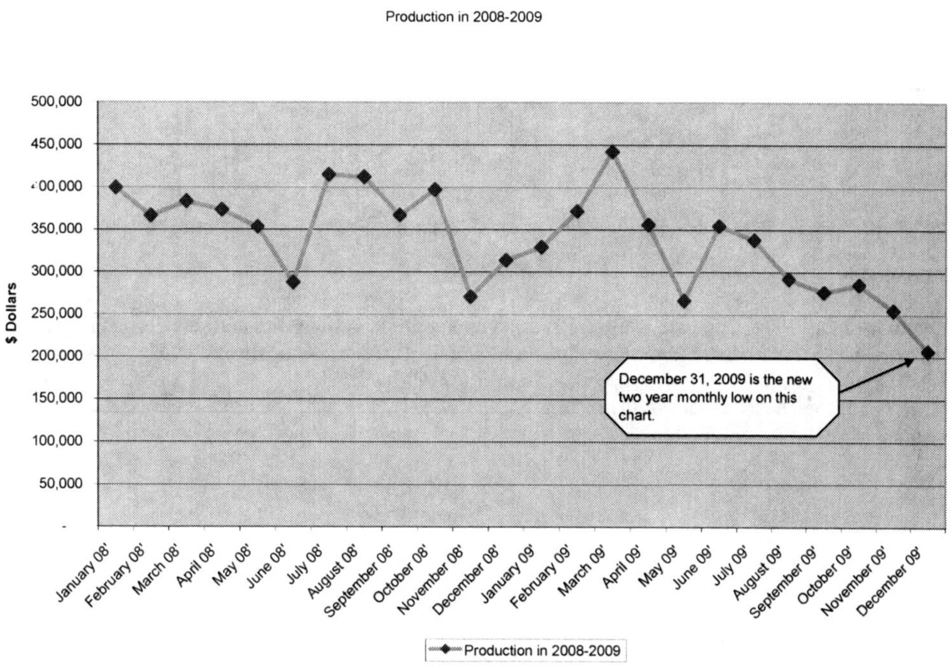

Customer Base and Concentration

The subject company serves a variety of small customers, being an individual patient-based provider. It has no one large customer, since its patients are primarily individuals. The subject company does have a great number of transactions with several major insurance providers such as Tenn Care, Blue Cross Blue Shield, and Delta Dental. On the practice fact sheet, the subject company gave the following information about its patient base:

Primary Patient Base:

1. Children
2. Adults
3. Special Needs
4. Hospital

Competitors

According to Dr. Wilcox, no other office in West Oregon provides as many dental services in one place. Therefore, there is considered to be no competition for the multi-discipline office of DDS Dental Care Clinics, PLC except in larger cities such as N, M, or K. Dr. Wilcox believes that thus far there has not been any pressure from the local dentist offices towards DDS Dental Care Clinics, PLC. Below is the geographic location of Columbia Springs Dental (G), as well as some of the area's surrounding dental clinics:

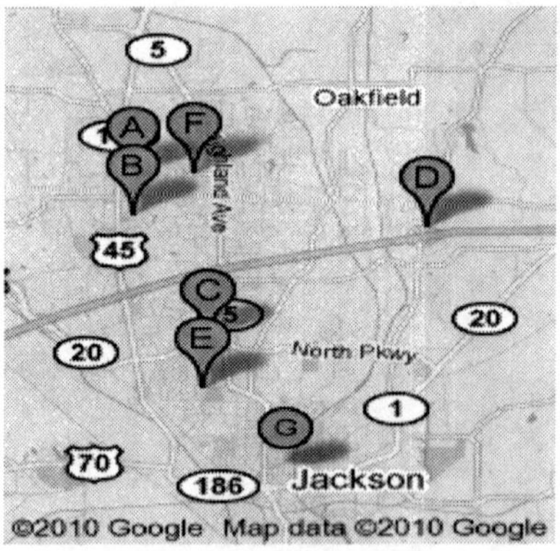

(Names of A-G deleted)

Physical Practices & Headquarters

The main office location of the subject company is located at 382 Oregon Avenue North, Plains, OR 97204.

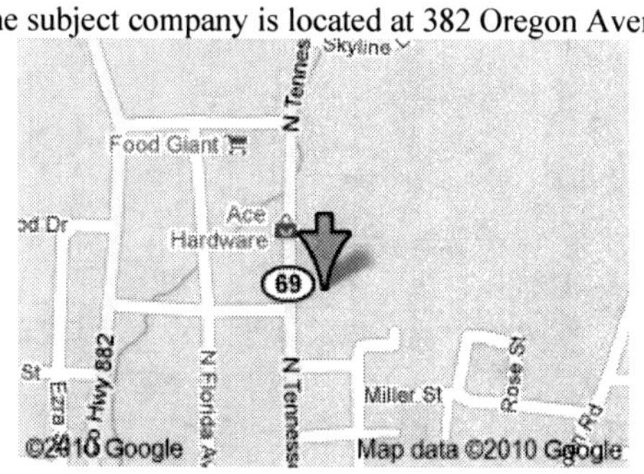

The most recent addition to DDS Dental Care Clinics, PLC is located at 21 Columbia Springs Dr., Vernonia, OR 97201 (Point A).

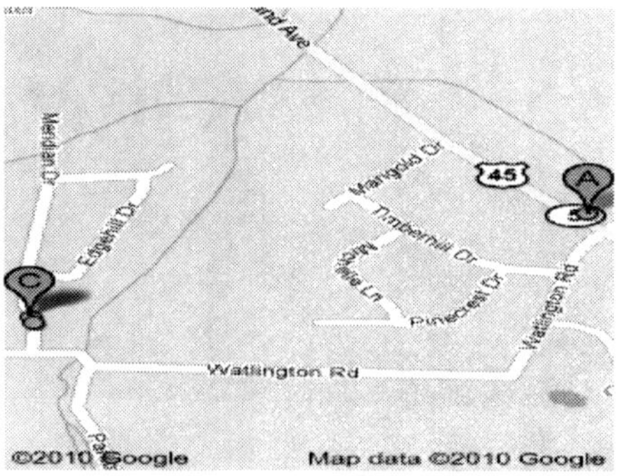

The subject also has a dental clinic located at 25 Stone Ridge Cove, Hermiston, OR 97222.

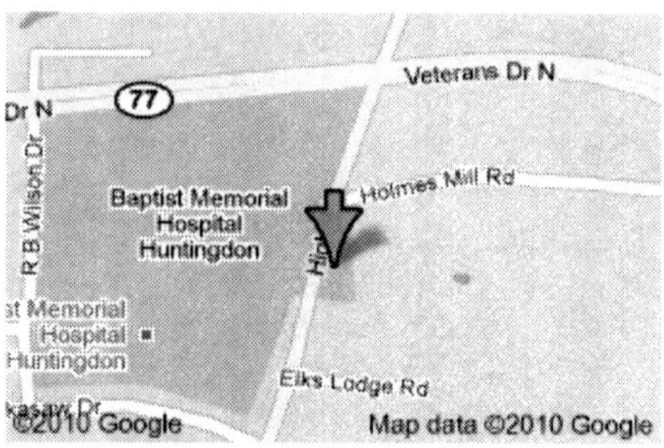

Appendix B: Sample Report

Valuation of 100.00% of the Sole Proprietorship of DDS Dental Care Clinics, PLC
As of September 30, 2010

The following map displays all three locations of DDS Dental Care Clinics, PLC.

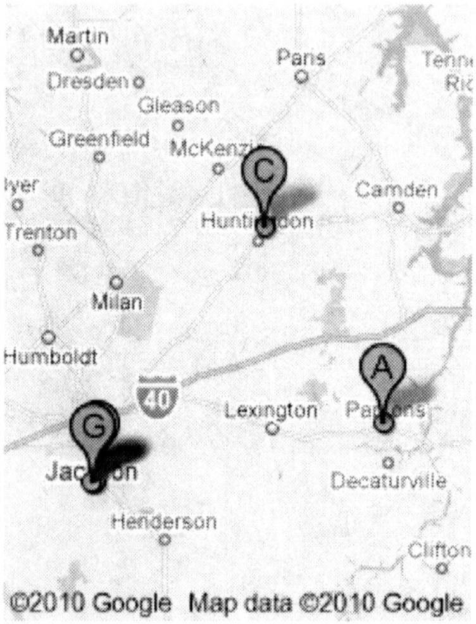

ECONOMIC AND INDUSTRY FACTORS AFFECTING THE COMPANY

As with any business operating as a going concern, the status of the economy and the particular industry will certainly impact revenues, operations and profitability. This section is used to inform the reader of the economic and industry factors considered relevant and material to the valuation process and value conclusion.

The Overall Affect of the Economy on this Valuation

Every business is directly or indirectly affected in some way by the economy… some more significantly and some less severe. The significance of effect the economy has on the business will be based on the elasticity of the demand for the product of the company. On the other hand, some businesses have products and services that are inelastic and suffer little affect when the economy turns sour. These are products and services that the buying customers see as a necessity. An example of a small product in this area of inelasticity might be a toothbrush. Toothbrush sales are only slightly affected, if at all, by changes in the economies.

The Valuator will routinely examine and consider the economic conditions of the national, regional, and local economies as well as the industry in which the subject company operates to gather insight as to the economic environment in which the company operates today and in the future.

The economies can be seen as a river, which has currents moving back and forth. Most objects in the river will be strongly affected by the current. Some will not. The amount of the affect will depend on how the river is moving at any particular time.

The "river theory" is the reason a business Valuator will look at the various economies and industry. The Valuator is trying to determine the affect of these outside influences on the subject business and their impact on his or her Valuation.

The single event that remains a cornerstone of the economy over the last 25 years is the lowering of inflation from it 12.1% rate in 1980 to the 3.6% rate in 1982. Inflation has remained under tight control because of the careful and prudent policies of the Federal Reserve System.

National Economy Overview

The United States' economy is projected to slowdown slightly through the middle of 2010 and will continue to experience a cooling down period in the housing market. The Federal Reserve's Federal Open Market Committee had previously stated that the slowdown will continue and the first sign of recovery is unlikely until at least the second half of 2009. The pace of growth rebounded somewhat in the middle of 2009 but drastically slowed during the first quarter of 2010. Projections are for continued slow growth of inflation-adjusted GDP through 2010. The U.S. Department of Commerce reported that the nation's economy decreased at a rate of 0.5%[5] in the third quarter of 2008, as indicated by the GDP, and marked the greatest decrease since the third quarter of 2001, when the economy shrank by a 1.4%[6] rate. The Bureau of Economic Analysis reported on August 27, 2010, that GDP increased at an annual rate of 1.6 percent in the second quarter of 2010.

Exhibit 5
DDS Dental Care Clinics, PLC
Graph of Real GDP[7]

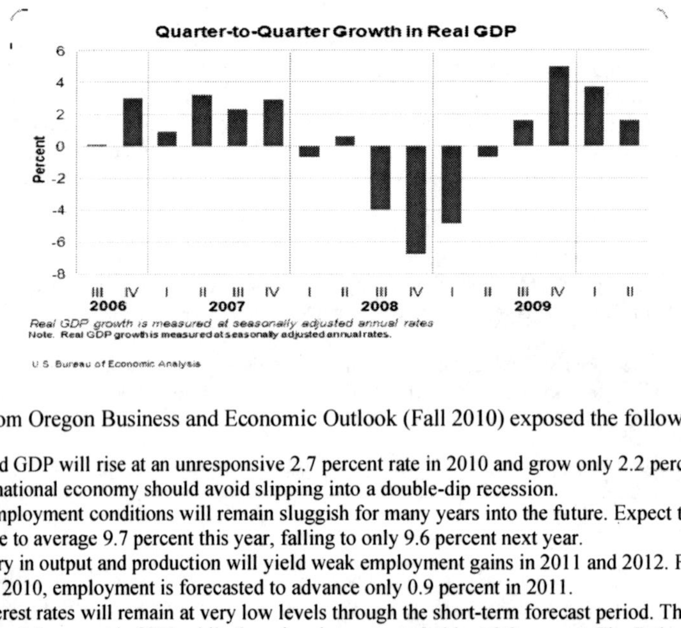

Data gathered from Oregon Business and Economic Outlook (Fall 2010) exposed the following result:[8]

- Inflation-adjusted GDP will rise at an unresponsive 2.7 percent rate in 2010 and grow only 2.2 percent in 2011. It is expected that the national economy should avoid slipping into a double-dip recession.
- The current unemployment conditions will remain sluggish for many years into the future. Expect the nation's unemployment rate to average 9.7 percent this year, falling to only 9.6 percent next year.
- The slow recovery in output and production will yield weak employment gains in 2011 and 2012. Following a 0.5 percent setback in 2010, employment is forecasted to advance only 0.9 percent in 2011.
- Inflation and interest rates will remain at very low levels through the short-term forecast period. The Consumer Price Index will rise 1.6 percent in 2011 while the prime interest rate holds at 3.3 percent. The Federal Reserve is not expected to begin increasing interest rates until 2012.

---

[5] BEA National Economic Accounts, Gross Domestic Product, Percent Change

[6] ibid

[7] http://www.bea.gov/newsreleases/national/gdp/gdp_glance.htm

[8] http://cber.bus.utk.edu/tefs/fall10.pdf

The nation's labor market will feel the pinch of the slowdown. The unemployment rate is expected to drift up to 10 percent by the third quarter of the year 2010.

Exhibit 6
DDS Dental Care Clinics, PLC
Unemployment Rate 2000-2010[9]

Age: 16 years and over

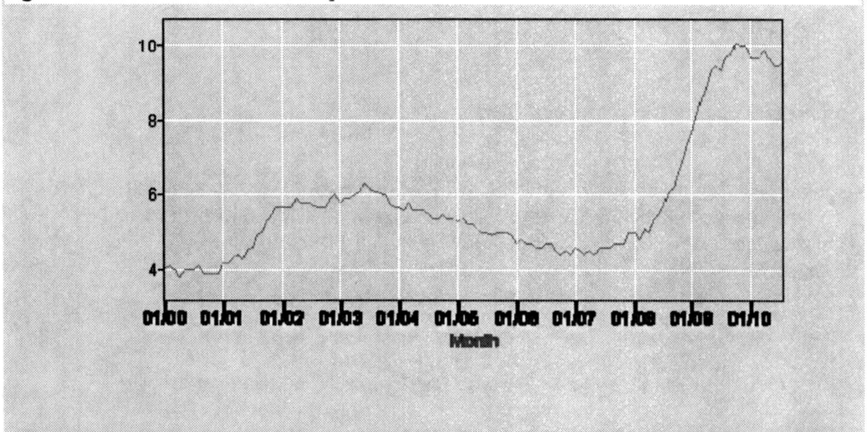

Year	Jan	Feb	Mar	Apr	May	Jun	Jul	Aug	Sep	Oct	Nov	Dec	Annual
2000	4.0	4.1	4.0	3.8	4.0	4.0	4.0	4.1	3.9	3.9	3.9	3.9	
2001	4.2	4.2	4.3	4.4	4.3	4.5	4.6	4.9	5.0	5.3	5.5	5.7	
2002	5.7	5.7	5.7	5.9	5.8	5.8	5.8	5.7	5.7	5.7	5.9	6.0	
2003	5.8	5.9	5.9	6.0	6.1	6.3	6.2	6.1	6.1	6.0	5.8	5.7	
2004	5.7	5.6	5.8	5.6	5.6	5.6	5.5	5.4	5.4	5.5	5.4	5.4	
2005	5.3	5.4	5.2	5.2	5.1	5.0	5.0	4.9	5.0	5.0	5.0	4.9	
2006	4.7	4.8	4.7	4.7	4.6	4.6	4.7	4.7	4.5	4.4	4.5	4.4	
2007	4.6	4.5	4.4	4.5	4.4	4.6	4.6	4.6	4.7	4.7	4.7	5.0	
2008	5.0	4.8	5.1	5.0	5.4	5.5	5.8	6.1	6.2	6.6	6.9	7.4	
2009	7.7	8.2	8.6	8.9	9.4	9.5	9.4	9.7	9.8	10.1	10.0	10.0	
2010	9.7	9.7	9.7	9.9	9.7	9.5	9.5	9.6	9.6				

The entire year of, 2011 is expected to yield employment growth of 0.9 percent.[10] The severity of the recent economic downturn and its resulted layoffs, along with a slow employment recovery, will convert into prolonged periods of high rates of unemployment for the nation. Unemployment rates are especially high in states east of the Mississippi River and in California and Nevada. The national unemployment rate was only 4.6 percent in 2007 but will likely average 9.7 percent in 2010. While the national unemployment rate will edge down beginning in 2011, it is forecasted to still average close to around 9.0 percent as far out as the third quarter of 2012.

---

[9] http://data.bls.gov/PDQ/servlet/SurveyOutputServlet?data_tool=latest_numbers&series_id=LNS14000000

[10] http://cber.bus.utk.edu/tefs/fall10.pdf

The Oregon Economy

It appears that the worst of the current economic downturn may now be in the past. Oregon's rate of unemployment is finally beginning to ease and the state's sales tax revenues are minimizing their losses.[11] According to Oregon's Department of Economic and Community Development the first seasonally-adjusted quarterly employment gains since 2007 should be seen this year. Primary factors weighing down on the economy in the near term include a sluggish national recovery, further setbacks in the agricultural and manufacturing industries, and an abnormally high unemployment rate.

Oregon Economic Overview – Current Conditions

Oregon has experienced a strong economic growth in the past five years. From 2006 to 2007, Oregon experienced a 3.44% change in Real Gross State Product putting the state rated fortieth in the U.S.[12] GDP levels have slightly fluctuated in both directions, but as shown in the Exhibit below it is decreasing over the years 2008 through 2009.

Exhibit 7
DDS Dental Care Clinics, PLC
Chart of Gross Domestic Product for Oregon from 2000-2009[13]

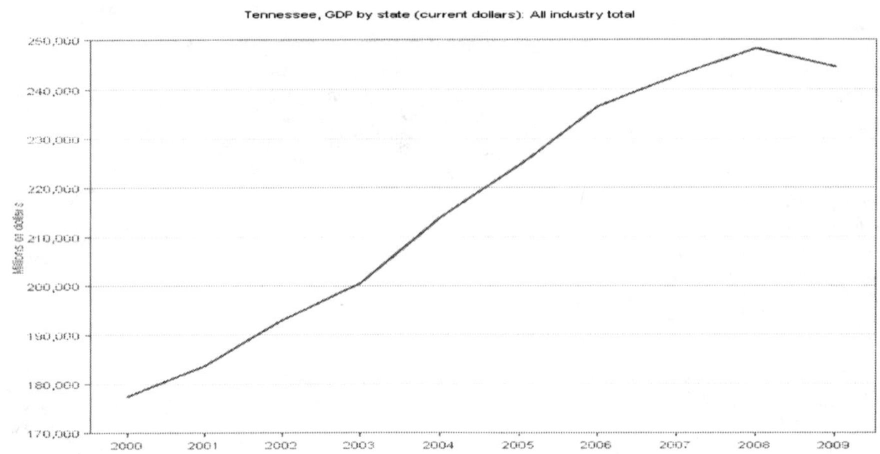

Source: Bureau of Economic Analysis

---

[11] http://cber.utk.edu/erg/erg10c2.pdf

[12] http://www.bea.gov/newsreleases/regional/gdp_state/gsp_newsrelease.htm

[13] http://www.bea.gov/regional/REMDchart/default.cfm#chart_top

Exhibit 8
DDS Dental Care Clinics, PLC
Employment Level in Oregon[14]

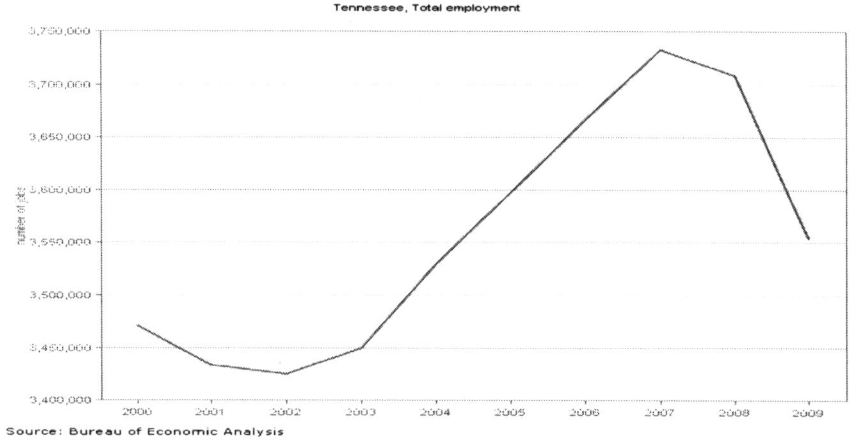

The downward hook, beginning in year 2007, represented in exhibit 6 illustrates a major decline in the employment levels throughout Oregon. Until 2007, Oregon had experienced continuous employment growth. However, as a result of our nation's previous economic downturn the employment rates in Oregon could continue to fall in the near future.

14 http://www.bea.gov/regional/REMDchart/default.cfm#chart_top

Valuation of 100.00% of the Sole Proprietorship of DDS Dental Care Clinics, PLC
As of September 30, 2010

Local Economic Overview

Exhibit 9
DDS Dental Care Clinics, PLC
Employment Rate in Decatur County, Oregon[15]

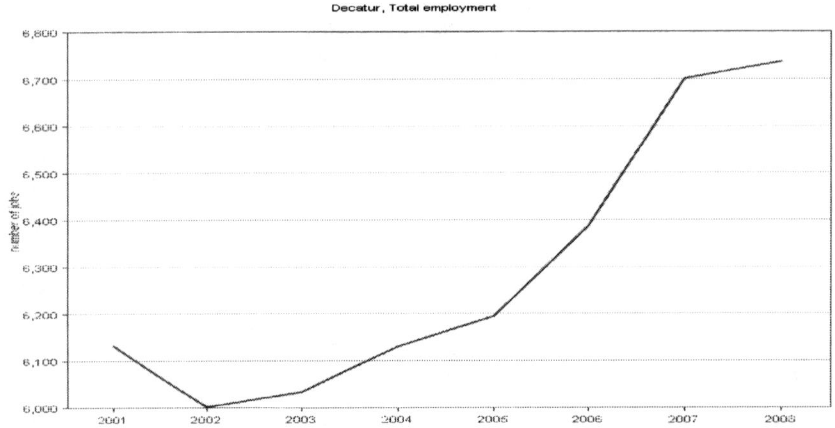

Source: Bureau of Economic Analysis

On the local level, the Decatur County, OR area has experienced a significant continued increase in employment rates. However, as the graph illustrates, employment rates have nearly leveled from 2007 to 2008.

Exhibit 10
DDS Dental Care Clinics, PLC
Population in Decatur County, OR[16]

	2009	2000	1990
Population	11,525	11,731	10,472

As shown in the above table, Decatur County, OR has had a varying population for the past 20 years in which a census was taken. Population increased 10.06% from 1990-2009 and decreased by only 1.52% from 2000-2009.

[15] http://www.bea.gov/regional/REMDchart/default.cfm#chart_top

[16] Source: U.S. Census Bureau, 2006 Population Estimates, Census 2000, 1990 Census

Exhibit 11
DDS Dental Care Clinics, PLC
Employment Rate in ABC County, Oregon[17]

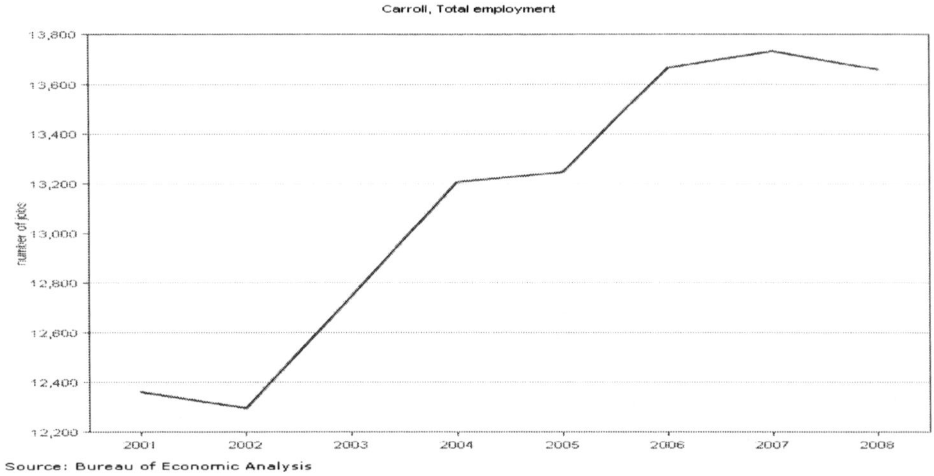

On the local level, the ABC County, OR area has experienced a significant continued increase in employment rates. However, as the graph illustrates, employment rates have began to decline during the year 2007 and have continued to decline into 2008.

Exhibit 12
DDS Dental Care Clinics, PLC
Population in ABC County, OR[18]

	2009	2000	1990
Population	28,517	29,475	27,514

As shown in the above table, ABC County, OR has had experienced increases and decreases in population for the past 20 years in which a census was taken. Population increased 7.13% from 1990-2000 and decreased only 3.25% from 2000-2009.

---

[17] http://www.bea.gov/regional/REMDchart/default.cfm#chart_top

[18] Source: U.S. Census Bureau, 2006 Population Estimates, Census 2000, 1990 Census

Exhibit 13
DDS Dental Care Clinics, PLC
Employment Rate in Madison County, Oregon[19]

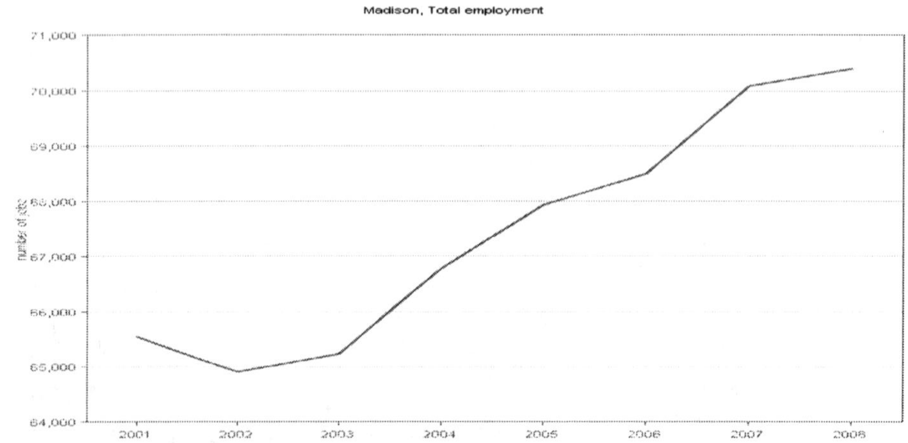

Source: Bureau of Economic Analysis

On the local level, the Madison County, OR area has experienced a significant continued increase in employment rates. However, as the graph illustrates, employment rates have nearly leveled from 2007 to 2008.

Exhibit 14
DDS Dental Care Clinics, PLC
Population in Madison County, OR[20]

	2009	2000	1990
Population	97,317	91,837	77,982

As shown in the above table, Madison County, OR has had an increase in population for the past 20 years in which a census was taken. Population increased 17.77% from 1990-2000 and only 5.97% from 2000-2009.

[19] http://www.bea.gov/regional/REMDchart/default.cfm#chart_top

[20] Source: U.S. Census Bureau, 2006 Population Estimates, Census 2000, 1990 Census

Industry Overview

For this report, the industry overview will focus on trends and norms in the dentist's offices and clinics service industry. The dentist's offices and clinics industry is made-up of about 130,000 companies that generate $100 billion of annual revenue[21]. Most companies have a large range of services, such as general dentistry, dental hygiene, routine cleanings, cosmetic dentistry, oral surgery, and gum disease treatments. No one single company, or small group of companies, dominates the dentistry industry, which is highly fragmented with the fifty largest offices generating only 5% of total revenue.

Industry demand is largely driven by demographics. The profitability of the smaller individual companies depends on effective marketing and ability to estimate future payments. By specializing in specific dental services or patient type, smaller companies can compete effectively. Due to the nature of operations, the industry is very labor intensive: annual revenue per employee is about $120,000.

American citizens with dental insurance usually visit the dentist every six months. As a result, the average individual spends nearly $350 annually on dental care services. This amount of revenue is derived from operations such as composite fillings, regular teeth cleaning, and oral surgery. In fact, the prices for dental procedures vary from around $80 to $130 for a normal checkup, and $600 to $1,500 per tooth for a root canal.[22] More often than none these the basic types of services (routine teeth cleaning) are being performed by dental hygienists. The fact that these duties have shifted from the dentist to the dental hygienist enables the dentist to conduct more complex procedures, which in turn leads to higher profits.

National Medicaid Growth Trends

Nationally, total Medicaid spending growth averaged 8.8 percent states in FY 2010. This is considered to be the highest rate of growth in eight years and well above original projections for FY 2010 of 6.3 percent growth. Enrollment growth averaged 8.5 percent in FY 2010, significantly higher than the 6.6 percent growth projected at the start of FY 2010. Many states predicted that Medicaid enrollment would grow at a somewhat sluggish rate of 6.1 percent for FY 2011. For Medicaid spending in FY 2011, initial legislative appropriations authorized total spending growth that would average 7.4 percent above FY 2010 spending.[23] Nationally, Medicaid has continued to increase every six-month interval since December of 1998.

---

[21] First research Industry Profile-Dentists Offices and Clinics, 7/12/2010.

[22] Ibid

[23] The Kaiser Commission on Medicaid and the Uninsured - Prepared by Vernon K. Smith, Ph.D., Kathleen Gifford, and Eileen Ellis, on September 2010.

Oregon Medicaid Growth Trends

Forty-nine percent of the children in Oregon are enrolled in Medicaid. However, children of Oregon account for only 19% of the state's Medicaid spending, which is an indication that the majority of Medicaid spending is on adults or the elderly. Each Medicaid-eligible child costs Oregon $1,227 per year, on average, compared to the average costs per adult Medicaid enrollee of $3,931.[24] Even though these numbers, in relation to Oregon's Medicaid enrollees, may sound attractive the Oregon program still has a lot of room left to grow. For example, it is estimated that 158,678 Oregon children are uninsured, which is 10.8 percent of the children in Oregon.[25]

Long-term Growth Prospects

Growth in the dentist's offices and clinics industry depends on the condition of the U.S. economy, number of individuals holding a dental insurance plan, and the number of patients willing to give positive referrals. The majority, 55%, of dental care procedures are paid for by private health insurance and other-third party payers (government plans).[26] Growth rates from 2010 to 2015 (projected) have been, and are expected to continue steadily increasing.

Several opportunities do exist, such as the increase in the overall condition of the U.S. economy, including increases in consumer spending, the prospect to attract more insurance paying patients (government healthcare reform), the increased popularity of cosmetic dentistry, the millions of Americans that are currently seeking dental care services are continuing to remain steady, and periodontic treatments are increasing in demand.[27] After all, dental care services are something that almost everyone seeks to acquire.

Some disadvantages include tighter government regulation, over saturation, and competition from low-cost dental providers.

---

[24] http://www.aap.org/advocacy/washing/elections/mfs_OR.pdf

[25] Ibid

[26] First research Industry Profile-Dentists Offices and Clinics, 7/12/2010.

[27] Ibid.

Exhibit 15
DDS Dental Care Clinics, PLC
Projected Growth for the Dental Industry[28]

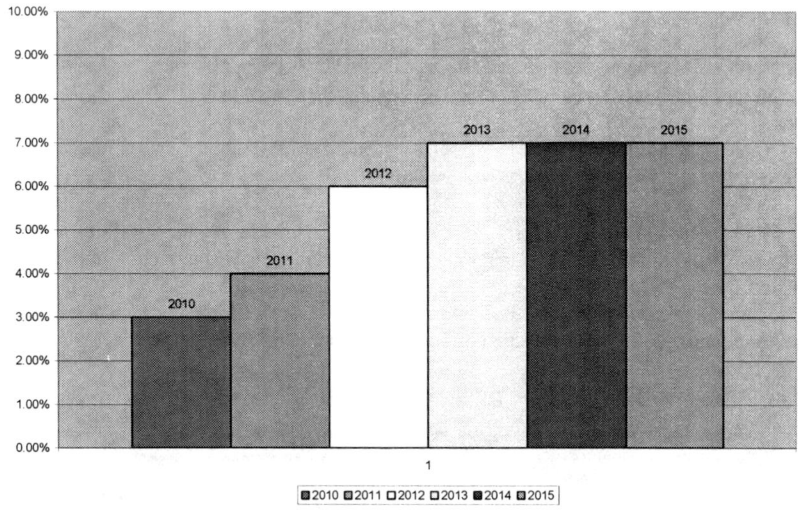

Implications for the Subject

The U. S. Economy is forecasting a continued somewhat negative performance for the subject company. The Oregon economic picture is also forecasting a slow recovery. In fact, the professional and business services sector has recovered quite quickly and should record 2.8 percent job growth this year and 4.8 percent growth next year.[29] Most industry experts predict minor future growth in the dental service industry; a minor increase will be a result from the increase in the general condition of the U.S. economy, as healthcare providers will began to provide more coverage. According to First Research, the dental industry is mostly driven by children ages 5-19 and adults over 55. As a result, the dental service industry is also expected to experience minor growth due to an increase in the age demographic among U.S. citizens.

These economic trends are neutral to slightly positive for the subject.

---

[28] First Research Industry Profile-Dentists Offices and Clinics, 7/12/2010.

[29] Ibid.

FINANCIAL ANALYSIS OF THE COMPANY

This section contains an analysis of the company's historical financial statements. The analysis and the normalized financial statements produced in this report are included solely to aid the valuation process and assist in determining the opinion of value. They should not be used for accounting or tax reporting, to obtain credit, or for any other purpose.

Financial Information provided to us by the company management and others.

The business valuator will often rely on the financial statements of the subject company as a primary source of financial information concerning the company.

- The Balance Sheet(s) are a point in time statement that list the assets and liabilities of a company at a particular point in time. This statement has often been compared to a photograph or snapshot.
- The Income Statement(s) display the performance of the subject company over a period of time, sometimes annually for 12 consecutive months, but also monthly or quarterly.

Financial statement(s) were provided to us as indicated below.

Form	*Basis*	*FYE*	*2003*	*2004*	*2005*	*2006*	*2007*	*2008*	*2009*	*2010*
Financial Statements	Income-Tax Basis	December	X	X	X	X	X	X	X	X
Federal Income Tax Returns	Cash	December	X	X	X	X	X	X	X	

Noted is several cases the Financial Statement's line item numbers did not tie to the Tax Return's items numbers. For example, the fiscal year ended December 31, 2008 Financial Statements reported a Depreciation Expense of $897,034, whereas the Tax Return reported a Depreciation Expense of $ 891,368

What is Financial Statement Analysis?

In a general way, the analysis portion of the valuation process is to assist the valuator as he looks at the financial statements of the subject company. The analysis consists of looking at and measuring trends, comparing the subject company to similarly situated companies in the industry using common size statements and ratio analysis, and other analytical techniques.

What will the financial statement analysis reveal?

While the analytical techniques of financial analysis are far from perfect, they can and often do reveal some or all of the following:

- Trends in the financial numbers.
- Unusual, nonrecurring and extraordinary items.
- Non Operating Assets.
- Accounts that need to be considered for normalization adjustments.

An Overview of the Subject Company's Historic Financial Performance before Adjustment

Summary

The subject company's gross revenue followed a steady increasing trend except for the 2008 year end, and the period ended September 30, 2010. The periods resulted in a decreasing gross revenue total. Operating Profit was also mixed for the subject. Expenses for the subject company have been following an overall steady upward trend. The subject company showed a historical net profit for all years reviewed.

Revenue and Sales

Revenue for the subject company ranged from a high $4,705,627 in 2009 to $1,726,466 for year ended December 31, 2003, and they averaged $3,120,663 dollars for the 7 ¾ -year period of December 31, 2004 through September 30, 2010. Revenues followed an upward trend except for year ended December 31, 2008 in which sales followed a downward trend.

Operating Profits

Operating Profit for the 7 ¾ -year period ranged from $ -186,303 on the low side for the year ending December 31, 2008 to $1,020,785 on the high side for the year ending December 31, 2007. Operating Profit also followed a mostly mixed trend for the most recent 7 ¾ -year period. Operating Profit averaged about $585,136 for the most recent 7 ¾ -year period.

Operating Expenses

Operating Expenses for the 7 ¾ -year period ranged from a low $958,594 for the year ending December 31, 2003 to $4,239,869 on the high side for the year ending 2009. Operating expenses averaged $2,535,527 for the most recent 7 ¾ -year period. Operating Expenses followed a consistent upward trend, except for period ended June 30, 2010, for the years being reviewed for valuation purposes.

Profitability

Net Income for the subject company ranged from $(261,840) on the low side for the year ending December 31, 2008 to $961,612 on the high side for the year ending 2007. Net Income followed a mixed trend for the years ended December 31, 2004 through period ended September 30, 2010.

The following exhibits display the performance of DDS Dental Care Clinics, PLC in both table and graph format.

Exhibit 16
DDS Dental Care Clinics, PLC
Historical Performance, as reported

Historic Summary Income Statements

	Period Ending September 30, 2010	Year Ending December 31, 2009	Year Ending December 31, 2008	Year Ending December 31, 2007	Year Ending December 31, 2006	Year Ending December 31, 2005	Year Ending December 31, 2004	Year Ending December 31, 2003
Revenue	2,935,001	4,705,627	3,935,559	4,115,755	2,447,885	2,285,466	2,033,382	1,726,466
Operating Expenses	2,629,922	4,239,869	4,121,862	3,094,970	2,079,556	1,393,511	1,132,050	958,594
Operating Profit	305,079	465,758	-186,303	1,020,785	368,329	891,954	901,332	767,872
Other Income/(Expense)	-70,871	-112,054	-75,537	-59,173	-34,388	-46,006	-37,625	-64,737
Income Before Taxes	234,208	353,704	-261,840	961,612	333,941	845,948	863,707	703,135
Income Taxes	0	0	0	0	0	0	0	0
Net Income	234,208	353,704	-261,840	961,612	333,941	845,948	863,707	703,135

Exhibit 17
DDS Dental Care Clinics, PLC

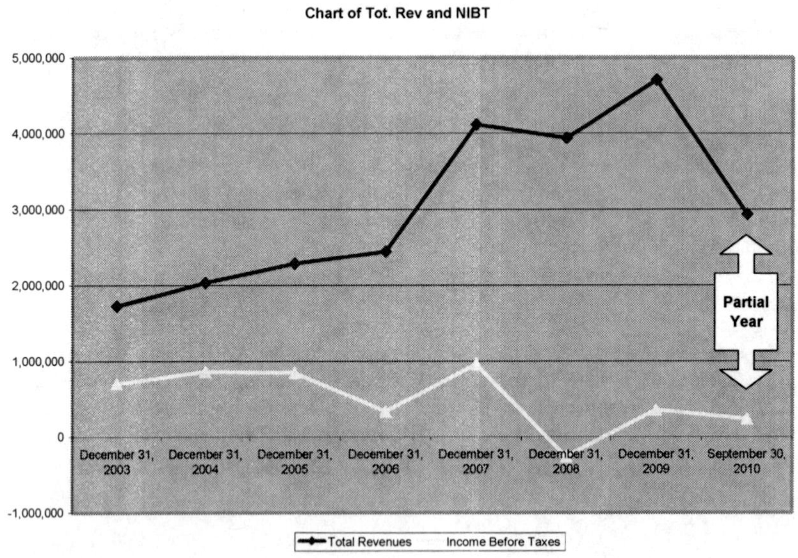

Overview of the Subject's Financial Position

Exhibit 18
DDS Dental Care Clinics, PLC
Pie Graph of Historic Assets at Sept 30, 2010

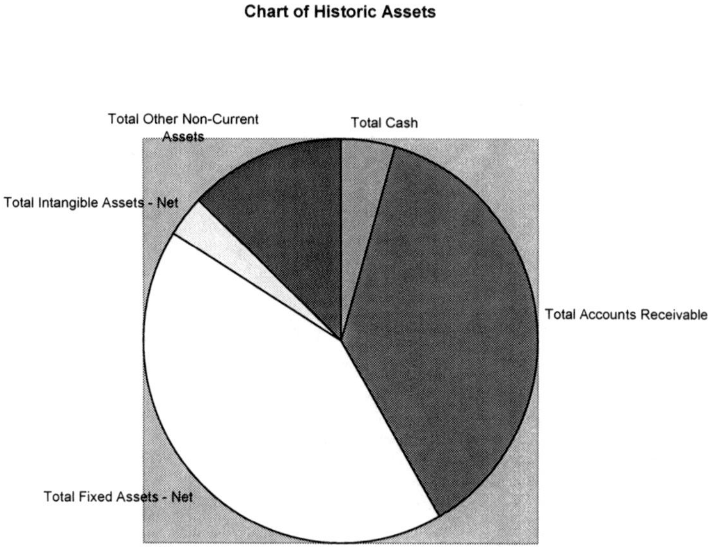

Above is a simple "pie" chart of the major unadjusted balance sheet asset accounts for the subject for the period ended September 30, 2010. The Current Asset classifications are generally on the right hand side of the chart and the various Fixed Asset classifications are generally to the left.

The pie chart shows that from a historical cost prospective that the major classes of assets were Total Fixed Assets and the major part of Total Fixed Assets is Dental Equipment.

The distinguishing feature of the left side of the chart shows the larger Fixed Asset section. When compared to the other Asset accounts it is relatively easy to notice that the majority of the subject's assets are comprised of Fixed Assets.

Exhibit 19
DDS Dental Care Clinics, PLC

Chart of Historic Total Liabilities

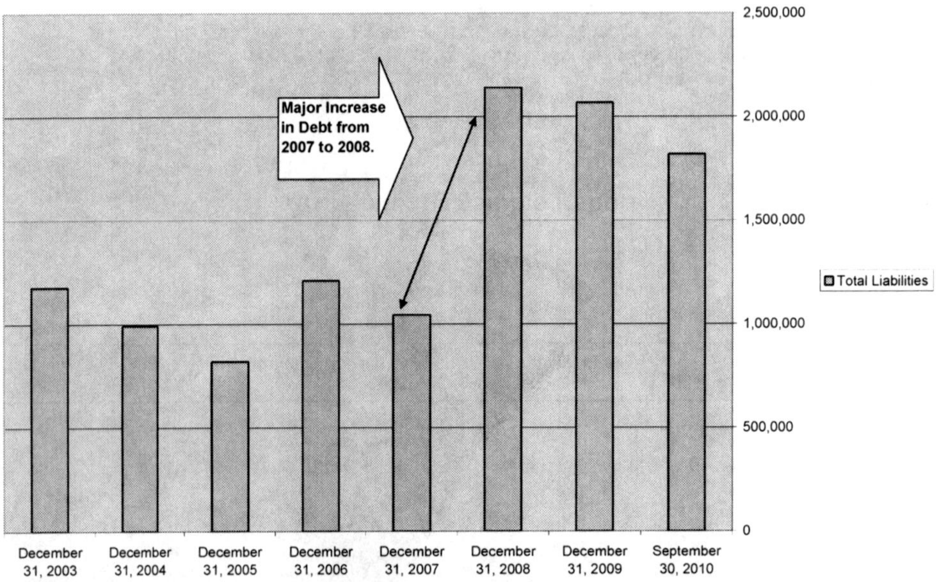

Above is a simple vertical bar chart of total liabilities from the fiscal year ended balance sheets from 2003 through period ended September 30, 2010. The time line moves from left to right.

Most notably this graph shows that the company's total liabilities had increased significantly over the one year period of December 31, 2007 through December 31, 2008. The major increase in liabilities during the 2008 fiscal year was in part a result of the subject acquiring an increase of $1,048,399 in long-term debt.

The practice's liabilities primarily come from a First State Bank Loan for Vernonia's Dental Equipment, along with other Liabilities like a First State Bank Loan for Hermiston's Dental Equipment. The large increase in Liabilities in 2008 came about because of the increase in a First State Bank Loan, for Vernonia's Dental Equipment, which totaled $1,200,000.

This graph is a negative indicator for the subject and debt has doubled in one year's time.

Exhibit 20
DDS Dental Care Clinics, PLC

Chart of Historic Assets, Liabilities and Equity

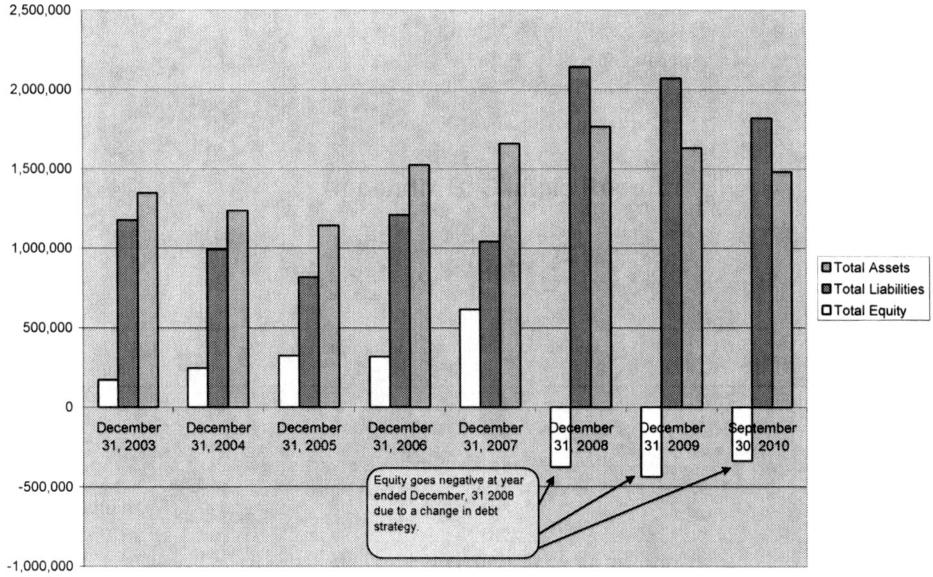

Above is a vertical bar chart showing total assets, liabilities, and the difference, which is called equity for the last day of each fiscal year 2004 through period ended September 30, 2010. The most notable feature to the valuator is that liabilities have significantly increased from fiscal year end December 31, 2007 to December 31, 2008 and total equity is also mixed (currently on the negative side) for the 7 ¾ - year period reviewed.

This chart shows the balance of assets to liabilities and equity that the practice has achieved over the 7 ¾ year period. A healthy company maintains a stable mix of assets and equity to counterbalance liabilities which are necessary if the practice wants to experience continued grow.

As can be seen from the chart the subject began to go into negative ground in year 2008, which is a negative indicator for the company.

Valuation of 100.00% of the Sole Proprietorship of DDS Dental Care Clinics, PLC
As of September 30, 2010

Exhibit 21
DDS Dental Care Clinics, PLC

Chart Comparison of Total Equity to Total Debt

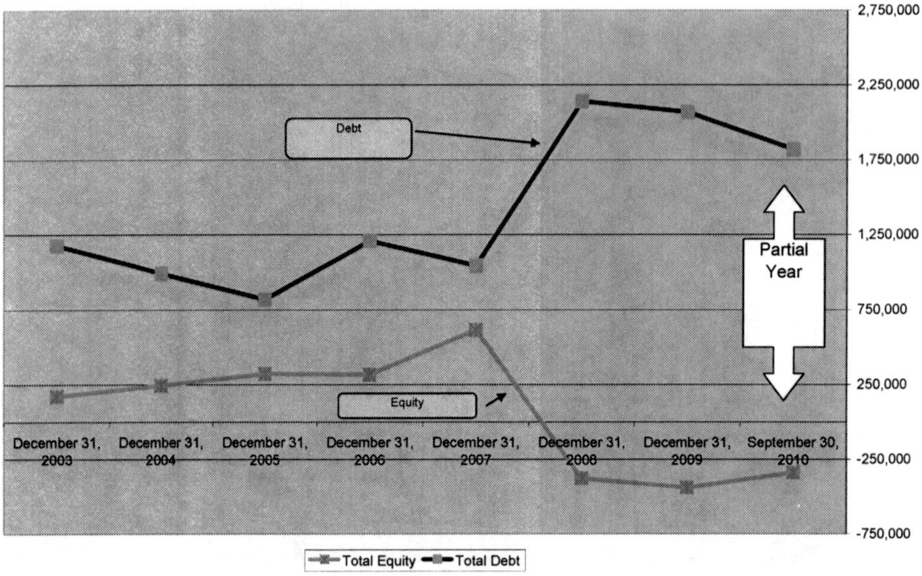

Above is a common line chart illustrating total equity to total debt for the last day of each fiscal year 2003 through period ended September 30, 2010. The graph illustrates that the company's equity has been below zero for 2 ¾ consecutive years. However, the most distinguishing feature to the Valuator is that the equity account has continued to decrease further into the negative numbers until period ended September 30, 2010. During this year the subject decreased its negative equity account.

The subject's total debt nearly mirrors its total equity. In other words, the subject's total debt will normally increase for each decrease in total equity. The graph shows that the total debt account of the subject drastically increased from fiscal year ended December 31, 2007 to December 31, 2008, because a large amount of long-term debt was obtained during 2008. However, the total debt of the subject is currently decreasing, while the total equity in increasing.

This graph is a very negative indicator for the subject and indicates a considerable risk to the practice.

Statement of Cash Flows

The subject does not prepare a statement of cash flow for internal use. The statement below was prepared by the valuation analyst from information provided to us by the subject:

Historic Summary Cash Flow

	Period Ended September 30, 2010	Year Ended December 31, 2009	Year Ended December 31, 2008	Year Ended December 31, 2007	Year Ended December 31, 2006	Year Ended December 31, 2005	Year Ended December 31, 2004
Cash Provided by (used for) Operations							
Net Income (Loss)	234,208	353,704	-261,840	961,612	333,941	845,948	863,707
Plus Depreciation & Amortization	186,655	432,751	897,034	242,348	156,034	145,021	89,264
Plus Non Cash Expenses	0	0	0	0	0	0	0
(Increase)/Decrease in Accounts Receivable	27,518	-61,880	91,166	-93,165	-321,336	65,384	-5,921
(Increase)/Decrease in Other Current Assets	0	0	0	0	-3,000	0	0
(Increase)/Decrease in Other Non-Current Assets	0	-37,386	-45,678	-41,000	-66,337	0	0
Increase/(Decrease) in Accounts Payable	0	0	0	0	0	0	0
Increase/(Decrease) in Other Current Liabilities	-70,227	159,051	49,670	-36,573	46,474	-73,095	184,122
Increase/(Decrease) in Other Non-Current Liabilities	0	0	0	0	0	0	0
Total Cash Provided by (used for) Operations	378,154	846,240	730,352	1,033,222	145,776	983,258	1,131,172
Cash Provided by (used for) Investing Activities							
(Increase)/Decrease in Net Fixed Assets	-32,280	-226,035	-1,253,379	-107,740	-161,264	-28,034	-18,785
(Increase)/Decrease in Net Intangible	0	0	5,666	5,667	0	0	0
Total Cash Provided by (used for) Operations	-32,280	-226,035	-1,247,713	-102,073	-161,264	-28,034	-18,785
Cash Provided by (used for) Financing Activities							
Net Additions to/(reductions in) Notes Payable	-178,733	-231,712	1,048,399	-128,987	343,302	-100,433	-368,708
Net Investment in/(distribution of) Equity	-133,753	-415,397	-730,563	-661,647	-339,983	-768,027	-790,435
Total Cash Provided by (used for) Operations	-312,486	-647,109	317,836	-790,634	3,319	-868,460	-1,159,143
Total Increase/(Decrease) in Cash	33,388	-26,904	-199,525	140,515	-12,169	86,764	-46,756
Beginning Cash Balance	31,431	58,335	257,860	117,345	129,514	42,750	89,506
Ending Cash Balance	64,819	31,431	58,335	257,860	117,345	129,514	42,750

Common Size Analysis

Common size analysis is a tool used by business valuators to examine the various financial statements. It shows the numbers in the financial statement as a percentage of total sales rather than the more traditional absolute figures using dollars. The valuator is generally looking for year-to-year relationship changes as they compare to the total assets of the subject company. It can provide "clues" as to where the business valuator might wish to extend his analysis. Summary statements in common size format are provided below.

Complete Dental Income Statements

Based On Historical Statements	Complete Dental Annualized September 30, 2010	Complete Dental December 31 2009	Complete Dental December 31 2008	Complete Dental December 31 2007	Complete Dental December 31 2006	Complete Dental December 31 2005	Complete Dental December 31 2004	Complete Dental December 31 2003
Revenue	100.00%	100.00%	100.00%	100.00%	100.00%	100.00%	100.00%	100.00%
Cost of Goods	0.00%	0.00%	0.00%	0.00%	0.00%	0.00%	0.00%	0.00%
Gross Profit	100.00%	100.00%	100.00%	100.00%	100.00%	100.00%	100.00%	100.00%
Total Operating Expenses	89.61%	90.10%	104.73%	75.20%	84.95%	60.97%	55.67%	55.52%
Operating Profit	10.39%	9.90%	-4.73%	24.80%	15.05%	39.03%	44.33%	44.48%
Other Income/(Expense) Net	-2.41%	-2.38%	-1.92%	-1.44%	-1.40%	-2.01%	-1.85%	-3.75%
Pre-Tax Profit	7.98%	7.52%	-6.65%	23.36%	13.64%	37.01%	42.48%	40.73%

Comparison to Industry Peers

One of the analytical techniques often used by valuators to glean insight into the company and its strengths and weaknesses is by comparison to others companies in the industry group. Information about the industry peers is occasionally useful because it allows comparison with others companies operating under assumed similar circumstances and business environment.

RMA Peer Comparisons

For purposes of comparison with industry financial measures available from non-public company sources, I reviewed the *Annual Statement Studies*, published by The Risk Management Association (RMA). RMA compiled average percentage income statement and balance sheets and key financial ratios of companies classified under Standard Industrial Classification (SIC) # 8021. The selected RMA group includes 1,165 companies. I believe the RMA data provides limited comparative perspective and strict comparisons should be made carefully and with caution.

According to their web site, RMA is an organization of 2850 members (banks and non-bank financial institutions) that gathers data from the financial statements of companies in similar avenues of business. With that information RMA hones this data into benchmark (or composite) data for use by the users of its service. The RMA data is not of a single company by rather a picture of the entire group of industry peers with which our subject company has been identified.

To summarize the data information in a table:

NAICS Code	621210
Code Classification Name	Dentists Offices and Clinics
Number of Companies in RMA Class	516[31]
Size of the Class	From $1-$3 MM
Class sorted by Assets or Revenues	Sales

SIC Code 8021	Offices of Dentists
Description of Code	Companies in the industry provide services that include general dentistry, oral pathology, oral surgery, orthodontics, pediatric dentistry, and periodontics. However, most clinics specialize in general dentistry services such as amalgam and composite fillings, regular teeth cleanings, and cosmetic dentistry.
Corresponding NAICS Code 621210	Dentists Offices and Clinics

[31] Of the 516 members of the group, 2 provided unqualified financial statements, 1 provided reviewed statements, 93 provided compilations, 297 provided Tax Returns, and 123 provided some other form of document.

Selected Comparative Ratio Analysis

Exhibit 22
DDS Dental Care Clinics, PLC
Chart of RMA and Subject Company Current Ratio

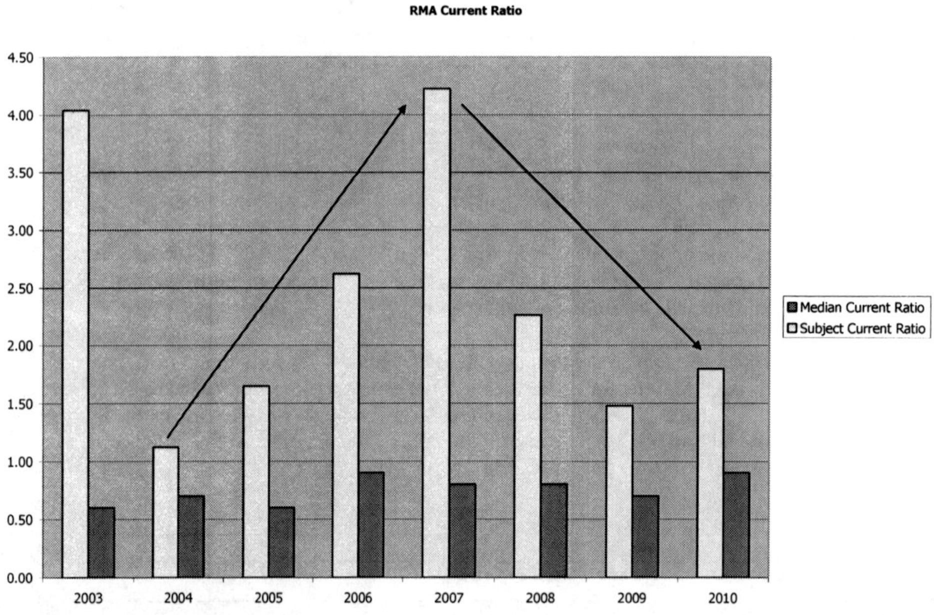

The graph above is a visual of the current ratio of the subject company compared to its industry peers (RMA). The current ratio indicates the ability of the subject to pay its current obligations as they become due from their current assets. A higher number is better.

This graph shows the subject having mixed trends for the years ended December 31, 2003 through period ended September 30, 2010. The year 2006 showed a very moderate ratio, high compared to 2004 but very low compared to 2007. Overall, the current ratio of the subject company is well above 1.0 at 1.80 for the period ended September 30, 2010. A ratio that exceeds 1.0 suggests that a company would be able to pay all of its current liabilities with its current assets if they all came due at once. In other words, since the subject's current ratio exceeds 1 this indicates that it would be able to pay all debt due.

While still positive there has been a large decrease in the current ratio from year ended December 31, 2007 to period ended September 30, 2010, which is a negative indicator for the subject.

Valuation of 100.00% of the Sole Proprietorship of DDS Dental Care Clinics, PLC
As of September 30, 2010

Exhibit 23
DDS Dental Care Clinics, PLC

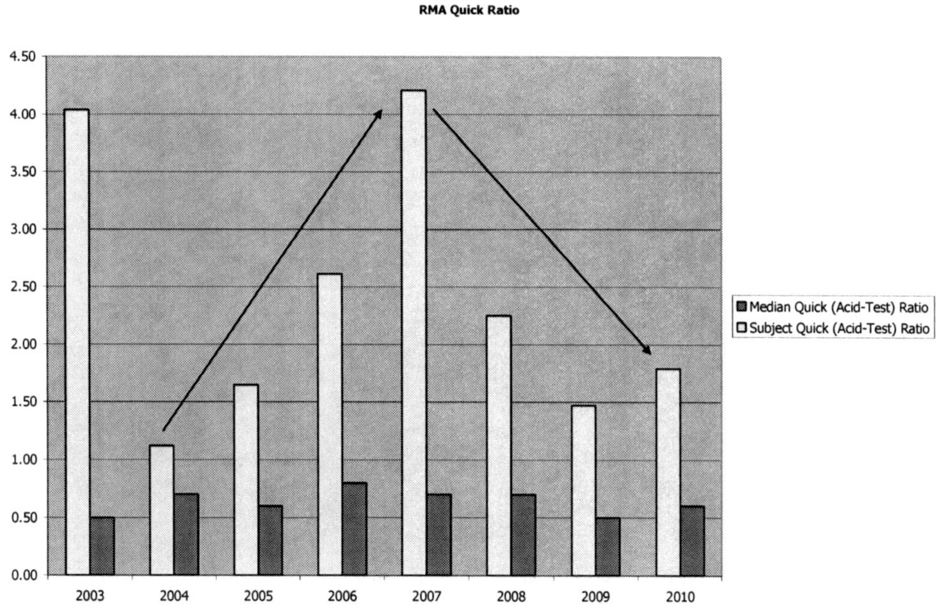

The Quick Ratio provides a more conservative view of creditor protection than the previously displayed Current Ratio because it does not include Inventory and Prepaid items in its calculation. The reason these accounts are not included is that these accounts are not readily converted into cash. This is the reason for the name "quick ratio." As a general rule, a company is in a favorable position to pay creditors when its Quick Assets (Cash, Cash Equivalents, and Net Receivables) exceed the Current Liabilities.

This graph shows that although it has been mixed over the 7 ¾ years, the subject company's quick ratio is still well above the median for its industry and is more than capable of quickly converting assets to cash. In fact, the subject's quick ratio for the period ended September 30, 2010 is 1.79, which is above an acceptable ratio amount.

While still positive there has been a large decrease in the quick ratio from year ended December 31, 2007 to period ended September 30, 2010, which is a negative indicator for the practice.

Exhibit 24
DDS Dental Care Clinics, PLC
Chart of RMA and Subject Debt to Equity

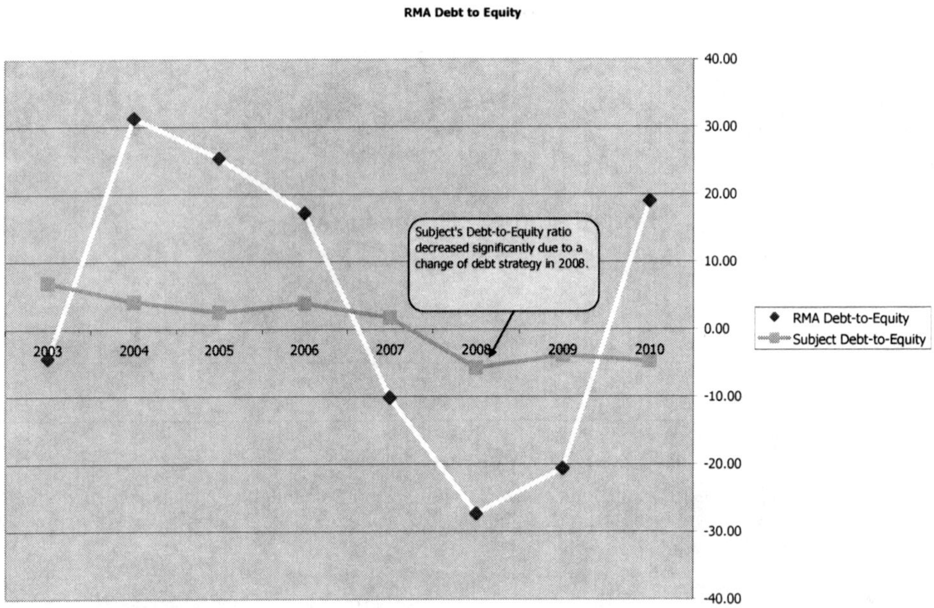

The debt to equity ratio is a ratio that allows comparison of the subject's funding of its assets. It shows how much of the subject's assets are funded by equity and how much is funded by outsiders (debt). It provides insight into whether a company is adequately capitalized for business. A lower number (above 0) is better.

For this graph I choose to use Total Liabilities to Equity.

This graph shows that the subject company does not have a debt-to-equity ratio (i.e. not above 0) for 2 ¾ consecutive years. This type of debt-to-equity ratio is rare, but it is a result of the subject company containing less equity than liabilities within its capital structure. A high debt-to-equity ratio, which indicates very aggressive financing, results in very volatile earnings and high risks. In contrast, a low debt-to-equity ratio, which indicates conservative financing and low risk, results in fewer possibilities of large losses.

This ratio is very negative for the subject company.

Exhibit 25
DDS Dental Care Clinics, PLC
Chart of RMA and Subject Times Interest Earned

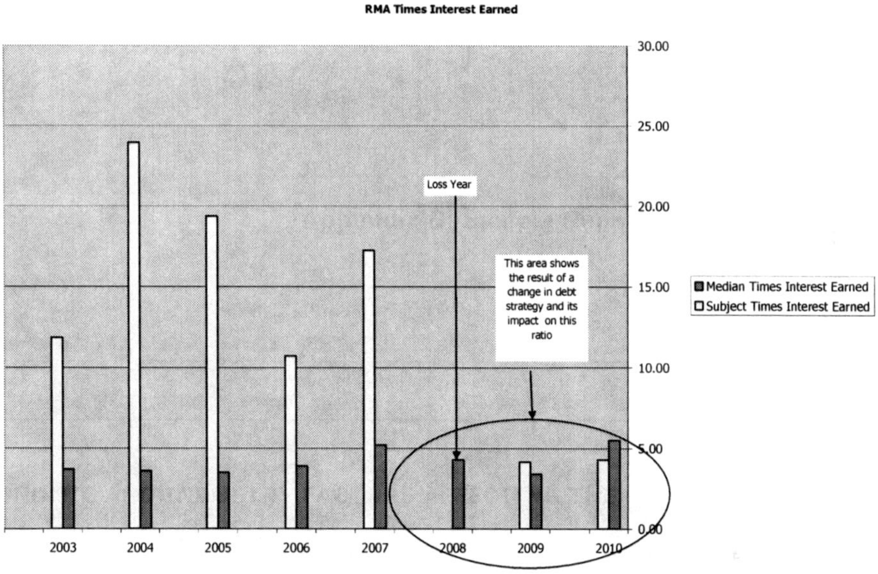

The times interest earned ratio is another debt ratio that measures the long-term solvency of a business. It measures how well a company can meet its interest expense obligations.

For example, if a company owes interest on its long-term loans or mortgages, the times interest earned ratio can measure how easily the company can come up with the money to pay the interest on that debt.

The number of times indicates how well the firm meets its interest obligations. The higher the number, the better the firm can pay its interest expense on debt. If the times interest earned ratio is less than 1.0, then the firm cannot meet its total interest expense on its debt. The times interest earned ratio for the subject's period ended September 30, 2010 was 4.30, which is well above and successful ratio. The above graph does not present a times interest earned ratio, above 0 for year ended 2008 because during this year the subject incurred a large loss, which is used to compute the times interest earned ratio. This large loss created a significant risk for the subject in the sense that it could not potentially meet its interest expense when due. The subject has not been able to regenerate a times interest earned ratio such as the one produced at year end December 31, 2007, because its net income has taken a dramatic decrease of $727,404 since that year.

This graph and its results, which indicate high risks, are a negative indicator for the subject.

Summary of Ratio Analysis

Exhibit 26
DDS Dental Care Clinics, PLC
Summary of Ratio Analysis

Ratio that was analyzed	Results of Analysis as compared to Peer
Current Ratio	Declining Trend
Quick Ratio	Declining Trend
Debt To Equity	Negative
Times Interest Earned	Negative

Balance Sheet Components Compared to Industry Peers

RMA Common Size Balance Sheets

Based On Historical Statements	Complete Dental Historic September 30, 2010		RMA 2009	Complete Dental December 31 2009		RMA 2008	Complete Dental December 31 2008		RMA 2007
ASSETS									
Cash	64,819	4.37%	23.20%	31,431	1.93%	20.40%	58,335	3.31%	20.80%
Accounts Receivable	550,234	37.13%	2.40%	577,752	35.44%	2.90%	515,872	29.23%	4.20%
Inventory	0	0.00%	0.30%	0	0.00%	0.20%	0	0.00%	0.50%
Other Current	3,000	0.20%	3.70%	3,000	0.18%	2.40%	3,000	0.17%	3.90%
Total Current Assets	618,053	41.71%	29.60%	612,183	37.55%	25.90%	577,207	32.71%	29.40%
Fixed Assets	626,044	42.25%	44.70%	776,169	47.61%	47.00%	977,219	55.38%	45.20%
Net Intangible	47,225	3.19%	16.00%	51,475	3.16%	16.40%	57,141	3.24%	16.20%
All Other Non-Current	190,401	12.85%	9.70%	190,401	11.68%	10.80%	153,015	8.67%	9.10%
Total Assets	1,481,723	100.00%	100.00%	1,630,228	100.00%	100.00% [SIC]	1,764,582	100.00%	100.00% [SIC]
LIABILITIES & EQUITY									
Accounts Payable	0	0.00%	1.30%	0	0.00%	1.70%	0	0.00%	2.30%
Short Term Notes Payable	0	0.00%	13.30%	0	0.00%	15.40%	0	0.00%	11.80%
Current Portion of LT Debt	0	0.00%	10.00%	0	0.00%	9.60%	0	0.00%	8.10%
Other Current Liabilities	343,957	23.21%	15.30%	414,184	25.41%	16.90%	255,133	14.46%	22.40%
Total Current Liabilities	343,957	23.21%	39.90%	414,184	25.41%	43.50%	255,133	14.46%	44.60%
Long Term Debt	1,475,075	99.55%	51.10%	1,653,808	101.45%	54.60%	1,885,520	106.85%	53.60%
All Other Liabilities	0	0.00%	4.00%	0	0.00%	7.00%	0	0.00%	5.60%
Total Liabilities	1,819,032	122.76%		2,067,992	126.85%		2,140,653	121.31%	
Total Equity	-337,309	-22.76%	5.00%	-437,764	-26.85%	-5.10%	-376,071	-21.31%	-3.80%
Total Liabilities & Equity	1,481,723	100.00%	100.00%	1,630,228	100.00%	100.00% [SIC]	1,764,582	100.00%	100.00%

Analysis of the Balance Sheet

The above Balance Sheet is a common sized and comparative Balance Sheet. A common size statement shows each group of assets as a percentage of total assets and each group of liabilities and equity as a percentage of total liabilities and equity. The above statement also compares the subject company to that of its industry peers. The subject company has a high amount of current assets, primarily accounts receivable, as a percentage of total assets as compared to its industry peers. The portion of Long-Term Debt as a percentage of total liabilities and equity is higher for the subject company than that of its industry peers, but the portion of Current Liabilities as a percentage of total liabilities and equity is lower for the subject company than for that of its industry peers. A very notable feature that can be observed by examining the above common size balance sheet in that the subject's Equity account is negative. The negative Equity account is a result of the subject acquiring a large amount of debt (often times the debt is 100% over the total Equity and Liabilities line item), which exceeds the assets that the subject currently holds.

The risk associated with high debt began in 2008 when the subject increased its total debt by $1,098,069, which is an increase of over 100% of the total debt from that of the previous year end.

Valuation of 100.00% of the Sole Proprietorship of DDS Dental Care Clinics, PLC
As of September 30, 2010

Income Statement Components Compared to Industry Peers

RMA Comparative Income Statements

Based On Historical Statements	Complete Dental Annualized December 31, 2010		RMA 2009	Complete Dental December 31 2009		RMA 2008	Complete Dental December 31 2008		RMA 2007
Revenue	3,913,335	100.00%	100.00%	4,705,627	100.00%	100.00%	3,935,559	100.00%	100.00%
Cost of Goods	0	0.00%	0.00%	0	0.00%	0.00%	0	0.00%	0.00%
Gross Profit	3,913,335	100.00%	100.00%	4,705,627	100.00%	100.00%	3,935,559	100.00%	100.00%
Total Operating Expenses	3,506,563	89.61%	87.40%	4,239,869	90.10%	85.50%	4,121,862	104.73%	84.70%
Operating Profit	406,772	10.39%	12.60%	465,758	9.90%	14.50%	-186,303	-4.73%	15.30%
Other Income/(Expense) Net	-94,495	-2.41%	-1.60%	-112,054	-2.38%	-4.80%	-75,537	-1.92%	-3.30%
Pre-Tax Profit	312,277	7.98%	11.00%	353,704	7.52%	9.70%	-261,840	-6.65%	12.00%

Analysis of the Income Statement

The above Income Statement is a common sized Income Statement. A common size statement shows all items as a percentage of total revenue. The above statement also compares the subject company to that of its industry peers. The Income Statement above shows the company having the same gross profit as a percentage of total sales than that of its industry peers. It also shows Operating Expenses as a percentage of total sales being higher than the peers in the industry. Operating Profit and Pre-Tax Profit as a percentage of total sales is lower for the subject company than for those of the peers in the industry. As a result, the company is not a profitable as its peer, which is a considerable risk factor.

The user of this report is warned that the subject dental practice is a Professional Liability Company that files an individual tax return (form 1040) for federal tax purposes and therefore historical statements show owners' distributions as withdrawals of profits rather than as expenses. This is different treatment than in a corporation where the distributions would be salary and shown as an expense. In such circumstances net income can be deceiving and give the uninformed user an erroneous impression about the financial health, or lack of health, of net profits.

Concluding thoughts on the RMA Peer analysis and implications

I think that DDS Dental Care Clinics, PLC is debt heavy practice, with slightly declining financial health. The industry also appears to be in a state of slow growth. This industry is considered to be dynamic, in part due to a financially recovering population, changes in insurance payments, and a recovering economy. The subject company is performing above its industry peers for most measures. The subject is in a patient-dependent industry in a relatively densely populated area with historically high disposable incomes. Also, the company has had 6 ¾ profitable years in its 7 ¾ year period of analysis and this would normally indicate less risk.

However; as discussed in the section on the income statement, a sole proprietor's profits can be deceptive to the uninformed user because distributions to owners are not offset against income as they are in the corporate entity. In this case, because the owner (dentists) "eats what he kills" net profits would, if restated in the historical statements as a corporation, be materially smaller. Also, adjusted statements in the analysis show that 2 out of the last five years with normalized losses.

NORMALIZATION ADJUSTMENTS

This section of the report considers adjustments often referred to as normalization adjustments. These adjustments reformulate the balance sheet to the fair market value that could be realized on sale and the income statement to indicate the true economic profit of the business without regard to owner efforts to reduce taxes and remove tax free income from the business. Adjusted (Normalized) statements allow financial statements to be presented on a basis comparable to that of other companies. The type of valuation of the subject – control or minority interest – often will have an impact on the adjustments considered and made by the valuation analyst.

Normalization adjustments are often required to adjust the historical financial statements so that they are representative of a business with a true profit motive as of the valuation date. Adjustments are made by the valuator to present the subject company in more realistic economic "light" -- free from the influence of such issues as the owner's desire to reduce taxes or remove "perks" from the company. The adjustments are often approximations and recast the financial statements so that a prospective investor in the subject company will have a better understanding of the economic reality for the company and its future.

Normalization adjustments generally fall into three classes:

- GAAP Adjustments: Adjustments to correct errors or omissions in generally accepted accounting principles.
- Control Adjustments: Adjustments to provide the prospective investor a clearer picture of the economic reality of a company.
- Non-Operating and Excess Assets Adjustments: Adjustments to remove assets or liabilities not germane to the company, or to remove "excess" assets.

GAAP Adjustments are generally made, if indicated, in all business valuations. Control Adjustments and Non-Operating and Excess Assets Adjustments are, as a rule, made only in a valuation where "control" is indicated. The reason they are not always considered appropriate in a minority valuation, which would be a less than fifty (50) percent interest valuation, is that the minority owner or prospective minority owner cannot control or force changes within the company.

Financial statement adjustments would include:

- Unrecorded assets or liabilities as well as Depreciation Methods are examples of Generally Accepted Accounting Principles (GAAP) Adjustments.

- An owner's salary in excess of the true value provided by that individual to his company. In other words, part of the economic profits of the company being converted to salary, rent or some other accounting or tax device in order to remove funds from the company and/or minimize taxes. This is an example of a control adjustment.

- A Non- Operating asset on the company books, i.e. a personal boat, a condo, or some asset is in excess (for example Inventory) of the normal operating requirements of the subject company. This is an example of a Non-Operating or Excess Asset Adjustment.

Balance Sheet Adjustments

As previously mentioned, the purpose of balance sheet adjustments are to re-cast the values reported by the subject company to new amounts that would approximate what would be realized in a fair market value sale between a hypothetical willing buyer and the same type of willing seller. The reason these adjustments are often required is because balance sheet numbers are required by accounting convention to be reported at historical costs, but these same values may have little relation to current economic reality.

The balance sheet adjustments are discussed below along with the reasoning for each. The line items of the adjustments are displayed in the balance sheet listed in Appendix A.

- **Dental Equipment:** The dental equipment of the subject was marked down from its previous historical cost to fair market value. The fair market value determination of the dental equipment was provided to us by Liston Dental Supplies, Inc. Liston Dental Supplies, Inc. conducted a thorough review of DDS Dental Care Clinics' equipment in order to yield a Fair Market Value of $1,355,565.

- **Furniture and Fixtures:** An analysis in relation to DDS Dental Care Clinics' furniture and fixtures was provided by Tom Sawyer's Office Outfitters. This report indicated that the furniture and fixtures needed to be markdown by $49,248 in order to reflect the Fair Market Value.

- **Improvements:** This account was reduced to zero in order to remove the improvements item from the balance sheet, because they were considered to have no value.

- **Software:** This account was reduced to zero in order to remove the software item from the balance sheet, because they were considered to have no value. The purchaser has a license to use the software, and this license generally cannot be transferred from one individual to another.

- **Vehicles:** This adjusting entry was made in order to replace the historical cost of the vehicles with a more accurate fair market value. After consulting with Kelly Blue Book per Nick Gaunt, Esq. at Docker and Charter, PLLC they estimated that the vehicles' total fair market value is $43,700. Therefore, an adjusting entry of $96,065 was made to the vehicles account in order to mirror this value.

- **Accumulated Depreciation:** This account was reduced to zero because the Fair Market Value is now solely reflected in the Asset value.

- **Goodwill and Accumulated Amortization:** These accounts were reduced to zero.

- **Due From Real Estate Holdings:** This is an inter company account with affiliate Dr. Mark Wilcox, and the balance was reduced to zero.

- **Computer Equipment:** The Computer Equipment account was appraised by Mr. Jeff Davis of Summit Computer, which is located in Lexington, OR. This account was reduced to $19,135 in order to reflect its Fair Market Value.

When the above adjustments had been made the summary adjusted balance sheet at the valuation date appeared as follows:

Exhibit 27

DDS Dental Care Clinics, PLC

2010 Balance Sheet Adjustments

		Period Ended September 30, 2010	Normalize /Adjust	Normalized /Adjusted September 30, 2010
Assets:				
Current Assets				
Cash				
Checking		32,231		32,231
Medical Savings - Fortis		9,495		9,495
Money Market		21,086		21,086
Parsons Dental Clinic		3,000		3,000
Payroll Clearing Account		-1,293		-1,293
Marketable Securities				
Petty Cash		300		300
Total Cash		64,819	0	64,819
Accounts Receivable				
Accounts Receivable		550,234		550,234
Loans to Shareholders				
Employee Loans				
Total Accounts Receivable		550,234	0	550,234
Other Current Assets				
Utility Deposits		3,000		3,000
Total Other Current Assets		3,000	0	3,000
Total Current Assets		618,053	0	618,053
Fixed Assets - Net				
Fixed Assets - Cost				
Computer	1a	202,173	-183,038	19,135
Dental Equipment	2a	1,792,283	-436,718	1,355,565
Furniture and Fixtures	3a	700,852	-49,248	651,604
Improvements	4a	248,804	-248,804	0
Software	5a	36,059	-36,059	0
Vehicles	6a	139,765	-96,065	43,700
Building				
Land				
New Building				
Leasehold Improvements				
Total Fixed Assets - Cost		3,119,936	-1,049,932	2,070,004
Accumulated Depreciation	7a	-2,493,892	2,493,892	0
Machinery & Equipment				
Vehicles				
Leasehold Improvements				
Total Accumulated Depreciation		-2,493,892	2,493,892	0
Total Fixed Assets - Net		626,044	1,443,960	2,070,004
Intangible Assets - Net				
Goodwill	8a	85,000	-85,000	0
Accumulated Amortization - Goodwill	9a	-37,775	37,775	0
Total Intangible Assets - Net		47,225	-47,225	0
Other Non-Current Assets				
Other Assets				
Due from RE Holdings	10a	190,401	-190,401	0
Total Other Assets		190,401	-190,401	0
Non-Operating Assets				
Total Other Non-Current Assets		190,401	-190,401	0
Total Assets		1,481,723	1,206,334	2,688,057
Liabilities and Equity:				
Liabilities				
Current Liabilities				
Accounts Payable				
Other Current Liabilities				
401K Payroll Deduction		1,451		1,451
Cafeteria Payroll Deduction		-1,668		-1,668
Note Payable#54491				
Note Payable#106714		4,467		4,467
Note Payable#56288				
Note Payable#76589				
Note Payable#76594				
Note Payable-BMW		21,853		21,853
Note Payable-Equipment #6624034		36,376		36,376
Note Payable-Farm Credit		225,819		225,819
Note Payable-Lexus Financial				
Note Payable-Patterson Dental Cerec				
Note Payable-Van#6622679				
Payroll Liabilities		9,282		9,282
Profit Sharing Accrual		46,377		46,377
Bank of Madison Co.-#9809				
NP-Bank of Madison Co..#9779				
NP-Bank of Madison Co#4626793				
NP-First Bank -Bldg#8500				
NP-First Commerical				
Total Other Current Liabilities		343,957	0	343,957
Total Current Liabilities		343,957	0	343,957
Long-Term Debt				
Loans from Shareholders				
First State Bank-Jackson Equipment Loan		1,019,281		1,019,281
First State Bank-Huntingdon Equipment Loan		455,794		455,794
Bank of Madison Co-#9809				
Bank of Madison Co.-#4626793				
Bank of Madison Co.-#9779				
First Bank-Bldg#8500				
First Commerical				
Total Long-Term Debt		1,475,075	0	1,475,075
Other Non-Current Liabilities				
Other Liabilities				
Deferred Income Taxes				
Non-Operating Liabilities				
Total Other Non-Current Liablilities		0	0	0
Total Liabilities		1,819,032	0	1,819,032
Equity				
Capital Stock				
Other Equity				
Uncollected Revenue		550,234		550,234
Adjustments to Shareholders Equity				
Owners' Equity		-887,543	1,206,334	318,791
Total Equity		-337,309	1,206,334	869,025
Total Liabilities and Equity		1,481,723	1,206,334	2,688,057

Notes
(1a) - Fair Market Value of Computers
(2a) - Adjustment to FMV Per Patterson Dental Supplies
(3a) - Markdown of Office Furniture (FMV) Per Tom Lawler's Office Outfitters
(4a) - Removal of Improvements
(5a) - Removal of Software
(6a) - FMV of Vehicles Per Noble Grant and Kelly Blue Book
(7a) - Return Excess Depreciation
(8a) - Removal of Goodwill
(9a) - Removal of Accum Amort - Goodwill
(10a) - Removal of Intercompany Account

Income Statement Adjustments

The purpose of income statement adjustments is to clarify the statements to the benefit stream (often some type of cash flow) that would likely be available to the shareholders if the subject company were managed "free" of influences to reduce taxes and "free" of the desire to remove cash flow from the company either tax free or with reduced tax consequences. Making the adjustments to the company reflects a more accurate assessment of the true economic profit of the enterprise, and its future possibilities, if the subject company were run free of the normal owner bias previously mentioned.

Control adjustments are made only when the prerogatives of control can be exercised. Control is defined as ownership of 50% or more of the company. Here we are valuating a controlling interest. Therefore, control adjustments are appropriate since the controlling interest has these prerogatives of control. Appendix A contains a detailed listing of each income statement adjustment. The adjustment(s) and their reasoning and assumptions are discussed below:

One of our usual procedures is to look at accounts that are the "usual suspects" or adjustments. Among these are officer's compensation, depreciation and leases from an owner or related parties. I made the adjustments indicated by my analysis in order to reflect our best estimate of the true economic profit of the company if it were operated free of owner bias to reduce taxes and remove tax free income from the company. The reasons and the assumptions for the adjustments are discussed below:

- **Adjustments to Officer's Compensation:** Because this entity is a sole proprietorship, draws of the profits distributed to owners are not shown on the tax return or financial statement as compensation. The Officer's Compensation adjustment was made by applying the professional opinion of Mr. Scott M. Davis who is employed by Carlson Davis Consulting. Mr. Davis produced a report, dated on November 29, 2010, that expressed an estimate of annual compensation earned by independent dentists of similar scope and complexity of Dr. Wilcox's dental clinics. Mr. Davis's report relied on compensation surveys produced by the American Dental Association (ADA).

- **Rent:** This adjustment was made to reflect the change from historical rent to necessary economic rent. A DDS calculation was conducted diligently by the Valuator at Sipes and Seaton CPAs, by using Smith and Associates' real estate appraisal reports, which were dated on October 22, 2010 (Columbia Springs Clinic), October 28, 2010 (Plains Clinic), and November 4, 2010 (Hermiston Clinic). These reports, along with the potential gross income of each individual clinic, were used to determine the adjusted rental expense of DDS Dental Care Clinics.

- **Depreciation:** Depreciation adjustments were required to reflect the true economic condition of the subject. To arrive at the appropriate adjustment for depreciation we used RMA depreciation data for NAICS # 621210.

- **Automobile:** The automobile expense on the income statement was reduced to zero because Dr. Wilcox informed us that this was a perquisite.

- **Meals and Entertainment:** The meals and entertainment expense on the income statement was reduced to zero because this account is considered to be a result of an owner's perk.

When the previous adjustments had been made the summary adjusted income statement at the valuation date appeared as follows:

Exhibit 28
DDS Dental Care Clinics, PLC

Net Income to Adjusted Income Reconciliation

		Annualized Year Ending December 31, 2010	Year Ending December 31, 2009	Year Ending December 31, 2008	Year Ending December 31, 2007	Year Ending December 31, 2006	Year Ending December 31, 2005	Year Ending December 31, 2004	Year Ending December 31, 2003
Historic Net Income		234,208	353,704	-261,840	961,612	333,941	845,948	863,707	703,135
Automobiles	1,1,1,1	-4,537	-3,744	-3,040	-1,568				
Depreciation Expense	2,2,2,2,1,1,1,1	-82,615	-267,094	-763,225	-102,412	-72,806	-67,315	-20,129	-25,362
Meals/Entertainment	3,3,3,3,2,2,2	-3,179	-5,453	-1,959	-3,542	-1,870	-818		-80
Officer Compensation	4,4,4,4,3,3,2,3	300,000	400,000	400,000	400,000	400,000	400,000	400,000	400,000
Rent	5,5,5,5,4,4,3,4	-56,554	-52,672	153,444	-103,360	35,906	80,418	80,418	80,418
Income Taxes	Tax,Tax,Tax,Tax,Tax,Tax,Tax,Tax	15,822	93,490	0	262,648	0	147,445	137,162	80,032
Annualization		21,757							
Adjusted Net Income		87,028	189,177	-47,060	509,846	-27,289	286,218	266,256	168,127

Annualized Year Ending December 31, 2010
(1) - Removal of Owner's Perk
(2) - RMA Depreciation Adjustment
(3) - Removal of Owner's Perk
(4) - Officer's Compensation Per Carlson Dettmann Consulting
(5) - Adjust to Economic Rent
(Tax) - As Per Tax Table

Year Ending December 31, 2009
(1) - Removal of Owner's Perk
(2) - RMA Depreciation Adjust
(3) - Removal of Owner's Perk
(4) - Officer's Compensation Per Carlson Dettmann Consulting
(5) - Adjust to Economic Rent
(Tax) - As per tax table

Year Ending December 31, 2008
(1) - Removal of Owner's Perk
(2) - Adjust for excess depreciation
(3) - Removal of Owner's Perk
(4) - Officer's Compensation Per Carlson Dettmann Consulting
(5) - Adjust to Economic Rent
(Tax) - As per tax table

Year Ending December 31, 2007
(1) - Removal of Owner's Perk
(2) - Adjust for Excess Depreciation
(3) - Removal of Owner's Perk
(4) - Officer's Compensation Per Carlson Dettmann Consulting
(5) - Adjust to Economic Rent
(Tax) - As per tax table

Year Ending December 31, 2006
(1) - RMA Depreciation Adjustment
(2) - Removal of Owner's Perk
(3) - Officer's Compensation Per Carlson Dettmann Consulting
(4) - Adjust for Economic Rent
(Tax) - As per tax table

Year Ending December 31, 2005
(1) - Adjust for excess depreciation
(2) - Removal of Owner's Perk
(3) - Officer's Compensation Per Carlson Dettmann Consulting
(4) - Adjust to Economic Rent
(Tax) - As per tax table

Year Ending December 31, 2004
(1) - RMA Depreciation
(2) - Officer's Compensation Per Carlson Dettmann Consulting
(3) - Rent Adjustment
(Tax) - As per tax table

Year Ending December 31, 2003
(1) - RMA Depreciation
(2) - Removal of Owner's Perks
(3) - Officer's Compensation Per Carlson Dettmann Consulting
(4) - Rent Adjsutment
(Tax) - As per tax table

Exhibit 29
DDS Dental Care Clinics, PLC

Chart of Adjusted Net Income

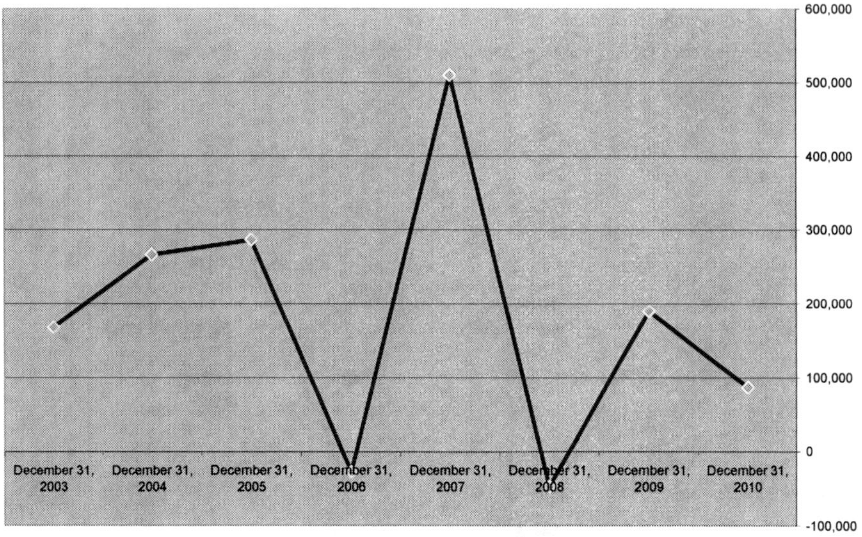

As mentioned previously, adjusted net income usually contains these line items below from the business financials and tax returns—these numbers are "added back" or "deductions" to the net income at the end of the year to obtain the "adjusted net income" of the business.

1. Owner's Salary
2. Depreciation
3. Amortization
4. Owners Personal Expenses (Auto expenses, entertainment, travel)
5. Rent

The above line graph of adjusted net income shows that the subject has experienced adjusted net income losses in two of the 5 years. Although it has been mixed from one year to another, the subject's adjusted net income has been below zero during two of the last five successive years. The subject's current annualized adjusted net income for future period ending December 31, 2010 is $87,028.

THE APPROACH TO VALUE

There are three traditional approaches to value; the cost (asset) approach, the income approach, and the market approach. Internal Revenue Ruling 59-60 which is the "bible" of business valuation provides the valuator a map to valuation principles. The company may be valued by using either an equity approach or an invested capital approach to value.

Revenue Ruling 59-60

Internal Revenue Ruling 59-60 states:

> .01 It is advisable to emphasize that in the valuation of the stock of closely held corporations or the stock of corporations where market quotations are either lacking or too scarce to be recognized, all available financial data, as well as all relevant factors affecting the fair market value, should be considered. The following factors, although not all- inclusive are fundamental and require careful analysis in each case:
>
> (a) The nature of the business and the history of the enterprise from its inception.
>
> (b) The economic outlook in general and the condition and outlook of the specific industry in particular.
>
> (c) The book value of the stock and the financial condition of the business.
>
> (d) The earning capacity of the company.
>
> (e) The dividend-paying capacity.
>
> (f) Whether or not the enterprise has goodwill or other intangible value.
>
> (g) Sales of the stock and the size of the block of stock to be valued.
>
> (h) The market price of stocks of corporations engaged in the same or a similar line of business having their stocks actively traded in a free and open market, either on an exchange or over-the-counter.

My approach gives careful consideration to all these factors.

Three Basic Approaches to Value

Asset (Cost) Based Approach: A general way of determining a value indication of a business's assets and/or equity using one or more methods based directly on the value of the assets of the business less liabilities.

Income Approach: A general way of determining a value indication of a business's assets and/or equity using one or more methods wherein a value is determined by converting anticipated benefits.

Market Approach: A general way of determining a value indication of a business's assets and/or equity using one or more methods that compares the subject to similar investments that have been sold.

The various methods of valuation that valuators use are typically considered as subdivisions of these broad approaches. Valuation methods under the Market and Income approaches generally contain common characteristics such as measures of earning power, discount rates and/or capitalization rates and multiples.

Valuation of Equity or Invested Capital: Equity means the value of the company's assets after subtracting all the liabilities. Invested Capital means the assessed value of the company's Equity plus its debt. The invested capital value would be the total price the willing seller would receive for the sale of their car. Equity value is the value of the same car after the note on the car had been paid. Our valuation here calls for an equity valuation of the subject company.

VALUATION OF THE SUBJECT COMPANY

This Section of the report discusses the valuation approaches and methods rejected and the most appropriate method(s) for the valuation selected by the valuator. The value developed here is not the final opinion of value. A later section will consider whether any premiums, discounts or other adjustments are appropriate

The Basis for Valuation

The three approaches to value were all considered to value the subject as were the eight considerations outlined in Revenue Ruling 59-60.

The approaches and methods chosen are a judgment of the valuator based on the facts, circumstances and purpose of the valuation.

The value of this subject is, in my view, best indicated by approaches and methods that rely on the net accumulated assets to determine value. In this section the valuator has provided indication of value from the methods chosen from these approaches that he considered as most appropriate and most likely to provide the best indications of value.

Methodologies Considered But Rejected

While there are certain methods that can be used to determine the fair market value of a company, the fact and circumstances in the specific case of DDS Dental Care Clinics, PLC dictates that certain methodologies are inappropriate and should therefore be rejected. The following lists those methods and the reasons why they were rejected for this subject.

Dividend Paying Capacity
This is not really a method in the truest sense of the word, but more of an ability of the subject.

The "bible" of business valuation, in my view, is Revenue Ruling 59-60, which states:

> (e) Primary consideration should be given to the dividend-paying capacity of the company rather than to dividends actually paid in the past. Recognition must be given to the necessity of retaining a reasonable portion of profits in a company to meet competition. Dividend-paying capacity is a factor that must be considered in an appraisal, but dividends actually paid in the past may not have any relation to dividend-paying capacity. Specifically, the dividends paid by a closely held family company may be measured by the income needs of the stockholders or by their desire to avoid taxes on dividend receipts, instead of by the ability of the company to pay dividends. Where an actual or effective controlling interest in a corporation is to be valued, the dividend factor is not a material element, since the payment of such dividends is discretionary with the controlling stockholders. The individual or group in control can substitute salaries and bonuses for dividends, thus reducing net income and understating the dividend-paying capacity of the company. It follows, therefore, that dividends are less reliable criteria of fair market value than other applicable factors.

Clearly, Revenue Ruling 59-60 holds dividend paying capacity in high regard as it says dividend paying capacity is a factor that must be considered.

While this method was rejected in a technical sense, the factors in dividend paying capacity were well considered in other parts of the valuation of the subject.

Book Value Method
The book value method falls within the cost (asset) approach to value.

The book value method is an accounting based value that is calculated by subtracting the book value of total liabilities from the book value of total assets. This method takes as fact that the underlying assets, stated at historical costs as required by accounting convention, are the seminal factor in the valuation of the company and that the fair market value is approximated by the book value.

The book value methodology was rejected for determining the value of DDS Dental Care Clinics, PLC because my review indicated that the value of the enterprise was driven by the ability of the collection of assets in place to generate a benefit stream[32] that is more important in terms of valuation than the value in the underlying assets themselves. In other words, the value of the individual assets and their associated liabilities are less important than the manner in which management has utilized them.

Additionally, my review indicated that the fair market value of the underlying assets less the fair market value of the liabilities was different than the book value of the assets. This due, as previously mentioned, to the fact that the accounting standards[33] do not allow for the recognition of appreciation in value.

This method was rejected.

---

[32] Normally Cash Flow or Earnings

[33] Also called accounting principles or accounting theory in the literature

Liquidation Value Method

The liquidation Value Method is generally thought to fall within the cost (asset) approach.

The definition of liquidation value for purposes of this report is:

> *The net amount that can be realized if the business is terminated and the assets are sold piecemeal.*[34]

Liquidation can be either orderly or forced, however orderly is normally assumed.

This method values a business by first adjusting the assets and liabilities to their fair market value. Next the assets are reduced by a discount that estimates the diminished value of the assets for a quick but orderly sale. Lastly, the liabilities are subjected from the diminished asset value to estimate the value of the business in orderly liquidation.

The Formula for this method might be represented as follows:

(Fair Market Value of Assets times Liquidation Discount) minus Liabilities equals the indicated value of the business

This method is generally suitable for subjects where:

- The Ownership being valued can cause liquidation.
- The liquidated assets less liabilities are more value than the capitalized income stream.
- The company is worth more dead than alive.

The method is generally not suitable for subjects:

- That are a Going Concern business.
- Where the current or projected benefit stream indicates goodwill.

In this case, we were instructed to value the company as a going concern.

This method was rejected.

---

[34] Business Valuation Body of Knowledge by Shannon Pratt, page 62

Discounted Future Cash Flow Method

The discounted future cash flow method, also known as the multi-period cash flow method is generally thought to fall within the income method.

This method looks to income rather than the underlying assets to indicate a value to the valuator. Almost without exception, the valuation community looks to this method as the best method, if available, to determine value. The Business Valuation Body of Knowledge says:

> *"In economic theory, the discounted economic income method is the proper way to value any investment."* [35]

This method develops a value by summing all the present values of discreet benefit streams that vary in future periods until the point in time when the benefit stream becomes stable and sustainable. At that point in time the present value of the terminal or benefit stream is determined and added to the sum of the previously calculated present values.

This method is generally suitable for valuations where:

- Reliable amounts of income are projected.
- Earnings of the subject contribute materially to the value.
- Future benefit streams are expected to differ from current benefit streams.
- The company is a start up business.
- The company is expecting to be acquired in the market.

This method is generally not suitable for:

- A holding company, or a company with large liquid assets
- A company where cash flow or earnings is not material.

The Subject Company did not prepare a forecast of future cash flows. The lack of a reliable estimate of stable, sustainable, terminal, or ongoing benefit stream cash flows will produce unreliable results when using this method.

This method was rejected.

[35] Page 105

Market Approach Methods

The Market Approach Method, also known as the Guideline Company Method, is usually thought to be a market method.

This method is based on the principle of substitution and relies on the concept that if one thing is like another and it can be substituted without compunction for another then their values should be quite similar.

The determination of value with this method relies on stocks traded in the open and public markets and which are alike or similar to the subject company. The value indication with this method rests on ratios developed from publicly traded companies such as the P/E (Price to Earnings Ratio) and the P/R (Price to Revenue) ratio.

This method would be suitable if sufficient and similar companies to the subject could be found for the comparison. The more similar the companies found the fewer that are needed. Companies used as market comparisons also need to be near the same in size.

This method is most often used to value companies much larger than the subject of this valuation, and in the experience of the valuator can and often will lead to unpredictable, unexpected, and inaccurate results when used to approach a small company the size of the subject.

The theory of substitution does not work with the valuation because the public guideline companies' stock and the subject company stock, due to the wide variance in size, are not in any sense an equal substitution.

Because the subject company is small in relation to the public guideline companies, this method is rejected.

Company Transactions Method

This method is generally considered to fall within the market approach.

This method uses prior sales of the subject company's stock to indicate a value of the company. Obviously, if prior transactions are available, the valuator must investigate and determine if those transactions are similar enough and recent enough to the current situation to be useful.

An inquiry of Dr. Mark Wilcox revealed that there has been no transaction involving the subject's ownership units.

This method was rejected.

Valuation Methods Selected

The choice of valuation approaches and methods is one the valuator makes based on the facts and circumstances involved. This choice includes:

- The law
- The purpose of the valuation
- The unique character of the business enterprise
- The Valuator's estimate of how the hypothetical buyer and seller will react to those unique items
- The amount of reliable information

Considering the methods previously rejected as unsuitable for this valuation, I selected the following methods as the most likely to provide a good estimate of the fair market value of the subject company.

- Asset or Cost Approach: Adjusted Book Value
- Income Approach: Capitalized Cash Flow
- Market Approach: Transaction Method

Application of the Asset Approach: Adjusted Book Value Method

Concept: The adjusted book value - going concern method develops a valuation indication by adjusting the reported book values of a subject company's assets to their actual or estimated fair market values and then subtracting its liabilities (adjusted to fair market value, if appropriate). The specific adjustments were described in the analysis of the balance sheet.

This method is generally only appropriate for control valuations where the control owner has prerogatives of control, which is the ability to dispose of the assets locked in the subject. However, there are occasions when valuing a minority interest, which cannot reach the locked in assets, that the Adjusted Asset Method can be useful. Those occasions would include when the value could be effectively changed from a majority interest value to a minority interest value.

To apply this method the process requires that the physical assets be recast to their current fair market value, as closely as can be estimated.

For purposes of this assignment all assets and liabilities have been included.

Valuation of the Tangible Assets

Tangible assets consist primarily of cash, accounts receivable, and operating equipment. Each tangible is valued at fair market value as far as can be reasonably determined. Adjustment details moving the values from historical cost (book value) to fair market value were discussed in the *normalization adjustments* section of this report and are shown in detail in Appendix A. The fair market value of the tangible assets is:

$ 2,688,057

Valuation of Intangible Assets

Step One: The valuation of intangibles is a multi-step process as outlined in Revenue Ruling 68-609[36] as published by the Internal Revenue Service. Net Tangible assets as generally defined is presented in the table below.

Exhibit 30
DDS Dental Care Clinics, PLC
Calculation of Tangible Assets

	Fair Market Value of Tangible Assets	$ 2,688,057
-	Less: Non-operating Assets	($ 0)
-	Less: Liabilities	($ 1,819,032)
=	Net Tangible Assets	$ 869,025

Step two: Next a more difficult step which is to estimate our tangible assets using an appropriate rate of return. This would probably be the return prevailing in the industry on the valuation data.[37] There is no reference book where this number can be looked up. It would seem reasonable that the very minimum rate would be what a borrower who purchased assets would pay to the lender in interest. I checked with Mr. Scott Heathman, a local banker, who told me that the likely rate at the date of valuation to the average borrower would be about 6.5% for a 5 year fixed rate loan. I also checked with Ms. Betty Billings at Dr. Wilcox's bank and she told me the note would be 5% (the floor), which is what I used.

Exhibit 31
DDS Dental Care Clinics, PLC
Calculation of Return on Net Tangible Assets

	Fair Market Value of Tangible Assets	$869,025
x	Required Rate of Return on Net Tangible Assets	5.00 %
=	Fair Return on Net Tangible Assets Liabilities	$ 43,451

Because the required minimum return of $43,451 is greater than the expected return on tangible assets $-136,578[38] I conclude that the intangible assets have no value.

[36] This is often called the "formula method" or the excess earnings method.

[37] See Revenue Ruling 59 - 60

[38] Net of Debt After Tax Cash Flow with the 3% Growth Rate applied.

Valuation of Intangible Assets

Step One: The valuation of intangibles is a multi-step process as outlined in Revenue Ruling 68-609[36] as published by the Internal Revenue Service. Net Tangible assets as generally defined is presented in the table below.

Exhibit 30
DDS Dental Care Clinics, PLC
Calculation of Tangible Assets

	Fair Market Value of Tangible Assets	$ 2,688,057
-	Less: Non-operating Assets	($ 0)
-	Less: Liabilities	($ 1,819,032)
=	Net Tangible Assets	$ 869,025

Step two: Next a more difficult step which is to estimate our tangible assets using an appropriate rate of return. This would probably be the return prevailing in the industry on the valuation data.[37] There is no reference book where this number can be looked up. It would seem reasonable that the very minimum rate would be what a borrower who purchased assets would pay to the lender in interest. I checked with Mr. Scott Heathman, a local banker, who told me that the likely rate at the date of valuation to the average borrower would be about 6.5% for a 5 year fixed rate loan. I also checked with Ms. Betty Billings at Dr. Wilcox's bank and she told me the note would be 5% (the floor), which is what I used.

Exhibit 31
DDS Dental Care Clinics, PLC
Calculation of Return on Net Tangible Assets

	Fair Market Value of Tangible Assets	$869,025
x	Required Rate of Return on Net Tangible Assets	5.00 %
=	Fair Return on Net Tangible Assets Liabilities	$ 43,451

Because the required minimum return of $43,451 is greater than the expected return on tangible assets $-136,578[38] I conclude that the intangible assets have no value.

[36] This is often called the "formula method" or the excess earnings method.

[37] See Revenue Ruling 59 - 60

[38] Net of Debt After Tax Cash Flow with the 3% Growth Rate applied.

Summary and Indicated Value Calculation

In the exhibit below, the intangible and tangible values of the subject are combined to provide a total value from this method.

Exhibit 32
DDS Dental Care Clinics, PLC
Value Indicated by Adjusted Book Value Method

	Fair Market Value of Tangible Assets	$ 2,688,057
-	Liabilities	$ 1,819,032
+	Estimated Value of Intangible Assets	$ 0
=	Indicated Value of Entire Subject	$ 869,025
=	Rounded	**$ 869,000**

The level of the value is a vital component to value. The above base is on a **control** and **marketable** basis.

Income Approach: Capitalization of Cash Flow Method

Concept: The Capitalization of Cash Flow Method derives its value from an income benefit rather than looking to the company assets. This method converts the expected benefits that an investor expects to receive as future periodic benefits to a singular current value. This, or a variation, is the approach used by most investors to estimate the value of nearly any investment. It is based on the principle of substitution.

The Capitalization of Cash Flow Method is proper when the current and recent operations of the subject are stable and expected to be continued into the future and the long term sustainable growth rate can be reasonably estimated.

This method can be defined as:

> *"Dividing a single historical or projected economic benefit (such as net cash flow) by a capitalization rate (or multiplying the same benefit by a capitalization multiple) that represents the discount rate for that benefit less the expected sustainable long-term growth rate."*

Stated another way, the use of the Capitalization of cash flow method requires

- an estimate of an steady and ongoing benefit stream and,
- a capitalization multiple, consisting of a risk factor and a growth factor.

The value indicated by this method is a very good estimate of the amount a willing buyer and a willing seller would exchange for the business.

Selection of Ongoing Benefit Stream to be Capitalized

The ongoing benefit stream should be a reasonable estimate of the likely future benefits available to the interest being valued.[39]

The analysis presented below represents the calculation of the ongoing economic benefit stream. It depicts the calculation of the after tax cash flow benefit stream.

I selected the after tax cash flow benefit stream because this is the amount that would be available to an investor or a shareholder. It is, in the valuator's opinion, the dividend paying capacity that was discussed earlier when we talked about the requirements of Revenue Ruling 59-60.

The cash flow benefit stream has been "annualized" to twelve months for year 2010. Annualized means that a time period of less than one year has been recast to be a full year based on the pro-rata relationships that were there on the date of valuation. Annualized data is necessary to make meaningful comparisons between years.

---

[39] Minority and Control interest cannot reasonably expect the same benefit stream because the control owner can force changes that the minority holder cannot.

Calculation of the Ongoing Economic Benefit Stream

Capitalization of Earnings Benefit Stream

	Annualized Year Ending December 31, 2010	Year Ending December 31, 2009	Year Ending December 31, 2008	Year Ending December 31, 2007	Year Ending December 31, 2006
Earning Power Based on Net of Debt After Tax Cash Flow					
Adjusted Pretax Income	108,124	282,667	-47,060	772,494	-27,289
Add Depreciation/Amortization and Other Non-Cash Expenses	138,720	165,657	133,809	139,936	83,228
Total	246,844	448,324	86,749	912,430	55,939
Weight	1	1	1	0	0
Ongoing Earning Power	260,639				
Less Ongoing Depreciation/Amortization	146,062				
Taxable Base	114,577				
Less Estimated State Income Taxes - Effective Rate:	0.00%				
Before Federal Taxes	114,577				
Less Federal Taxes	27,935				
Subtotal	86,642				
Depreciation/Amortization	146,062				
Subtotal	232,704				
Adjust for Working Capital Requirements	0				
Adjust for Capital Expenditure Requirements	-60,000				
Adjust for Long Term Debt Requirements	-305,298				
Calculated Ongoing Net of Debt After Tax Cash Flow	-132,594				
SELECTED ONGOING NET OF DEBT AFTER TAX CASH FLOW	-132,600				

Weighting of the Net Cash Flow to Equity

The weighting of cash flows can often be a difficult decision. In this case, the weighting of the Cash Flow was evenly distributed through the years 2008-2010 because of the change in business model and strategy from a dental practice with less debt and larger net income to a dental practice with large amounts of debt and normalized losses in one of the last three years. I chose not to include the years prior to 2008 since they were not relevant based on the change in policy. Our examination of the prior years did indicate that strategy change had made an impact on the performance and reporting of the subject company. I would have preferred the use the average of all years reviewed which might have better covered an operating cycle for the subject. That was not possible in this valuation due to the change in strategy and to include those years might have skewed our numbers.

Taxes

Taxes were calculated as $0 for the state and $27,935 for federal. The ongoing benefit stream was reduced by these outflows.

Cash Flow

A cash flow stream needs to define the changes in working capital, capital expenditures and long term debt. The ongoing change in working capital is $0. The ongoing decrease in capital expenditures is $60,000.[40] The decrease in long term debt amounts to $305,298. This amount was provided to us by Ms. Anita Hill-independent CPA for Dr. Wilcox. The amounts were rounded and based on the assumptions discussed below.

[40] Estimated and provided by Dr. Wilcox.

Assumptions Used in Adjusting from Net Income to Net Cash Flow to Equity

- Depreciation: Historically, the subject has reported high depreciation compared to its net revenue when compared to the industry cohorts. The RMA industry data for NAICS #621210 indicates that the subject, if typical, would have depreciation of approximately between 2.7% and 4.4% of Sales.

  The DDS Dental Care Real Estate Holding Group, an affiliate of this dental practice, has as its economic purpose to purchase and then rent dental real estate buildings to the DDS Dental Care Clinics entity. The result of that strategy is that the depreciation expense and interest expense that this practice might incur under different circumstances is transferred to the Real Estate Holding affiliate.

  One purpose of depreciation is to provide for a consumption of the assets so that a new capital expenditure can be made at the appropriate time. With this in mind, the valuator looked to use the depreciation expense averaged over three years as the proxy for the on going depreciation expense required.

- Required Capital Expenditures: Capacity must be maintained by the company and so the subject will need to acquire fixed assets. Without acquiring these assets to take the place of consumed assets the company would eventually reach a place where they could not maintain their place in the marketplace. According to Dr. Wilcox, the practice anticipates an ongoing $60,000 capital expenditures and our benefit stream reflects that amount.

- No Change in the Working Capital Required: Every company must have adequate working capital from its cash flow to reinvest in the business to assure its continued success. My review of working capital of this subject indicated that working capital of the subject has not been a problem in the past. My analysis of the working capital ratio indicated that no adjustment is required on the part of the subject, because the subject's working capital ratio exceeds that of its peers.

- Long Term Debt: Many companies and professional practices require both short term and long term debt to assist in the financing of current and future operations. Long-term debt was provided to us by Ms. Anita H., whom is a Partner at H. CPA Firm.[41] I also spoke with Ms. Betty B. at 1st State bank who provided us the principle for the next 12 months.[42]

---

[41] Estimate provided by Mr. Tony Jones, CPA and Anita Hamilton, CPA at Horne LLP is $305,298.

[42] During a personal conversation between Betty Baker at 1st State Bank and Bill Sipes, CPA at 2:54 pm on November 29, 2010, Ms. Baker revealed that the principle on the debt is for the next 12 months is $280,905.

Selection of a Suitable Capitalization Rate

Capitalization Rates

The Capitalization rate is a rate of return which is defined as follows:

"*...an amount of income (loss) and/or change in value realized or anticipated on an investment, expressed as a percentage of that investment.*"[43]

Master Certified Business Appraiser Steve Schroeder states that investors may not all demand the same rate but you can be sure they will demand a rate of return that will satisfy them that they have invested their money appropriately.

Like other aspects of valuation the use of the capitalization rate is based on the principle of substitution. As you may recall, that principle says that the valuator must consider alternative investments. To do that the valuator must put himself in the "shoes" of the potential investor, or fair market value financial buyer, and consider the factors he would consider. Those factors would in this valuator's opinion include size, liquidity, risk and the very nature of the subject business.

The discount rate/capitalization rate represents the risk an investor is willing to take on for the potential reward an investment in the subject company will return. Different rates apply to different types of businesses. It can also be considered the rate of return that an investor requires on an ongoing basis.

The Capitalization Rate can be shown as follows:

Capitalization Rate = Risk Free Rate + Risk Premiums – Long Term Growth Rate

This risk is not calculated in a vacuum or a sterile environment but rather it is calculated based on the factors that can be contrasted against the investment in other vehicles that are available (alternatives, or substitutes) and in the specific environment as of the valuation date.

It is common for the valuator to use a build-up method to determine his capitalization rate. The buildup method layers different risk estimates starting from the least risky and moving to the most risky to "build up" a discount rate. The discount rate is then reduced by sustainable long-term growth to yield the capitalization rate.

Rate to Factor Conversion

The capitalization rate developed using the buildup method is 25.26%. The reciprocal of this measure (1/25.26%) provides a capitalization multiple of 4.077593.

---

[43] Hitchner, James, *Financial Valuation: Applications and Models*, page 15 (Hoboken, New Jersey:Wiley,2003).

Calculation of the Multiple

The schedule below shows how the multiple was calculated.

Exhibit 33
DDS Dental Care Clinics, PLC
The Build-up of the Discount Rate and the Capitalization Rate

Capitalization of Earnings Capitalization Rate

BUILDUP CAPITALIZATION RATE

Risk-Free Rate of Return	3.38%	
Equity Risk Premium	6.60%	
Small Stock Risk Premium	6.28%	
Company Specific Premium	12.00%	
Net Cash Flow Discount Rate	28.26%	
Discount Rate		28.26%
Sustainable Growth		3.00%
Capitalization Rate To Apply To Next Year Stream		25.26%
Selected Rate		25.26%

Each part of the build-up rate is explained below.

Risk Free Rate

The risk free rate measures the rate of return an investor can earn without taking any additional risk. Examples of risk free returns are the United States Treasury bonds. As of the valuation date September 30, 2010, this yield was 3.38%. The rate applied to the buildup was

3.38%[44]

Equity Risk Premium

The equity risk premium represents the incremental risk an investor takes on for investing in large public companies. This risk is measured by taking the returns of large public companies since the year 1926 and subtracting the risk free return since 1926 (average annual returns for large capitalization stocks minus average annual returns for long-term government bonds). This information is published by Ibbotson Associates. As of December 31, 2009, the equity risk premium was 6.60%. We used this rate as a proxy for our September 30, 2010 rate. The rate applied to DDS Dental Care Clinics, PLC was

6.60%[45]

[44] http://www.treas.gov/offices/domestic-finance/debt-management/interest-rate/yield_historical.shtml

[45] We used the 12/31/2009 note, as determined by SBBI data, as the proxy for the 9/30/2010 note.

Size Risk Premium

Empirical evidence shows that the risk reward principle (the greater the risk the greater the reward) holds true in the size or capitalization of the company. The size premium represents average annual returns for small capitalization stocks minus average annual returns for large capitalization stocks. Based on Stocks, Bonds, Bills, and Inflation Yearbook, a publication of Ibbotson & Associates, the small stock risk premium averaged 6.28% from 1926 to 2009. We used the December 31, 2009 rate as a proxy for the September 30, 2010 rate. The rate applied to DDS Dental Care Clinics, PLC was

6.28%[46]

Company Specific Risk Premium

Based upon Company specific factors - cyclical risk, risks of competitive encroachment, Management, Financial Risk, size and various operating concentrations (key executive dependency, customer concentration, and other issues discussed below) - the risk associated with the company requires an additional risk premium of

12.00%

The company Specific Risk Premium is a unique component of the buildup and as Indicated is specific to and only appropriate to the subject company. The Specific Risk Premium has been defined as

> *"additional return required if risks of the subject company [are] greater than those reflected in [comparable] companies on which the risk premium elements are based"*[26]

My estimate of the most appropriate specific risk premium for the subject carefully considered all of the follow factors:

Depth of Subject Company Management: The Company has good and experienced management that are thoroughly familiar with the practice and its capabilities.

The Importance of Key People: Several people appear to be key people to this company, especially Dr. Wilcox. The loss of this person could negatively impact the subject. Unfortunately, Dr. Wilcox has a medical condition that may end his career soon. Two doctors from V. Medical Center, Thomas L. D., M.D. and Harry F. G., M.D., have diagnosed and treated Dr. Wilcox for a hand tremor. However, despite treatment with multiple medications, Dr. Wilcox's tremor has worsened over the years.

Succession Plan: The Company does not have a succession plan. This is a serious flaw in the strategic makeup for the practice.

Growth Potential of the Company: The geographic location is a very good location for the practice due to a considerably dense population in continuous need of dental health care.

---

[46] We used the 12/31/2009 rate, as determined by SBBI data, as the proxy for the 9/30/2010 rate.

Stability of the Company's Profits: Due to a change in business strategy in 2007-2008 and the worsening of economic conditions beginning in 2007, as well as a number of other reasons, the adjusted income statement indicates no stability in profits over the last 7 ¾ periods. This has a negative impact on the subject.

Company Gross Revenue: Looking at the subject's gross revenue indicates a mixed bag as well. Gross revenue is fiscal year ended 2009 was higher than any preceding year.

Location of the Company: The Company has 3 operating locations, which are located in Vernonia, OR; Hermiston, OR; and Plains, OR (see the discussion of the local economy in the Economic and Industry Section). These are mid-sized and progressive communities in West Oregon with a growing population in need of continuous dental health care.

Risk: In 2008, the practice more than doubled its debt by $1,098,069. This adds a considerable element of risk to this practice and places the bottom line of this practice in jeopardy.

The Concentration of the Company's Customer Base: The practice reported occasional larger billings to patients, but said none were really of a size to consider them for patient concentration. Dental surgery procedures by their nature can and do get expensive.

It is the valuator's hope that someday there will be empirical methods that will allow the valuator a better way to express the use and development of this part of the build up rate. However, for now, the best we can do is to explain our reasoning. With this in mind, based on the previous discussion I selected the specific company discount rate.

Expected Sustainable Long-Term Growth Rate

The valuator estimates 3.00% long-term compound annual growth. This cash flow growth estimate is based upon my assessment of the Company's prospects for sustained growth in relationship to the estimate of ongoing earning power developed above and the assumption that the subject will continue to grow at approximately the rate a little above inflation which the valuator assumes will continue to be in the range of 3 percent.

Check of Total Capitalization rate against findings in the literature: The capitalization rate selected is comparable to other sources.[47] My analysis placed the subject in the slightly more risky side of the table because of a heavy debt load. The specific risk premium selected by the valuator represents the opinion of the most likely entire risk faced by the subject.

[47] In a private conversation that I had with Steve Schroeder, who is chairman emeritus of the Institute of Business Appraisers Review Qualification Committee, he informed me that a study of the IBA Transaction Data Base revealed that the average rate of return on a business or professional practice listed in their database was approximately 25%, which is very near the rate used in this report.

Summary and Indicated Value

Capitalization of Earnings Indicated Value

Net of Debt After Tax Cash Flow	-132,600	
Sustainable Growth Rate	3.00%	
Net of Debt After Tax Cash Flow		-136,578
Capitalization Rate		25.26%
Indicated Equity Value		-540,689
SELECTED EQUITY VALUE		-541,000

To calculate an indicated value for DDS Dental Care Clinics, PLC, the first step is to calculate next year's cash flow by adding 3% to this year's cash flow. The second step is to divide projected cash flow by the selected capitalization rate, as shown above.

Indicated Value Capitalization of Earnings Method

As calculated, the indicated fair market value of the subject is $-540,689 which has been rounded to

$-541,000.

Direct Market Data Method (Transaction)

How this Method Works (the Conceptual Basis)

The Direct Market Data Method relies on actual transactions. These transactions are actual sales of ownership interest in companies similar to the subject. Usually business brokers report these transactions, but business valuators sometimes report these transactions also.

I queried the IBA[48] database for sales transactions because of its size and long standing acceptance in the Business Valuation community. The database is comprised of nearly 30,000 transactions and is commonly used in the valuation community for business "comps". The institute reports that it is the largest database of its kind in the world.

To use this method the business valuator must first gather a list of appropriate sales transactions. The next step -- based on the transactions -- a "multiplier is formed" that will project a value from the list of appropriate comparables to the subject company. This is accomplished by the final step which is to determine Revenue, and possibly a Seller's Discretionary Cash Flow base, so the multiplier may be applied to determine value.

The general problem with this method is that often little is known of the companies and additional research must be done to determine if the list of sales transactions are from companies truly comparable to our company. Sometimes this research is successful and sometimes it is not.

Selection of Transactions for Comparison to the subject

I obtained the market comparison data from the IBA (Institute of Business Appraisers) to begin our use of this method. I requested all of the transactions for the SIC code 8021. This included 2,545 transaction actions in companies that operate by reference to that code. I narrowed the list, by use of the business type column to the 27 comparables that are included in the exhibit which follows on the next page. I removed a number of transactions by looking at the company descriptions because they were obviously not comparable (i.e. Medical Practice Primary, Oral and Maxillofacial Surgery, etc.). Next I removed all transactions with Gross Sales of less than 2.0 Million dollars, because for the past 7 ¾ years that are currently being reviewed the subject has experienced only 1 year ending revenue amount of less than $2.0 million. Again this action was taken to allow for better comparability.

The average revenues of the comparable companies are around $2,636,000 but the median is smaller—around $2,500,000. The range of the Price/Gross Sales[49] ratio has a high of 1.43 and a low of .35. The dates of the transactions for these companies were mixed with some transactions dating as far back as 2003. The most recent transaction was in 2008.

[48] Institute of Business Appraisers, Plantation, Florida

[49] Also the Sales Price Received divided by Annual Revenues of the company

Valuation of 100.00% of the Sole Proprietorship of DDS Dental Care Clinics, PLC
As of September 30, 2010

The exhibit below shows the comparables selected for this valuation.

Exhibit 34
DDS Dental Care Clinics, PLC
Table of potential comparables from the IBA Database

Business Type	Annual Sales $000's	Annual Earnings $000's	Sales Price $000's	Sales Price/ Annual Sales	Sales Price/ Annual Earnings	Location	Sale Date
General Dentistry	2,000		400	0.63		PA	12/01/04
General Dental	2,071		329	0.56		NM	07/01/05
General Dental	2,078		635	0.47		NM	04/01/05
General Dental	2,079		329	0.64		NM	01/01/05
General Dental	2,100		514	0.56		NM	10/01/04
General Dental	2,100		325	0.80		NM	05/01/03
General Dental	2,100		260	0.64		NM	12/01/03
General Dental	2,124		550	0.64		NM	12/01/03
General Dental	2,125		479	0.67		NM	02/01/04
Dentists' office	2,200		48				01/01/06
General Dentistry	2,500	260	567	0.85	2.18	TX	05/01/06
General Dentistry	2,500	202	394	0.68	1.95	TX	04/04/06
General Dentistry	2,500	65	140	0.67	2.15	TX	04/04/06
General Dentistry	2,500	91	140	0.51	1.54	TX	09/01/06
General Dentistry	2,558	170	275	0.70	1.62	TX	09/01/06
General Dentistry	2,567	75	150	1.43	2.00	TX	08/01/06
General Dentistry	2,600	350	498	0.60	1.42	TX	07/01/06
General Dentistry	2,620	225	350	0.68	1.56	TX	11/01/05
General Dentistry	2,673	255	200	0.35	0.78	TX	09/01/05
General Dentistry	2,713	770	759	0.70	0.99	TX	05/01/05
General Dentistry	2,730	230	482	0.74	2.10	TX	04/01/05
General Dentistry	3,175		430	0.63		OR	07/01/07
Dental Related|Dental Practice	3,249	77	395	0.75	5.13	RI	01/17/06
Dental Related|Dental Practice	3,310	0	275	0.44		IN	03/20/06
Dental Related|Dental Practice	3,325	160	0			SC	12/05/06
General dentistry	4,132		116	0.37		PA	12/01/07
General Dentistry	4,555		140	0.45		PA	12/01/08

27 Transactions Selected

	Annual Sales $000's	Annual Earnings $000's	Sales Price $000's	Sales Price/ Annual Sales	Sales Price/ Annual Earnings
Number of Observations				25	12
Low	$2,000	$0	$0	0.35	0.78
High	$4,555	$770	$759	1.43	5.13
25th Percentile				0.56	1.51
Mean	$2,636	$209	$340	0.65	1.95
Median	$2,500	$186	$329	0.64	1.78
75th Percentile				0.70	2.11
Standard Deviation	$637	$188	$187	0.21	1.10
Coefficient of Variation				0.32	0.56

A scatter gram of the above table appears below:

Exhibit 35
DDS Dental Care Clinics, PLC
Scatter Gram IBA Price to Revenue Scatter Gram

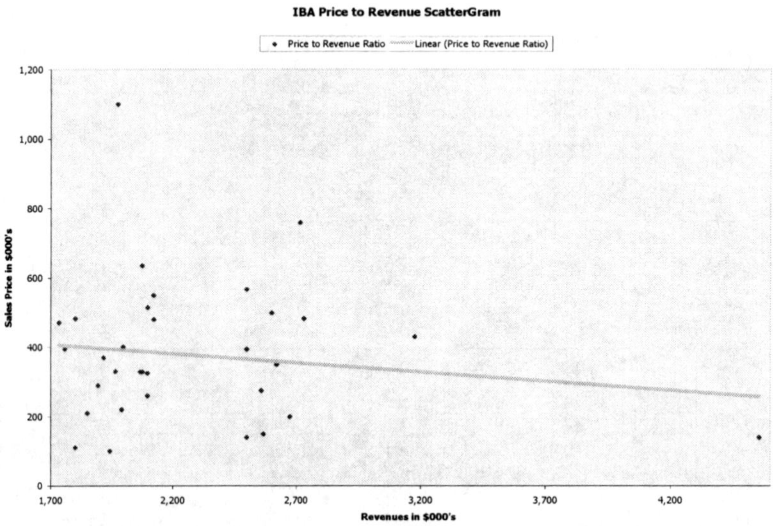

The main feature, in this valuator view of this scatter gram is the various distributions of the transactions above and below the trend line. As the line is extended, less outliers appear underneath or above the line. Overall, the line does not seem to at least identify a rough to positive correlation between price and revenue, but rather a slightly negative correlation. Therefore, larger revenue does not necessarily equal larger sales price.

One good question is: Does the database lose some of its ability to predict value when using older transactions. The answer is provided by IBA as follows: "...transaction data on closely held businesses do not become obsolete with the passage of time."[50] The study goes on to say that the multiples developed by the database, according to empirical proprietary research by IBA, are acceptable ways to develop market ratios of Price/Gross and Price/Earnings ratios and are unrelated to the data of the transaction.[51] Clearly IBA suggest using transactions from their database in the market method regardless of the dates of the transaction. However, this is an area of some controversy and other experts think the transactions should be much closer to the effective date of the report to be used as a comparable transaction.

---

[50] Institute of Business Appraisers, How to use the IBA market database, Part XXV, page 4 published 1999

[51] Ibid

Selection of a suitable multiplier

As shown above a statistical analysis of the data yields the following: a mean Sales Price to Revenue of 65 % and a median for the same ratio of 64%. Even though the range of data is narrowly defined[52] it is the valuator's view that the median, that is the middle number, is more apt to provide a meaningful estimate of the value than the mean. The mean, also known as the average, can be skewed by high or low numbers and is often replaced by the median to provide a truer economic picture for that reason.

Conclusion: I selected the median Sales Price to Revenue as my multiplier.

---

[52]Statisticians generally feel a narrowly defined and close range between the mean and the median provide the user a more meaningful and useful amount of data and that the data is more reliable than data with a wider dispersion between the mean and the median.

Exhibit 36
DDS Dental Care Clinics, PLC

Calculation of the Revenue Base for use with the IBA Data Base and using the Price to Sales Method

IBA Revenue Base

	Annualized Year Ending December 31, 2010	Year Ending December 31, 2009	Year Ending December 31, 2008	Year Ending December 31, 2007	Year Ending December 31, 2006
Adjusted Revenue	3,913,335	4,705,627	3,935,559	4,115,755	2,447,885
Additional Adjustment					
Total	3,913,335	4,705,627	3,935,559	4,115,755	2,447,885
Weight On Revenue	1	1	1	0	0
Ongoing Revenue	4,184,840				
SELECTED ONGOING REVENUE BASE	4,184,800				

Once again, I chose not to include the years prior to 2008 since they were not relevant based on the change in debt policy. Our examination of the prior years did indicate that strategy change had made an impact on the performance and reporting of the subject company. I would have preferred the use the average of all years reviewed which might have better covered an operating cycle for the subject. That was not possible in this valuation due to the change in strategy and to include those years might have skewed our numbers.

Summary and Indicated Value

I developed a value for this method by multiplying the selected multiplier by the expected, or normalized gross revenue.

Exhibit 37
DDS Dental Care Clinics, PLC
Table to develop the Value Indicated by the Direct Market Method[53]
IBA Indicated Value

	SDE Multiple	Revenue Multiple
Base	608,600	4,184,800
Multiple	1.78	0.64
Subtotal	1,083,308	2,678,272
Net Operating Assets	-1,200,979	-1,200,979
Subtotal	-117,671	1,477,293
Weight	0	1
Ongoing Value	1,477,293	
Adjustment	-147,730	
Indicated Equity Value	1,329,563	
SELECTED EQUITY VALUE	1,329,600	

Estimate of Sellers' Discretionary Earnings[54]

Normally, I make no analysis of the discretionary earnings. After discussions with IBA it was concluded that these estimates are largely unreliable because of the various bias of owners and their constant desire to reduce taxes to the lowest possible level. Further, IBA studies indicate that the Price to Sales Ratio is probably the best indicator of value.[55] Further, the coefficient of variation indicated that the revenue multiple provided a better indicator of potential value.

Seller's Commission

The -147,730 adjustment to the Price to Sales Ratio is the costs of sale of the practice in the private sector by a business broker at estimated ten percent commission sale.

1,329,600

[53] This method includes what is known as "packaging" differences. These differences make the assumption that the transactions used in this method did not include the buyers receiving the cash or accounts receivable of the company. It also assumes that the liabilities of the company remain with the seller. This adjustment is shown above as Net Operating Assets.

[54] Valuation Resources.com states that seller's discretionary earnings (SDE) is defined as net income before the primary owner's compensation, other discretionary, nonoperating, or nonrecurring income or expenses, depreciation, interest, and taxes.

[55] Technical Studies of the IBA Transactional Database published by the Institute of Business Appraisers in 2002.

ADJUSTMENTS

Before we provide our final conclusion of value, there are additional considerations to be made. Often these are called adjustments. The valuator must consider and determine if any additional adjustments are necessary and appropriate. This section will identify the adjustments and provide reasoning for their application to reach a final conclusion of value.

Adjustment for Non-Operating and/or Excess Assets

The purpose of this adjustment is to recognize certain assets in the subject that do not contribute to the operation of the company because they are either personal in nature, are normally used for the personal benefit of owner(s), or they are not necessary to the operation of the business.

Examples of often seen Non-Operating Assets include:

- A pleasure boat
- Airplane or automobile
- Skybox
- Securities
- Real Estate

Excess assets, as previously mentioned are assets over and above what would be required to operate the business under most business conditions. These assets are harder to identify than the Non-Operating Assets discussed above. The method used to identify these "excess" assets is to compare the assets i.e. cash, inventory to the average of the peers in the industry to see if you can discovery a pattern of overinvestment for which little or no benefit is provided to the company.

Examples of "Excess" Assets include:

- Cash
- Inventory

Both the Non-Operating Assets adjustment and the "Excess" adjustment are normally only applied in the case of a "control" appraisal…one in which the owners of the interest could affect the changes implied by the adjustments. My analysis found no assets of this type.

Conclusion: The amount of the adjustment for non-operating and/or excess assets is:

$ -0-

Adjustment for Control

The Concept: *Cravens v. Welch* describes the plight of minority stockholders as "minority stock interests in a 'closed' corporation are usually worth much less than the proportionate share of the assets to which they attach."[56] If no protective measures are taken, the controlling block of shares will hold more worth than the minority block of shares. These minority shareholders may even receive a small fraction of the sum received by majority shareholders when interest is sold.[57]

This disadvantage generally comes from the minority shareholder's lack of control over the financial and operational performance of the company. They have little say in the election of officers, the spending of company funds, and the distribution of dividends. They also have no control over the underlying assets, as they cannot force liquidation to realize asset values. Controlling shareholders often pay themselves higher salaries rather than distributing profits to minority shareholders through dividends. They usually have management prerogatives of the following:

Exhibit 38
DDS Dental Care Clinics, PLC
Common Prerogatives of Control

1. Set Management compensation & perks.
2. Liquidate assets.
3. Dissolve the subject.
4. Retire stock or partnership interest.
5. Determine distributions.
6. Do business with friends.

[56] *Cravens v. Welch*, 10 Fed.Supp 94 (1935)

[57] Cf. *Claget v. Hutchinson*, 583 F.2d 1259 (CA4, 1978); and *Ritchie v. McGrath*, 571 P2d 17 (1977)

In order to fully understand the disparity of value between controlling interests and non-controlling interests, a full analysis of rights continues in the following exhibit:

Exhibit 39
DDS Dental Care Clinics, PLC
Analysis of Effect on Value of Aspects of Control

Qualitative Characteristic	*Control Interest*	*Subject Interest*	*Effect on Discount*	*Comments*
Authority Characteristics				
Voting Control	Yes	Yes	**N/A**	Non control owners have little impact
Swing-vote Ability	Yes	No	**N/A**	Control concentrated in swing voter
Ability to amend by laws and agreements	Yes	Yes	**N/A**	Minority owner cannot amend by laws or agreements.
Control Accounting Methods	Yes	Yes	**N/A**	Set by Control owner(s)
Change Management	Yes	Yes	**N/A**	Controlled exclusively by Control Owner(s)
Dist. Of Benefits Characteristics				
Control Distributions/Dividends	Yes	Yes	**N/A**	Decision made by control owner(s)
Control Timing of Distributions	Yes	Yes	**N/A**	Decision made by Control owner(s)
Pay Prerequisites	Yes	Yes	**N/A**	Decision made by Control owner(s)

A minority interest is worth less than a control interest. Because minority interests are worth less than controlling interests, an adjustment known as the Minority Discount or Adjustment for Lack of Control is made to the results of valuation methods and is defined as "reduction from the pro rata share of the whole business, to reflect the absence of the power of control."[58] If the controlling owner has DDS power over pay decisions, liquidation of assets, and dividend distribution, the minority owner has no way to realize the value of their assets. As such, no potential buyer would purchase stock that promises no foreseeable return and thus a permanent minority discount exists.

Analysis and application to subject: Here I am valuing a control interest. The subject interest can control any element of the business.

Conclusion: My conclusion is that a zero percent (0%) discount is appropriate for lack of contro!, because the subject is controlled 100% by its sole proprietor, Dr. Wilcox.

[58] Business Valuation Committee of American Society of Appraisers.

Adjustment for Lack of Liquidity

The Concept: Investors love liquidity i.e. the ability to quickly convert an asset or equity into cash. To the extent this ability is missing from an assets or equity it becomes less desirable to hold.

Publicly traded companies are usually quite large and can be quickly sold and converted into cash.[59] Jack Sanders, the owner of BizComps[60], says that the average small company takes, on average, 180 days to sell.[61] The relative difference in time to sell a large freely traded public company stock versus smaller company equity requires recognition. This recognition traditionally takes the form of a liquidity discount.

The purpose of the liquidity discount is to bridge the gap quantitatively between the public marketplace and the "market" for the small privately held company. It does this by assigning a number to compensate for the difference in one side of the bridge versus the other. This is necessary because public market data was used to develop our capitalization rate but this rate was applied to a private company benefit stream.

Private companies also often have stock restriction agreements and often have restrictions in loan documents.

The Framework of our analysis: To know the basis of our analysis I point to two well known studies which provide the valuation community empirical evidence on which to benchmark this discount. The studies provide a range of reasonable discounts. Our analysis provides a point for our discount and the reason why.

The adjustment is always relative: The valuator must also be aware of what level of value his selected method has produced, and carefully apply the indicated liquidity discount, if required, relative to the value produced by the method used. The reason for this is that different methods can produce different values, i.e. control or minority values.

A Review of the Empirical Evidence: A number of empirical studies have been made in an attempt to quantity the liquidity discount. These studies fall into two basic classes:

- Restricted stock studies comparing the restricted stock to the same shares of unrestricted and freely traded stock,
- Studies of private placements which compared the price of shares of small companies sold to the price at which the shares were later sold in public offerings.

Probable range of Liquidity Discount Values: These studies point to a reasonable discount range of approximately 35% to approximately 50% for levels of value determined using public market data.

[59] This is commonly called a T3 in the securities industry, which means settlement, is made in cash in 3 days.

[60] BizComps is a database of small company transactions whose home base is San Diego, California

[61] Private conversation on June 2, 2006 at the NACVA Conference in San Francisco, California

Purpose of the Liquidity Discount: This adjustment is intended to balance the difference between the liquidity of minority interest and the liquidity of the basis for valuation. The difference often results because minority interest cannot be readily sold due to limits of control. Similar reasoning is given to the difference between liquidity of minority interest and that of publicly-traded stock that are the basis for the rate of return for projected cash flows. Both theory and practice prove that liquidity has greater value than the lack of liquidity.

Conclusion: In view of the facts above and understanding that the discount is relative to the base I have chosen a liquidity discount of zero percent (0%). No liquidity adjustment is needed for the subject because the Business is 100% owned by its sole proprietor, Dr. Wilcox.[62]

[62] This is an area of current controversy within the Business Appraisal community. There are a number of members of the community that think a discount for liquidity is appropriate for a control business. Currently there is no empirical research to suggest any type of liquidity discount is appropriate.

REACHING AND RECONCILING A CONGRUENCE OF VALUE

The valuator at this point in the valuation process has reached the point where he must coalesce the values indicated from the various methods, or pick one or several that he has the most confidence will yield the most accurate and most appropriate results. This is a key area and requires careful and diligent thought because methods may produce value indications with a large variance between them. This is the final step to the conclusion of value.

Now comes decision time. The valuator has value indications from several methods and must use his best judgment to determine which one method, or averaging of several methods, provides the most meaningful answer in the current circumstances.

There is no book where the answer can be found. The valuator must now use more of his judgment and business acumen to reach a final conclusion. Also, the valuator must thoughtfully consider which of the various value indicators would reflect his analysis of how the hypothetical buyer and hypothetical seller would think. The valuator must then express his level of confidence in each value indicator. Further, he should explain his reasoning for the confidence.

The **Adjusted Book Value** is often used, especially by neophytes. It is also easy to understand. Assets and Liabilities are adjusted to their fair market values, unrecorded assets or liabilities are added, and the resulting difference after subtracting the adjusted liabilities from the adjusted assets is Fair Market Value.

As a general rule, asset based methods are less suitable for valuation indicators than the income or market methods. The reason for this is that the profits of a business, rather than the possession of assets, motivate most enterprises. The primary question is "What would the hypothetical buyer and hypothetical seller do?"

The Asset Method provides us with a threshold of value or a floor, if you will. The process then goes on to the Income Method and the Market Method, in which these methods are usually expected to indicate a higher value. Here, because we have a negative net free cash flow, which provides a zero value for the income method and also makes our market value indicator suspect, we are left at the Asset Method by default.

Conclusion: I choose to give this method a weight of one hundred percent (100%).

The **Capitalized Cash Flow Method** is an example of a use of a pure investment activity. Refer to the foreword on page 4 of this document and locate the principle of future benefits. You are informed that the value of any investment is the future estimated benefit discounted back to the present date at an appropriate and suitable cost of capital. An operating company is treated as if it were an investment, similar to a stock that provides its investor a dividend, and is valued accordingly.

The bible of valuation, Revenue Ruling 59-60 provides a loud and clear message to the valuation community:

"*...In general, the appraiser will accord primary consideration to earnings, when valuing stocks of companies which sell products or services to the public...*"[63]

Estimating the benefit stream and building a discount rate and capitalization rate are central to the use of this method. We diligently analyzed and carefully computed each of those two parts of this method. Our analysis of the benefit stream provided us with a negative amount. Therefore, the Income Approach provided us with no value indicator to the hypothetical investor, as no hypothetical investor would purchase an investment without expecting a return on his/her money.

Conclusion: This method receives a weight of zero percent (0%)

[63] Internal Revenue Ruling 59-60, Section 5(a)

The **Direct Market Data Method** is based on actual transaction in the marketplace and is easy to understand. It is very similar to a real estate valuator using the comparable house across the street, which just sold to value your house. This is another method that on the face is easy to understand...but sometimes not so easy to apply.

First, it is often difficult to find a comparable business. That is why it is often called similar business rather than comparable.

Again, I refer to Revenue Ruling 59-60, which states:

"The market price of stocks of corporations engaged in the same or similar lines of business having their stocks actively traded in a free and open market, either on an exchange or over the counter."[64]

We found potential comparable companies, but were not able to find out much additional information about any of the companies. As such, we have a general indication of the industry more than comparable to one particular company. Most practices sell on a term price and are self-financed. We have no idea how many are in the IBA Database that fit this description, but for all that did the Cash Equivalent price would be materially lower. Here we seek a Cash Equivalent Price. In addition, some of the data was old which makes it of questionable comparability.

Finally we performed a "sanity test" on the indication of value provided by the Direct Market Data Method. That test is also called a justification of purchase test. Using the indicated value of $1,329,600 and common terms in the industry, I found that the amount obtained from this method could not be justified as a reasonable transaction price.

Conclusion: Because of lack of additional information about the transactions, and the older age of some of the transactions, I am not confident with this method and afford it a weight of zero percent (0%).

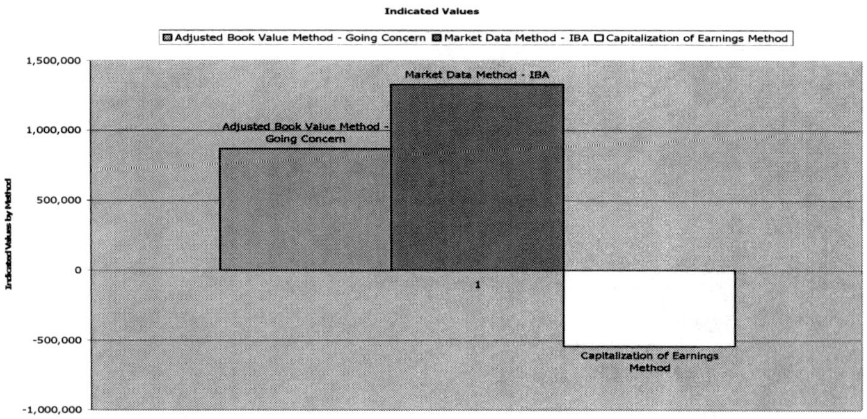

---

64 Ibid.

CONCLUSION OF VALUE

In the opinion of the valuator(s), using accepted methods of valuation, and subject to the assumptions and limiting conditions herein, the fair market value of **100.00%** of DDS Dental Care Clinics, PLC, at September 30, 2010 is:

$869,000

APPENDIX A: ADJUSTED FINANCIAL STATEMENTS

2010 Balance Sheet Adjustments

		Period Ended September 30, 2010	Normalize /Adjust	Normalized /Adjusted September 30, 2010
Assets:				
Current Assets				
Cash				
Checking		32,231		32,231
Medical Savings - Fortis		9,495		9,495
Money Market		21,086		21,086
Parsons Dental Clinic		3,000		3,000
Payroll Clearing Account		-1,293		-1,293
Marketable Securities				
Petty Cash		300		300
Total Cash		64,819	0	64,819
Accounts Receivable				
Accounts Receivable		550,234		550,234
Loans to Shareholders				
Employee Loans				
Total Accounts Receivable		550,234	0	550,234
Other Current Assets				
Utility Deposits		3,000		3,000
Total Other Current Assets		3,000	0	3,000
Total Current Assets		618,053	0	618,053
Fixed Assets - Net				
Fixed Assets - Cost				
Computer	1a	202,173	-183,038	19,135
Dental Equipment	2a	1,792,283	-436,718	1,355,565
Furniture and Fixtures	3a	700,852	-49,248	651,604
Improvements	4a	248,804	-248,804	0
Software	5a	36,059	-36,059	0
Vehicles	6a	139,765	-96,065	43,700
Building				
Land				
New Building				
Leasehold Improvements				
Total Fixed Assets - Cost		3,119,936	-1,049,932	2,070,004
Accumulated Depreciation	7a	-2,493,892	2,493,892	0
Machinery & Equipment				
Vehicles				
Leasehold Improvements				
Total Accumulated Depreciation		-2,493,892	2,493,892	0
Total Fixed Assets - Net		626,044	1,443,960	2,070,004
Intangible Assets - Net				
Goodwill	8a	85,000	-85,000	0
Accumulated Amortization - Goodwill	9a	-37,775	37,775	0
Total Intangible Assets - Net		47,225	-47,225	0
Other Non-Current Assets				
Other Assets				
Due from RE Holdings	10a	190,401	-190,401	0
Total Other Assets		190,401	-190,401	0
Non-Operating Assets				
Total Other Non-Current Assets		190,401	-190,401	0
Total Assets		1,481,723	1,206,334	2,688,057
Liabilities and Equity:				
Liabilities				
Current Liabilities				
Accounts Payable				
Other Current Liabilities				
401K Payroll Deduction		1,451		1,451
Cafeteria Payroll Deduction		-1,668		-1,668
Note Payable#54491				
Note Payable#106714		4,467		4,467
Note Payable#56288				
Note Payable#76589				
Note Payable#76594				
Note Payable-BMW		21,853		21,853
Note Payable-Equipment #6624034		36,376		36,376
Note Payable-Farm Credit		225,819		225,819
Note Payable-Lexus Financial				
Note Payable-Patterson Dental Cerec				
Note Payable-Van#6622679				
Payroll Liabilities		9,282		9,282
Profit Sharing Accrual		46,377		46,377
Bank of Madison Co.-#9809				
NP-Bank of Madison Co..#9779				
NP-Bank of Madison Co#4626793				
NP-First Bank -Bldg#8500				
NP-First Commerical				
Total Other Current Liabilities		343,957	0	343,957
Total Current Liabilities		343,957	0	343,957
Long-Term Debt				
Loans from Shareholders				
First State Bank-Jackson Equipment Loan		1,019,281		1,019,281
First State Bank-Huntingdon Equipment Loan		455,794		455,794
Bank of Madison Co-#9809				
Bank of Madison Co.-#4626793				
Bank of Madison Co.-#9779				
First Bank-Bldg#8500				
First Commerical				
Total Long-Term Debt		1,475,075	0	1,475,075
Other Non-Current Liablilities				
Other Liabilities				
Deferred Income Taxes				
Non-Operating Liabilities				
Total Other Non-Current Liablilities		0	0	0
Total Liabilities		1,819,032	0	1,819,032
Equity				
Capital Stock				
Other Equity				
Uncollected Revenue		550,234		550,234
Adjustments to Shareholders Equity				
Owners' Equity		-887,543	1,206,334	318,791
Total Equity		-337,309	1,206,334	869,025
Total Liabilities and Equity		1,481,723	1,206,334	2,688,057

Notes
(1a) - Fair Market Value of Computers
(2a) - Adjustment to FMV Per Patterson Dental Supplies
(3a) - Markdown of Office Furniture (FMV) Per Tom Lawler's Office Outfitters
(4a) - Removal of Improvements
(5a) - Removal of Software
(6a) - FMV of Vehicles Per Noble Grant and Kelly Blue Book
(7a) - Return Excess Depreciation
(8a) - Removal of Goodwill
(9a) - Removal of Accum Amort - Goodwill
(10a) - Removal of Intercompany Account

Valuation of 100.00% of the Sole Proprietorship of DDS Dental Care Clinics, PLC
As of September 30, 2010

2010 Adjusted Income Statement

	Historic Period Ending September 30, 2010	Normalize /Adjust	Normalized /Adjusted September 30, 2010	Annualized Year Ending December 31, 2010	Notes
Revenues					
Refunds	-4,899		-4,899	-6,532	
Patient Fees	1,598,674		1,598,674	2,131,565	
Rent Income	26,000		26,000	34,667	
Miscellaneous Income	26,536		26,536	35,381	
Tenncare	1,288,806		1,288,806	1,718,408	
Returned Checks	-116		-116	-155	
Total Revenues	2,935,001	0	2,935,001	3,913,335	
Operating Expenses					
Accounting Fees	47,016		47,016	62,688	
Advertising	54,785		54,785	73,047	
Amortization Expense	4,250		4,250	5,667	
Automobiles	4,537	-4,537	0	0	1 - Removal of Owner's Perk
Bad Debts					
Bank Charges	12,471		12,471	16,628	
Building					
Cleaning Services	20,888		20,888	27,851	
Collections					
Computer	8,743		8,743	11,657	
Credit Card Fees					
Dental Services	188,836		188,836	251,781	
Depreciation Expense	182,405	-82,615	99,790	133,053	2 - RMA Depreciation Adjustment
Donations	4,060		4,060	5,413	
Dues and Subscriptions	1,200		1,200	1,600	
Education/Seminars	1,128		1,128	1,504	
Employee Benefits	4,810		4,810	6,413	
Employee License and Dues	4,555		4,555	6,073	
Employee Lunches					
Equipment Lease					
Flowers and Gifts	533		533	711	
Fuel/Travel/Hotels	15,898		15,898	21,197	
Insurance-Building	3,843		3,843	5,124	
Insurance-Disability					
Insurance-Employee Group					
Insurance-General	33,867		33,867	45,156	
Insurance-Malpractice	2,950		2,950	3,933	
Insurance-Workmens Comp					
Lab	100,877		100,877	134,503	
Legal					
Loan Fees					
Meals/Entertainment	3,179	-3,179	0	0	3 - Removal of Owner's Perk
Miscellaneous	1,117		1,117	1,489	
Officer Compensation		300,000	300,000	400,000	4 - Officer's Compensation Per Carlson Dettmann Consulting
Pager Expense					
Patient Reimbursement					
Payroll Taxes	86,774		86,774	115,699	
Payroll Wages	1,102,604		1,102,604	1,470,139	
Penalties and Late Fees	856		856	1,141	
Postage	3,505		3,505	4,673	
Professional Fees	10,327		10,327	13,769	
Profit Sharing Expense					
Rent	350,957	-56,554	294,403	392,537	5 - Adjust to Economic Rent
Repairs & Maintenance	24,745		24,745	32,993	
Security	56		56	75	
Supplies	230,809		230,809	307,745	
Taxes & Licenses	24,550		24,550	32,733	
Telephone	30,054		30,054	40,072	
Uniforms	754		754	1,005	
Utilities	59,855		59,855	79,807	
Waste Disposal	2,128		2,128	2,837	
Total Operating Expenses	2,629,922	153,115	2,783,037	3,710,716	
Operating Profit	305,079	-153,115	151,964	202,619	
Other Income/(Expense)					
Interest Income	337		337	449	
Interest Expense	-71,208		-71,208	-94,944	
Gain/Loss on Sale of Fixed Assets					
Other Income					
Key Man Life Insurance					
Other Expense					
Total Other Income/(Expense)	-70,871	0	-70,871	-94,495	
Income Before Taxes	234,208	-153,115	81,093	108,124	
Income Taxes		15,822	15,822	21,096	Tax - As Per Tax Table
Net Income/(Loss)	234,208	-168,937	65,271	87,028	

DDS Dental Care Clinics, PLC Page 99 of 117

Valuation of 100.00% of the Sole Proprietorship of DDS Dental Care Clinics, PLC
As of September 30, 2010

2009 Adjusted Income Statement

	Historic Year Ending December 31, 2009	Normalize /Adjust	Normalized /Adjusted December 31, 2009	Notes
Revenues				
Refunds	-14,422		-14,422	
Patient Fees	2,313,018		2,313,018	
Rent Income	13,500		13,500	
Miscellaneous Income	13,242		13,242	
Tenncare	2,380,511		2,380,511	
Returned Checks	-222		-222	
Total Revenues	4,705,627	0	4,705,627	
Operating Expenses				
Accounting Fees	48,174		48,174	
Advertising	48,825		48,825	
Amortization Expense	5,666		5,666	
Automobiles	3,744	-3,744	0	1 - Removal of Owner's Perk
Bad Debts				
Bank Charges	20,444		20,444	
Building	151,028		151,028	
Cleaning Services	34,295		34,295	
Collections	1,646		1,646	
Computer	7,187		7,187	
Credit Card Fees	800		800	
Dental Services	292,604		292,604	
Depreciation Expense	427,085	-267,094	159,991	2 - RMA Depreciation Adjust
Donations	10,944		10,944	
Dues and Subscriptions	3,425		3,425	
Education/Seminars	10,226		10,226	
Employee Benefits	2,669		2,669	
Employee License and Dues	435		435	
Employee Lunches	1,913		1,913	
Equipment Lease	0		0	
Flowers and Gifts	1,669		1,669	
Fuel/Travel/Hotels	19,104		19,104	
Insurance-Building	0		0	
Insurance-Disability	4,600		4,600	
Insurance-Employee Group	12,529		12,529	
Insurance-General	0		0	
Insurance-Malpractice	5,216		5,216	
Insurance-Workmens Comp				
Lab	180,897		180,897	
Legal	4,396		4,396	
Loan Fees	1,347		1,347	
Meals/Entertainment	5,453	-5,453	0	3 - Removal of Owner's Perk
Miscellaneous	2,246		2,246	
Officer Compensation		400,000	400,000	4 - Officer's Compensation Per Carlson Dettmann Consulting
Pager Expense				
Patient Reimbursement	0		0	
Payroll Taxes	132,207		132,207	
Payroll Wages	1,835,568		1,835,568	
Penalties and Late Fees				
Postage				
Professional Fees	0		0	
Profit Sharing Expense	39,027		39,027	
Rent	445,209	-52,672	392,537	5 - Adjust to Economic Rent
Repairs & Maintenance	2,749		2,749	
Security	3,531		3,531	
Supplies	394,321	0	394,321	
Taxes & Licenses	75,640	0	75,640	
Telephone				
Uniforms	3,052		3,052	
Utilities				
Waste Disposal				
Total Operating Expenses	4,239,869	71,037	4,310,906	
Operating Profit	465,758	-71,037	394,721	
Other Income/(Expense)				
Interest Income	768		768	
Interest Expense	-112,822		-112,822	
Gain/Loss on Sale of Fixed Assets		0	0	
Other Income				
Key Man Life Insurance		0	0	
Other Expense				
Total Other Income/(Expense)	-112,054	0	-112,054	
Income Before Taxes	353,704	-71,037	282,667	
Income Taxes		93,490	93,490	Tax - As per tax table
Net Income/(Loss)	353,704	-164,527	189,177	

Valuation of 100.00% of the Sole Proprietorship of DDS Dental Care Clinics, PLC
As of September 30, 2010

2008 Adjusted Income Statement

	Historic Year Ending December 31, 2008	Normalize /Adjust	Normalized /Adjusted December 31, 2008	Notes
Revenues				
Refunds	-15,703		-15,703	
Patient Fees	1,662,129		1,662,129	
Rent Income	28,500		28,500	
Miscellaneous Income	0		0	
Tenncare	2,263,766		2,263,766	
Returned Checks	-3,132		-3,132	
Total Revenues	3,935,559	0	3,935,559	
Operating Expenses				
Accounting Fees	22,265		22,265	
Advertising	57,994		57,994	
Amortization Expense	0		0	
Automobiles	3,040	-3,040	0	1 - Removal of Owner's Perk
Bad Debts				
Bank Charges	13,597		13,597	
Building	107,275		107,275	
Cleaning Services	28,306		28,306	
Collections	1,043		1,043	
Computer	10,708		10,708	
Credit Card Fees	120		120	
Dental Services	223,701		223,701	
Depreciation Expense	897,034	-763,225	133,809	2 - Adjust for excess depreciation
Donations	8,050		8,050	
Dues and Subscriptions	1,967		1,967	
Education/Seminars	26,242		26,242	
Employee Benefits	3,746		3,746	
Employee License and Dues	500		500	
Employee Lunches	1,606		1,606	
Equipment Lease	4,369		4,369	
Flowers and Gifts	1,299		1,299	
Fuel/Travel/Hotels	28,246		28,246	
Insurance-Building	0		0	
Insurance-Disability	4,585		4,585	
Insurance-Employee Group	8,006		8,006	
Insurance-General	464		464	
Insurance-Malpractice	2,925		2,925	
Insurance-Workmens Comp				
Lab	176,895		176,895	
Legal	4,314		4,314	
Loan Fees	0		0	
Meals/Entertainment	1,959	-1,959	0	3 - Removal of Owner's Perk
Miscellaneous	0		0	
Officer Compensation		400,000	400,000	4 - Officer's Compensation Per Carlson Dettmann Consulting
Pager Expense				
Patient Reimbursement	0		0	
Payroll Taxes	113,871		113,871	
Payroll Wages	1,569,820		1,569,820	
Penalties and Late Fees				
Postage				
Professional Fees	2,750		2,750	
Profit Sharing Expense	34,047		34,047	
Rent	239,093	153,444	392,537	5 - Adjust to Economic Rent
Repairs & Maintenance	731		731	
Security	1,458		1,458	
Supplies	498,416	0	498,416	
Taxes & Licenses	18,563		18,563	
Telephone				
Uniforms	2,857		2,857	
Utilities				
Waste Disposal				
Total Operating Expenses	4,121,862	-214,780	3,907,082	
Operating Profit	-186,303	214,780	28,477	
Other Income/(Expense)				
Interest Income	1,635		1,635	
Interest Expense	-77,172		-77,172	
Gain/Loss on Sale of Fixed Assets				
Other Income				
Key Man Life Insurance				
Other Expense				
Total Other Income/(Expense)	-75,537	0	-75,537	
Income Before Taxes	-261,840	214,780	-47,060	
Income Taxes		0	0	Tax - As per tax table
Net Income/(Loss)	-261,840	214,780	-47,060	

Valuation of 100.00% of the Sole Proprietorship of DDS Dental Care Clinics, PLC
As of September 30, 2010

2007 Adjusted Income Statement

	Historic Year Ending December 31, 2007	Normalize /Adjust	Normalized /Adjusted December 31, 2007	Notes
Revenues				
Refunds	-7,967		-7,967	
Patient Fees	2,177,952		2,177,952	
Rent Income	35,000		35,000	
Miscellaneous Income				
Tenncare	1,914,344		1,914,344	
Returned Checks	-3,573		-3,573	
Total Revenues	4,115,755	0	4,115,755	
Operating Expenses				
Accounting Fees	39,006		39,006	
Advertising	20,612		20,612	
Amortization Expense				
Automobiles	1,568	-1,568	0	1 - Removal of Owner's Perk
Bad Debts				
Bank Charges	7,894		7,894	
Building	106,061		106,061	
Cleaning Services	21,920		21,920	
Collections	4,239		4,239	
Computer	7,935		7,935	
Credit Card Fees	1,173		1,173	
Dental Services	258,193		258,193	
Depreciation Expense	242,348	-102,412	139,936	2 - Adjust for Excess Depreciation
Donations	7,840		7,840	
Dues and Subscriptions	1,723		1,723	
Education/Seminars	21,655		21,655	
Employee Benefits	2,263		2,263	
Employee License and Dues	295		295	
Employee Lunches	4,865		4,865	
Equipment Lease				
Flowers and Gifts	1,466		1,466	
Fuel/Travel/Hotels	19,153		19,153	
Insurance-Building	1,730		1,730	
Insurance-Disability	5,281		5,281	
Insurance-Employee Group	6,421		6,421	
Insurance-General	0		0	
Insurance-Malpractice	6,676		6,676	
Insurance-Workmens Comp	9,044		9,044	
Lab	228,614		228,614	
Legal	1,766		1,766	
Loan Fees				
Meals/Entertainment	3,542	-3,542	0	3 - Removal of Owner's Perk
Miscellaneous	8,959		8,959	
Officer Compensation		400,000	400,000	4 - Officer's Compensation Per Carlson Dettmann Consulting
Pager Expense	900		900	
Patient Reimbursement	0		0	
Payroll Taxes	84,228		84,228	
Payroll Wages	1,266,052		1,266,052	
Penalties and Late Fees				
Postage				
Professional Fees				
Profit Sharing Expense	47,453		47,453	
Rent	277,114	-103,360	173,754	5 - Adjust to Economic Rent
Repairs & Maintenance				
Security	1,404		1,404	
Supplies	352,596	0	352,596	
Taxes & Licenses	20,089		20,089	
Telephone				
Uniforms	2,890		2,890	
Utilities				
Waste Disposal				
Total Operating Expenses	3,094,970	189,118	3,284,088	
Operating Profit	1,020,785	-189,118	831,667	
Other Income/(Expense)				
Interest Income	6,349		6,349	
Interest Expense	-65,522		-65,522	
Gain/Loss on Sale of Fixed Assets				
Other Income				
Key Man Life Insurance				
Other Expense				
Total Other Income/(Expense)	-59,173	0	-59,173	
Income Before Taxes	961,612	-189,118	772,494	
Income Taxes		262,648	262,648	Tax - As per tax table
Net Income/(Loss)	961,612	-451,766	509,846	

Valuation of 100.00% of the Sole Proprietorship of DDS Dental Care Clinics, PLC
As of September 30, 2010

2006 Adjusted Income Statement

	Historic Year Ending December 31, 2006	Normalize /Adjust	Normalized /Adjusted December 31, 2006	Notes
Revenues				
Refunds	-4,003		-4,003	
Patient Fees	984,332		984,332	
Rent Income	35,000		35,000	
Miscellaneous Income				
Tenncare	1,434,345		1,434,345	
Returned Checks	-1,789		-1,789	
Total Revenues	2,447,885	0	2,447,885	
Operating Expenses				
Accounting Fees	30,185		30,185	
Advertising	9,441		9,441	
Amortization Expense				
Automobiles				
Bad Debts				
Bank Charges	4,614		4,614	
Building	75,453		75,453	
Cleaning Services	13,160		13,160	
Collections	1,505		1,505	
Computer	2,962		2,962	
Credit Card Fees	276		276	
Dental Services	169,917		169,917	
Depreciation Expense	156,034	-72,806	83,228	1 - RMA Depreciation Adjustment
Donations	2,230		2,230	
Dues and Subscriptions	3,440		3,440	
Education/Seminars	40,613		40,613	
Employee Benefits	1,827		1,827	
Employee License and Dues				
Employee Lunches	3,112		3,112	
Equipment Lease				
Flowers and Gifts	259		259	
Fuel/Travel/Hotels	20,033		20,033	
Insurance-Building	6,430		6,430	
Insurance-Disability	3,754		3,754	
Insurance-Employee Group	5,054		5,054	
Insurance-General	416		416	
Insurance-Malpractice	5,197		5,197	
Insurance-Workmens Comp	5,277		5,277	
Lab	154,620		154,620	
Legal	9,605		9,605	
Loan Fees				
Meals/Entertainment	1,870	-1,870	0	2 - Removal of Owner's Perk
Miscellaneous	1,715		1,715	
Officer Compensation		400,000	400,000	3 - Officer's Compensation Per Carlson Dettmann Consulting
Pager Expense	1,800		1,800	
Patient Reimbursement	0		0	
Payroll Taxes	55,301		55,301	
Payroll Wages	741,398		741,398	
Penalties and Late Fees				
Postage				
Professional Fees				
Profit Sharing Expense	38,888		38,888	
Rent	137,848	35,906	173,754	4 - Adjust for Economic Rent
Repairs & Maintenance				
Security	675		675	
Supplies	367,747		367,747	
Taxes & Licenses	3,045	0	3,045	
Telephone				
Uniforms	3,856		3,856	
Utilities				
Waste Disposal				
Total Operating Expenses	2,079,556	361,230	2,440,786	
Operating Profit	368,329	-361,230	7,099	
Other Income/(Expense)				
Interest Income	746	0	746	
Interest Expense	-35,134		-35,134	
Gain/Loss on Sale of Fixed Assets				
Other Income				
Key Man Life Insurance				
Other Expense				
Total Other Income/(Expense)	-34,388	0	-34,388	
Income Before Taxes	333,941	-361,230	-27,289	
Income Taxes		0	0	Tax - As per tax table
Net Income/(Loss)	333,941	-361,230	-27,289	

Valuation of 100.00% of the Sole Proprietorship of DDS Dental Care Clinics, PLC
As of September 30, 2010

2005 Adjusted Income Statement

	Historic Year Ending December 31, 2005	Normalize /Adjust	Normalized /Adjusted December 31, 2005	Notes
Revenues				
Refunds	-5,539		-5,539	
Patient Fees	761,443		761,443	
Rent Income	36,000		36,000	
Miscellaneous Income	17,014		17,014	
Tenncare	1,476,548		1,476,548	
Returned Checks				
Total Revenues	2,285,466	0	2,285,466	
Operating Expenses				
Accounting Fees	32,248		32,248	
Advertising	3,317		3,317	
Amortization Expense				
Automobiles				
Bad Debts				
Bank Charges	3,696		3,696	
Building	64,842		64,842	
Cleaning Services	8,960		8,960	
Collections	1,307		1,307	
Computer	983		983	
Credit Card Fees	501		501	
Dental Services	245,521		245,521	
Depreciation Expense	145,021	-67,315	77,706	1 - Adjust for excess depreciation
Donations	4,211		4,211	
Dues and Subscriptions	1,583		1,583	
Education/Seminars	12,088		12,088	
Employee Benefits	77		77	
Employee License and Dues				
Employee Lunches	5,392		5,392	
Equipment Lease				
Flowers and Gifts	418		418	
Fuel/Travel/Hotels	4,507		4,507	
Insurance-Building	4,671		4,671	
Insurance-Disability	2,988		2,988	
Insurance-Employee Group	660		660	
Insurance-General	2,025		2,025	
Insurance-Malpractice	1,830		1,830	
Insurance-Workmens Comp	1,634		1,634	
Lab	95,518		95,518	
Legal	24,638		24,638	
Loan Fees				
Meals/Entertainment	818	-818	0	2 - Removal of Owner's Perk
Miscellaneous	1,467		1,467	
Officer Compensation		400,000	400,000	3 - Officer's Compensation Per Carlson Dettmann Consulting
Pager Expense	1,800		1,800	
Patient Reimbursement	660		660	
Payroll Taxes	31,269		31,269	
Payroll Wages	423,088		423,088	
Penalties and Late Fees				
Postage				
Professional Fees				
Profit Sharing Expense	57,801		57,801	
Rent		80,418	80,418	4 - Adjust to Economic Rent
Repairs & Maintenance				
Security	462		462	
Supplies	189,533	0	189,533	
Taxes & Licenses	13,344		13,344	
Telephone				
Uniforms	4,632		4,632	
Utilities				
Waste Disposal				
Total Operating Expenses	1,393,511	412,285	1,805,796	
Operating Profit	891,954	-412,285	479,669	
Other Income/(Expense)				
Interest Income	867	0	867	
Interest Expense	-46,873		-46,873	
Gain/Loss on Sale of Fixed Assets				
Other Income				
Key Man Life Insurance				
Other Expense				
Total Other Income/(Expense)	-46,006	0	-46,006	
Income Before Taxes	845,948	-412,285	433,663	
Income Taxes		147,445	147,445	Tax - As per tax table
Net Income/(Loss)	845,948	-559,730	286,218	

Valuation of 100.00% of the Sole Proprietorship of DDS Dental Care Clinics, PLC
As of September 30, 2010

2004 Adjusted Income Statement

	Historic Year Ending December 31, 2004	Normalize /Adjust	Normalized /Adjusted December 31, 2004	Notes
Revenues				
Refunds	-10,875		-10,875	
Patient Fees	860,279		860,279	
Rent Income	42,500		42,500	
Miscellaneous Income				
Tenncare	1,141,478		1,141,478	
Returned Checks				
Total Revenues	2,033,382	0	2,033,382	
Operating Expenses				
Accounting Fees	15,408		15,408	
Advertising	4,401		4,401	
Amortization Expense				
Automobiles				
Bad Debts				
Bank Charges	1,862		1,862	
Building	64,598		64,598	
Cleaning Services	10,480		10,480	
Collections				
Computer	160		160	
Credit Card Fees	1,732		1,732	
Dental Services	175,976		175,976	
Depreciation Expense	89,264	-20,129	69,135	1 - RMA Depreciation
Donations	6,728		6,728	
Dues and Subscriptions	292		292	
Education/Seminars	33,189		33,189	
Employee Benefits	1,880		1,880	
Employee License and Dues				
Employee Lunches	4,176		4,176	
Equipment Lease				
Flowers and Gifts	550		550	
Fuel/Travel/Hotels	803		803	
Insurance-Building	4,414		4,414	
Insurance-Disability	2,988		2,988	
Insurance-Employee Group	660		660	
Insurance-General				
Insurance-Malpractice	1,687		1,687	
Insurance-Workmens Comp	1,732		1,732	
Lab	79,744		79,744	
Legal	12,934		12,934	
Loan Fees				
Meals/Entertainment	0		0	
Miscellaneous	722		722	
Officer Compensation		400,000	400,000	2 - Officer's Compensation Per Carlson Dettmann Consulting
Pager Expense	1,500		1,500	
Patient Reimbursement	1,721		1,721	
Payroll Taxes	26,275		26,275	
Payroll Wages	349,183		349,183	
Penalties and Late Fees				
Postage				
Professional Fees				
Profit Sharing Expense	57,879		57,879	
Rent		80,418	80,418	3 - Rent Adjustment
Repairs & Maintenance				
Security	512		512	
Supplies	169,709		169,709	
Taxes & Licenses	2,142		2,142	
Telephone				
Uniforms	6,752		6,752	
Utilities				
Waste Disposal				
Total Operating Expenses	1,132,050	460,289	1,592,339	
Operating Profit	901,332	-460,289	441,043	
Other Income/(Expense)				
Interest Income	1,075		1,075	
Interest Expense	-38,700		-38,700	
Gain/Loss on Sale of Fixed Assets				
Other Income				
Key Man Life Insurance				
Other Expense				
Total Other Income/(Expense)	-37,625	0	-37,625	
Income Before Taxes	863,707	-460,289	403,418	
Income Taxes		137,162	137,162	Tax - As per tax table
Net Income/(Loss)	863,707	-597,451	266,256	

Valuation of 100.00% of the Sole Proprietorship of DDS Dental Care Clinics, PLC
As of September 30, 2010

2003 Adjusted Income Statement

Revenues	Historic Year Ending December 31, 2003	Normalize /Adjust	Normalized /Adjusted December 31, 2003	Notes
Revenues				
Refunds	-2,259		-2,259	
Patient Fees	753,806		753,806	
Rent Income	31,700		31,700	
Miscellaneous Income				
Tenncare	943,219		943,219	
Returned Checks				
Total Revenues	1,726,466	0	1,726,466	
Operating Expenses				
Accounting Fees	17,527		17,527	
Advertising	3,681		3,681	
Amortization Expense				
Automobiles				
Bad Debts				
Bank Charges	3,432		3,432	
Building	55,462		55,462	
Cleaning Services	9,787		9,787	
Collections	898		898	
Computer	377		377	
Credit Card Fees	1,730		1,730	
Dental Services	152,049		152,049	
Depreciation Expense	84,062	-25,362	58,700	1 - RMA Depreciation
Donations	4,231		4,231	
Dues and Subscriptions	1,163		1,163	
Education/Seminars	6,556		6,556	
Employee Benefits	216		216	
Employee License and Dues				
Employee Lunches	-6,360		-6,360	
Equipment Lease				
Flowers and Gifts	130		130	
Fuel/Travel/Hotels	321		321	
Insurance-Building	3,423		3,423	
Insurance-Disability	2,988		2,988	
Insurance-Employee Group	620		620	
Insurance-General				
Insurance-Malpractice				
Insurance-Workmens Comp	1,601		1,601	
Lab	57,435		57,435	
Legal	7,165		7,165	
Loan Fees				
Meals/Entertainment	80	-80	0	2 - Removal of Owner's Perks
Miscellaneous	2,715		2,715	
Officer Compensation		400,000	400,000	3 - Officer's Compensation Per Carlson Dettmann Consulting
Pager Expense				
Patient Reimbursement	521		521	
Payroll Taxes	22,790		22,790	
Payroll Wages	308,460		308,460	
Penalties and Late Fees				
Postage				
Professional Fees				
Profit Sharing Expense	55,930		55,930	
Rent		80,418	80,418	4 - Rent Adjsutment
Repairs & Maintenance				
Security	462		462	
Supplies	149,077		149,077	
Taxes & Licenses	7,327		7,327	
Telephone				
Uniforms	2,736		2,736	
Utilities				
Waste Disposal				
Total Operating Expenses	958,594	454,976	1,413,570	
Operating Profit	767,872	-454,976	312,896	
Other Income/(Expense)				
Interest Income	591		591	
Interest Expense	-65,328		-65,328	
Gain/Loss on Sale of Fixed Assets				
Other Income				
Key Man Life Insurance				
Other Expense				
Total Other Income/(Expense)	-64,737	0	-64,737	
Income Before Taxes	703,135	-454,976	248,159	
Income Taxes		80,032	80,032	Tax - As per tax table
Net Income/(Loss)	703,135	-535,008	168,127	

APPENDIX B: ADDITIONAL LIMITING CONDITIONS

Preparation of this report involved the review of substantial documentation with respect to the Company, the industry and the national economy. Information reviewed relative to the Company is summarized in Appendix C. Sources of information related to the industry and the national economy are cited specifically at appropriate sections of the report.

In conjunction with the preparation of this report, William H. Sipes, Jr. of Sipes and Seaton PC., CPAs and Business Appraisers visited with management of DDS Dental Care Clinics, PLC. This visit, together with other conversations with management, provided important perspective to my understanding of the information reviewed and analyzed in the preparation of this valuation opinion.

In all cases, I have relied upon the referenced information without independent verification. This report is, therefore, dependent upon the information provided. A material change in critical information relied upon in this report would be cause for a reassessment to determine the effect, if any, upon my conclusion.

Users of this business valuation report should be aware that business valuations are based on future earnings potential that may or may not materialize. Therefore, the actual results achieved during the projection period will vary from the projections utilized in this valuation, and the variations may be material.

Some assumptions invariably will not materialize, and unanticipated events and circumstances may occur. Therefore, the actual performance in any areas forecasted/projected will vary from the forecast/projection, and the variations may be material. Sipes and Seaton PC., CPAs and Business Appraisers will not express any form of assurance on the likelihood of achieving the forecast/projection or on the reasonableness of the used assumptions. Any such forecast/projection is presented as part of the valuation and is not intended to be used separately.

The value premise(s) cited in this report are fundamental to the value opinions rendered herein, and I reserve the right to reconsider such premise(s) should subsequent or additional information be discovered, although no such obligation exists.

We have relied upon the representations of the owners, management and other third parties concerning the value and useful condition of all equipment, real estate, investments used in the business, and any other assets or liabilities except as specifically stated to the contrary in this report. I have not attempted to confirm whether or not all assets of the business are free and clear of liens and encumbrances, or that DDS Dental Care Clinics, PLC has good title to all assets.

The estimate of value included in this report assumes that DDS Dental Care Clinics, PLC will maintain the character and integrity of the company through any sale, reorganization or reduction of any owner's/manager's participation in the existing activities of the company.

Since neither DDS Dental Care Clinics, PLC management nor advisors have advised me otherwise, I assume that there is full compliance with all applicable federal, state, and local laws and regulations unless the lack of compliance is stated, defined, and considered in the valuation report.

Public information, purchased private information and industry statistical information are from sources I deem to be reliable; however, I make no representation as to the accuracy or DDSness of such information, and have accepted the information without further verification.

This report and its related calculations were prepared using various software applications potentially including Microsoft Word and Microsoft Excel, ValuSource Pro, and/or various Internet-related software, third-party data (as indicated) and information.

I assume no responsibility for the legal description or matters including legal or title considerations. Title to the subject assets, properties, or business interests is assumed to be good and marketable as represented by owners, management and advisors of DDS Dental Care Clinics, PLC unless otherwise stated.

We assume no hidden or unapparent conditions regarding the subject assets, properties or business interests.

Unless otherwise stated in this report, I did not observe, and I have no knowledge of, the existence of hazardous materials with regard to the subject assets, properties, or business interests. However, I am not qualified to detect such substances. I assume no responsibility for such conditions or for any expertise required to discover them.

No opinion, counsel or interpretation is intended in matters that require legal or other appropriate professional advice. It is assumed that such opinions, counsel or interpretations have been or will be obtained from the appropriate professional sources.

The analyses, opinions, and conclusions presented in this report apply to this engagement only and may not be used out of the context presented herein. This report is valid only for the effective date(s) specified and only for the purpose(s) specified herein.

Although I have exerted considerable diligence and applied my best efforts in constructing this document, immaterial anomalies, if any, may arise. Even so, I am confident that my overall conclusion would still fall within a materially consistent conclusion.

While the client has not informed DDS Dental Care Clinics, PLC of any intent to do so, any third parties to whom this report is shown may be assured that this report, while performed in the employ of the client, was materially prepared on a non-advocacy basis. Any third persons, however, are cautioned that Sipes and Seaton PC., CPAs and Business Appraisers has no duty to you and, therefore, no warranty is expressed or implied. Nothing in this report is intended to replace your independent sole judgment, due diligence, or decision to seek professional legal, accounting, or valuation counsel.

This report has been prepared solely for the use of the party or parties named and specifically for the purposes set out therein. In accordance with normal, I hereby disclaim liability to any other person. Any other person should not rely upon the information and conclusions reached nor should any statement in this report be used for any other purpose without written consent from DDS Dental Care Clinics, PLC.

The statements and opinions given in this report are given in good faith and in the belief that such statements are not false or misleading. In preparing this report I have relied upon information believed to be reliable and accurate provided by the owners, management and advisors of DDS Dental Care Clinics, PLC and other sources. I have no reason to believe that any material facts have been withheld from me, nor do I warrant that my investigation has revealed all of the matters in which an audit or more extensive examination might disclose.

This valuation reflects facts and conditions existing at the date of this valuation. Subsequent events have not been considered, and I have no obligation to update my report for such events and conditions.

Sipes and Seaton PC., CPAs and Business Appraisers does not purport to be a guarantor of value. Valuation of closely held companies is an imprecise science, with value being a question of fact, and reasonable people can differ in their estimates of value. Sipes and Seaton PC., CPAs and Business Appraisers, however, performed conceptually sound and commonly accepted methods and procedures of valuation in determining the estimate of value included in this report. Sipes and Seaton PC., CPAs and Business Appraisers is not liable for any use, reliance, financial applications, report distribution or other utilization of any kind, by any party not having written authorization from Sipes and Seaton PC., CPAs and Business Appraisers.

The valuated estimate of fair market value in this report is based on the definition applied throughout such report. An actual transaction in the shares may be DDSd at a value higher, lower or equal to the value rendered herein. I make no guarantee of any kind with regard to the likely or ultimate amount that may result in any future transaction. The opinion(s) offered in this report do not constitute an offer to buy or sell the shares.

APPENDIX C: THE APPRAISER'S QUALIFICATIONS

William H. Sipes, Jr.
Managing Shareholder, Sipes & Seaton, PC
166 B West University Parkway
Vernonia, OR 38305
(731) 664-7777
bill@sipescpa.com

RANGE OF EXPERIENCE

With more than 40 years of experience and expertise, Bill Sipes has the knowledge, training, skills and education to provide consulting or independent expert observations and, if necessary, to provide personal expert testimony in the areas of commercial and economic damages, business valuation, wrongful death and wrongful termination matters.

CREDENTIALS AND LICENSES

CPA – Certified Public Accountant licensed in Oregon
ABV – Accredited in Business Valuation (AICPA)
ASA- Accredited Senior Appraiser (ASA)
CBA – Certified Business Appraiser (IBA)
CFF – Certified in Financial Forensics (AICPA)
BVAL – Business Valuator Accredited for Litigation (IBA)
ABAR – Accredited in Business and Appraisal Review (IBA)
Roster of Neutrals for commercial damages – American Arbitration Association
NASD Series 7 General Securities License
NASD Series 63 Securities License
PFS – Personal Financial Specialist (AICPA)

PROFESSIONAL ORGANIZATIONS (Current)

American Institute of Certified Public Accountants (AICPA)
Institute of Business Appraisers (IBA)
Oregon Society of CPAs (TSCPA)
American Society of Appraisers (ASA)

PROFESSIONAL ORGANIZATIONS (Past)

AICPA "Key" Contact Committee (1990-2001)
Oregon State Board of Accountancy (1995-1999)
TSCPA Legislative Services Committee (1992-1999)

PROFESSIONAL COMMITTEES

AICPA "Yeanpolos" Committee to make recommendations to improve the national ABV Examination (2005-2006)

American Institute of Certified Public Accountants Business Valuation "Virtual Committee" (1998 – 2001)

National Association of State Boards of Accountancy Annual convention planning committee (1999)

AICPA ABV (Accredited in Business Valuation) Credentials Committee (2007-2010)

AICPA ABV (Accredited in Business Valuation) Exam Review Specifications Outline (CSO) Committee Co-Chairman (2010)

Chairman, AICPA ABV Exam Review Task Force (2005-2007)

AICPA ABV Exam Review Task Force Liaison to AICPA Credentials Committee (2008-2010)

Co-Chairman of AICPA Exam Review Task Force for "Credential" Committee (2010-2011)

IBA (Institute of Business Appraiser) Roster of CBA Demonstration Requests Reviewer (2010-Open)

EDUCATION

B.B.A., Accounting, University of Mississippi (1968)
M.A. Music Education, University of Southern Mississippi (1972)

PROFESSIONAL AND BUSINESS HISTORY

Sipes & Seaton, PC
Managing Shareholder, September 1975 to present

PUBLICATIONS

Author of "The Music Store," Chapter 45 in the third edition of Portfolio of Accounting Systems for Small and Medium Sized Businesses published by Prentice-Hall, 1992

Co-Author of Financial Coaching: How to be a Hero and Get Paid for It, *Oregon CPA Journal*, April, 2000 and *Hawaii CPA Journal*, August 2000

Author and editor of 2010 Business Appraisal Sourcebook published by Business Valuation Resources (BVR)

Technical Review editor of Investigative and Forensic Accounting published by Commerce Clearing House (CCH) February 2004

SELECTED SPEECHES

Business Appraisal Basics: An Interactive Approach, 2000
Accountancy Weekend at the University of Mississippi, January 2000, Oxford, Mississippi

	"The Impact of Oregon Case Law on Your Business Valuation," TSCPA Oregon Super Conference held at the Franklin Marriott – Cool Springs, Franklin, Oregon, October 2000
QUOTED	The Wall Street Journal online edition in the article *"How to Prepare for a Death in a Business"* July 15, 1999
HONORS	*Appreciation for Excellence* award presented by the Oregon Society of Public Accountants (1991)
CASES IN WHICH TRIAL TESTIMONY WAS GIVEN	Dr. Susan Johnson v. Wal-Mart, a damages case, Circuit Court of Weakley County, Oregon (2001)
	Dunlap v. Dunlap, a divorce, concerning a business valuation of Dunlap Insurance Agency, Inc., Chancery Court of Haywood County, Oregon (2000)
	Whirley v. Whirley, a divorce, concerning a business valuation of Good Connections, Inc. Chancery Court of Madison County, Oregon (1999)
	Moore v. Moore, a divorce, concerning a business valuation of Moore Pumps, Inc., Chancery Court of Crockett County, Oregon (1997)
	Beal v. Beal, a divorce, concerning a business valuation of certain minority interest in selected business enterprises, and rebuttal of expert testimony of the defendant's expert Madison County, Oregon Chancery Court (1997)
	Estate of Danita Hawkins concerning the fair market value of three separately capitalized Subway franchises, Probate Court of Madison County, Oregon (1997)
CASES IN WHICH DEPOSITION TESTIMONY GIVEN	Goodmark, Inc. vs. Reflexxion, Inc., a damages case, Federal District Court of Oregon, Western Division (2002)
	Raven Industries, Inc. vs. Western Rivers, Inc., a damages case, Federal District Court of South Dakota (2002)
	Harrison v Harrison, a divorce case with a business valuation for the husband and one for the wife, Gibson County (OR) Chancery Court (2001)
	Dr. Susan Johnson v Wal-Mart, a damages case, Weakley County (OR), District Court (2001)
	Locke Brother Supply, Co. v. BancorpSouth, a lender liability damages case, McNairy County (OR) District Court (1995)
	Willis vs. Ford, a damages case, Dyer County (OR) District Court (2010)

APPENDIX D: GLOSSARY

This Glossary was developed jointly by representatives of the American Institute of CPAs, the American Society of Appraisers, the Canadian Institute of Business Valuers, the Institute of Business Appraisers, and the National Association of Certified Valuation Analysts.

Adjusted Book Value - the value that results after one or more asset(s) or liability amounts are added, deleted, or changed from their respective financial statement amounts.
Appraisal - See Valuation.
Appraisal Approach - See Valuation Approach.
Appraisal Date - See Valuation Date.
Appraisal Method - See Valuation Method.
Appraisal Procedure - See Valuation Procedure.
Asset (Asset-Based) Approach - a general way of determining a value indication of a business, business ownership interest, or security by using one or more methods based on the value of the assets of that business net of liabilities.
Benefit Stream - any level of income, cash flow, or earnings generated by an asset, group of assets, or business enterprise. When the term is used, it should be supplemented by a definition of exactly what it means in the given valuation context.
Beta - a measure of systematic risk of a security; the tendency of a security's returns to correlate with swings in the broad market.
Blockage Discount - an amount or percentage deducted from the current market price of a publicly traded security to reflect the decrease in the per share value of a block of those securities that is of a size that could not be sold in a reasonable period of time given normal trading volume.
Business - see Business Enterprise.
Business Enterprise - a commercial, industrial, service, or investment entity, or a combination thereof, which pursues an economic activity.
Business Valuation - the act or process of determining the value of a business enterprise or ownership interest therein.
Capital Asset Pricing Model (CAPM) - a model in which the cost of capital for any security or portfolio of securities equals a risk free rate plus a risk premium that is proportionate to the systematic risk of the security or portfolio.
Capitalization - a conversion of a single period stream of benefits into value.
Capitalization Factor - any multiple or divisor used to convert anticipated benefits into value.
Capitalization Rate - any divisor (usually expressed as a percentage) used to convert anticipated benefits into value.
Capital Structure - the composition of the invested capital of a business enterprise; the mix of debt and equity financing.
Cash Flow - cash that is generated over a period of time by an asset, group of assets, or business enterprise. It may be used in a general sense to encompass various levels of specifically defined cash flows. When the term is used, it should be supplemented by a qualifier (for example, "discretionary" or "operating") and a definition of exactly what it means in the given valuation context.
Control - the power to direct the management and policies of a business enterprise.
Control Premium - an amount (expressed in either dollar or percentage form) by which the pro rata value (calculated, in proportion value) of a controlling interest exceeds the pro rata value of a noncontrolling interest in a business enterprise, that reflects the power of control.
Cost Approach - a general way of estimating a value indication of an individual asset by quantifying the amount of money that would be required to replace the future service capability of that asset.

Cost of Capital - the expected rate of return (discount rate) that the market requires in order to attract funds to a particular investment.
Discount - a reduction in value or the act of reducing value.
Discount for Lack of Control - an amount or percentage deducted from the pro rata share of value of one hundred percent (100%) of an equity interest in a business to reflect the absence of some or all of the powers of control.
Discount for Lack of Marketability - an amount or percentage deducted from the value of an ownership interest to reflect the relative absence of marketability.
Discount Rate - a rate of return (cost of capital) used to convert a monetary sum, payable or receivable in the future, into present value.
Economic Life - the period of time over which property may generate economic benefits.
Effective Date - See Valuation Date.
Enterprise - See Business Enterprise.
Equity Net Cash Flows - those cash flows available to pay out to equity holders (in the form of dividends) after funding operations of the business enterprise, making necessary capital investments, and reflecting increases or decreases in debt financing.
Equity Risk Premium - a rate of return in addition to a risk free rate to compensate for investing in equity instruments because they have a higher degree of probable risk than risk free instruments (a component of the cost of equity capital or equity discount rate).
Excess Earnings - that amount of anticipated benefits that exceeds a fair rate of return on the value of a selected asset base (often net tangible assets) used to generate those anticipated benefits.
Excess Earnings Method - a specific way of determining a value indication of a business, business ownership interest, or security determined as the sum of the value of the assets obtained by capitalizing excess earnings and the value of the selected asset base. Also frequently used to value intangible assets. See Excess Earnings.
Fair Market Value - the price, expressed in terms of cash equivalents, at which property would change hands between a hypothetical willing and able buyer and a hypothetical willing and able seller, acting at arm's length in an open and unrestricted market, when neither is under compulsion to buy or sell and when both have reasonable knowledge of the relevant facts. {NOTE: In Canada, the term "price" should be replaced with the term "highest price".}
Forced Liquidation Value - liquidation value at which the asset or assets are sold as quickly as possible, such as at an auction.
Going Concern - an ongoing operating business enterprise.
Going Concern Value - the value of a business enterprise that is expected to continue to operate into the future. The intangible elements of Going Concern Value result from factors such as having a trained work force, an operational plant, and the necessary licenses, systems, and procedures in place.
Goodwill - that intangible asset arising as a result of name, reputation, customer loyalty, location, products, and similar factors not separately identified.
Goodwill Value - the value attributable to goodwill.
Income (Income-Based) Approach - a general way of determining a value indication of a business, business ownership interest, security, or intangible asset using one or more methods that convert anticipated benefits into a present single amount.
Intangible Assets - nonphysical assets (such as franchises, trademarks, patents, copyrights, goodwill, equities, mineral rights, securities and contracts as distinguished from physical assets) that grant rights, privileges, and have economic benefits for the owner.
Invested Capital - the sum of equity and debt in a business enterprise. Debt is typically long term liabilities or the sum of short term interest bearing debt and long term liabilities. When the term is used, it should be supplemented by a definition of exactly what it means in the given valuation context.

Invested Capital Net Cash Flows - those cash flows available to pay out to equity holders (in the form of dividends) and debt investors (in the form of principle and interest) after funding operations of the business enterprise and making necessary capital investments.
Investment Risk - the degree of uncertainty as to the realization of expected returns.
Investment Value - the value to a particular investor based on individual investment requirements and expectations. {NOTE: In Canada, the term used is "Value to the Owner."}
Key Person Discount - an amount or percentage deducted from the value of an ownership interest to reflect the reduction in value resulting from the actual or potential loss of a key person in a business enterprise.
Levered Beta - the beta reflecting a capital structure that includes debt.
Liquidity - the ability to quickly convert property to cash or pay a liability.
Liquidation Value - the net amount that can be realized if the business is terminated and the assets are sold piecemeal. Liquidation can be either "orderly" or "forced".
Majority Control - the degree of control provided by a majority position.
Majority Interest - an ownership interest greater than fifty percent (50%) of the voting interest in a business enterprise.
Market (Market-Based) Approach - a general way of determining a value indication of a business, business ownership interest, security, or intangible asset by using one or more methods that compare the subject to similar businesses, business ownership interests, securities, or intangible assets that have been sold.
Marketability - the ability to quickly convert property to cash at minimal cost.
Marketability Discount - See Discount for Lack of Marketability.
Minority Discount - a discount for lack of control applicable to a minority interest.
Minority Interest - an ownership interest less than fifty percent (50%) of the voting interest in a business enterprise.
Net Book Value - with respect to a business enterprise, the difference between total assets (net of accumulated depreciation, depletion, and amortization) and total liabilities of a business enterprise as they appear on the balance sheet (synonymous with Shareholder's Equity); with respect to an intangible asset, the capitalized cost of an intangible asset less accumulated amortization as it appears on the accounting books of the business enterprise.
Net Cash Flow - a form of cash flow. When the term is used, it should be supplemented by a qualifier (for example, "Equity" or "Invested Capital") and a definition of exactly what it means in the given valuation context.
Net Tangible Asset Value - the value of the business enterprise's tangible assets (excluding excess assets and nonoperating assets) minus the value of its liabilities. {NOTE: In Canada, tangible assets also include identifiable intangible assets.}
Nonoperating Assets - assets not necessary to ongoing operations of the business enterprise. {NOTE: In Canada, the term used is "Redundant Assets."}
Orderly Liquidation Value - liquidation value at which the asset or assets are sold over a reasonable period of time to maximize proceeds received.
Premise of Value - an assumption regarding the most likely set of transactional circumstances that may be applicable to the subject valuation; e.g. going concern, liquidation.
Portfolio Discount - an amount or percentage that may be deducted from the value of a business enterprise to reflect the fact that it owns dissimilar operations or assets that may not fit well together.
Rate of Return - an amount of income (loss) and/or change in value realized or anticipated on an investment, expressed as a percentage of that investment.
Redundant Assets - {NOTE: In Canada, see "Nonoperating Assets."}
Report Date - the date conclusions are transmitted to the client.

Replacement Cost New - the current cost of a similar new property having the nearest equivalent utility to the property being valued.

Reproduction Cost New - the current cost of an identical new property.
Residual Value - the prospective value as of the end of the discrete projection period in a discounted benefit streams model.
Risk Free Rate - the rate of return available in the market on an investment free of default risk.
Risk Premium - a rate of return in addition to a risk free rate to compensate the investor for accepting risk.
Rule of Thumb - a mathematical relationship between or among variables based on experience, observation, hearsay, or a combination of these, usually applicable to a specific industry.
Special Interest Purchasers - acquirers who believe they can enjoy post-acquisition economies of scale, synergy, or strategic advantages by combining the acquired business interest with their own.
Standard of Value - the identification of the type of value being utilized in a specific engagement; e.g. fair market value, fair value, investment value.
Sustaining Capital Reinvestment - the periodic capital outlay required to maintain operations at existing levels, net of the tax shield available from such outlays.
Systematic Risk - the risk that is common to all risky securities and cannot be eliminated through diversification. When using the capital asset pricing model, systematic risk is measured by beta.
Terminal Value - See Residual Value.
Unlevered Beta - the beta reflecting a capital structure without debt.
The Risk Management Association – Formerly know as Robert Morris Associates .
Unsystematic Risk - the portion of total risk specific to an individual security that can be avoided through diversification.
Valuation - the act or process of determining the value of a business, business ownership interest, security, or intangible asset.
Valuation Approach - a general way of determining a value indication of a business, business ownership interest, security, or intangible asset using one or more valuation methods.
Valuation Date - the specific point in time as of which the valuator's opinion of value applies (also referred to as "Effective Date" or "Valuation Date").
Valuation Method - within approaches, a specific way to determine value.
Valuation Procedure - the act, manner, and technique of performing the steps of an valuation method.
Valuation Ratio - a fraction in which a value or price serves as the numerator and financial, operating, or physical data serve as the denominator.
Value to the Owner - {NOTE: In Canada, see Investment Value.}
Weighted Average Cost of Capital (WACC) - the cost of capital (discount rate) determined by the weighted average at market value of the cost of all financing sources in the business enterprise's capital structure.

APPENDIX E: PICTURES FROM THE SITE

Pictures showing building, equipment, parking, waiting area, etc…should be included in this portion of the report.

Valuing Dental Practices: A BVR Teleconference

Presenters: Jim Anderson, Ron Seigneur, Stephen Persichetti
Business Valuation Resources, May 14, 2009/10:00 a.m. PDT

Blake Lyman: Welcome to *Valuing Dental Practices*, a BVR teleconference featuring Jim Andersen, Ron Seigneur, and Dr. Stephen Persichetti. I am Blake Lyman, Professional Program Manager for BV Resources.

As of 2006 there were more than 160,000 practicing dentists of all types in the United States, 63 percent of whom ran practices in which they were the only licensed dentist. With an aging population of baby boomers getting ready to retire, the volatile economy, and technological and administrative changes already underway, dentistry valuation is an increasingly tricky practice. Valuing dental practices is also the second installment of our industry spotlight series, a collection of teleconferences focused on the characteristics of specific industries, businesses, and business models.

Next up in the series is Valuing Intellectual Property in Entertainment and the Arts on June 10 featuring Kevin Yeanoplos, Bill Sipes, and Mike Pellegrino.

But joining us today to discuss classic considerations and emerging trends in dentistry valuation are three distinguished professionals.

Jim Andersen is a Partner in the Consulting Business Valuation Litigation Practice at Burr Pilger Mayer. Over the past 20 years he has been involved in more than 700 business valuation and litigation assignments and has testified as an expert witness throughout California. He is Chairman of the Business Valuation Section of the CAL CPA Litigation Section and an instructor with the AICPA and CAL CPA Litigation Foundation.

Ronald Seigneur is a Partner with Seigneur Gustafson LLP, a CPA firm located in Lakewood, Colorado. He holds the AICPA Specialty Designation of Accredited in Business Valuation and is a Certified Valuation Analyst with the National Association of Certified Valuation Analysts. He has published over a hundred articles on business valuation, commercial damages, leadership, and other related subjects.

Dr. Stephen Persichetti, DDS, MBA, is a practicing dentist in Portland, Oregon, and a professor of dental practice management at Oregon Health and Science University. A graduate of the Baltimore College of Dental Surgery and at the University of Maryland he is a fellow in the Academy of General Dentistry and the American College of Dentists, and the International College of Dentists.

We are thrilled to have Jim, Ron, and Steve join us today. You can read much more about them on the webpage for today's teleconference.

Before we begin, I would like to lead you through the administrative details of our teleconference. Your attendance to this 100-minute presentation is eligible for two CPE credits. In order to receive these credits you must complete a brief survey on today's teleconference at the conclusion of our presentation. A link to our survey is included with your registration email which included instructions on how to dial in today.

A link is also available on the reading page for today's teleconference. The survey will be active for five business days and will require you to fill in three four-digit CPE codes. Simply write down the codes as they are read and fill them in when asked in the survey. I will read the CPE codes three times during today's teleconference: one hour through the presentation, at the conclusion of the presentation, and right now.

The three four-digit CPE codes for today's teleconference are: 8014, 6841, and 1034; once again, 8014, 6841, and 1034.

We will be taking questions during the session today by email only. Please send questions to *tc-questions@bvresources.com.* With that, we welcome Jim Andersen, Ron Seigneur, and Dr. Stephen Persichetti.

Jim Andersen: Thank you very much Blake. This is Jim Andersen. I just thought I would lead off the process with a few comments and I feel very honored to have as my colleagues, Ron and Stephen, to assist in what I think is going to be a very enlightening presentation.

Just to give you kind of an overview of what we hope to talk about, we are going to be leading it off initially with Steve talking about an industry overview to give everybody a flavor for what the dentistry industry is doing and how Steve sees things as an actual practice guy and practice management guy. Ron is going to lead in with some information regarding various purposes for valuing the practices and give us a little overview on the differences between the general practices and specialty practices. I am going to talk a little bit more about dealing with how practices are valued for by sale purposes.

We can refer to some of the materials we have. Ron will then talk a little bit about the litigation and divorce stuff. I am sure a lot of you in here get involved heavily in that area. I know that Ron and I are both people who have testified in a number of these types of cases. There are some nuances that go with litigation in divorce. I am probably going to get into some of the resource materials. We have some costs and so forth on what some of this stuff does cost and so forth. We will go over it all.

Ron is going to talk a little bit about gathering compensation data. Where this compensation becomes a very relevant and important situation is particularly in regards to when you are dealing with stuff in the litigation arena. Sometimes in these specialty practices, at least in California, you have issues that are personal versus practice goodwill issues, and it is different on a state by state basis.

Anyway, he is going to go into some of those things and what they provide for us. Then I am going to finish up. I have a sample report that we have some information that everybody has access to. I am going to walk people through that process. Then we are going to go from there. That gives us an opening statement. At this time I would really like Steve to basically open up and talk to us about the industry and his experiences and what he sees.

Dr. S. Persichetti: Thank you, Jim, and welcome everybody. I am pleased to be here. It is a nice experience for me. I am a practicing dentist fulltime and I teach up at the dental school at the Oregon Health Sciences University. It is a great position to be in. I am one of the few dentists who gets to practice what they preach and preach what they practice.

You have asked me to outline what might be some current dental industry trends. It is a little bit of a tough nut to crack. There is obviously no published current data, and I have also found that a lot of the anecdotal information reporting I've heard can be misleading at best.

The opinions I share are a mix of personal experience, certainly discussion with my dental colleagues on a national basis, also the opinions of well-respected CPAs and appraisers and lawyers who I involve in my curriculum. I would think that if you are putting together a curriculum for dental students you probably would approach it the same way I do and that is you want to have a dentist teaching the courses, but on the other hand there are lots of resources to tap into. We do that quite a bit.

A lot of the information I get is from CPAs and attorneys and appraisers that I know who have shared information with their colleagues on a national basis. I thought I would review a little bit of that from that perspective putting out that kind of composite view of the industry.

The trend that I am seeing is that general practicing dentists have shown increasing sales and collections over the end of 2008 and into 2009, and this is overall nationally. Certainly not all practices are doing well. It is my opinion that practices that were doing poorly prior to the economic downturn have probably seen their problems amplified a little bit. I have noticed a lot of changes in what I refer to as the niche dental practices such as those dental practices that limit their services such as limit the practice to cosmetic dentistry, temporal mandibular joint treatment, implant dentistry, and even treatment for sleep disorders.

I find that these practices are changing their service mix and going to broader levels of service. My favorite story is a billboard in town that had a dentist advertising his cosmetic dentistry practice. That billboard was changed a couple of months ago and now it says his "cosmetic and family dentistry practice." There are some changes going on along that road, too.

I see a trend where general practitioners with solid dental prevention and dental hygiene departments that offer wide variety of services are typically trending upwards. They are growing. That growth may not be what it was at previous rates, but I still see the nose is up.

I find that most dentists relate to me that they are not booked out as far in advance as they used to be. It was typical before 2008 for a general dentist to be scheduled four, six weeks in advance. The reporting that I am getting back is that that has changed. It is not that the schedule has fallen apart, but the depth of the schedule has gone away a little bit.

I think the value of an efficient prevention and hygiene system is illustrated in this down economy. Those dentists who have stuck to offering services to patients who are going to help them out and continue with their dental health through preventive efforts because the dividends that are paid by preventive dentistry are certainly marvelous.

One of the things that I find is that the offices that have these very efficient hygiene systems, what we typically see is that about 40 percent of the dentist's schedule is filled with treatments for problems that are identified when patients are coming back in to see the dental hygienist in the office. That is a huge influx of treatment needs that are diagnosed in the dental hygiene department.

I see some trends for specialty practices. I don't think specialty practices are seeing the continued growth as the general practitioners are. I have heard reports about orthodontists especially being down. It is probably the hardest hit group of the dental specialties. The orthodontists report recording fewer starts in the last quarter of 2008 and the first quarter of 2009.

Other specialists such as the endodontist, who is a dentist who specializes in root canal therapy, and oral and maxillofacial surgeons have reported slight downward trending. I think that a lot of it is that more general practitioners are getting involved in the specialty arenas, and probably a little less likely to refer cases that they could normally handle easily in their office.

The pediatric dentists continue to do gangbusters. Pediatric dentistry is a huge growing field. I think it continues to be. Pediatric dentistry has been growing. They are very efficient. I think these practices are probably the best of the specialists. They have not been immune to the economic downturn, but I haven't seen their numbers being reported down.

Ron, if you want to jump in and ask any other questions about that industry overview, I would be happy to review some of that with you.

Ron Seigneur: Steve, that is very helpful. I would chime in with what Jim said as well—I am very pleased to have Steve on the line as someone who works in the field everyday. We are the outsiders looking in trying to figure out what values are. I also have a couple of dentists who are traditional practices of our CPA firm. I think one of them is on the line today listening.

It has been interesting because he is also a good friend of mine and a golf buddy. I have been listening to him over the last few years as his practice has evolved. I think it is embracing several of the things that Steve mentioned.

There are a few slides that we have up on industry overview that Steve touched on. I think some of the things I will expand on a little bit and then ask for Steve to chime in if he has any additional comments.

What I am hearing and seeing in the valuation work we are doing and just the professional reading, there is a huge amount of technological change in the industry that has been following pace with the healthcare industry generally in terms of computerized patient charts. When I go into the dentist now, I am just amazed at the technology. Everything is on the computer.

They will take the x-rays digitally as opposed to the old x-ray and all that kind of environmental issue where they put the old lead thing over you. I don't know if you folks have been around long enough to remember that. Now it is just a digital thing. Then it shows up on the computer screen. You are sitting there in the chair, and what Steve said I think is really true; the hygienist is oftentimes the one who is doing that process under the supervision of the licensed dentist. They look at that and then the dentist will come in and pick it up from there which seems like good patient management and delegation and that type of thing.

It is just amazing to me how it is all integrated with the patient scheduling and the charts. I am hearing in the background the stuff we don't see as a patient which is the third party billing and those types of things. I have found that at my dentist, one of the keys is the frontline staff.

It is kind of like when someone comes into our firm and they need a tax return done. It is the staff and the manager that they meet with and make the impression first. Then you see the licensed practitioner. I think that is happening a lot in the practice of dentistry. If you have good, capable, personable, hygienists and staff, they bring in patients and they retain patients.

This slide that is presently on the screen is something that I pulled out of First Research which is an industry research tool that many valuators use and will be familiar with. It gave just an overview of some of the range of pricing for different types of services. I think it is instructive because we have the general practitioner who is doing routine cleanings and checkups. There is a charge for that which is often in the range of $100 to $200.

Then you have things that go up from there. When someone has a root canal—fortunately I haven't had to have that experience yet—or you start doing dental implants. I did just get sold by my dentist on having my teeth laser whitened and it was a $500 charge. I was very happy with the service and happy with the result. It was something that he has promoted.

You can see it visibly when I walk into the office that it is not just the old family dentist anymore. The image of walking into my dentist office is there are other things that we can do. A good example is my daughter and my wife both had braces recently. In the past, our dentist, the same dentist, would refer us to the orthodontist. When my kids were little, it would be the pediatric orthodontist, if that is the right term.

They send him over to the specialist and that person would take care of the orthodontia. Now, my dentist has gone through training to be capable to do—and I don't think to do all the types of orthodontia—but did it for my daughter and just recently did it for my wife—as a way to expand his capabilities and the higher value services as opposed to one and two hundred dollar cleanings comparatively to doing 1040 tax returns; it is doing valuation projects probably, if there is an analogy there.

I thought it was also interesting on this slide the range of per capita spending with a $275 national average on dental needs with a low in the southern states of $175 in Louisiana to $400 in Washington State. I think there is a geographic issue there maybe in terms of—I don't know what you can take away from that, but there might be something. If you are in an affluent market or community and you have a dentist, they are probably more likely to be selling the laser whitening and some of the cosmetic procedures that are out there today.

I think Slide #6 talks about some of the things that are happening. This is also from the First Research about identifying disease issues in terms of mouth cancer and things like that, that I think dentists have always been clued into. I think they are seeing more of that. I understand that the meth issue has awful effects on folks' teeth. I have seen pictures. It is just drastically bad.

There is also an issue about the old fillings that many people have in their mouths. Some of those are being replaced. I think now they are using more non-hazardous substances for filling the compounds. The old stuff has mercury in it and mercury is not good, and they are making sure that is properly disposed of so we don't get mercury in the soil and the water.

There was a mention in the First Research about the exposure to nitrous oxide that many dentists have used in the past. It is not good for the clinicians who have had routine exposure to that.

There was a mention made that I thought was instructive. I don't know how valid this is, but when you see the statistic there, roughly 4,000 new dentists graduating and going through their residency programs and entering the marketplace with roughly 6,000 retiring annually in the current market; that is significant from a valuation standpoint. I think we are seeing that.

I know some dentists I have talked to are saying, "I would really like to start my exit plan, succession plan, whatever you label it." I know Jim has been very involved with this in various industries. When you have less candidates coming into the market it definitely drives the practice values if that is the focus of the valuation exercise.

Dr. S. Persichetti: Ron, can I interject there a bit on that point you had about the 4,000 new dentists? Think about the complexion that the dental schools deal with in terms of entering students and exiting students and class sizes, etc. It takes a lot to open up the faucet for increasing the number of dental school graduates. I will just give you some statistics on it.

Right now Oregon Health Sciences School of Dentistry has about a thousand plus applications for 75 spots. We are looking at grade point averages about 3.70 on average. So there is a high hurdle getting into the dental school. Once you are in, the education process is such that we can't just throw a few more chairs in the back of the lecture hall. With the clinics and the labor intensity and the technology intensity that has to be provided for students to learn in these kinds of clinical environments, these class sizes are really hard to change.

When we see these similar class sizes to graduating classes the size in 1962 basically, we are graduating about as many dentists as we were then, and we are seeing a population increase, that is a pretty strong impact on the dental industry in my view. It is really something that we have to deal a lot with at the dental school trying to make sure, particularly in Oregon, areas that are less successful to this kind of care that the physicians and dentists go to these more remote areas to practice. So it is a big deal.

Jim Andersen: Steve, I have a question for you. This is Jim speaking. As we are talking about the stuff where we are having these general practitioners and so forth that are now trying to take on other practice specialties as part of their overall practice obviously in order to keep the bacon on the table and so forth, my question is, "What are they doing from a training standpoint in order to avoid what I would consider some potential malpractice issues?"

I am sure the specialists are trying to throw this back at the general dentist and say, "You guys aren't qualified." What do they do? For instance, what do the pediadontists, who I know do a fair amount of the orthodontic work, do? What has been your experience as far as what your colleagues who are in general dentistry are doing as far as training in order to take on some of these more advanced procedures?

Dr. S. Persichetti: That is a very good point. The mantra is, "Don't practice on your patients." If you have techniques as a dentist that you want to learn, if you want to change the mix of services in your practice, dentists are very good at this particular type of learning called Study Clubs.

A number of dentists get together; they find a mentor. Somebody comes in and there are over a period of a year a number of get-togethers where under the guidance of a mentor, dentists are basically given extra added training in a specialty area. It is a marvelous situation because you watch what your colleagues are doing. You learn from watching them perform procedures. You learn from performing your own procedures on your own patients under the guidance of a mentor.

I like to think that there are many opportunities for dentists to get good, consistent training so that they can practice at the level of a specialist in certain limited areas. You are not going to become an endodontist doing root canals on a weekend course at a Hilton somewhere. But on the other hand, there are a lot of opportunities to expand a dentist's capabilities and practice. I think that is a good way to approach it—expanding your practice.

There are just not enough endodontists, oral surgeons, and pediatric dentists around to handle all the demands, so it is going to have to be shuffled back to the general practitioner. Those who take care and get the extra training are going to enjoy the benefits from that. The liability issue is there because as a practicing general dentist, if you choose to do specialty treatment, you are held to the level of standard of care of the specialist. There is just no way around that. There are ramifications there if dentists aren't trained properly and don't execute properly.

Ron Seigneur: Steve, there has to be a huge difference. I think you alluded to it. The setting of the dental practitioner being in a robust urban market where maybe there is a dental school close by and a lot of competitive force versus that rural dentist that is out in Colorado. I think the difference between an urban dental practice here in Denver versus something that is down in Lamar where maybe there are two dentists in town, if you need something out of the ordinary, you might be out of luck in terms of finding that in the community.

Dr. S. Persichetti: That is true. If you are a general practitioner in a less metropolitan area, there is probably going to be a burden on you to be able to provide this greater mix of services.

When I look at the type of practices, urban versus remote practices in Oregon guess where I see the most productive practices and the most profitable practices? They are in the more remote areas. That might seem contrary to conventional wisdom. I also see an issue there with when a practice goes for sale in downtown Portland, there might be a queue of 10, 15 interested buyers. If you are out in an area where there is not a lot of population, it might take a selling dentist five or six years just to identify somebody who might be interested in coming to that area.

Those are real concerns.

Ron Seigneur: There is a slide up on the screen here, Slide #8, that actually should be labeled ADA, not ASA, 9 Recognized Specialties, the American Dental Association. Those were also pulled from the First Research. These are just some of the specialty areas that are at least designated by that professional organization.

A question I have to maybe build on that point a little further, Steve, I don't know if you know this or not, but I know that for healthcare practitioners, a lot of the rural communities have actually provided some stimulus to bring physicians in to the local area just because we need a local Doc or practice. I don't know if that same type of thing has been in the dental field. It is like if a community is without a dentist, maybe the chamber of commerce or whatever says, "What can we do to create an incentive to bring a practitioner into the area?"

Dr. S. Persichetti: I have seen efforts like that and campaigns like that. My opinion is they haven't been very successful. I find that some dentists who are selling their practices in less metropolitan areas are actually looking at high school students who might have an interest and trying to guide them through to choosing dentistry as a career.

I know an oral surgeon in a remote county in Oregon who has basically sent a kid who was on his basketball team way back when who is now finishing up his oral surgery residency and is going to come and join the surgeon in practice. That was about an eight year glide path into his practice. That takes a lot of planning.

Ron Seigneur: On Slide #7, I made note of this again from the background research that we have. As I understand it we have two different types of practicing licensed doctors. We have a doctor dental surgery DDS and a doctor of dental medicine. In your view, is there any distinction that the listeners ought to be aware of between those two?

Dr. S. Persichetti: There is absolutely no distinction. The University of Maryland, Baltimore College of Dental Surgery where I went to school, it was touted to be the first dental school in the world. They offered a Doctor of Dental Surgery. Harvard came along a couple of schools later and had to be different so they offered a DMD. There is no difference in the licensure or education or curriculum. It is all following the same accreditation policies by the American Dental Association.

Jim Andersen: Before we move on, I want one of these questions. Steve, I think we have had a few questions pop up on the board from Will Gere. This on I think is more down your aisle. I think we ought to address this one now since we are talking about basic practice issues.

Basically the question is, "Discuss the issues with older retiring dentist practices meshing with the new younger dentists familiar with new technology expectations."

How are we doing? That is the same problem that Ron and I have with the old guys in the accounting and valuation professions with the new young people that are a little more on top of some things. Why don't you talk to us a little bit about that?

Dr. S. Persichetti: That is a multifaceted issue. You have these students coming out of school. They are getting their hands on the newest and latest. They have opportunities to get experience in some of these emerging technologies, etc. Then they are looking to approach as a practice in a certain locale. The dentist who is there has been there for 40 years, had a great career, longtime staff people, and you can see that there may not be great equilibration there in terms of philosophy, etc.

One of the things the dental students are told over and over and over again, is to practice where you want to live. I think that is a very important message that the students have to get. When a student goes to an area, it is what is available for sale at that point. If you have a particular spot where you want to be, well that is where you need to go.

The message that I give to students is that there are certain things you can change and there are certain things that you can't. All the issues about philosophy practice, the technology that is introduced to the practice by a new dentist who assumes it and transitions it to meet their goals, all those things can be changed.

I don't really find a need to match identically the philosophy of practice of the older retiring dentist and the new dentist. I like to think that the older retiring dentist is looking for a great match, someone who can take over their practice, take care of these patients who they have nurtured for all these years. Once they find that, I don't think it really matters what the incoming dentist does as long as they maintain that obligation to the patient.

Ron Seigneur: I suspect with many folks being in the same world as the rest of us where as I heard it called recently, their 401k has turned to 201k that some of the older practitioners who were looking for an exit strategy maybe a couple of years ago are saying, "Maybe I'm going to stick around and practice a little longer before I try to find that new generation."

Dr. S. Persichetti: I would have to say that is absolutely the case. The appraisers I speak to and what they check in with their national organizations, there is the divorce valuation, there is the disability valuation, but maybe a little dropping off on the number of valuations done for retiring dentists wanting to sell the practice. I am seeing that hit too on the younger dentists because it was very typical three or four years ago to see graduating seniors finding an employees position in a dental practice where they can transition over a year or two and then assume the practice. They can either buy in or buy out.

I have seen since, in my opinion, the supply of dental practices for sale on the marketplace have diminished. I am finding that this year's class of graduating students and last year's, too, we are looking at one or two employee positions just to fill their week up. Dentists who are anticipating retirement are now digging their heels in a little bit and saying, "You know what? I'm not really sure I want to move on yet."

That is a big deal for these dental students because they have a fire under them. That fire is their student indebtedness. It is not atypical for me to see dental students graduating with about $250,000 of just dental school debt. That is very significant. What that translates to for them is that they cannot stumble coming out of the starting gate. They can't make bad choices; they can't make bad decisions.

They are in a situation where they probably have—they sit around the table with the accountant, the attorney, the appraiser, and the retiring dentist, and of everybody at the table, they know the least. That is a real tough situation for these new dentists transitioning into practice.

Ron Seigneur: Steve, there is another question that has come in. I think it kind of relates to this discussion so I will put it on the table and see if you have any insight. This comes from Linda Holmes Rubin. "What considerations are important in a multi-office, multi-dentist company if they are adding offices quickly, incoming cash flow is impacted negatively as so much cash is being used in growth?"

I think that is partly a question for Jim and I, but the point I wanted to ask you is we have been talking to a great degree about these solo practices or a practice that is maybe bringing in a younger practitioner, maybe one or two or three practitioner offices with a complement of support staff versus some of the larger dental concerns that I am not fully knowledgeable of, but maybe if you have some insight to the lay of the land in terms of some of the bigger dental companies versus the small practices and how that fits into the dynamic.

Dr. S. Persichetti: That is a very good question. We don't see that many of these large, large groups. They certainly exist, but 85, 90 percent of the practices will have one or a few dentists in them. Cash flow is always the crucial issue here with any size practice. I have known some groups that have grown too fast.

The thing about dental practices, and you had it up on an earlier slide, was just how labor intensive they are. Approximately 30 percent of our expenses are focused on our staff. With all the technology, the overhead can get pretty high very quickly. These growth issues are difficult to call.

Ron Seigneur: I moved us back to Slide #2. Instructive for me was the lay of the land in the dental profession, but to move us into this next area, the purpose for valuing a practice, which is kind of why we are on this call today, valuing a dental practice. We want to run through that to set the groundwork for what Jim and I can lead here going forward.

Obviously we have three general areas identified here. There is the transactional aspect of someone who is buying into a practice, these younger practitioners who Steve was talking about, or the older practitioner who is looking to sell all or a portion of the practice. Also, there is how we can be involved to set price. That price may be changing over time as the older guys are hanging on and the younger guys are motivated because of the debt they have coming out of school and so forth.

I think there is a lot of opportunity there, not only from buying and selling, but the value engineering as I call it in terms of going into these practices and saying, "Look, we know value. We can help value your practice. We can help you figure out how you can optimize that value by reducing your risk, expanding your practice." These are some things that they might not see fully because they are involved on a day to day basis practicing dentistry. I think that is part of the transactional scheme of things.

There is the litigation standpoint. Most of that is captured in that sub-bullet—Dissolution of Marriage Proceedings. We get involved because a dentist is going through divorce and we are representing either the practitioner or that practitioner's spouse and setting a value for the practice. That is going to be very jurisdictional as probably most of the people on the call know fully in terms of how you value that practice, in terms of methodology. What flies and what doesn't is going to depend on where you are at in the case law and the statutes in your particular jurisdiction.

Jim and I will come back to that in terms of more on that to follow.

Then there is the estate planning. You are doing estate planning for a dentist who has sufficient value to warrant it upfront, or the dentist passes away and his part of the estate needs to be valued. There is that opportunity as well in terms of the reasons we get called to value dental practices.

We have valued a number over the years. It does seem like the landscape is changing quite rapidly, but I think it is changing very much in line with some of the things we are seeing in the other professions.

Jim Andersen: One comment that I wanted to add to that, too, is I agree with you, Ron, that I think it is in some ways changing favorably because as all of us know, to do a startup from fresh start is very difficult in today's economy. I don't care if it is an accounting practice, if it is a dental practice, or whatever.

Basically, there is a premium for quality practices, like a good dental practice. I think that market has, if you run a tight ship, has gotten better and will continue to get better. That is just my perspective from talking to dental people that I know. I think that is a real positive. I just wanted to add that.

Ron Seigneur: We have now bounced back forward to Slide #9 where we are going to now talk about some of the specifics of valuation and how it applies to dental practices. This first slide here is labeled valuation for buy/sell purposes which is probably somewhat of a misnomer. The valuation based upon a multiple of gross revenue is a very, very common methodology used in the valuation of dental practices from my experience.

I was talking to another individual I know and highly respect who does all healthcare and some dental, but that is his entire practice. He is nationally known for it. I was asking his input in advance of this call. One of his comments was, "Whenever you value a practice and you are using advanced techniques that you think are good, if your valuation is outside the range of somewhere between 50 and 70 percent a multiple of gross revenues, you better do a gut check because you might have to justify why it is worth less or more than that top line indication."

I find that fascinating. As a guy who has been doing valuation for two plus decades because a multiple of gross revenues is simply that. There is so much more involved based upon the almost 45 minutes of discussion we have had to this point in terms of where the practice is located, what kind of technology they have, what kind of staffing do they have, what kind of computerization, where are they at on technology, what ancillary services are they offering, how well trained are they, what age are their patients? We haven't even talked about that in terms of looking at the demographic of the patient mix.

All of that that lends itself to what the value of the underlying practice should be. How much are they paying for their leasehold? Do they own their building? Do they have a short term lease? They might have to move out of their location.

When you say that it ought to be a 45 to 75 percent of gross revenues, it is like, "Wow! That doesn't seem like a very sophisticated approach valuation-wise comparatively to what we often encounter elsewhere Jim."

It does seem like something that has held the test of time to some degree at least I would say as a first pass indication. What is a 60 to 75 percent of gross revenues? What does that tell you? Then work from there to apply some of these more advanced concepts to see if you can refine it.

Jim Andersen: Ron, I am going to add to that also. I agree 100 percent with what you are saying. There are very few of these things that, and Ron and I have always run into problems in the many years that we have been valuation specialists, we run into competitors and so forth that try to always rely on these rules of thumb and we roll our eyes. I tell you, in the dentistry industry, whether it was 20 years ago or it is now, basically what happens is these rules of 45, 50, to 70 percent for better practices is the absolute starting point, still the stuff that we weight the heaviest when we are dealing with our valuation conclusion.

Then we start peeling back the onion. There are a couple of slides coming forward here that are included in our packet that talk about the differentiation between using an example of a million dollar practice to talk about why one would go at 70 percent and why another would only go at 55 percent. We will get there.

I do think it is pretty darn amazing that that is the case.

Ron Seigneur: A comparative benchmark as well is the valuation of a traditional accounting practice where the old "rule of thumb"—I hate to even use the term—but one times gross revenue for a traditional accounting practice, a little more, a little less, depending on the client demographics, the service mix, the desirability of location, those same attributes for an accounting practice that people said, "You can start there and then you can go up or down."

But it is interesting to see that change over time for someone who is very involved in that dynamic right now where it has really never been one times gross revenue because it is typically on an earn out basis. Most of these deals, a buy/sell deal in a dental practice is going to be on an earn out basis where it might be, "We are going to pay you 70 percent of gross revenue, but we are going to give you 20 percent down and then we are going to pay you the rest over the next two to three years," similar to an accounting practice.

"We are going to pay you one times gross revenue, but 20 percent of this years trailing 12 months revenues, and then 20 percent for the next four years." You win or lose and typically when you take time value of money right off the top, that is less than one times today's earnings. When you look at the patient attrition, it typically ends up working out less.

I have seen lots of arguments to where the one times gross for accounting practice really translates into a 60 to 70 percent of current revenue if you wanted to do a cash on the barrelhead deal. I think that same dynamic applies here.

There is a question that relates to this that came in that I will toss out. "What is a reasonable patient attrition percentage to use in a general dentistry practice?"

I am going to take the first shot at this and them maybe see what Steve and Jim have to add. It is going to totally depend on looking at the demographics of the practice. If you have a traditional practice that has a baby boomer-based patient base, you are going to have higher attrition. You might have those older patients coming in for some of those advanced needs, the root canals, and the dental needs that happen with age versus if you are in a location where there are a lot of people moving in or out, that attrition percentage is going to change.

If you are a dental practitioner in Detroit, you might see a lot of your patients who are moving out to different parts of the country versus the opposite. To answer the question, "What is a reasonable patient attrition percentage?" it is probably harder than ever in today's economy to answer that question, but it is going to depend on a lot of other factors.

Jim Andersen: I agree with that. I can't put a percentage on that one. I don't know if Steve can. I haven't seen anything that is very consistent.

Dr. S. Persichetti: I am seeing and hearing that in a properly executed transition where the selling dentist sends out a letter to the patient population, "I have been looking for a buyer for my practice for so many years. I finally found that person. I want you to meet him or her," and set up a way that patients can come in and feel comfortable about what is going on, I have heard that the attrition rate is low, less than five percent.

If you want a number then that is the one I would give. As far as I am concerned, what I counsel the students on is if there is not an adequate transition set up in the sale, it does take away from the value of the practice.

Ron Seigneur: Steve, I would also expect that a younger practitioner coming out of a quality dental program with today's training, just like somebody coming into an old, staid accounting practice, say, "You have all these patients and you haven't really extended the other types of services to these patients. You have them coming in for their checkups and their cleanings, but you haven't talked to them about whitening, or cosmetic, or apnea devices, all those things that if you are competent as you very well stressed and qualified to provide, you can increase that annual return per patient with just those additional skills.

Dr. S. Persichetti: Absolutely.

Ron Seigneur: We have the next slide, Slide #10, Valuation for Litigation/Divorce Purposes. I did mention that most of the litigation is in matrimonial related instances, but you can have situations where you have multiple players in a practice. One is leaving or has a dispute. You can have instances where we get involved from a valuation standpoint because they are arguing over a buy/sell agreement that they have that might be poorly worded. They might be arguing over someone's theft of the patients in the practice.

As a matter of fact, one of the ancillary reading materials from BV Update is about a practice. It is the *Gammel v. Elias Practice* that is an interesting read because it has to do with a practitioner who left and took some patients and took some records and was sued for a conversion. This was an Ohio case back in 2004. The claim was that even though you didn't take any hardware with you, you didn't take equipment, you took the value of the practice because you took the patients and you owe me something for it.

We can get involved from that standpoint as well. Do you have any comments there, Jim?

Jim Andersen: No, I absolutely agree with you. I think that is very good information and I see nothing that I don't agree with you on that at all. Are you going to start the specialty practices?

Ron Seigneur: We have a couple of slides up here on the valuation information. Do we have some comments on the specialty practices?

Jim Andersen: I do. In fact, some of them relate to one or two of the questions that have been coming through there. There is one here from Newt Rumbel, "Do these generic overviews and buy/sell multiples apply to niche practices like oral surgeons? Did I understand that the niche practices in desirable urban markets are holding their values better?"

No, I think it is the opposite. I think niche practices, and this is just my gut, and again, I am going to need some assistance from what Steve sees, but I can tell you that my view is that the specialized practices, even though the oral surgeons and some of these endodontists may make more money than your general practitioners, these practices are often worth considerably less.

The reason being is the fact that these niche practices are based upon relationships with general dentists. Your general practices, you have a true patient ongoing list that you are selling, even though I do realize some of them you may have a periodontist. My wife sees one and has two appointments a year with her periodontist. That is kind of a patient list, but not really.

I think what makes these things tough or it is no different than like with Ron and me. I have a substantial business valuation litigation practice. Well, that is not worth the same thing as your audits and these repeat customer bases and so forth. My view on that when you are looking at them, they may make more money, but I think they are worth less in the marketplace. I haven't seen anything that has indicated anything else.

Ron Seigneur: I would agree with that, Jim, because I agree that in most instances those niche specialists, as you indicated, are relying on referrals from other professionals for their work. My mom taught me that you ought to get your teeth checked twice a year. Unfortunately, I am doing it about once a year.

It is very analogous again to compliance work in a CPA firm. You have somebody coming in doing their tax return every year and you are making a reasonable return. If you treat them right and you give them good service, they are going to be back every year. You have an annuity and that is very attractive from an investment value perspective. But if you are doing valuation work and you are relying on referrals primarily from attorneys, and in my neighborhood we do get repeat business from those referral sources, but it is much harder to transition the value proposition in that instance.

There is a question here that I think builds on that. This is also from Will Gere. "How would you reconcile these sales multiples with the higher sales multiple for accounting or CPA firms (1.0 to 1.25) if the dental practice has repeat business?"

It just builds on what we have said here that if you have a good stable demographic of patients that are not too old, that are going to continue to need services, or maybe they have family and kids who will come into that same practitioner for their routine hygiene, and I think that is a good issue here—their dental hygiene—in an area where, and this is something we haven't even touched on, where there is good insurance coverage, there is a good demographic for folks being employed in situations where they have dental coverage as part of their insurance coverage, then that repeat business is going to be huge in terms of the value of proposition versus being a specialty practitioner in a down economy where folks aren't getting dental insurance coverage.

Jim Andersen: There is no question about it. I don't know if we are going to get to that one slide, Ron, which I thought was an excellent slide which I believe you put together which shows the comparison on the $2 practices.

Ron Seigneur: Yes, we can do that. We will get back to that. I think that would be a good way to recap in a bit.

Jim Andersen: Absolutely.

Ron Seigneur: Let's move forward through this next area. We are going to talk a little bit in general terms about sources of valuation information. We have four bullets up here on Slide #11. We are talking about information from business brokers who have experience in selling and marketing dental practices. That is a good source if you have access to that. As a good example, Colorado has the Colorado Association of Business Intermediaries that I have become very involved with. These are folks who do business brokerage and there are 80 individuals in Colorado that are fulltime business brokers which is stunning to me.

There are a lot of fringe players. Well, not all the 80, but they are pretty well involved in business brokerage. Not all of those are going to be experts in valuing dental practices, but it just tells me that there is a big group of people out there that are out brokering businesses.

Jim Andersen: Can I stop you for one quick second? One thing that I want to point out is on business brokers, and I just think these guys are great sources, but I just want to point something out here. You don't want to get involved with anybody who is a jack of all trades. We have two of them here in the northern California area. That is all they do is dental practices. That is different than your standard mom and pop practice brokers.

I run into a lot of these guys and there is a lot of flim flam out there who do this stuff. They sell coin laundromats and try everything. I just want to make sure the people who are doing that are in strictly professional practices where they might do accounting practices and dental practices because there are some nuances, but you don't get somebody who is just a generalist.

Ron Seigneur: That is a very good point. I will also make reference to another item in the ancillary reading materials. There is an article about an individual, Pepper Veatch, who works with the Patterson Dental Group, and is billed as Arizona's largest dental broker. So here is an individual in that market who holds herself out as someone who specializes in brokerage of dental practices. That is a very good point, Jim, to try to seek out to see if there are some folks who have particular expertise.

Before we go on to these other resources, in preparing for this call I found interesting a group of CPAs who hold themselves out as specialists in working with dental practices. There is a website—and I am not here to advocate any of these individuals or resources, but just as a point of reference—*www.DentalCPAs.com*. This is a website that is pretty interesting because it is a group of CPAs around the country that belong to a group that have a bunch of areas listed on how they can help dental practitioners because they profess to know the area better than the basic CPA. It is an interesting twist that they are there for traditional CPA practitioners.

The next item on this Slide #11 is the Goodwill Registry. It has an approximate cost of $500. I have been aware of the Goodwill Registry for a number of years. It has a lot of information about the value multiples, and I will use the term loosely here, for different types of healthcare practitioners including dental specialists by practice specialty.

I have always been persuaded particularly by some others that I highly respect that do a lot more healthcare than I do, that there is some bias in the information in terms of where it comes from and how reliable it is and how defendable it is if you are an expert witness in litigation particularly. We are familiar with it; we don't subscribe to it, but it is a source of information that you should be aware of.

Jim Andersen: The only thing I will add to that is I agree with what you are saying. It has a lot of statistical stuff. Quite frankly, what it does for you is that it basically gets you right back to your 45, 50, to 70 percent of gross revenue. That is what it does. It is very interesting. I think that there are a number of outliers that don't make sense, but I will say that it reaffirms what we originally talked about earlier.

Ron Seigneur: I am going to pause here for just a second and let Blake come on the line to give the CPE code.

Blake Lyman: Thank you, Ron. The three four-digit CPE codes for today's teleconference are: 8014, 6841, 1034. Once again the three four-digit CPE codes for today are: 8014, 6841, 1034. As a reminder, please send questions to *tc-questions@bvresources.com.* Ron?

Ron Seigneur: Thanks, Blake. The next bullet on Slide #11 is Pratt's Stats. It has next to it an approximate cost of $600. We have used Pratt's Stats routinely on a number of engagements. It is the database that was originally founded by Shannon Pratt, the original founder of Business Valuation Resources, and a wonderful man, a great contributor to our profession.

Most people on the call will likely be familiar with Pratt's Stats, but for those who aren't, it is a database of transactions that have actually occurred in the marketplace. They are sorted by SIC code. The nice thing about Pratt's Stats is compared to some of the other transactional databases that we will make reference to including the next one, BizComps, is Pratt's Stats tends to be more robust in terms of the information you get about the underlying transaction.

Also, if the data is available, they will give you more multiples that you can use in actually applying the information to come up with indications of values. We like Pratt's Stats when it is in the right environment for the target. There are a number of dental practices that have reported data in Pratt's Stats. You can get Pratt's Stats through Business Valuation Resources. There are different options in terms of the pricing, so just be familiar with that. I think you can buy individual transactions versus having an annual license if you will to pull it down if you are using the information routinely.

It is widely used by business brokers. It is widely used by valuation practitioners. It is a good source of market data for practices like dental practices and other types of businesses.

There is also BizComps. BizComps has been around for a long time. It is founded by Jack Sanders out of San Diego. It is a very large database of transactions as well. It doesn't quite have nearly as much underlying data to help you analyze the specific transactions similar to Pratt's Stats, but they do have a large number of dental practice transactions that are reported in that particular database.

One other that isn't here that I will make mention of is the Institute of Business Appraisers. They have a database as well that dates transactions back to the mid 1970s. At last count I think they had 24,000 plus transactions. It is also a source of information. Again, the data there is very limited in terms of what you get. For the transaction that has occurred you get the gross revenues, the sale price, the state that the transaction took place, the month and the year of the transaction, and sometimes you will get what is called seller's discretionary earnings, and sometimes not.

The real differentiation element here is you don't know whether there was a non-compete agreement; you don't know whether there was a carry back financing arrangement, all of those things that can greatly affect the price. That is really important to understand when you are using these transactional databases.

I will also make reference to a question that came in from Newt Rumbel. "The industry historic multiple inclusive of net fixed assets and leaseholds, what about accounts receivable and accounts payable, especially for larger better known niche practices in desirable markets like Portland, Seattle, Spokane, Boise? How do insider buy/sell transactions affect these questions?"

The point I wanted to make off of this question is when you are using these databases, it is something that I have learned the hard way on the witness stand in the last couple of years. There are often transactions that are duplicated in the different databases and they have different results. One will say, here is a practice in Portland that sold and it was 70 percent of gross revenues. That same transaction might be reported in BizComps and it is 85 percent of gross revenues. You can determine that it is the same practice, but it has two different multiples. Why would that be?

The answer is the first part of this question. It is because they are calculated differently for the different databases. Some use the last tax return as their base for the gross revenues. Others use trailing 12 months for the revenue. Some include fixed assets; some don't. You need to filter through how the databases are calculating their multiples. Make sure as you apply those multiples from a particular database to your particular target that your understanding of what base to apply it to and what that result gives you. Is it just the goodwill value or does it include fixed assets?

Jim Andersen: I would like to add a little bit. One of the things that I see popping up on our screen right now is we are getting a plethora of questions regarding databases. Ron has done an excellent job going over some of his experiences. There was one question regarding the Goodwill Registry of giving something a little more precise than I can give right now off the top of my head as far as why it maybe not as reliable. We use it. I am just saying that my view is that what you have to do, first of all, anytime you use any database you have to understand what the statistical nuances are and what is really in it because they present it differently. That is the first thing.

The second thing is the more that you can use, the merrier. If you can find some of the same transactions and then try to ferret out why there is a difference, that will help you with getting your little scope and what I call your scatter gun when you are trying to do an almost mini regression analysis to get this thing tightened up to say, "Yeah, I think I am going to go with 60 or 63 percent or something like this."

When we teach these types of classes and things, it is not an exact science. These things are negotiated off of these parameters. I just think that you have to sit there and take a look at as much data as you can that is feasibly possible. Then use your good judgment and come to your conclusion.

Ron Seigneur: Good points there. I am going to move on. We do have a number of questions and we will try to round back to as many of those as we can. The second leg of the slide we are looking at are these other sources. I am going to run through these quite quickly.

Done Deals is another source of transactions typically for larger firms and practices. In my experience there is less application to dental practices, but if you have a large multi-office practice, it might be a place that you want to peak.

Thomas West does a guide every year that has information about valuing different types of industry segments. There is some good information in that guide for valuing dental practices in terms of some good sources of information.

Jim Andersen: I want to stop you real quickly there, Ron, and I'll let you finish. I think Tom West Business Reference Guide at a buck and a quarter is the best deal in the marketplace. You can get a lot of good stuff out of it. Particularly, and you guys have this information, is that the information related to the dental practice stuff is very good in this one here. I am just saying for any of you CPA or business valuation type people out there, Tom West, if you don't own that Business Reference Guide, I think it is a must in every library.

Ron Seigneur: Absolutely. I totally agree with that. We have limited time left so I am going to move us forward a little bit faster. We have Dental Economics which is a website that focuses on the economics related to dental practices. A lot of practitioners look at that on a regular basis. It has a lot of information about ways that practitioners can enhance the economics of their practice. They have some survey information on what practices should be worth and how to benchmark practices and those types of things. There is information from both Dental Economics itself, which is actually a publication—I don't know if it is monthly or bimonthly, but it is a publication that comes out.

They have a nice robust website, as does the ADA. It has some economic survey information as well. We are going to jump forward here. Before we take this next one and move into compensation, I am going to answer one other question that has come in. This is from George Leslie.

"How has the current difficulty in obtaining financing affected the purchase price of dental practices?" I am going to make one particular comment here. There have been some huge restrictions lately with SBA financing that include a component for goodwill. There have been a large number of transactions of professional practices generally including accounting practices and dental practices where the buyer has used SBA financing, all or a portion of, to buy the practice.

Now, just recently, in this current year the SBA has mandated a Statement of Operating Procedure 5010A that says that the goodwill component of an SBA backed loan cannot exceed $250,000 maximum. I think there are still some rumblings of exceptions to that, but that has greatly reduced the access to SBA funding for some of these practices. That is something to be aware of.

Moving forward into compensation information, I am going to make reference here to Dental Economics. It has compensation information that you can get if you subscribe to that. It comes out annually. I think we have that in our library.

Economic Research Institute is the first place we look for compensation information generally in the valuation work we do. It is a very well recognized entity that does compensation and benefits work. Their primary focus is the Fortune 1000 market on compensation for upper and middle management. They have a great deal of empirical data on compensation for different types of positions based upon size and region of the entity in the niche that they operate in—manufacturing, dental.

They also have relocation. What would be the difference in this person's salary in this position in St. Louis versus Pueblo, Colorado? There are those types of things. It is not inexpensive and it takes a little training to get up to speed to be able to handle and appropriately utilize. We have a staff person who has undertaken some training and has become our in-house compensation expert.

I think there is a learning point just for valuation generally. If you are trying to come up with what should the compensation of the dental practitioner be and it is really important because of this next area we go to when you are using an excess earnings approach, it can make all the difference in your conclusion. The support for the compensation determination is kind of the whole ballgame.

The point I make is we have now invested in having someone on our staff who we view as our compensation analyst. When we have this type of question, and it is really paramount to the overall determination, we start out by saying, "Matt, go dig out everything you can on compensation from ERI and otherwise," and then we will figure out how that fits into the overall valuation analysis.

Jim Andersen: Ron has brought up a very good point. For all of you CPA/ASA types that are basically smaller practitioners, sometimes it is tough to be all things to everybody. We even do some of this work for other firms now. There are outside people who do this type of stuff, but we have one fulltime person that does nothing but this industry research and compensation analysis. That is her fulltime job. That is a full 40 plus hours a week force based on our workload.

Ron Seigneur: One question came in, "Why do you omit the IBA's database?" We didn't have a bullet point for it on that slide but we do use it and we do subscribe to it. The one limitation as I said similar to BizComp is that it has very limited information in terms of what the underlying elements are of the transaction.

Moving forward to stay on schedule, we are going to get into a case study here that has a report that I think Jim can help walk us through. It was done for marital dissolution purposes. Jim, I will let you walk us through this next one.

Jim Andersen: We have one and it is also the full report just to let you know. It is in your materials. I think for all of you who are true valuation people, I think this can literally be a template report. I am going to make one comment on it to all the CPAs that are in our audience today as opposed to some of the people who are of the ASA variety. This report was issued prior to the AICPA's SSVS-1 standard that came out. You will notice when you go through this report it doesn't go through the fact that it says it is in conformity with SSVS-1. That would be the only thing that would change this.

It is a pretty recent report. It was done in 2008, December 31, 2007 valuation. This particular report that we are also talking about, as Ron had said, it is a valuation for marital dissolution purposes. In this type of a report, since it is a litigation assignment, it is a little bit of a different animal. We considered about three or four different things here because the thing is actually not for sale. In other words, the willing (the term in California anyway)—you have your willing buyer who basically is the in-spouse who is going to continue on in the practice.

As part of this type of step, this is what we call a letter report. As we know, we are dealing within the framework of fully contained reports, letter reports, and what they now call calculation engagements which are what the AICPA is basically done their standard over.

As we are going through there, we basically talk about what methodologies we used. We used an asset approach and we used an excess earnings method. Ron alluded to earlier that we had to do our compensation research. Quite frankly, this is all redacted information; these aren't our real people obviously.

This marriage of this Susan Allen—this is not a practice of great stature. When you see what the overall value is, you will find that it didn't happen. Guess what? We did an analysis and we didn't have excess earnings.

But when you do an underlying asset approach, this is standard in any business valuation that you do. The first thing you have to look at is you have to come up with the net tangible assets. The balance sheet is adjusted because typically your dental and all your professional practices are dealt with on a cash basis. You have to add your receivables and you have to get this thing set up so it is on a true accounting standard basis, maybe not gap statements, but accounting stuff.

In front of your face right now we have a balance sheet in front of us. We basically took that cash basis adjustment. The first thing we had to do there was to sit there and say we added accounts receivable. Then you will notice down below that we also got information regarding all these fully depreciated assets and so forth. We ended up having to footnote all of this. That is why I say this is an excellent report for people who are doing their litigation or just doing valuations in general, but there are some nuances that show the fixed assets were basically adjusted to what was fair market value.

We have a footnote that explains in the report itself how we got to that fair market value number. One of the comments I am going to make to you is one of these situations and problems. A lot of it is going to be cost effective problems. One of the things that Ron and I have talked about in the past and are constantly dealing with is that we are licensed business appraisers, but we are not licensed equipment appraisers.

For any of you who are doing a valuation like this where you have fixed assets in there, you have two options. If you don't have a ton of equipment in there and so forth, you may have to sit down with your perspective dentist and so forth, talk to them, have he or she give you some sort of guesstimate of what the value may be, or you may try to take some of the tax depreciation and apply some sort of an economic depreciation.

The key to that would be to explain it in your footnote. In a perfect world, although it gets very expensive, what you then have to deal with is the following: you have to make darn sure that what you have done is to—if you can't get an equipment appraiser because it is not cost effective—explain what you did. Then in your assumptions you would state that this could be subject to change based on a full equipment appraisal and it could be worth more or less. That is just to cover yourself.

Ron Seigneur: Let me interject briefly here because that point resonates with me. We are working on the valuation of a medical practice right now. It is a sole practitioner. We are not qualified to appraise it all because it is a surgical clinic and we are not qualified to appraise the equipment. There is some high end equipment in this practice.

The doctor goes out and finds somebody that he likes that brokers medical equipment and gets a number; it's a low number. The other side comes in who is an ASA equipment appraiser and it is a high number. It is like a $400,000 swing in equipment value. So $400,000, we will split the difference and figure out how to get the deal done.

But what it does is when you take that $400,000 to the next phase of what you are going to go to, it gets magnified because of the math of the excess earnings. The point made is sometimes you have to figure out how to justify those equipment values. Sometimes we may need to step back and say, "We need to go call an expert in." And even those experts differ.

Jim Andersen: I agree. Would you go back to the prior slide, please?

Ron Seigneur: Absolutely.

Jim Andersen: In the prior slide, we basically reconciled the owner's equity and we reconciled what this practice would be worth if you used an underlying asset methodology based on the fact of considering excess earnings and then considering what those assets are worth. As you can see here, we did an adjustment. Basically what we ended up with under this methodology, the thing is worth $75,000.

Again, I think it is invaluable for everybody who has all the materials we sent. The materials are worth the price of admission, all the great stuff Ron provided, and Steve and myself. There is some great stuff. There are a couple of these good reports. They work real well. Anyway, go ahead to the next slide Ron.

Ron Seigneur: Okay.

Jim Andersen: Basically, this just describes the excess earnings methodology. As I said earlier, when you look at the report in detail, guess what? We did our comps study and there are no excess earnings because this is an underperforming practice. So the answer to the question is "no goodwill" based upon a marital dissolution standard in this practice.

On the next slide we show how we lay out schedules. We took a look at the typical valuation schedules where you show five years, we show adjustments for comp, and then again it gets you down to normalized earnings. Guess what? There are no excess earnings.

I already told you what the value was. Here is your value resolution.

Then in this report here, we then looked at the market approach. Again, under the market approach, we applied on a weighting basis. This is where we analyzed various databases. What were the databases we used for this specific practice? We went through and thoroughly worked with Pratt's Stats. We worked with BizComps and we worked with Done Deals.

Then we basically determined appropriate multiples to apply to the subject company, the various price to sales, the price to discretionary cash flow. That was another indication that we haven't spent a lot of time talking about because I basically still think the price to revenue is still the strongest.

Then here is what we basically ended up doing. Here is an example for the Susan Allen DDS. We thought that Pratt's Stats had the most meaningful information. We used a multiplier of 0.56 based upon our best judgment to come up with what the total value of the furniture, fixtures, equipment, and goodwill is. To that we added the cash receivables and other assets. We subtracted off the debt.

Guess what? We had estimated equity value under the market approach and that was based under a revenue multiplier. That is in the left hand column.

In the right hand column under the seller's discretionary cash flows, we basically took the earnings, what her income was, multiplied it by what we felt would be correct. The seller's discretionary cash flow multiple, added the same cash receivables, etc. Then we came up with a value under the seller's discretionary cash flow method of $168,000.

Next schedule.

Ron Seigneur: I think we are back to...

Jim Andersen: What I will then do in summary, again, since we have limited time in this webinar being that it is 100 minutes, please spend some time going through this. You are more than welcome to email me or Ron later with questions regarding this stuff. I am always happy to help other people who are doing this. It has a lot of interesting stuff here and in this report also.

In summary, since it was done for marital dissolution purposes, for any of you who are in California, we also had to do a separate versus community property allocation, community property state, so we were relying on a complex Parrer versus Vancamp analysis which is something we are obviously beyond the scope of this.

Ron Seigneur: I apologize. I stuck some slides in here. I am coming back to that last slide you were expecting.

Jim Andersen: Good call. Obviously when we went through this in rapid fire, you have to ultimately have a value conclusion. We gave the least amount of allocation to the excess earnings method. We felt that had the weakest argument. If it was a buy/sell deal, we wouldn't have used it at all, but for marital dissolution purposes, we would throw it in there.

Then we took a look at it and gave the greatest allocation to the market approach using the multiple of sales. We weighted it 50 percent. Then on the sellers discretionary earnings we did give that a significant weighting and that was 30 percent. When you take a look at those weighted averages, our estimate of conclusion of value for marital dissolution purposes was $177,000.

Again, this was an underperforming practice. But this gives you an idea of how you can do reports like this. When we start talking about value conclusions, it is not mandatory that you do various types and that you have to use three or four things in the final conclusion and weight them differently. You can use one if you so choose, but you just need to consider everything.

I think that is it. I will let everybody else go through that report in more detail so that Ron can go to this next section here because this is a really good wrap up portion for the discussions we are having.

Ron Seigneur: Thanks, Jim. I apologize for having that slide out of order, but there is a question that I think tees up this next set of slides. This comes from Bill Mason. "If revenues are generated from hygienists, etc., in addition to the dentist's services, why would you not do a discounted cash flow valuation?" And that makes a good question.

I think this is going to bring that out. We have two practices—Practice #1 and Practice #2. The both have a million dollars of gross. We have just learned that you ought to start with a 60, 65, 70 percent of gross to see what that gives you as an indication. Then figure out where you go from there.

Both of these practices have a sole practitioner who is a DDS. The net to the DDS after expenses is $350,000. Wouldn't they have the same value? They have the same revenue, same net, and same one practitioner. Well, maybe not so quick.

Let's take a look under the covers a little bit. Practice #1 is in an urban location. It has a couple of part time hygienists. Let's assume that they are personable and capable of taking on more if work was there. They have modern office space in the lobby of a building, maybe a bank that has lots of traffic coming through it. They have already gone through the computerization of patient records. They have nice new laser technology. They know how to market the practice in terms of their image and their follow up and reminding people of their next appointment and those types of things. The dentist is working three and a half days a week. He's playing golf, taking a little time off.

Practice #2 is in a rural location. They have one fulltime hygienist who is hard to replace because there aren't a lot of hygienists in that rural location. They have average space, in a middle income neighborhood. They have traditional patient records, a little dated technology. It is a second generation practice with maybe some older patients. The dentist is working five days a week. That tells you there is a little bit more to that bottom line of $350,000.

Look a little further. Practice #1 has a younger, more affluent patient mix that can maybe be attracted to cosmetic procedures and some of those additional things. It is increasing its revenues from teeth leaching, Invisiline braces and some of the elected things that folks can do. But they are experiencing a drop off in the cleanings and checkups.

I think as Steve alluded to earlier, people are waiting longer to go in to get their cleaning and not doing it quite as often because of economic issues. They both have that in common.

Practice #2, maybe the patients are the same age or older than the doctor himself or herself, and most of the revenues are coming from traditional services. I think you can look at that and say that there are some real issues there in terms of how you go about valuing that. It leads back to Bill Mason's question in terms of what happens if you have more revenues coming from the hygienist. You have to take that into the mix.

I have an accounting practice. I have folks who work in our practice that generate a lot of profits and revenues. It is good for me because I can do some of the things I want to do and bring in more work and I have people to do the work. It is the same thing if you have a young dental guy or gal out of school and a good hygienist who can bring in work and relate to the patients. There is a lot to be said for that in terms of how you apply the value proposition.

I am also going to make reference to a couple of things in the ancillary reading materials. One is another valuation report that I am not going to take a lot of time to go through, but it is in the materials you can pull down and walk through. It is a report also for marital dissolution. It is the valuation of 100 percent interest of James M. Walter Jr. as of August 16, 1996.

Like Jim said, it is a pre-SSVS-1 report so it is not compliant for those disclosures, but I think it is a pretty darn decent report. It is a little larger practice, a little bit more value in the practice. There were three valuation methodologies that were employed. It has a very good write-up of the practice profile in terms of the mix of staffing, the patient mix, the location, and the qualifications of the dental practitioner. It has the standard stuff about the industry economics.

Then it goes into some industry analysis. A lot of that came from Risk Management Associates in terms of the information that can be gleaned from there in terms of some comparative benchmarking. The practice itself is kind of interesting. There is an excess earnings approach applied. This is on page 15 of that sample report that is included. Again, I am just running through it because folks can pull this down and read through it.

There are some excess earnings in this example comparing what is called a typical salary pulled from the American Dental Association data compared to what this sole practitioner was earning. They come up with $259,000 of excess earnings. They apply a 25 percent cap rate. There is not a whole lot of support for how they came up with that cap rate which seems a bit low in my experience. That is just a conceptual issue.

They apply a five percent marketability discount on the result for that 100 percent interest which is also a separate issue in valuation science. It gives another comparative benchmark to the report that Jim walked us through. They apply a market data approach and they use the IBA database. In this report they indicate there were 780 transactions for dental practices identified in the IBA database. That is a big number of dental practices compared to some of the others you find.

The last issue I will point out on this is there was also a prior valuation done of this practice as noted on page 16 and 17 of the report. It doesn't give a whole lot of details in terms of the purpose of that prior valuation. In the end, just like Jim summarized, they have the three approaches that were used—the excess earnings method, the IBA market data method and the prior valuation that was done. There is no weight given to the prior valuation. It could be because maybe they didn't have enough information to relate it to the current purpose.

In any event, this is also a report that talks about how it is done for North Carolina equitable distribution. It talks a little bit about North Carolina case law. I think that is important to also relate to the issue when you are valuing a practice of this sort.

I think we are right at our closing time. I would like to turn it back to Jim to see if there is anything we've missed.

Jim Andersen: First of all, one apology—I am going to address one or two of the questions. Some of the questions that are here are literally worthy of a separate discussion. I know Bill Mason who has obviously done a lot of high end sophisticated valuation tests and really good questions regarding regression analysis and other questions regarding multiples and choosing things.

Some of the stuff quite frankly, I don't think we can get to, but I want to acknowledge. I would be happy to talk at any given time to you Bill as a listener. I do want to address one because it is a good, good solid question here. There may be one or two questions that Ron sees that we can get through quickly.

This is a very important question regarding using excess earnings. I think Will Gere had asked the question, "Where do you get your information regarding cap rate on excess earnings?" Here is the point I want to make. This is on valuation in general. I have often seen practitioners use some of the standard Ibbotson, Duff & Phelps data as a buildup approach when they are using an excess earnings methodology. They think they will use that because that is what they used when they tried to capitalize earnings under a normal income approach. That is totally incorrect.

Basically, when you are using excess earnings, I hate to say it this way, but it is basically appraiser judgment. Ron had been talking about this prior report he had been dealing with. On that report he said that 25 seems a little low to me. I couldn't agree more with him.

When you are using excess earnings, what you have to understand is in an excess earnings analysis you are only valuing the goodwill portion on the cap rates. In other words, on a capitalized earnings or income approach, that includes all the fixed assets and everything.

Taking that into account, your cap rate has to be traditionally larger and somewhat significantly larger. I often see 40 to 60 to 70 percent as potential rates. Again, it is appraiser judgment depending on the quality of the practice. I just wanted to get that one in because that is a very important point. Ron, do you have anything?

Ron Seigneur: I'm good, Jim.

Jim Andersen: Okay, we are basically at 11:40. This has been a lot of fun. I am sure we could go for two more hours. We have tons and tons of questions here. My biggest recommendation that I would like to throw out to everybody is to really go through the materials that have been supplied to you. I learned a ton today myself just by looking and going back through the stuff and listening to these questions and responding and so forth.

We obviously have some great participants here. I wish everybody in our conference all the success in the world.

Blake Lyman: Thank you very much, Jim. This concludes our presentation today. BVR would like to thank Jim Andersen, Ron Seigneur, and Stephen Persichetti for their expertise as well as all of our listeners for attending.

Be sure to check BVR's training and CPE page at *bvresources.com/training* for more information on upcoming teleconferences and live events. Transcripts and recordings of this and all teleconferences are available for purchase via our on-demand packs. You can find more information on the conference on-demand packs at *bvresources.com/training*.

As a reminder, to receive CPE credit, listeners must complete and submit a brief survey on this teleconference. The link to this survey is provided in your registration email and on the reading page for today's teleconference. The survey will be active for five business days and must be completed before we can process surveys. After five business days we will process all surveys and CPE certificates via email.

Once again, the three four-digit CPE codes for today's teleconference are: 8014, 6841, and 1034. Once again, 8014, 6841, and 1034. If you have any questions related to content or format of this teleconference, please email BVR at *tc-questions@bvresources.com*. Thank you and you may now disconnect.

VALUING DENTAL PRACTICES

BVR
What It's Worth

Business Valuation Resources, LLC
(888) 287-8258 or (503) 291-7963
www.BVResources.com

James Andersen
CPA/ABV/CFF, ASA, MBA | Burr Pilger Mayer
Ron Seigneur
MBA, CPA/ABV/CFF, CVA | Seigneur Gustafson
Dr. Stephen Persichetti
DDS, MBA | Downtown Dental Associates

Send questions to:
TC-Questions@BVResources.com

Purpose of valuing the practice

- **Transactions:**
  - Buying the practice
  - Selling the practice
- **Litigation:**
  - Marital dissolution
- **Estate Planning**

Send questions to: TC-Questions@BVResources.com 2

 Valuing Dental Practices

Industry Overview

- Roughly 120,000 dental offices nationwide, generating annual revenues of over $80 billion
  - Large majority are sole practitioners, focused on general dentistry
  - Smaller portion focused on orthodontics, oral surgery, periodontics, and pediatric dentistry
- Demand for services driven largely by demographics
  - Slowing growth in number of children
  - Baby boomer generation impacts demand
  - Americans are generally healthier, reducing demand

Send questions to: TC-Questions@BVResources.com 3

 Valuing Dental Practices

Industry Overview

- Labor intensive
  - Hygienists and staff
- Rapid technological changes
  - Laser drills, improved analgesics, computer imaging, laser bleaching
- Computerized management systems
  - Patient scheduling and charts
  - Third party billing
- Continued increase in dental insurance coverage
  - Least Expensive Alternative Treatment (LEAT)

Send questions to: TC-Questions@BVResources.com 4

 Valuing Dental Practices

Industry Overview

- Pricing
  - ~ $100 - $200 for normal check up and cleaning
  - ~ $1,500 - $3,000 for implants
  - ~ $400 to $600 for root canal
  - ~ $500 for laser teeth whitening
- Per capita spending
  - ~ $275 national average
  - ~ $175 Louisiana to $400 Washington State

Send questions to: TC-Questions@BVResources.com 5

Valuing Dental Practices

Industry Overview

- Challenges
  - Heavy competition, particularly in urban markets
  - Larger practices have marketing advantage
  - Regulatory issues
    - Disease transmission issues
    - Mercury in fillings
    - Exposure to Nitrous Oxide
- ~ 4,000 new dentists entering market, with roughly 6,000 retiring annually

Send questions to: TC-Questions@BVResources.com 6

Valuing Dental Practices

General vs. Specialty Practices

- **General Practices**
  - Repeat business
  - Patient list is a commodity
- **Specialty Practices**
  - Oral Surgeons, Endodontists, Periodontists, etc.
  - Rely on referrals
- **Doctor of Dental Surgery(DDS)/Doctor of Dental Medicine(DMD)**

Send questions to: TC-Questions@BVResources.com 7

 Valuing Dental Practices

ASA 9 Recognized Specialties

- Dental Public Health
- Endodontics
- Oral and Maxillofacial Pathology
- Oral and Maxillofacial Radiology
- Oral and Maxillofacial Surgery
- Orthodontics and Dentofacial Orthopedics
- Pediatric Dentistry
- Periodontics
- Prosthodontics

Send questions to: TC-Questions@BVResources.com 8

 Valuing Dental Practices

Valuation for Buy/Sell Purposes

Typically, valuation based on multiple of gross revenue:

- Includes fixed assets and leasehold improvements
- Multiple will change with:
  - Profitability
  - Patient demographics
  - Service mix
  - Desirability of location
- Multiples range from 45% - 70%

Send questions to: TC-Questions@BVResources.com 9

Valuing Dental Practices

Valuation for Litigation/Divorce Purposes

General Practices:

- Similar to buy/sell

Specialty Practices:

- Possible goodwill issues:
  - Lack of repeat client base
  - Greater earnings than median

Send questions to: TC-Questions@BVResources.com 10

© 2009, Business Valuation Resources, LLC

Valuing Dental Practices

Sources of Valuation Information

- Business brokers
- Goodwill Registry ~ $500
- Pratt's Stats ~ $600
- BizComps ~ $400

Send questions to: TC-Questions@BVResources.com 11

 Valuing Dental Practices

Sources of Valuation Information

- Done Deals ~ $400
- Tom West's Business Reference Guide ~ $125
- Dental Economics – free surveys on website
- American Dental Association ~ $300 per survey

Send questions to: TC-Questions@BVResources.com 12

 Valuing Dental Practices

Sources of Compensation Information

- Economic Research Institute
- Dental Economics – Practice Survey (free)
- A.D.A.

Send questions to: TC-Questions@BVResources.com 13

 Valuing Dental Practices

Case Study

- Valuation for marital dissolution purposes
- Valuation methodologies used
  - Asset Approach
    - Excess Earnings Method
  - Market Approach
    - Transaction Method

Send questions to: TC-Questions@BVResources.com 14

 Valuing Dental Practices

Case Study

- Asset Approach
  - Determine value of net tangible assets
    - Balance sheet is adjusted for accounts receivable, depreciation, and other items as appropriate
    - The net adjustments flow through to owner's equity

Send questions to: TC-Questions@BVResources.com 15

 Valuing Dental Practices

Balance Sheet

	(a) 05/02/07	Dr	Cr		Estimated Fair Market Value 05/02/07
CURRENT ASSETS					
Cash	$ 25,145		67	[1]	$ 25,078
Accounts Receivable	-	21,430		[2]	21,430
TOTAL CURRENT ASSETS	25,145				46,508
FIXED ASSETS (and year purchased)					
Furniture & Fixtures (12/1999)	23,624		23,624	[3]	-
Leasehold Improvements (12/1999)	10,813		10,813	[3]	-
Furniture & Fixtures (7/2000)	14,730		14,730	[3]	-
Toyota Sequoia (12/01)	42,114		42,114	[3]	-
Office Equipment (12/2002)	14,801		14,801	[3]	-
Hand Pieces & Autoclave (11/2003)	8,695		8,695	[3]	-
Dentrix Dental System (7/2004)	1,071		1,071	[3]	-
Dental Equipment (2004)	9,806		9,806	[3]	-
Office Equipment (11/2004)	1,005		1,005	[3]	-
Adjust to Estimated Fair Market Vallue	-	36,130		[3]	36,130
Gross Fixed Assets	126,659				36,130
Less adjustments & accumulated depreciation	(96,315)	96,315		[3]	-
NET FIXED ASSETS	30,344				36,130
OTHER NON-CURRENT ASSETS	-				-
TOTAL ASSETS	**$ 55,489**				**$ 82,638**

Send questions to: TC-Questions@BVResources.com

© 2009, Business Valuation Resources, LLC Valuing Dental Practices

Balance Sheet

CURRENT LIABILITIES					
Accounts Payable	$ -			$ -	
Accrued Liabilities and Payables	-			-	
Est taxes on Net A/R & A/P	-	7,500	[4]	7,500	
TOTAL CURRENT LIABILITIES	-			7,500	
TOTAL LONG-TERM LIABILITIES	-			-	
TOTAL LIABILITIES	-			7,500	
TOTAL OWNER'S EQUITY	55,489	19,649	[5]	75,138	$ 75,100 (rounded)
TOTAL LIABILITIES & EQUITY	**$ 55,489**			**$ 82,638**	

Send questions to: TC-Questions@BVResources.com 17

 Valuing Dental Practices

Case Study

- Excess Earnings
  - Determine value of intangible assets, or "goodwill"
    - Net income is adjusted for reasonable compensation, resulting in a normalized earnings stream
    - Since normalized earnings are zero, there is deemed to be no "goodwill"

Calculated value is equal to the value of the tangible assets

Send questions to: TC-Questions@BVResources.com 18

 Valuing Dental Practices

Normalized Earnings

For the Year Ending		12/31/01	12/31/02	12/31/03	12/31/04	12/31/05	12/31/06
TOTAL SALES	[1]	**$ 279,890**	**$ 309,176**	**$ 339,064**	**$ 330,881**	**$ 338,866**	**$ 318,182**
BOOK INCOME	[1]	**$ 75,857**	**$ 91,106**	**$ 93,291**	**$ 97,757**	**$ 101,151**	**$ 90,655**
NORMALIZATION ADJUSTMENTS:	[2]						
Other		-	-	-	-	-	-
Adjustments Total		-	-	-	-	-	-
NORMALIZED EARNINGS BEFORE COMP ADJ.		**75,857**	**91,106**	**93,291**	**97,757**	**101,151**	**90,655**
Adjustment for Owner's Compensation	[3]	(75,857)	(91,106)	(93,291)	(97,757)	(101,151)	(90,655)
NORMALIZED EARNINGS		-	-	-	-	-	-
Weight Factors	[4]	-	-	-	-	-	-
Weighted Net Income		-	-	-	-	-	-
TOTAL WEIGHTED NET INCOME							-
Divided by Total Weight							-
NORMALIZED EARNINGS							**$ -**

Send questions to: TC-Questions@BVResources.com 19

Valuing Dental Practices

Case Study

Asset Approach /
Excess Earnings
Conclusion

Excess Earnings	[1]	-
Goodwill Value of Excess Earnings	[1]	$ -
Fair Market Value of Net Tangible Assets	Sch VI	75,100
Estimated Equity Value under the Excess Earnings Approach (rounded)		**$ 75,000**

Send questions to: TC-Questions@BVResources.com 20

Valuing Dental Practices

Case Study

- Market Approach
  - Transaction Method
    - Analyze databases for sales transactions of similar companies
      - Pratt's Stats
      - BizComps
      - Done Deals

Send questions to: TC-Questions@BVResources.com 21

 Valuing Dental Practices

Case Study

- Market Approach
  - Transaction Method
    - Determine appropriate multiples to apply to subject company
      - Price to sales
      - Price to seller's discretionary cash flow

Send questions to: TC-Questions@BVResources.com 22

 Valuing Dental Practices

Market Approach

	Average 2005-06 Sales	[2]	Seller's Discretionary Cash Flows
Measure of Earnings - Susan Allen, DDS	$ 329,000		$ 98,000
Market multiple - Pratt's Stats	0.56		1.32
Furniture, Fixtures, Equipment & Goodwill	184,240		129,360
Plus: Cash	25,078		25,078
A/R	21,430		21,430
Other Assets	-		-
	230,748		175,868
Less: Current Liabilities	(7,500)		(7,500)
Long-term Debt	-		-
Estimated Equity Value Under the Market Approach	**$ 223,000**		**$ 168,000**

Send questions to: TC-Questions@BVResources.com 23

 Valuing Dental Practices

Differentiation Elements – The Tale of Two Practices

Practice #1	**Practice #2**
• Gross Revenues = $1,000,000	• Gross Revenues = $1,000,000
• Sole Practitioner/DDS	• Sole Practitioner/DDS
• Net to DDS = $350,000	• Net to DDS = $350,000

Both practices would sell for the same price.....right?
Well....lets look under the covers......

Send questions to: TC-Questions@BVResources.com 24

 Valuing Dental Practices

Differentiation Elements – The Tale of Two Practices

Practice #1

- Urban location
- Two part time hygienists
- Modern office space in lobby of A office bldg
- Computerized patient records
- Laser technology
- Marketing savvy
- DDS works 3.5 days a week

Practice #2

- Rural location
- One full time hygienist
- Average space in middle income neighborhood
- Traditional patient records
- Dated technology
- Second generation practice
- DDS works 5 days a week

Send questions to: TC-Questions@BVResources.com 25

Valuing Dental Practices

Differentiation Elements – The Tale of Two Practices

Practice #1

- Younger more affluent patient mix
- Increasing revenues from teeth bleaching, cosmetic electives, Invisalign, etc.
- Experiencing drop off in cleanings and check ups

Practice #2

- Many of the patients are same age or older than DDS
- Most revenues come from traditional services
- Experiencing drop off in cleanings and check ups

Send questions to: TC-Questions@BVResources.com 26

Valuing Dental Practices

Case Study

- Value Conclusion
  - Weight the various methodologies based on
    - Valuator's experience
    - Accuracy of information provided

Send questions to: TC-Questions@BVResources.com 27

 Valuing Dental Practices

Case Study

Value Conclusion

		Values	Weight	Weighted Values
Excess Earnings Value	Sch II	$ 75,000	20.0%	$ 15,000
Market Approach Value - MVIC to Sales	Sch IV	$ 223,000	50.0%	$ 111,500
Market Approach Value - MVIC to Discretionary Earnings	Sch IV	$ 168,000	30.0%	$ 50,400
Value Conclusion: Estimated Fair Value for Marital Dissolution Purposes of 100% of the Owner's Equity in Susan Allen, DDS Sole Proprietorship at June 30, 2007 (rounded)			100.0%	**$ 177,000**

Send questions to: TC-Questions@BVResources.com 28

 Valuing Dental Practices

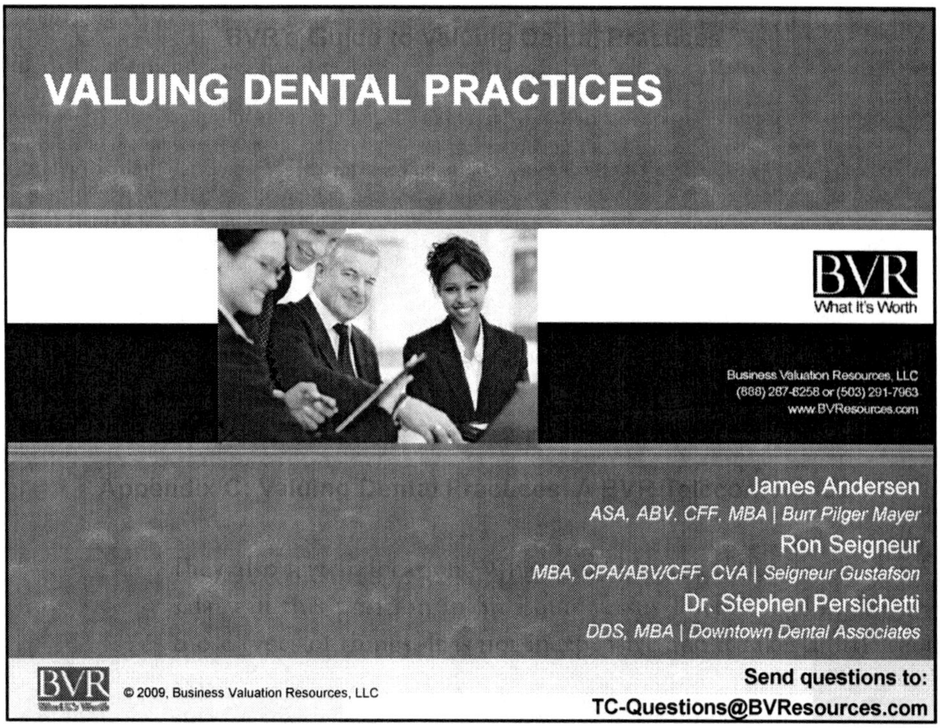
VALUING DENTAL PRACTICES
BVR
What It's Worth
Business Valuation Resources, LLC
(888) 287-8258 or (503) 291-7963
www.BVResources.com
James Andersen
ASA, ABV, CFF, MBA | Burr Pilger Mayer
Ron Seigneur
MBA, CPA/ABV/CFF, CVA | Seigneur Gustafson
Dr. Stephen Persichetti
DDS, MBA | Downtown Dental Associates
BVR
© 2009, Business Valuation Resources, LLC
Send questions to:
TC-Questions@BVResources.com

CPSIA information can be obtained at www.ICGtesting.com
Printed in the USA
LVOW09*0714260914

405996LV00005B/74/P

9 781935 081753